Marvin Richardson Vincent

The Age of Hildebrand

Marvin Richardson Vincent
The Age of Hildebrand
ISBN/EAN: 9783743309050
Manufactured in Europe, USA, Canada, Australia, Japa
Cover: Foto ©Lupo / pixelio.de

Manufactured and distributed by brebook publishing software (www.brebook.com)

Marvin Richardson Vincent

The Age of Hildebrand

'*By a bright, attractive appearance, by a very comfortable typography, by the participation of dignified scholars and experienced writers, this Series is likely to enjoy a deserved popularity.*'—THE NEW WORLD.

Eras

of

The Christian Church.

EDITED BY

JOHN FULTON, D.D., LL.D.,

AUTHOR OF 'INDEX CANONUM,' 'CHALCEDONIAN DECREE,' ETC.

MESSRS. T. & T. CLARK have pleasure in announcing the Serial Publication of 'ERAS OF THE CHRISTIAN CHURCH.'

Christians of all denominations have begun to understand that many of the existing divisions of Christendom had their origin partly in misapprehensions and partly in causes which have long since passed away, and that the cause of unity will be most surely promoted by a calm and impartial study of the history of the Church in its long and varied experience under the guidance of the Holy Spirit.

It is impossible, however, for persons of ordinary leisure and opportunity to make a profound study of ecclesiastical history. It has therefore been suggested that a series of popular monographs, giving, so to speak, a bird's-eye view of the most important epochs in the life of the Church, would supply a real want, and this Series is intended to furnish such monographs.

The Series will be completed in Ten Volumes,

Price Six Shillings each.

† [P.T.O.

ERAS OF THE CHRISTIAN CHURCH.

Three Volumes are now ready, price 6s. each.

I.

The Age of Hildebrand.

BY PROFESSOR M. R. VINCENT, D.D.,

PROFESSOR OF NEW TESTAMENT EXEGESIS, UNION THEOLOGICAL SEMINARY, NEW YORK.

The magnificent scheme of ecclesiastical supremacy projected by Hildebrand; the bold attempt of Boniface VIII. to absorb the power of the Empire into the papacy, which led at last to the temporary extinction of papal power, though not of papal claims, at the Council of Constance; the rise of the Franciscan and Dominican Orders; the conditions of monastic and clerical life; the beginnings of the modern national spirit; the establishment and progress of universities.

II.

The Age of the Great Western Schism.

BY REV. CLINTON LOCKE, D.D.,

CHICAGO.

The Great Schism, dividing European Christendom for generations into two hostile camps, which was terminated by a supreme humiliation of the papacy; the Popes at Avignon; the persecution of the Templars; the rival Popes, and the Councils of Pisa, Constance, and Basle.

III.

The Age of the Crusaders.

BY J. M. LUDLOW, D.D.,

AUTHOR OF
'CAPTAIN OF THE JANIZARIES,' 'A KING OF TYRE,' ETC.

The Crusades, with their heroic personalities, their dramatic, tragic, and romantic histories; the real religiousness out of which the crusading movement grew, and its unconscious preparation for intellectual and spiritual movements which no man could then have imagined.

ERAS OF THE CHRISTIAN CHURCH.

The following Volumes are in Preparation—

The Apostolic Age.
By the Right Rev. A. C. COXE, D.D., LL.D.

> *The death of Bishop Coxe makes it necessary to place this Volume in the hands of a new Author, whose name will be announced later. The four chapters completed by the Bishop prior to his death (his last literary work), will be published either as an Appendix or Supplement to this Volume.*

The constitution, the fundamental polity, the doctrine, the worship, and the social and the spiritual life of the Apostolic Church.

The Post=Apostolic Age.
By the Right Rev. H. C. POTTER, D.D., LL.D.,
BISHOP OF NEW YORK;
And Archdeacon C. C. TIFFANY, D.D.

The development of doctrine in the Second and Third Centuries, and the influence of Greek thought in suggesting questions which rose into paramount importance in the Fourth; the growth of liturgical forms, and the gradual self-adjustment of the Episcopal and Conciliar Constitution of the Church; the ascetic and monastic tendencies in which there was so much good purpose and the beginning of so much evil practice; and the universal evidence of a genuinely new power working in humanity.

The Ecumenical Councils.
By Professor W. P. DUBOSE, D.D.,
DEAN AND PROFESSOR OF EXEGESIS AND MORAL SCIENCE, UNIVERSITY OF THE SOUTH, TENNESSEE.

The age of the Ecumenical Councils, with its tragic importance and its incidental comedies, with its majestic figures and its incomparable saintliness in contrast with contemptible intrigue; and, above all, the ultimate and authoritative definition of the essentials of the Christian faith.

The Age of Charlemagne.
By Professor CHARLES L. WELLS, Ph.D.,
UNIVERSITY OF MINNESOTA.

The formative period of the Ninth Century, with its picturesque figures and stirring events, and the laying of the foundations of the mediæval system, ecclesiastical and civil.

ERAS OF THE CHRISTIAN CHURCH.

Volumes in Preparation—*continued*.

The Age of the Renaissance.

BY HENRY VAN DYKE, D.D., AND PAUL VAN DYKE.

The intellectual and political movements which preceded and anticipated the Reformation, including the Italian Renaissance, with the extravagances and sanities of the Humanists; the general growth of universities and great cities; the fuller development of a national spirit, especially in France and Germany; the religious fervour and the awakened spirituality which appeared most conspicuously in such tragedies as that of John Huss and Jerome of Prague, in the Lollard movement in England, and in many abortive attempts at reformation elsewhere.

The Protestant Reformation.

BY PROFESSOR WILLISTON WALKER, PH.D., D.D.,
HARTFORD THEOLOGICAL SEMINARY.

The Protestant Reformation in Germany, Scandinavia, Holland, Switzerland, and Scotland, in which the life and labours of Luther, Calvin, Melancthon, Erasmus, John Knox, and other worthies, will be appreciatively described.

The Anglican Reformation.

BY WILLIAM R. CLARK, LL.D., D.C.L., ETC.,
PROFESSOR OF PHILOSOPHY IN TRINITY COLLEGE, TORONTO, TRANSLATOR OF BISHOP HEFELE'S 'HISTORY OF THE COUNCILS OF THE CHURCH.'

A graphic survey of the Anglican Reformation which had so much in common with the Continental and Scottish movements, and yet was differentiated from them by peculiarities of principle and action which remain to the present time.

Such are the topics of the 'ERAS OF THE CHRISTIAN CHURCH.' Their perennial interest to Christian people is unquestionable, and no pains will be spared, either by the writers or by the publishers, to make the volumes worthy of their several themes.

EDINBURGH: T. & T. CLARK, 38 GEORGE STREET.
LONDON: SIMPKIN, MARSHALL, HAMILTON, KENT, & CO. LIMITED.

Eras of the Christian Church

Edited By
John Fulton, D.D., LL.D.

The Age of Hildebrand

Marvin R. Vincent, D.D.

CONTENTS.

	PAGE
PREFACE	ix
BIBLIOGRAPHY	xv

CHAP. I.—THE CHURCH AND THE EMPIRE.—The Church Imitates the Empire.—The Church Subordinate to the Empire.—The Benedictines.—Donation of Pepin.— The Clergy Refuse Vassalage.—Degradation of the Papacy   1

CHAP. II.—HENRY III.—CLUGNY—LEO IX.—HILDEBRAND. —Gregory VI.—Clugny.—Early Days of Hildebrand.— Bruno of Toul Chosen as Pope.—Isidorian Decretals   14

CHAP. III.—SIMONY—CLERICAL CELIBACY—TRANSUBSTANTIATION.—Domestic Relations of the Clergy.—The Policy of Celibacy.—Leo IX. at Rheims.—Berengar and Transubstantiation   24

CHAP. IV.—THE NORMANS—VICTOR II.—BEATRIX AND MATHILDE.—Rise of the Norman Power in Italy.—Death of Leo IX.—Gebhard of Eichstadt as Victor II.—Death of Henry III, and Regency of Agnes   32

CHAP. V.—FOUR POPES—THE ELECTION DECREE—THE PAPAL ALLIANCE WITH THE NORMANS.—Death of Stephen. —Benedict X.—Preliminary Treaty with the Normans.— Norman Alliance Concluded.—Death of Nicholas.—Election of Alexander II   41

CHAP. VI.—CADALOUS—BENZO—HENRY IV.—MILAN.—Cadalous Elected Antipope.—Battle of Monte Mario.—The Empress Agnes a Penitent.—Retirement of Cadalous.— Fight in Milan over Clerical Marriage.—Great Festival at Monte Cassino   52

CHAP. VII.—HILDEBRAND POPE—GREGORY AND HENRY IV. —THE REFORM SYNOD.—Hildebrand Chosen by Acclamation.—Hildebrand Asserts Himself.—He Demands the Emperor's Submission.—The Saxons Revolt.—The Pope Con-

	PAGE
templates a Crusade.—Ban and Interdict.—Orgies in St. Peter's...	64
CHAP. VIII.—THE INVESTITURE DECREE—CENCIUS ATTACKS THE POPE—THE SYNOD OF WORMS—GREGORY'S ABDICATION DEMANDED.—Summons to a Crusade.—The Synod Abolishes Lay Investiture.—Henry Openly Breaks with Gregory.—The Pope a Prisoner.—Gregory's Abdication Demanded.—Right to Dethrone Kings Claimed.............	78
CHAP. IX.—CANOSA—RUDOLPH OF SUABIA—GREGORY AND WILLIAM THE CONQUEROR.—The Oath to the Empress Disregarded.—Henry Crosses Mount Cenis.—A Brutal Pope.—Rudolph of Suabia Elected King.—Death of the Empress Agnes.—Berengar's Case Finally Decided.—Gregory Meets his Match	90
CHAP. X.—HENRY BESIEGES ROME—GREGORY'S FATAL TRIUMPH—HIS DEATH.—Henry Again Deposed.—Death of Rudolph.—Henry's League with Alexius.—An Orthodox Abbot among Heretics.—A Venal and Fickle City.—Guiscard Comes to Gregory's Relief.—Gregory Rests at Salerno.	104
CHAP. XI.—CHARACTER AND POLICY OF GREGORY VII.—His Principles Included his Policy.—A Fatal Sincerity.—The Pope is Lord of Kings and Princes	118
CHAP. XII.—URBAN II.—MATHILDE—CONRAD'S TREACHERY—SYNOD OF PIACENZA—THE FIRST CRUSADE.—Mathilde Marries Welf of Bavaria.—The Synod of Piacenza and Praxedis.—Urban Preaches the Crusade.—Praxedis Canonized	125
CHAP. XIII.—PASCHAL II.—DEATH OF HENRY IV.—HENRY V.—THE INVESTITURE CONTEST.—An Antipope on Horseback.—Peace in Germany.—The Liégers Speak Their Mind.—Another Antipope.—Papal Spite Vented on the Dead.—Henry V. Marches into Italy.—A Great Papal Concession..	134
CHAP. XIV.—THE CORONATION RIOT—PASCHAL'S BROKEN OATH—DEATH OF MATHILDE—GELASIUS II.—CALIXTUS II.—The Right of Investiture Conceded.—The Pope Repents his Concession.—A New Saxon Insurrection.—Flight of Gelasius.—Synod of Rheims..................... .	149
CHAP. XV.—THE CISTERCIANS—TREATY OF WORMS—THE FRANGIPANI AND PIERLEONI—HONORIUS II.—Treaty of Worms.—Influence of the Treaty.—The Triumph of the Church Pictured.—The Pierleoni.....................	161

Contents.

	PAGE
CHAP. XVI.—LOTHAIR THE SAXON—THE SOUTH-ITALIAN KINGDOM—INNOCENT AND ANACLETUS—BERNARD OF CLAIRVAUX.—Roger Masters the Pope.—Innocent Flees to France.—Bernard's Early Life.—Rapid Growth of the Cistercians	171
CHAP. XVII.—MYSTICAL PIETY—BERNARD AND HUGO OF ST. VICTOR—NORBERT AND THE PRÆMONSTRANTS.—Scholasticism of Erigena.—Contemplation of Jesus.—Mysticism and the Scholastics.—Norbert of Xanthen	180
CHAP. XVIII.—THE PAPACY AND ROGER OF SICILY—INNOCENT AND ANACLETUS—SCHOLASTICISM.—Bernard Ends the Milan Schism.—Anacletus Losing Ground.—Roger Receives Sicily.—Erigena and Aristotle.—Nominalist and Realist	189
CHAP. XIX.—ABÉLARD—LAST DAYS OF INNOCENT II.—TIVOLI—THE ROMANS PROCLAIM A REPUBLIC.—Bernard and Abélard.—Bernard Takes the Offensive.—Abélard as a Theologian.—Romans Proclaim a Republic	201
CHAP. XX.—EUGENIUS III.—ARNOLD OF BRESCIA—BERNARD'S CRUSADE.—Bernard of Pisa.—Eugenius Retires to France.—Arnold Denounces the Pope.—Bernard Preaches the Crusade.—Failure of the Crusade	210
CHAP. XXI.—BARBAROSSA—HADRIAN IV.—WILLIAM OF SICILY—BARBAROSSA AND THE ROMANS—THE GAUNTLET THROWN DOWN TO THE POPE.—A Clumsy Evasion.—The Stirrup Question.—The Emperor Attacked in Rome.—William of Sicily Submits.—The Gauntlet Thrown Down	221
CHAP. XXII.—RONCAGLIA—HADRIAN AND FREDERICK AT ISSUE—TWO POPES IN THE FIELD.—Papal Demands.—Sharp Words to the Pope.—Octavian Enthroned.—Octavian Acknowledged at Pavia.—Alexander Acknowledged at Toulouse.—Frederick Terrifies Italy	233
CHAP. XXIII.—THOMAS À BECKET—PASCHAL III.—ALEXANDER, BECKET, AND HENRY II.—Thomas à Becket.—"Constitutions of Clarendon."—Becket Condemned.—Diet at Würzburg.—Alexander Forced to Conciliate	246
CHAP. XXIV.—BATTLE OF MONTE PORZIO—BARBAROSSA'S DISASTERS—BECKET.—Storming the Leonina.—The Tide Turns.—Becket's Suspension Confirmed.—The Pope Checks Becket.—Becket Recalled.—Character of Becket	257

Contents.

	PAGE
CHAP. XXV.—Papal Transactions in France and England—Barbarossa in Lombardy—Battle of Legnano—Treaty of Venice—Close of Alexander's Pontificate.—Ireland and the Roman See.—Queen Eleanor's Treachery.—Legnano.—The Peace of Venice.—Alexander Returns to Rome.—The Pope's Bier Stoned	270
CHAP. XXVI.—Five Popes in Ten Years—Third Crusade—The New Roman Constitution—Death of Barbarossa—Henry VI. Emperor.—A Ghastly Procession.—Gregory VIII.—The Third Crusade.—Death of Barbarossa.—Tusculum Destroyed.—Richard of England Imprisoned	282
CHAP. XXVII.—The Emperor Master of Italy—Papal Complications in France and Spain—Death of Henry VI. and Cœlestine III.—The Great Heresies.—Philip and Ingeborg.—Ban upon Leon.—Character of Cœlestine III.—"The Poor of Lyons."—The Albigenses.—Obstinacy of the Heresy	294
CHAP. XXVIII.—Innocent III.—Steps towards Papal Supremacy in Italy—A New Crusade Proclaimed—The Contest for the German Crown.—Markwald of Anweiler.—Innocent's Administrative Skill.—Philip and Ingeborg.—Contest for the German Throne.—Papal Allegory	306
CHAP. XXIX.—Heresy Attacked in France—Innocent Decides for Otto—The Crusaders at Venice—The New Latin Empire in the East.—"Slay the Wolves."—The Pope Challenged.—Innocent Urges the Crusade.—Capture of Zara.—The New Latin Emperor	317
CHAP. XXX.—Stephen Langton—Otto's Cause Weakening—The Templars.—Stephen Langton.—Rise of the Templars.—Abuses and Corruptions	329
CHAP. XXXI.—The Albigensian Crusade.—Murder of Pierre de Castelnau.—Surrender of Carcassonne.—Toulouse Resists Montfort.—Innocent Inexorable.—Death of Montfort	337
CHAP. XXXII.—Innocent Abandons Otto—Troubles in the East—Murder of Philip and Recognition of Otto—A New Contest between Innocent and Otto—Frederick of Hohenstaufen Crowned.—The Greeks Defeat the Crusaders.—Otto Recognized.—Otto Excommunicated.—Frederick Accepts the Crown	349

Contents.

CHAP. XXXIII.—INNOCENT AND JOHN OF ENGLAND—THE CHILDREN'S CRUSADE—THE TWELFTH GENERAL COUNCIL—DEATH OF INNOCENT III.—John Encounters Pandolfo.—Cowardly Submission of John.—Fate of the Young Crusaders.—The Twelfth General Council.—Character of Innocent 359

CHAP. XXXIV.—THE POPES AND FREDERICK II.—THE PASTOUREAUX AND FLAGELLANTS—THE MENDICANT ORDERS.—Popularity of Frederick.—Manfred.—The Flagellants.—Error in the Monastic Ideal. 371

CHAP. XXXV.—THE DOMINICANS AND FRANCISCANS.—Francis of Assisi.—Institution of the Franciscan Order.—A Blow at the Episcopate.—Saved by Death. 381

CHAP. XXXVI.—THE INQUISITION.—Testes Synodales.—Commission of Gregory IX.—Bull of Innocent IV.—A Terrible Phenomenon 391

CHAP. XXXVII.—THE UNIVERSITIES.—The Crusades Strike at Feudalism.—Work of Justinian.—Student-Guilds.—The Clergy Study Civil Law.—Intellectual Fermentation 400

CHAP. XXXVIII.—BONIFACE VIII.—COLLAPSE OF THE HILDEBRANDIAN PAPACY.—Boniface and the Colonnas.—The Great Jubilee.—Events in Sicily.—Meeting of the States-General.—The Vengeance of the Colonnas.—" The Babylonish Captivity " 411

CHAP. XXXIX.—CONCLUSION.—The Papal Dominion Secular.—Hildebrand's Episcopal Policy.—The Isidorian Decretals.—Moral Obligations Disregarded.—Romanism and Protestantism.—How Much Allowance?—A Warning. 424

PREFACE.

HE period of mediæval history treated in this volume begins with the appearance of Hildebrand in the arena of papal politics under Leo IX. in 1049, and ends with the death of Boniface VIII. in 1303.

It is properly styled "the age of Hildebrand," because the theory of papal absolutism, which is its controlling factor, received its definite and practical embodiment from that Pontiff.

Strictly speaking, however, the historical development of this theory reaches its climax in Innocent III. The succeeding pontificates down to Boniface VIII. add to it no new elements, and are merely attempts to maintain the Papacy at the level attained by Innocent.

This age, in which the Papacy reaches the height of its power over the nations of Europe, is marked by the efforts of the Roman hierarchy to control the German empire and the kingdoms of France, Spain, and England. It is the age of the monastic orders in close alliance with the Papacy; the age of the crusades, of the scholastic philosophy and theology, of the great universities, and of the rise of the Inquisition.

The period is so significant historically, so crowded

with incident, and illustrated by a modern literature so rich and copious, that I have been constantly under a temptation to enlargement, which my prescribed limits have compelled me as constantly to resist.

The successive pontificates furnish the natural and convenient outline for the history. For obvious reasons the life of Hildebrand has been treated with greater fulness of detail than the others, but I have endeavored throughout to make all personalities and all historical details tributary to the main theme—the evolution of the Hildebrandian theocracy.

Among the large number and variety of sources upon which I have drawn, it is proper that I should acknowledge my special obligations to the following works: Dr. Joseph Langen's "Geschichte der Römischen Kirche von Gregor VII. bis Innocenz III." (1893); D. Karl Müller's "Kirchengeschichte," vol. i. (1892); Dean Milman's "History of Latin Christianity"; Henry C. Lea's "Historical Sketch of Sacerdotal Celibacy in the Christian Church" (2d ed., 1884), and the same author's "History of the Inquisition in the Middle Ages" (1888); Ferdinand Gregorovius's "Geschichte der Stadt Rom im Mittelalter" (4th ed., 1889); A. F. Villemain's "Histoire de Grégoire VII." (2d ed., 1874); and the valuable collections in Dr. John C. L. Gieseler's "Text-Book of Church History," translated by Davidson, American edition by Henry B. Smith (1876). I have also derived valuable aid from Robson's translation of Michaud's "Histoire des Croisades" (1854); Friedrich Hurter's "Geschichte Papst Innocenz des dritten und seiner Zeitgenossen" (2d ed., 1836); the two learned and exhaustive monographs of Carl Mirbt, "Die Absetzung Heinrichs IV. durch Gregor VII. in der Publicistik jener Zeit" (1890), and " Die Wahl Gregors VII." (1892); Mr. James Bryce's "Holy Roman Empire"; and Hallam's "History of the Middle Ages." For the guidance of any readers who may possibly be stimulated by this volume to a thorough study of the period which it covers, I have appended a catalogue of books, which, though by no means exhaustive, will be found useful.

MARVIN R. VINCENT.

UNION THEOLOGICAL SEMINARY,
December 26, 1895.

BIBLIOGRAPHY.

GENERAL LITERATURE ON THE HISTORY OF THE PAPACY AND THE EMPIRE.

L. A. MURATORI: Rerum Italicarum Scriptores ab anno aerae Christi quingentesimo ad millesimum quingentesimum; Milan, 1723-51, 25 vols. With supplemental vols., Florence, 1748 and 1770; Venice, 1771.

PERTZ, WAITZ, WILMANS, WATTENBACH (editors): Monumenta Germaniae Historica; Hannover, 1826 ff.

J. F. BÖHMER: Die Regesten des Kaiserreichs von 1198 bis 1254; Stuttgart, 1849; new ed.

The Papal "Regesta" from St. Peter to Innocent III., edited by Jaffé; Berlin, 1851. 2d ed., enlarged, by Wattenbach, Loewenthal, Kaltenbrunner, and Ewald; Leipzig, 1885-88. Continuation by Aug. Potthast, from Innocent III. to Benedict XI.; Berlin, 1874-75. Faucon and Thomas, Boniface VIII.; Paris, 1885.

P. HEINR. DENIFLE and P. FRANZ EHRLE: Archiv für Literatur- und Kirchengeschichte des Mittelalters; Freiburg, 1885 ff.

CÆSAR BARONIUS: Annales Ecclesiastici; A. Theiner's ed., Bar-le-Duc, 1864 ff.

PERIOD FROM 1049 TO 1085.

ABBÉ MIGNE: Patrologia Latina (Patrologiae Cursus Completus, etc., vols. cxl.-cxlviii.; Paris, 1844-66).

Damiani Epistolae (Migne, vol. cxliv.).

F. W. E. ROTH: Der heilige Petrus Damiani (Studien und Mitteilungen aus dem Benediktiner- und Cistercienserorden, vols. vii., viii.; 1886 ff.).

F. NEUKIRCH: Das Leben des Petrus Damiani bis 1059; Göttingen, 1875.

BONIZO or BONITHO (a great admirer of Gregory VII.): Libri ad Amicum, sive De Persecutione Ecclesiae (in Jaffé's Monumenta Gregoriana; Berlin, 1865).

PHIL. JAFFÉ: Regesta Pontificum Romanorum; 2d ed. by Wattenbach, Leipzig, 1883.

WATTENBACH: Deutschlands Geschichtsquellen im Mittelalter; 5th ed., Berlin, 1886.

WATTENBACH: Geschichte des Röm. Papstthums; Berlin, 1876.
HÖFLER: Deutsche Päpste; Regensburg, 1839.
C. WILL: Anfänge der Restauration der Kirche im XI. Jahrh.; Marburg, 1859-62.
THOMAS GREENWOOD: Cathedra Petri, bks. x., xi.; London, 1861.
W. GIESEBRECHT: Geschichte der Deutschen Kaiserzeit; 4th ed., Braunschweig, 1876.
RUD. BAXMANN: Die Politik der Päpste von Gregor I. auf Gregor VII.; Elberfeld, 1868-69.
FERDINAND GREGOROVIUS: Geschichte der Stadt Rom im Mittelalter, vom V. bis zum XVI. Jahrhundert; 3d ed., Stuttgart, 1877; 4th ed., vols. i., ii., 1889. An English translation by Annie Hamilton is in progress; 3 vols. published; London, 1894-95.
K. J. HEFELE: Conciliengeschichte, vol. iv., 2d ed., 1879; vol. v., 2d ed., Freiburg, 1886.
HENRY C. LEA: An Historical Sketch of Sacerdotal Celibacy in the Christian Church; 2d enlarged ed., Boston, 1884.

SPECIAL WORKS ON HILDEBRAND.

His Letters, "Registrum" (Migne, Patrologia Latina, vol. cxlviii.). Best in Jaffé's Monumenta Gregoriana (see above).
Biographies, in Muratori, Rer. Ital., vol. iii.
WATTERICH: Pontificum Roman. Vitae, vol. i.; Leipzig, 1862.
JOHANN VOIGT: Hildebrand als Papst Gregor VII. und sein Zeitalter; 1815; 2d rev. ed., 1846. The substance of Voigt is reproduced in J. W. Bowden, Life and Pontificate of Gregory VII.; London, 1840.
SIR JAMES STEPHEN: Hildebrand. Reprinted from Edinburgh Review, in Essays on Ecclesiastical Biography; 4th ed., London, 1860.
SÖLTL: Gregor VII.; Leipzig, 1847.
FLOTO: Kaiser Heinrich IV. und sein Zeitalter; 1855-56.
HELFINSTEIN: Gregors VII. Bestrebungen nach den Streitschriften seiner Zeit; Frankfort, 1856.
GFRÖRER: Papst Gregor VII. und sein Zeitalter; Schaffhausen, 1859-61.
W. GIESEBRECHT: Geschichte der Deutschen Kaiserzeit, vol. iii., pt. i. (see above).
JOS. LANGEN: Geschichte der Römischen Kirche von Gregor VII. bis Innocenz III.; Bonn, 1893.
A. F. VILLEMAIN: Histoire de Grégoire VII.; 2d ed., Paris, 1873. English translation by J. F. Brockley; London, 1874.
S. BARING-GOULD: Lives of the Saints for May 25th; London, 1873.
MARTENS: Die Besetzung des päpstlichen Stuhls unter den Kaisern Heinrich III. und Heinrich IV.; 1887.
W. R. W. STEPHENS: Hildebrand and his Times; London, 1888.

CARL MIRBT: Die Absetzung Heinrich IV. durch Gregor VII. in der Publicistik jener Zeit; Leipzig, 1890.
CARL MIRBT: Die Stellung Augustinus in der Publicistik des Gregorianischen Kirchenstreits; Leipzig, 1888. Showing the influence of Augustine on both parties in the Gregorian controversy concerning the relations of church and state.
CARL MIRBT: Die Wahl Gregors VII.; Marburg, 1892.
LEOP. V. RANKE: Weltgeschichte, vol. vii.; Leipzig, 1886.

ROMAN CATHOLIC AUTHORITIES.

K. J. HEFELE: see above.
HERGENRÖTHER, ROHRBACHER, J. GRETZER: Apologia pro Gregor VII. (in Migne, vol. clxxxix.).
ABBÉ GORINI: Défense de l'Église contre les erreurs historiques de MM. Guizot, Thierry, Michelet, Ampère, etc.; 6th ed., Lyons, 1872.

CHURCH HISTORIES.

HENRY H. MILMAN: History of Latin Christianity.
J. A. W. NEANDER: Allgemeine Geschichte der christlichen Religion und Kirche. English translation by Torrey; 12th ed., New York, 1882.
D. KARL MÜLLER: Kirchengeschichte, vol. i.; Freiburg, 1892.
W. MÖLLER: Lehrbuch der Kirchengeschichte; 1889-91. English translation.
FERD. CH. BAUR: Die christliche Kirche des Mittelalters; 1861.
J. K. L. GIESELER: Kirchengeschichte. English translation by Samuel Davidson. Amer. ed. revised and edited by Henry B. Smith; New York, 1876.

ROMAN CATHOLIC HISTORIES.

J. HERGENRÖTHER: Handbuch der allgemeinen Kirchengeschichte; 1884-86.
F. X. KRAUS: Lehrbuch der Kirchengeschichte; 1887.
F. X. FUNK: Lehrbuch der Kirchengeschichte; 1890.

THE INVESTITURE CONTEST.

STAUDENMAIER: Geschichte der Bischofswahlen; Tübingen, 1830.
MELTZER: Papst Gregor VII. und die Bischofswahlen; Dresden, 1876.
BERNHEIM: Zur Geschichte des Wormser Konkordates; Göttingen, 1878.
BERNHEIM: Lothair III. und das Wormser Konkordat; Strassburg, 1874.

SCHUM: Die Politik Papst Paschalis II. gegen Kaiser Heinrich V.; Erfurt, 1877.
JOS. LANGEN: see above.
G. PEISER: Der Deutsche Investiturstreit unter Heinrich V. bis 1111; Berlin, 1883.
UL. ROBERT: Étude sur les actes du Pape Calixte II.; Paris, 1874.
Text of the Worms Concordat in Gieseler's Church History, H. B. Smith's ed., vol. ii., p. 275.

MONASTICISM.

MIRÆUS: Regulae et Constitutiones Clericorum; Antwerp, 1638.
HOLSTENIUS: Codex Regularum Monasticarum; Rome, 1661.
HELYOT: Histoire des Ordres Religieux et Militaires; Paris, 1714-19.
HENDRION: Histoire des Ordres Religieux; Paris, 1835.
DAY: Monastic Institutions; London, 1846.
RUFFNER: The Fathers of the Desert; New York, 1850.
C. F. R. MONTALEMBERT: Histoire des Moines d'Occident; Paris, 1860. English translation by Mrs. Oliphant; 1861-67.
A. HARNACK: Das Mönchthum: seine Ideale und seine Geschichte; Giessen, 1882.
MÖHLER: Geschichte des Mönchthums; Regensburg, 1836.
J. A. W. NEANDER: Der heilige Bernhard von Clairvaux; 3d ed., 1854-58. English translation from 1st ed., by Matilda Wrench; London, 1843.
G. HÜFFER: Der heilige Bernard von Clairvaux, vol. i.; 1886.
R. S. STORRS: Bernard of Clairvaux; New York, 1893.
MORISON: Life and Times of St. Bernard; London, 1863.
THÉODORE RATISBONNE: Histoire de St. Bernard et de son Siècle; Paris, 1875.
R. ROSENMUND: Die ältesten Biographien des heiligen Norbert; 1874.
R. W. CHURCH: St. Anselm; London, 1892.
F. WINTER: Die Cisterzienser des nordöstlichen Deutschlands; 1868-71.
F. WINTER: Die Praemonstratenser des XII. Jhs., etc.; 1865.

MENDICANT ORDERS.

K. HASE: Franz von Assisi; 1856.
PAUL SABATIER: The Life of St. Francis of Assisi. Translated from the French by Louise S. Houghton, with critical study of the sources; New York, 1895.
K. MÜLLER: Die Anfänge des Minoritenordens und der Bussbruderschaften; 1885.
H. THODE: Franz von Assisi und die Anfänge der Kunst der Renaissance in Italien; 1885.
F. MORIN: St. François et les Franciscains; Paris, 1853.

DOMINIC AND THE DOMINICANS.

FRIEDRICH HURTER: Geschichte Innocenz des dritten, vol. iv.; 3d ed., Hamburg, 1841-43.
J. B. H. LACORDAIRE: Vie de St. Dominique; Paris, 1840.
CARO: Dominique et les Dominicains; Paris, 1853.
E. C. BAYONNE: Le Monastère des Dominicains de Langres; Langres, 1881.
HENRY C. LEA: History of the Inquisition in the Middle Ages; New York, 1888.

INDIVIDUAL POPES.

M. MAURER: Papst Calixtus II.; Munich, 1886.
M. F. STURN: Zur Biographie des Papstes Urbans II.; Halle, 1883.
H. REUTER: Geschichte Alexanders III.; 2d rev. ed., Leipzig, 1860-64.
F. HURTER: Geschichte Innocenz des dritten (see above).
F. DELITZSCH: Papst Innocenz III. und sein Einfluss auf die Kirche; Breslau, 1876.
JORRY: Histoire du Pape Innocent III.; Paris, 1853.
JOS. LANGEN: Geschichte der Römischen Kirche, vol. iv. (see above).
ABEL: König Philipp der Hohenstaufe; Berlin, 1852.
RAUMER: Geschichte der Hohenstaufen; Leipzig, 1857.
CHERRIER: Histoire de la Lutte des Papes et des Empereurs de la Maison de Souabe; 2d ed., Paris, 1858.
FICKER: Forschungen zur Reichs- und Rechtsgeschichte Italiens; Innsbruck, 1869.
SENTIS: De Monarchia Sicula; Freiburg, 1869.
WINKELMANN: Philipp von Schwaben und Otto IV.; Leipzig, 1873-78.
PRINZ: Markwald von Anweiler; Emden, 1875.
MAYR: Markwald von Anweiler; Innsbruck, 1876.
J. SCHULZ: Philipp August und Ingeborg; Kiel, 1804.
LAU: Die Entstehungsgeschichte der Magna Charta; Hamburg, 1857.
W. STUBBS: Constitutional History of England; Oxford, 1874.
K. J. HEFELE: Der Kreuzzug unter Innocenz III., etc. (in Beiträgen zur Kirchengeschichte, vol. i.; Tübingen, 1864).
KLIMKE: Die Quellen zur Geschichte des vierten Kreuzzugs; Breslau, 1875.
J. RUBEUS: Bonifacius VIII.; Rome, 1651.
L. TOSTI: Storia di Bonifazio VIII. e de suoi tempi; Monte Cassino, 1846. Both Rubeus and Tosti are glorifiers of Boniface.
W. DRUMANN: Geschichte Bonifacius VIII.; Königsberg, 1852.
CHANTREL: Boniface VIII.; Paris, 1862.
FERD. GREGOROVIUS: Geschichte der Stadt Rom, vol. v. (see above).

FREDERICK II.

H. H. MILMAN: History of Latin Christianity, bk. x.
HÖFLER: Kaiser Friedrich II.; Munich, 1844.
ABEL: Kaiser Otto IV. und König Friedrich II.; Berlin, 1856.
J. L. A. HUILLARD-BRÉHOLLES: Historia Diplomatica Friderici Secundi; Paris, 1859.
J. L. A. HUILLARD-BRÉHOLLES: Vie et Correspondance de Pierre de la Vigne, etc.; Paris, 1866.
T. L. KINGTON [OLIPHANT]: History of Frederick the Second, Emperor of the Romans; London, 1862.
E. A. FREEMAN: The Emperor Frederick the Second (Historical Essays, 1st series, 3d ed., London, 1875).

THE CRUSADES.

MICHAUD: Histoire des Croisades; Paris, 1825. English translation by Robson; London, 1854; reprinted in New York, 1880.
MILLS: History of the Crusades; London, 1828.
KEIGHTLEY: The Crusades; London, 1847.
G. W. COX: The Crusades; London, 1874.
R. RÖHRICHT: Beiträge zur Geschichte der Kreuzzüge; Berlin, 1874-78.
W. E. DUTTON: A History of the Crusades; London, 1877.
B. KÜGLER: Geschichte der Kreuzzüge; Berlin, 1880.
A. DE LAPORTE: Les Croisades et le pays Latin de Jerusalem; Paris, 1881.
H. SYBEL: Geschichte des ersten Kreuzzuges; 2d ed., Leipzig, 1881.
H. HAGENMEYER: Peter der Eremite; Leipzig, 1879.
KUGLER: Geschichte des zweiten Kreuzzuges; Stuttgart, 1866.
W. STUBBS (editor): Chronicles and Memorials of Richard I.; 1864.
GEOFFROI DE VILLE-HARDOUIN: Histoire de la Conquête de Constantinople; Paris, 1656.

THE TEMPLARS.

St. Bernhardi Opera, ed. of Mabillon, vol. i.
MURATORI: Rer. Ital. Script., vols. vii., ix.
MANSI: Conciliorum Acta, vols. xxi., xxv.; Venice, 1782.
DU PUY: Histoire de la Condamnation des Templiers; Bruxelles, 1751.
MOLDENHAWER: Process gegen den Orden der Tempelherren, aus den Akten der päpstlichen Commission; Hamburg, 1792.
FR. MÜNTER: Statutenbuch des Ordens der Tempelherren; Berlin, 1794.
MICHELET: Procès des Templiers; Paris, 1841.
W. F. WILCKE: Geschichte des Tempelherrenordens; 2d ed., Halle, 1860.

LOISELEUR: La Doctrine Secrète des Templiers; 1872.
HANS PRUTZ: Geheimlehre und Geheimstatuten des Templerordens; Berlin, 1879.
F. JACQUOT: Défense des Templiers, etc.; Paris, 1882.

HERESIES.

For original sources on the Waldenses, see Em. Comba's article "Waldenser" in Herzog's Real-Encyklopädie, vol. xvi.
ALEXIS MUSTON: Histoire des Vaudois; Paris, 1834.
ALEXIS MUSTON: L'Israel des Alpes; Paris, 1851. English translation by J. Montgomery; London, 1875.
MONASTIER: Histoire de l'Église Vaudois; Lausanne, 1847.
DIECKHOFF: Die Waldenser im Mittelalter; Göttingen, 1851.
HERZOG: Die Romanischen Waldenser; Halle, 1853.
MAITLAND: Facts and Documents of the Waldenses; London, 1862.
E. COMBA: Waldo and the Waldenses before the Reformation; New York, 1880.
E. COMBA: Storia della Riforma in Italia; Gotha, 1880.
G. F. OCHSENBEIN: Der Inquisitionsprozess wider die Waldenser, etc.; Bern; 1881.
ALLIX: History of the Albigenses; Oxford, 1821.
FABER: Theology of the Waldenses and Albigenses; London, 1838.
BARRAN and DARROGAN: Histoire des Croisades contre les Albigeois; Paris, 1840.
HENRY C. LEA: History of the Inquisition in the Middle Ages; New York; 1888.
SCHMIDT: Histoire et Doctrine de la Secte des Cathares; Paris, 1849.
See also, on the Cathari, Neander's and Gieseler's Church Histories, Lea on the Inquisition, and Hahn's Geschichte der Ketzer im Mittelalter.

SCHOLASTIC PHILOSOPHY AND THEOLOGY.

R. D. HAMPDEN: The Scholastic Philosophy Considered in its Relation to Christian Theology; 3d ed., London, 1838.
R. D. HAMPDEN: Life of Thomas Aquinas, etc.; 1848.
RITTER: Geschichte der Philosophie, vols. v.–viii.; Hamburg, 1836–53.
COUSIN: Fragmens Philosophiques; Philosophie Scolastique; Paris, 1840.
BARTHÉLEMY HAUREAU: Histoire de la Philosophie Scolastique; 2d ed., Paris, 1881.
LÖWE: Der Kampf zwischen dem Realismus und Nominalismus im Mittelalter; Prag, 1876.
W. T. TOWNSEND: The Great Schoolmen of the Middle Ages; London, 1882.

ABÉLARD.

Complete edition of his works by Cousin, Paris, 1849-59.
Life by Charles de Rémusat, Paris, 1845.
I. L. JACOBI: Abälard und Heloise; Berlin, 1853.
BONNIER: Abélard et St. Bernard; Paris, 1862.
KAHNIS: Drei Vorträge; Leipzig, 1865.
R. S. STORRS: Bernard of Clairvaux; New York, 1893.

THE UNIVERSITIES.

F. C. VON SAVIGNY: Geschichte des Römischen Rechts im Mittelalter; 1826-51.
DU BOULAY: Historia Universitatis Parisiensis; Paris, 1665.
SIR W. HAMILTON: Discussions, etc.; 1853.
ZARNCKE: Die Deutschen Universitäten im Mittelalter; Leipzig, 1857.
K. VON RAUMER: Geschichte der Pädagogik, vol. iv.; 4th ed., 1872.
ANTHONY WOOD: History and Antiquities of the University and of the Colleges and Halls of Oxford; 1786-96.
P. BLISS (editor): Athenae and Fasti Oxonienses; 1813-20.
H. C. MAXWELL LYTE: A History of the University of Oxford from the Earliest Times to 1530; Oxford, 1886.
HASTINGS RASHDALL: The Universities of Europe in the Middle Ages; Oxford, 1895.
C. H. COOPER: Annals of Cambridge; 1842-52.
J. B. MULLINGER: History of the University of Cambridge from the Earliest Times to the Accession of Charles I.; 1873-85.

THOMAS À BECKET.

HERBERT DE BOSEHAM: Vita S. Thomas Cantuariensis, etc.; edited by J. A. Giles; Oxford, 1845.
JOANNIS SARISBURIENSIS: Opera Omnia; coll. J. A. Giles; Oxford, 1848.
JOHN MORRIS: Life and Martyrdom of St. Thomas Becket, etc.; London, 1859.
JAMES CRAGIE ROBERTSON: Becket, Archbishop of Canterbury; London, 1859.
J. A. FROUDE: Life and Times of Thomas Becket; New York, 1878.
A. P. STANLEY: Historical Memorials of Canterbury; 10th ed., London, 1883.
E. A. FREEMAN: St. Thomas of Canterbury and his Biographers (Historical Essays, 1st series, 3d ed., London, 1875).

For Geographical References, Spruner-Menke Hand-Atlas für die Geschichte des Mittelalters und der neueren Zeit; 3d ed.; Gotha, 1880.

CHAPTER I.

THE CHURCH AND THE EMPIRE.

N the bleak height of Canosa, on the 25th of January, 1077, Henry IV., the Emperor of Germany, stood between the two outer walls of the Countess Mathilde's castle, barefoot and in the garb of a penitent. Within the castle was Hildebrand, Gregory VII., the Pope of Rome. Nearly a year before, the Pope had publicly cursed the Emperor, and had released his subjects from their allegiance. After standing for three days in the snow, Henry was at last admitted to the Pope's presence, and on humiliating terms, which placed him absolutely under the control of Gregory, received forgiveness and absolution.

It is not to the tragical pathos of this incident that its prominence in history is due. It is rather that the incident is the climax of a movement covering nearly seven centuries; the full flower of an idea which owed its first realization to Hildebrand—the idea of universal papal absolutism. The idea meant the freedom of the church in all things, and the elevation of its power above every other power. It meant that the head of the Roman Church should be the real Emperor of the world, and every king the creature and puppet of the Pope. These meanings are expressed in the "Dictates," drawn up by Hildebrand himself or under his direction, which contain the following propositions: The Roman Church was founded by the Lord alone. Only the Pope may wear the imperial insignia. All princes are to kiss the Pope's feet only. His name stands alone in the world. He can be judged by no one. No one can pass sentence on one who appeals to the apostolic throne. The Roman Church has never erred, and, according to the testimony of Scripture, never will err. The Pope can depose the Emperor. Only the Roman bishop is rightly styled universal.

These are claims to make a nineteenth-century head reel. The attempt to realize such a scheme might have appalled Charlemagne or Napoleon. It is the object of this volume to exhibit the mature embodiment of this startling conception during a century and a half, from the election of Leo IX., in 1049, to the close of the pontificate of Innocent III., in 1216, which marks the culmination of the papal power. This period rightly bears the name of Hildebrand, since his idea and his policy are its controlling factors. The story is a painful one, but its lessons are none the less salutary.

The idea of Hildebrand was no sudden birth. It was the resultant of forces some of which had been at work since the apostolic age. It was the crystallization of ideas and principles which had been held in solution in the minds of successive generations, tacitly accepted, but never carried out to their logical consequences. As a preliminary to the special history it will therefore be necessary to sketch hastily its rise and growth.

Hildebrand's ideal was the imperial ideal. It would have been strange if it had been anything else. The papal economy in its full flower was an evolution of Roman imperialism. The Christian religion and the empire of the Cæsars arose simultaneously. The society in which the Christian church developed had no other idea of organized power than the Roman empire and the Roman civil administration, and therefore no other idea of government than that of a centralized despotism. The church of the apostolic age concerned itself very little with secular affairs. Under the current belief that the world was soon to come to an end, it had no motive for attempting to build up a great organization. But as this belief weakened and persecution and heresy threw it upon its defence, as its borders extended and it became an administrator of property and a custodian of the poor and sick, a more elaborate and thorough organization became necessary, and the forms of this organization were naturally determined by those of the civil government. Accordingly the chief cities of the several Roman provinces came to represent the chief ecclesiastical centres. The eparchates, states, and dioceses of Constantine soon found their counterparts in the metropolitan bishoprics and patriarchates of the church, and the bishops of the great centres thus acquired a special prominence. From the time of Constantine onwards the imperial church was divided into the three great apostolic patriarchates of Rome, Alexandria, and Antioch, and by the side of these were formed the later non-apostolic patriarchates of Jerusalem and Constantinople. Rome was the world's metropolis, and as such naturally became the centre of the church, and the Roman bishop took rank as the bishop of bishops.

This tendency was seconded by the persistence with which the mind of Europe clung to the idea of the Holy Roman Empire long after the empire itself had ceased to exist—the idea that it was still a fact and a necessity in the world's order, though, as Voltaire observed, it was neither holy nor Roman nor an empire. It survived the division of the empire between Arcadius and Honorius in the fourth century, the reign of Charlemagne, and the downfall of the Hohenstaufen. It is Dante's political ideal, pervading the "Commedia" and elaborated in the "De Monarchia." The vision of the eagle in the eighteenth canto of the "Paradiso" is Heaven's indorsement of Roman imperialism.[1] Through all those later years the fond fancy prevailed that the Roman empire was "suspended, not extinct"; that the Roman empire of Charlemagne and Otto was still the Roman empire of the Flavians and Antonines. The place of each sovereign was numbered from Augustus, and the title of the Emperor under the Germans was "semper Augustus." Cherishing this fiction in common with society at large, the Roman Church gradually turned it to her own account by adroitly shifting its focus from the throne to the altar, from the Cæsar to the Pope, from the universal Roman empire to the universal Roman Church.

[1] See "Purgatorio," xxxiii., 58–60.

But it was long before the Roman Church assumed the character of a rival of the civil power. Her earlier efforts contemplated nothing more than recognition as the legitimate head of Christendom. She began as early as the second century to assert a certain precedence, a precedence not of the bishop, but of the church;[1] and this tendency was stimulated by the removal of the imperial seat to Constantinople in 330; only the ground of the claim was shifted, since the prospect of a rival city made it expedient to base it on the descent of the church from St. Peter rather than on the superior importance of the city.

The imperial edict of Valentinian III. in 445, issued at the instigation of Pope Leo the Great, declared the establishment of the Roman primacy on the threefold ground of the merits of St. Peter, the majesty of the Roman city, and the decree of a holy council. Reluctant as was the Patriarch of Constantinople to admit the supremacy of the Roman see, Boniface III., in 607, succeeded in procuring from the Emperor Phocas a decree declaring the Roman Church to be the head of all churches, and assumed the title of "Universal Bishop." Towards the close of the eighth century the germs of the principal papal claims were already in existence, and the Roman pontiff claimed the right of a universal metropolitan.

Yet the church, meanwhile, was subordinate to the empire, accepting its control and relying upon its protection, and seeking, not to supersede, but to imitate it. The powers of church and state were not two,

---

[1] See J. B. Lightfoot, "St. Clement of Rome," vol. i., p. 69 ff.; Dr. Schaff, "History of the Christian Church," vol. ii., p. 157 ff.

but one, represented by a single head, the Emperor. The antagonism which appears later was unknown to Constantine and his immediate successors. Charlemagne and Constantine were alike heads of the church. The Emperors summoned church councils, the clergy conferred under the superintendence of imperial commissioners, and their decrees were ratified or disapproved by the Emperor. The Emperor filled and vacated the most important episcopal sees. Between Gregory I. (590–604) and Gregory II. (715–731) were twenty-four popes, and during this period the Pope was a subject of the Eastern Empire, consecrated only with the Emperor's permission. The code of Justinian (527–565) assumes control of the religious no less than of the civil interests of his subjects Under Charlemagne the authority of ecclesiastical officers emanates from the Emperor, and the clergy enjoy no exemption from civil laws. During the subjection of Italy to the eastern emperors the Pope was appointed by the imperial mandate, dared not assume his seat without the imperial sanction, and was summoned to Constantinople at the Emperor's pleasure.

The secular character of the Papacy may be said to have been partly forced upon it at first by the barbarian invasions. While the feeble Emperor Honorius was feeding chickens at Ravenna, and Alaric and Rhadagaisus were threatening Rome, Innocent I. (402–417) was supreme in the city. The capture of Rome by Alaric (410) was one of the great steps in the advance of the Papacy to secular power. It placed Innocent in the position of a Cæsar. After the departure of the Vandals under Genseric (455) the church under Leo the Great furnished the only social organization of the city. By the Lombard invasion (568) Gregory the Great became the recognized head of Rome. In his person the Bishop of Rome first became a temporal sovereign, not in designed antagonism to the civil power, but as compelled to assume its functions in order to save the city from anarchy.

A powerful force in the establishment of papal supremacy was the monastic organization of Benedict of Nursia, begun by the foundation of the monastery of Monte Cassino in 529, from which the order spread rapidly throughout Italy, and into France, Spain, and England. The establishment of this order, with its severe rules of discipline which became the rules of all the monasteries of the Western Church,[1] fell in at a time when the political order of the empire was dissolved, and gave to the church the organization which was lacking in the state. A second force lay in the wealth which flowed into the church from numerous sources, especially in the form of landed property. Even as early as the time of Constantine the clergy were exempt from taxation and had the right of acquiring real estate by bequest. The Roman see had thus become enriched, and some of its possessions lay outside of Italy. Donations of land were continually being made to bishops and to monasteries, and the industry of the monks converted many uncultivated tracts into fertile farms and sources of large revenue. Gifts came, also, from dying penitents and as com-

---

[1] See Ed. Martène, "Commentarius in regulam S. P. Benedicti," Paris, 1690; Milman, "Latin Christianity," bk. iii., chap. vi.; Gregorovius, "Geschichte der Stadt Rom," chap. i.

mutations of penance, and an immense revenue was derived from the system of tithes adopted from the ancient Jewish economy. Gregory the Great was the richest landholder in Italy, possessing estates in Dalmatia, Illyria, Gaul, Sardinia, and Corsica.[1]

The schism between the East and the West, growing out of the attempt of the eastern Emperor, Leo the Isaurian (726), to abolish in the churches the use of statues and pictures of the Saviour, the Virgin, and the saints, greatly increased the temporal power of the Papacy. In the disorders which ensued upon the attempt to enforce this edict, Gregory II. (715-731) appeared as a political negotiator and an independent power. In his correspondence with the Emperor Leo he asserted that the successor of Peter might lawfully chastise the kings of the earth. Here, for the first time, the church and the state appear as opposing powers.

In the release of the Franks from their allegiance to Childeric III. by Pope Zacharias (751), and the anointing and coronation of Pepin by the papal legate (752), the Pope arrogated to himself the office of supreme arbiter between kings and their people, and proclaimed the principle that he possessed the power to bestow and to take away crowns. From this point the steps were rapid. Stephen II., the successor of Zacharias, reanointed Pepin and his two sons, forbade the Franks, under penalty of excommunication, to elect any king but one of the Carlovingian family, and assumed the privilege, hitherto residing only in

---

[1] For details of the church's possessions in the city of Rome itself, see Gregorovius, "Geschichte der Stadt Rom," vol. ii., p. 59.

the Emperor, of conferring the title of "Patrician," a title introduced by Constantine, and denoting the highest rank next to the Emperor and the consul. With the defeat of the Lombards in 756 went the celebrated "Donation of Pepin"—the district which included the territories of Ravenna, Bologna, Ferrara, and the Pentapolis, which was the country along the Adriatic from Rimini to Ancona and inland to the Apennines. This "Donation" conferred supreme and absolute dominion. A Christian bishop was now for the first time invested with the prerogatives of a temporal prince. Thus the foundation was laid of the "States of the Church," by which the unity of Italy was rendered impossible for centuries. The era is important. "The church and the hierarchy have become penetrated with the canons and the policy of imperialism. The church has assumed a political existence and the form of a permanent ecclesiastical state. With the establishment of such a state the purely episcopal and priestly period, the greatest and most honorable in the history of the Roman Church, has come to an end.

Charlemagne ratified the "Donation," and Hadrian I. openly claimed from the inhabitants the same allegiance which Charlemagne's subjects owed to him. In his letter to Charlemagne (777) he alludes to Constantine as "he through whom God had deigned to bestow everything on the holy church of the apostolic prince." This is the first allusion to that monstrous forgery known as the "Donation of Constantine," which served later popes as a pretence for wholesale appropriations of territory. By this, it was said, Constantine not only endowed the Pope with imperial powers and the Roman clergy with the prerogatives of the senate, but surrendered Rome and Italy into the hands of the Pope as his property.[1] Dante pathetically alludes to this:[2]

> "Ah, Constantine, of how much ill was mother,
> Not thy conversion, but that marriage dower
> Which the first wealthy father took from thee!"

Charlemagne was crowned by Leo III. at Rome in November, 800. The discussion of the bearing of this act on the papal claims to secular supremacy belongs to the fourth volume of this series. On the side of the church it is claimed that the Emperor received the crown solely by the favor of the Pope; on the side of the Emperor, that he received it from God, as the inalienable inheritance of the Cæsars. It requires notice, however, since this dispute as to the source of the imperial power continued throughout the middle ages.[3]

Charlemagne was by no means disposed to recognize the Pope as a temporal sovereign, and kept a strong hand on the church, assuming his own right to legislate in ecclesiastical as in civil affairs, and not admitting that the sovereignty of Rome or of Ravenna had been transferred to the Pope in any sense which should make him the rival of the Emperor. At the Council of Frankfort, which was both a parliament

---

[1] See Gibbon, "Decline and Fall," etc., chap. xlix.; Döllinger, "Die Pabst-Fabeln des Mittelalters," p. 52 ff.

[2] "Inferno," xix., 115.

[3] See Bryce, "Holy Roman Empire," 5th ed., p. 56 ff.; Gregorovius, "Geschichte der Stadt Rom," vol. ii., p. 486.

and an ecclesiastical council, Charlemagne presided, and the canons were issued in his name. Still the Pope and the hierarchy were aggrandized by Charlemagne's policy, and under his son and successor the scale turned in favor of the hierarchy. The feudal system had already struck its roots into the soil of Europe—that social organization based on ownership of land and personal relations created thereby; in which political rights were dependent on landed rights and the land was concentrated in the hands of a few. This system naturally extended to the hierarchy as the holders of vast landed estates. For the time being, Charlemagne, as Emperor, exercised over the clergy the same feudal authority as over the nobles. Their estates were held by the same tenure, and the leading ecclesiastics took the oath of vassalage on a change of sovereign. They were even bound to obey the summons to military service. But in the reign of Louis the revolt against the obligations of vassalage broke out among the clergy. It was boldly asserted that all property given to the church, the poor, and the servants of God was given absolutely and without reservation; that the King had no power over the church's fees; that the clergy and their estates belonged to another commonwealth, and held directly from God. The vast scheme of the reorganization of the clergy under the Benedictine rule was a step to the severance of the hierarchy from the control of the state, and to putting the whole property of the church absolutely under the control of the clergy.

It is unnecessary to prolong this sketch. Enough

has been said to show the gradual change in the aim and policy of the Roman Church. From the assertion of a primacy in the church universal she has advanced to the assertion of a supremacy over all other churches, and finally to the claim to be supreme over the kings of the earth. From sheltering herself under the shadow of the empire she now aspires to overshadow the empire.

With the pontificate of Benedict IV. (901) begins the "iron age." The most of the tenth century is marked by the degradation of the Papacy. Between the death of Charles the Bald (877) and the coronation of Otto the Great (962) the Carlovingian empire broke up, with disastrous results both to the Papacy and to the kingdom. The invasions of the Saracens, Northmen, and Magyars spread disorder and consternation. The feudal lords denied the authority of the King, and the bishops forsook their allegiance to the Pope. The popes became partisans of secular factions and were imprisoned and insulted. The disposal of the papal chair fell into the hands of courtesans; the bastard son, grandson, and great-grandson of a prostitute occupied the chair of St. Peter. The papal jurisdiction was limited almost wholly to Rome, and it is difficult to trace the succession of the popes.

Under Otto the Great (936–973) some signs of returning order appeared. Otto asserted himself as the Pope's master. He deposed John XII., established Leo VIII. in the papal chair, and compelled the Romans to swear never to ordain a Pope without the imperial sanction. Otto III. (983–1002), under the guidance of Pope Gerbert, aimed at making Rome again the seat of imperial power, but in vain. The young Emperor could not make head against the feudal nobles and the episcopal order which was their tool. The Papacy again lapsed into a degradation which continued until the period where this history properly begins.

CHAPTER II.

HENRY III.—CLUGNY—LEO IX.—HILDEBRAND.

IN 1039, Henry, the son of Conrad II., became Emperor of Germany at the age of twenty-three, under the title of Henry III. The papal succession had fallen into the hands of the Counts of Tusculum, descended from the courtesans Theodosia and Marozia, who, in the previous century, had for a considerable period controlled the papal elections, and had wielded an enormous influence by means of their personal charms and their brazen licentiousness. Three of this family in succession occupied the papal throne. After the death of John XIX. the Tusculans inducted into the papal office, in 1033, his nephew, a boy of ten or twelve years, under the title of Benedict IX. Even at that tender age he was an execrable wretch, abandoned to a life of shameless debauchery,[1] and with him the Papacy reached its lowest depth of moral depravity. "Christ was represented by a prelate more childish than Caligula, and as vicious as Heliogabalus." The people of Rome, wearied of his murders, robberies, and other abominations, drove him at last from the city,

---

[1] His portrait is drawn in strong colors by one of his contemporaries, Rudolf Glaber, a monk of Clugny, in his "Historia sui temporis," vol. iv., chap. v.

and elected John of Sabina as Silvester III.; but the Tusculans restored Benedict after a banishment of forty-nine days. Benedict, however, grew weary of his office. According to one story, he became enamoured of his cousin, whose father refused his consent to her marriage unless Benedict would resign the papal chair. This he agreed to do, and accordingly sold the office to John Gratian, who offered him more than he could make by his robberies, and who succeeded to the chair under the title of Gregory VI. John was possessed of large wealth, and, though popularly regarded as lacking in brains, he appears to have been a man of learning and of pure character and piety measured by the standard of his time.

The condition of Rome was pitiable. A hundred petty lords stood ready to pounce upon it at every opportunity. All the roads to the city were beset with robbers who plundered pilgrims; the churches were in ruins; daily assassinations made citizens afraid to walk the streets; and St. Peter's was thronged with nobles who waited, sword in hand, to snatch from the altars the offerings of pious devotees. With these abuses Gregory dealt promptly and vigorously. He called out the soldiery, reëstablished discipline, and regained possession of many strongholds within the city. Silvester, however, still claimed the papal seat, and there were thus three popes—one in the Lateran, one in St. Peter's, and the third in Santa Maria Maggiore—with their respective factions at deadly feud with one another.

But some faint sense of decency still survived in Rome, and a deputation was at length sent to solicit the interference of Henry III., who promptly acquiesced and advanced towards Rome. At Sutri, about three miles from the city, he held a council of bishops to examine the claims of the three popes, which resulted in the rejection of all three. He then entered the city amid great rejoicing, and with his entrance begins a new epoch in the history of the city and of the church.

Among the motives which led to Henry's prompt acceptance of the Romans' invitation was one which introduces us to an institution that played a prominent part in the movements of the century. In 910, William, Duke of Aquitaine, gave to the Abbot Bruno the monastery of Clugny, in Burgundy, north of Mâcon. The community was to be independent of all metropolitan or episcopal control, and under the immediate jurisdiction of the Pope. The rule of Benedict was adopted, though with some modifications on account of the severer climate. This was the starting-point of a great monastic reform. Clugny furnished a centre for other monasteries, which rapidly increased in number,[1] until the most important monasteries of Gaul and Italy were included. At the height of its prosperity Clugny ruled over two thou-

[1] In the tenth century, however, these were not banded into one organization under the rule of Clugny, as "the congregation of Clugny." The reformed monasteries were either not under Clugny, or were ruled by it for only a limited time, obtaining thereafter their own independent abbots. The placing of monasteries under the permanent direction of Clugny did not begin until the abbacy of Odilo (994–1048), and Odilo's successor first made this the fundamental principle of his policy. When the "congregation" of the Abbot of Clugny is spoken of in proclamations, the collection of the monks of Clugny is meant, and not an alliance of several monasteries. See Müller, "Kirchengeschichte," p. 392.

sand monastic establishments. Under Abbot Hugo, in 1089, was begun the construction of its vast basilica, which up to that time was the largest in the world, and was subsequently only a little surpassed by St. Peter's at Rome.[1] It was adorned with the finest works of art—glass, tapestries, gold and silver lamps, wall-paintings, and carvings. At this time the congregation of Clugny numbered ten thousand monks. Laymen of all conditions enriched the order with gifts, and the popes vied with each other in conferring privileges upon it. Among the highest nobles of France, Clugny, within twenty or thirty years after its foundation, was regarded as the nucleus of a party. It was favored by King Robert of France, promoted in Upper Italy by William of Dijon, and received in Spain the indorsement and alliance of Sancho the Great. Towards the end of the eleventh century, within a short space of time, three monks of Clugny succeeded to the chair of St. Peter—Gregory VII., Urban II., and Pascal II.

Henry, by his second marriage with Agnes, the daughter of William of Aquitaine, had come into close alliance with Clugny, and this fact furnished him a powerful motive for carrying out church reform in Rome, since Clugny was the chief representative of the reform-movement and practically controlled the reform-party.

The three popes having been deposed, a canonical Pope was now to be chosen. Henry knew that he

---

[1] That is, the present edifice, begun by Bramante in 1503, and completed by Giacomo della Porta in 1590. Constantine's basilica on the present site was founded in 306.

had no right in this election, and so expressed himself to the council of the Roman lords. "However foolishly," he said, "you may have acted hitherto, I nevertheless concede to you the election of the Pope according to ancient usage." Probably by previous agreement the right of nomination was now formally conveyed to him by the council. "Where the royal majesty is present," said they, "the consent to a choice does not pertain to us. It belongs to your imperial power to furnish the church the arm of the defender." Thus to hand over the election of a Pope to a temporal sovereign was a significant concession, fraught with bloody consequences at no distant date; but it betrays the suffering and the utter exhaustion of Rome. It was a humiliating confession, moreover, that Rome had within itself no one worthy or capable of filling the office.

Henry nominated Suidger, the Bishop of Bamberg, who was consecrated as Clement II. on Christmas, 1046. His first official act was to place the imperial crown on the heads of Henry and his wife.[1] Nobles, citizens, and clergy confirmed with acclamations the act which subjected the city and the apostolic see absolutely to the German Emperor. After his coronation the patrician power was conferred upon him, with the insignia of a green robe, a ring, and a golden diadem. Henry knew that, in the eyes of the Romans, this dignity represented the highest rights of the senate and people; and further that, since the tenth century, it had carried with it the power to nominate

---

[1] A very elaborate description of the coronation ceremonies may be found in Gregorovius, vol. iv., p. 55.

the Pope, according to Pope Hadrian's conveyance to Charlemagne. As the church could be saved only by subjecting both the city and the Papacy to his will, Henry did not hesitate to introduce this power regularly into the empire. Amid the rejoicings of the hour only a few paused to forecast the future. Rome was too thankful for her release from the Tusculan tyranny to measure the more formidable tyranny which she had invoked. There was one at least who saw and measured the danger, and that one was Hildebrand.

When Gregory VI., on his surrender of the chair, retired into Germany, he was accompanied by a young monk who had been his chaplain during his brief pontificate. Popular rumor had so exaggerated Gregory's mental deficiencies as to declare that he was compelled to appear in public by deputy. Whether or not the young chaplain had been accustomed to discharge that duty, it is certain that Gregory gave no evidence of imbecility in selecting him for a confidential position. He was born at Savona, in Tuscany, probably between 1015 and 1020, for the exact date is uncertain. His father was said to have been a carpenter, and his later fame called forth a multitude of legends concerning the portents of greatness which attended his earlier years. His name, Hildebrand, which the Italians softened into Hellebrand, was naturally the subject of sundry puns by his German enemies, who interpreted it Hellbrand ("pure flame") and Höllebrand ("brand of hell").

At an early age he was sent to the monastery of Santa Maria on the Aventine at Rome. More than the instruction which he there received in the liberal arts, in the use of Latin, in the rules of rhetoric and dialectic, and in the writings of the fathers, was the atmosphere of churchliness which he daily breathed, the continual reminders of the venerableness of the city and of the authority of the apostolic see. The science and the sanctity of the world alike converged thither. In later stormy years he wrote that St. Peter had nourished him from infancy beneath his wings, and had fostered him in the lap of his clemency. Odilo, the Abbot of Clugny, often visited the monastery, and it was perhaps owing to his influence that Hildebrand withdrew to Clugny, where he passed several years. He practised the severe discipline of the Benedictines, with whom he formed intimate relations. Whether he completed his novitiate at Clugny or returned to Rome is unknown. It is not impossible that he may have spent some time in Germany, though the stories of his residence at the court of Henry have little foundation. He returned to Rome to find the city occupied by the factions of the three rival popes, and the church in utter confusion. Soon after he took his place in the suite of Gregory VI., whom he always styled his master, whose exile he shared, and whose pontifical name he assumed when he himself succeeded to the office of Pope.

Clement II. died before the end of his first year in the pontificate, and Benedict IX. reappeared and succeeded in holding the chair for nine months, when Poppo of Brixen succeeded as Damasus II., and died after twenty-three days—the Germans declared, by poison. On the application of the Romans to the Emperor for the nomination of a successor, his choice fell upon Bruno, the Bishop of Toul, in Lorraine. Content with a humble position, this prelate had distinguished himself by his piety and gentleness no less than by his vigorous assertion of all ecclesiastical prerogatives. He was versed in all the knowledge of the age, beautiful in person, and eloquent in speech.

Hildebrand at this time was at Worms with the Emperor, and the new Pope offered to take him with him to Rome. His best friends never claimed for him excessive modesty, and his reply foreshadowed the insolence which marked him in later years: "I cannot, because, without canonical institution, and by the royal and secular power alone, you are going to seize upon the Roman Church." If the story is to be credited it shows very clearly what was Hildebrand's opinion concerning the appointment of a Pope by an Emperor. Possibly Bruno had already felt scruples on this point, which were confirmed by Hildebrand's words; at any rate, he refused to owe his election to the Emperor's will, and declared to the assembly at Worms and to the Roman deputies that he would not accept the papal throne save upon the free election of the Roman clergy and people.[1]

Accompanied by Hildebrand, he travelled to Rome as a pilgrim. His journey occupied two months, and legends relate how streams bared their channels at his approach, and voices of angels greeted him at his devotions. He knocked at the gate of the city and

---

[1] For other—colored—accounts, see Villemain, "Histoire de Grégoire VII.," vol. i., p. 281.

asked the Romans if they would receive him as Pope in the name of Christ. In St. Peter's he declared that though the Emperor had chosen him, he would return to his bishopric unless the dignity should be conferred by the unanimous voice of the people. The decree of election was drawn up in the name of the clergy and people, and he was enthroned as Leo IX. on the 12th of February, 1049. After the concession which the Romans had voluntarily made to the Emperor, such a ratification was little better than a farce; but whether so intended by Bruno or not, it was a stroke of policy which propitiated the people in advance. In demanding the assent of the Romans he cast contempt upon the imperial nomination. Hildebrand was by his side. He was the real genius of the new epoch, and of the new policy which was already beginning to take shape in the economy of the church; for the administration of Leo marked a crisis in the history of the Papacy. It was the inauguration of a great and radical reform in the high-catholic sense. He brought with him to Rome the spirit of Clugny, and responded to the demands of the Clugny party.

A feature of his policy which demands notice at this point is his use of the Pseudo-Isidorian Decretals. A decretal is an authoritative rescript of a Pope in reply to a question. The Isidorian Decretals consisted of a collection of spurious letters ascribed to the popes of the first three centuries, and opening with a preface attributed to one Isidorus Mercator, for which reason it was falsely assigned to Isidore, the Bishop of Seville, who died in 636. The letters were probably written between 829 and 845, and were first published

Isidorian Decretals. 23

at Mainz in a pretended Isidorian collection said to have been brought from Spain between 826 and 847. The objects of this forgery were the establishment of an absolute church authority over the laity, the securing of all church offices and positions against lay interference, the erection of the clergy into a community with absolute right to legislate in all church affairs without interference, with the free right of judgment over all its members, and their complete immunity against all complaints of the laity even before church courts. It also incorporated the Donation of Constantine. These rights, it was claimed, were conferred by the contents of the collection, which contains fifty-nine spurious letters of popes and thirty-five spurious decretals. Down to the fifteenth century their genuineness was not openly assailed. The fraud was fully exposed by the Magdeburg Centuriators [1] (1559-74). Their spuriousness is now generally admitted even by Roman Catholic historians and theologians.[2] These forgeries, which hitherto had operated only in the sphere of the French Clugniacs, were now made by Leo IX. the groundwork of his whole administration, and were persistently cited in his official deliverances.

---

[1] Compilers of the first great Protestant work on church history, which bore the name of "Centuriæ Magdeburgenses." The thirteenth volume appeared in 1574. It enlisted all the Protestant learning of the age.

[2] As Bellarmine and Baronius. For details and literature, see Gieseler, "Ecclesiastical History," Amer. ed., by Dr. H. B. Smith, vol. ii., p. 109 ff.

CHAPTER III.

SIMONY—CLERICAL CELIBACY—TRANSUBSTANTIATION.

LEO was committed to the work of clerical reform; but his task was a gigantic one. He was confronted with a veritable Augean stable in the life and habits of the clergy. The picture of the clerical morals of that age cannot be ascribed to Protestant prejudice or slander. It is drawn by contemporaries and by Romanists, especially by Peter Damiani, the friend of Hildebrand and the leader of the strict monastic party of which Clugny was the centre.[1] Fornication, incest, adultery, infanticide, unnatural vice, polluted the monastic life. The title of Damiani's book, "Gomorrhianus," is as suggestive as a description, and its pages will not bear translation. Added to these enormities was the widely spread evil of simony.

Simony, according to canon law, is the gravest of ecclesiastical crimes. The name was derived from the New Testament story, in the eighth chapter of Acts, of Simon Magus, who offered the apostles money for

---

[1] His eight books of Epistles, and especially his "Liber Gomorrhianus," addressed to Leo IX. in 1051. See also Henry C. Lea, "Historical Sketch of Sacerdotal Celibacy in the Christian Church," and Lecky, "History of European Morals," vol. ii., chap. v.

the gift of the Holy Ghost. As the imposition of bishops' hands was supposed to impart the Holy Spirit, the buying and selling of ordination was regarded as simony. The term was gradually extended to cover traffic in ecclesiastical offices and in the rights of ecclesiastical patronage, and to the purchase of admission to monastic orders. According to primitive usage, a candidate for an episcopal vacancy was elected by the clergy and people of the diocese, subject to the approval of the metropolitan bishop and his suffragans or assistant bishops. The Merovingian and Carlovingian kings of France and the Saxon emperors of Germany conferred bishoprics by direct nomination or by recommendatory letters to the electors; but the honors and estates of a see were often granted by sovereigns, prelates, and lay patrons of the tenth and eleventh centuries only on liberal payments by the recipients. Thus the power of nomination and investiture became an instrument of the grossest rapacity, and church offices were bestowed on the highest bidder.

The domestic relations of the clergy presented an equally difficult problem. From very early times celibacy had been enjoined upon the western clergy; but the prohibition of marriage had practically been confined to the letter of the canon. The secular or parochial clergy kept women in their houses by connivance with their spiritual superiors. A tax called *cullagium*, which was nothing more than a license to keep concubines, appears as early as 1080 in the prohibitions issued by a synod at Lillebonne, at which William the Conqueror was present; and this system was put in operation by Henry I. of England as a means of replenishing his exchequer, was stringently forbidden by a canon of the Fourth Lateran Council in 1215, but continued to flourish until the sixteenth century. The sons of priests were empowered to inherit by the laws of France and Castile; in Milan, in the middle of the eleventh century, all priests and deacons were married; Hadrian II. was married before he became Pope, and Benedict IX., as we have already seen, resigned the papal chair in order to marry.

The early fathers, following St. Paul, held celibacy to be a matter of individual choice. Even Jerome admitted that at the beginning of the church there was no absolute injunction to abstain from marriage. At the close of the third century bishops and abbots were allowed to retain the wives whom they had married before ordination, but not to marry after they were in orders; while deacons and subdeacons were permitted to marry after ordination. The first absolute command to the higher clergy to observe celibacy was the decretal of Pope Siricius in 385, which applied to bishops, priests, and deacons. This decree naturally encountered vigorous resistance; but the resistance was futile, and the prohibition was embodied in the canon law. Legal connections being thus forbidden, the clergy had recourse to concubinage, or else violated the law. In the sixth and seventh centuries the Spanish clergy openly lived with their wives. The Carlovingian efforts at reform accomplished little. The most convincing evidence of the debased morality of the clergy is furnished by the Isidorian Decretals in their palliation of lapses from virtue, " of which so few are guiltless." Even the greatly enlarged power of the Papacy added to the increasing license. Though Nicholas I. (861) ordered the deposition of all immoral priests, the forms of judicial procedure favored concealment of priestly amours. In the tenth century the clergy began openly to claim the privilege of matrimony. Marriage evoked from the ecclesiastical authorities more opposition than concubinage, because possessions previously held by laymen were becoming hereditary. Had marriage been allowed to the clergy their benefices would have been transmitted by descent, the result of which would have been a great hereditary caste—a feudal clergy bequeathing ecclesiastical benefices from father to son. It was of vital importance to the church to prevent this. The church was rich and its possessions inalienable, and these possessions were exposed to greater risks from clergy who to their personal ambitions added family interests. The policy of the church demanded that the priest should be bound absolutely and completely to itself; that the sacerdotal order should be separated from the rest of society and from common sympathies, interests, and affections. Yet, as the tenth century advanced, sacerdotal marriage became more common, and in 966, Rutherius, an Italian bishop, not only intimated that all his clergy were married, but declared that if he were to enforce the prohibitory canon only boys would be left in the church, while even they would be ejected under the rule which rendered bastards ineligible to sacred offices. The simple, summary mode of reform was to cut asunder the domestic tie.

Simony was far too vast an abuse to be dealt with at a stroke. To depose all who had obtained their benefices by simony would have been to leave most of the benefices throughout the church vacant. Leo was therefore compelled to adopt less summary measures for the time being, and to substitute confession, penance, and absolution for deposition. He found himself equally unable to cope successfully with clerical marriage and concubinage. The bishops assembled in synod acquiesced in the prohibition of marriage, but took no steps to enforce it, and on the subject of concubinage were ominously silent. The Pope meanwhile surrounded himself with men of a temper kindred to his own. Prominent among these was Peter Damiani, Abbot of Fontavella, in Umbria, a man who combined the superstitiousness of his age and order with liberal education, trained amid the austerities of a hermit's life, unpractical and timid in his dealings with men, but candid, pure in morals, inspired with horror and detestation of the foul abominations of monastic and clerical life, and portraying them in terms which, if not choice or classical, were unmistakable. With him was Hildebrand, whom the Pope had already made subdeacon and soon after appointed superior of the monastery of St. Paul, which afforded a sorry specimen of the debasement of clerical morals. Here Hildebrand at once displayed his rare administrative power, by restoring the ancient rule of the monastery, instituting a severe discipline, reëstablishing the revenues, and repelling the thieving incursions of the neighboring lords.

Efforts at reform and constant journeys between

Italy and Germany at first prevented Leo from giving his attention to the political condition of the state; but he was slowly reviving the sense of the papal institution in the minds of men who had well-nigh forgotten its existence. He now undertook a great religious visitation to the three principal kingdoms of western Europe. At Rheims he participated in the consecration of the new cathedral, and the removal of the remains of St. Rémy, the popular saint of France, who had baptized Clovis. At the council immediately following, simony, incestuous marriages, adulterous connections, the apostasy of monks and clergy, and vices against nature were discussed. Public confessions on these points were demanded of the different members of the council, and several were anathematized. Decrees were issued against divers secular and ecclesiastical abuses. Bishops must be elected by the clergy and people; holy orders must not be bought or sold; priests must not exact fees for burial, baptism, and visitation of the sick, and must refrain from usury and bearing arms.

Leo was politic enough to strike hard only where a blow was likely to tell. His most vigorous measures were taken where the political powers were on his side or where there was a prospect of carrying out his reforms. In Germany he did not disturb the existing method of possessing the episcopal chairs, even when this came through simple nomination by the King. In southern France, where bishoprics were regularly sold for large sums, he effected nothing; while in Normandy and Burgundy, where the churches, being united in a few hands, were more manageable, he broke through the former limits of the national church, boldly assumed the attitude of supreme head, summoned delinquents to his Roman synod, and issued, against the hitherto unlimited disposal of churches by the nobles, his decree that bishoprics and abbacies must be acquired only by canonical election by the clergy and people. His visitation, however, did much to restore the authority of the Papacy and to awaken the pride of Germany at having given such a Pope to the church. Yet, while the existing powers of reform were strengthened, passionate opposition was also excited by the new development of the Papacy and the Pope's appearance on the ground of the national churches of Germany and France. With all his vigorous efforts Leo succeeded in the end little better than his predecessors in reforming the scandals of the priesthood. The papal power was not yet sufficiently established to carry out a scheme of reform.

In the midst of this reformatory movement the Pope's attention was claimed by a dogmatic controversy concerning the manner of Christ's presence in the Eucharist, a matter which had never come into serious debate in the first eight centuries. Paschasius, a learned monk, issued in 831 a treatise entitled "The Sacrament of the Body and Blood of Christ," asserting that in priestly consecration the substance of the bread and wine is changed into the body and blood of Christ; yet so as that the "accidents"— the form, color, and taste of the elements—remain. The substance of the bread and wine is annihilated, and nothing exists but the body and blood of Christ. These positions were attacked by John Scotus, better

Berengar and Transubstantiation.

known as Erigena. Two centuries later, Berengar, director of the cathedral school at Tours, resumed the attack on Paschasius, and denied the doctrine of transubstantiation as taught by him, asserting with Erigena that the presence of Christ in the elements is real, but only symbolic and spiritually conceived.

Berengar was assailed by Lanfranc, afterwards Archbishop of Canterbury, at a council held by Leo in Rome in 1050, and was condemned, without citation and without hearing, on the strength of a private letter to Lanfranc in which he had avowed the position of Erigena. The council excommunicated him, but this did not finally dispose of the matter, which came before several different councils and synods, and was not finally settled until 1078, when Hildebrand, who had all along secretly befriended Berengar, and who has been supposed by many to have sympathized with his views, demanded and received his recantation and his subscription of a strict transubstantiational formula.

CHAPTER IV.

THE NORMANS—VICTOR II.—BEATRIX AND MATHILDE.

A NEW element now appears in our history and enters into the movements of the whole period with which we have to deal. This element is the Norman race. We shall see it persistently asserting itself in the long struggle between the Papacy and the empire; the object of solicitation and purchase by both parties; allied sometimes with the one and sometimes with the other; often turning the scale into which its sword is thrown; the instrument both of the humiliation and of the triumph of the Papacy.

The name "Norman" is a softened form of "Northman," which was first applied to the Scandinavian people in general, and afterwards, more strictly, to those of Norway. These hardy piratical adventurers first appeared in France in 912, when a band of them, led by one Rolf, gained possession of the land on either side of the mouth of the Seine and settled there. Although originally the same in name and descent, the Normans differed from the Northmen. With all the sturdy vigor of the race, they were marked by a singular adaptability to circumstances, so that they readily adopted the characteristics of any people among whom they came to live, and lost themselves in those whom they conquered. The change of the name from "Northman" to "Norman," therefore, marked a change in their religion, language, and social system. Their natural love of adventure dispersed them into different countries, and their plasticity allied them with warlike enterprises of the most different character. As a race they were ambitious and rapacious, cunning and enduring, warlike and independent. They displayed natural affinities for culture; though not inventive, they were appreciative and teachable, and welcomed men of genius of every race. They were versed in flattery and devoted to the study of eloquence, so that the very boys were orators. They were fond of legal forms and processes, and were lavish in their gifts and assiduous in their pilgrimages to holy places.

It was in religious pilgrimage that the Norman power in Italy began. Southern Italy and Sicily had from a very early period been occupied by Greeks, and the Saracens had come from Africa into Sicily in 827, and after fifty years had completed the conquest of that island by the capture of Syracuse. A party of Normans, returning from the Holy Land, rescued the city of Salerno from the hands of the Saracens, enlisted against the Greeks, and became allies of the princes of Capua, Benevento, Salerno, and Naples, usually insuring victory by their superior spirit and discipline. From their own country they drew fresh colonies of adventurers, stimulated by the prospect of conquest and pillage. By the gift of the Duke of

Naples in 1029, they obtained a permanent seat a few miles from Naples, where, under Robert Guiscard, they founded and fortified the town of Aversa. The people of Apulia, unable to resist, paid them tribute and even enlisted under their standards, so that Guiscard gradually established his sovereignty over a large territory. Henry III. of Germany gave them portions of the duchy of Benevento; and in the time of Leo IX. three Norman princes were ruling respectively at Salerno, Calabria, and Benevento.

But the church had long coveted Benevento, and the Beneventines, tired of both the Normans and the Lombards, finally put themselves, in 1051, into the hands of the Pope, as the least of evils. Leo had been unsuccessful in keeping the Normans from the city, and they resumed their depredations after the murder of the two princes to whose charge he had committed it, so that both bishops and citizens now besought his interference.

Leo applied to the German emperor for troops, but obtained only some hundreds of mercenaries and a swarm of adventurers of all sorts, accompanied by Godfrey of Lorraine and his brother Frederick, all of whom crossed the Alps in 1053. Some more troops were gathered from different provinces of Italy. The head of the church now assumed the temporal sword and took command in person, not, however, leaving behind his spiritual arsenal, since his first military measure was the excommunication of the Normans. He joined battle with the Norman army on the banks of the Fertorio, near Dragonata, where his army suffered a crushing defeat. He himself was taken prisoner, and was conducted, though with all marks of respect, to Benevento, where he remained all winter, practising the severest penances. He obtained his liberty at last at a high ransom, and granted to his captors, in the name of St. Peter, the investiture of all the territories conquered or to be conquered by them in Apulia, Calabria, and Sicily.

Much weakened by sickness, he returned to Rome, borne in a litter and escorted by a crowd of knights. He gave orders that he should be carried to his tomb in St. Peter's, where he was laid in the choir, which was hung with black and lighted with funeral torches. Dragging himself to his coffin, he stretched himself upon the marble sarcophagus, saying, " Of all my honors and dignities only this little dwelling remains." At sunrise the next morning he was supported to the altar, where he wept and prayed, lying at length upon the pavement; then, returning to his couch, he received the last sacraments, and expired on the 13th of April, 1054, in the fiftieth year of his age.

The Papacy, as we have seen, had recovered its strength by its submission to Henry III. and its concession of the right of nominating the Pope. It now demanded back the right, as a prelude to complete freedom from its deliverer. Hildebrand was the principal man in Rome, and as the leader of the reform-movement soon made all others his instruments—the monks, whose fanatical zeal he inspired; the popes, whom he directed; the Patarenes[1] of Lombardy,

---

[1] This name originated in Milan, and was derived from the district called Pataria, or "the rag-pickers' quarter," where the opponents of priestly marriage used to assemble. A full description of the sect will be given later.

whom he sent into the field against the aristocracy and the stubborn episcopacy; the powerful margraves of Tuscany; and the plundering Normans, in whom the church acquired vassals and defenders. In Hildebrand's programme the free election of the Pope, which from ancient times had been limited by the imperial power, did not at that time hold the first place. His efforts were directed principally against simony and the marriage and concubinage of the priesthood. The fear of the Emperor, and the insecurity in Rome, where the nobility, in the event of a breach with him, would again have controlled the papal election, constrained the priestly party to bide its time in patient submission to Henry.

On the death of Leo all eyes were turned upon Hildebrand as his successor; but nothing shows more clearly the far-seeing wisdom of the man than his refusal to hasten to his ends. There were weighty reasons which made a German Pope desirable. An Italian Pope could wield spiritual weapons only, at which the rich barons, who still held most of the papal domains, would merely have laughed. The Pope must be rich and able to command imperial protection against the Normans, who had again shown signs of hostility by imprisoning the papal legates on their journey from Constantinople. Moreover, the candidate must be approved by the Emperor; for the church was too feeble to attempt an election independently of him.

A deputation, headed by Hildebrand, was accordingly sent to Henry to request a nomination. In his own mind Hildebrand had already fixed upon Gebhard, the Bishop of Eichstadt, one of the wealthiest and ablest of the German prelates, and the confidential counsellor of the Emperor. He had been indirectly the cause of Leo's defeat in his unfortunate Norman campaign, since it was by his advice that Henry had withheld the greater part of his troops from going to the Pope's assistance. It was a shrewd stroke of policy to secure the full exertion of the imperial power to wrest from the Normans a portion of the papal estates. The voice which had withheld troops from Leo could command their services for the rescue of Rome. On the other hand, the Emperor, by Gebhard's election, would be deprived of a valuable instrument of the German policy of keeping the Pope in subjection to the empire; and, in the work of reëstablishing the Papacy, the churchman might be expected to predominate over the imperialist, " the Italian Pope over the German liegeman."

The negotiation was long. Gebhard was reluctant, and Henry was divided between his desire to retain him at court and his hope of having a strong ally in Italy; but Hildebrand at last prevailed, and Gebhard was inaugurated at Rome on the 13th of April, 1055, as Victor II.

The Emperor followed the new Pope into Italy with a large army, only to confront a new enemy. The Margrave Boniface of Tuscany had been murdered three years before, leaving three minor children under the care of his widow, Beatrix. Two of these died, leaving only Mathilde, eight years of age. Beatrix, two years later, contracted a second marriage with Godfrey, Duke of Lorraine, and committed to him

Tuscany and nearly all her other extensive possessions. By this marriage Henry's old and implacable enemy acquired control of the inheritance of the most powerful family in Italy, an inheritance which, in the possession of Mathilde, afterwards became the great source of Hildebrand's power and independence. If Godfrey now could ally himself with the Normans and bring all central Italy under one sceptre, he might win both the Italian and the Roman crown and dispose of the Papacy as he pleased.

At Florence Henry seized Beatrix and Mathilde and held them as hostages. Godfrey retorted by going into Lorraine and stirring up there a dangerous revolt against his authority. Henry returned to Germany, taking with him Beatrix and Mathilde. The latter, educated with much care, speaking several languages, beautiful in person, and with a high and fierce spirit, was inspired by her mother's captivity with a lively hatred of the imperial house, of which Henry's son and successor experienced the consequences.

Henry had committed to the Pope plenary power in Italy, with instructions to keep Godfrey within bounds. He commanded him also to seize Godfrey's brother Frederick, Leo's legate to Constantinople, on his return from that city; but Frederick eluded him, and concealed himself until he emerged, a short time after, as Pope. Henry, on his return to Germany, heard of Godfrey's uprising in Lorraine, and desiring to deal with this and also to have his son recognized by Italy, he sent for the Pope, his former counsellor, and received him at Goslar. Only a few days after, he died at Botfeldein, on the 5th of October, 1056, at the age of thirty-nine. His death was the beginning of confusion in Italy and Germany. The church saw in it her deliverance from imperial dictation. Victor might shed tears over the bier of his old friend, but Hildebrand was already forecasting his own triumph over Germany and Italy.

The Empress Agnes was regent for her son, Henry IV., scarcely six years old. Victor was in power both as Pope and as Emperor. Through Agnes's agency peace was concluded with Godfrey, the first condition being the release of Beatrix and Mathilde. Godfrey now became more powerful than ever, and his power gave him a greater influence in ecclesiastical affairs. Victor exerted himself to secure the adherence of the Lorraine family, and with that view Frederick, Godfrey's brother, was made Abbot of Monte Cassino, the richest monastery in Italy. Hildebrand had already selected him as the next Pope, with a view to placing between Rome and Germany this strong family, reconciled to Germany only in appearance, and to win by its aid the independence of the church. He was in Tuscany, near to Victor, inspiring him with his own hatred of the empire. He had won the confidence of Beatrix, and was, apparently, her confessor and counsellor. Mathilde revered him as the wisest and holiest of men, and he made good use of his opportunity to inspire her with that zeal for the Holy See which was the passion and the glory of his life. Victor began to assume a loftier tone, and to speak of the apostolic throne of Peter, the chief of the apostles, raised high above all people and all realms that it may pluck up and destroy, plant and build, in his name. He was preparing to cross the Alps again to arrange the affairs of Germany with the Empress, and was meditating a second great council at Rheims, when he suddenly died, on the 28th of July, 1057.

CHAPTER V.

FOUR POPES—THE ELECTION DECREE—THE PAPAL ALLIANCE WITH THE NORMANS.

REDERICK of Lorraine, Abbot of Monte Cassino and brother of the most powerful prince of Italy, had gone to Rome to be invested with his new dignity of cardinal priest of St. Chrysogonus in Trastevere, which Victor had conferred upon him shortly before his death. Scarcely had he taken possession of his church when the news was received that Victor was dead. The highest ambitions of the house of Lorraine seemed about to be realized. The Franconian house of Germany was represented only by the Empress and her young son. Godfrey and his wife had been admitted by Victor as joint representatives of the empire and rulers of Italy; with Victor had fallen the last prop of the empire in Italy; Frederick, through Henry III.'s persecutions, had become the hereditary enemy of the imperial house of Germany, and the time seemed ripe for the Roman clergy and people to elect a Pope without imperial interference. Instead, therefore, of sending to Germany for a nomination, the chiefs of the clergy and nobility consulted Frederick as to the succession. Hil-

debrand was absent in Florence. Frederick named five candidates, among whom was Hildebrand, but the dominant party insisted upon Frederick himself. Five days after Victor's death he was enthroned as Stephen IX.

Frederick was a man of princely nature, a churchman of the sternest and haughtiest type, and a rigid monk, with the spirit and aims of a secular potentate. Faithful to the plans of his predecessors, he contemplated the reform of morals, and especially the celibacy of the clergy. To this end he called to his side men like Hildebrand and Damiani, promoting the latter to the cardinalate. Frederick's elevation made the influence of the house of Lorraine in Italy practically unlimited. What was more natural than the thought that the new Pope had designed the imperial crown for his brother? By the aid of Godfrey he might expel the Normans and then elevate him to the imperial throne. He was without means for so vast an undertaking, but he was still Abbot of Monte Cassino, and the vaults of Monte Cassino were packed with treasure. Why should he not use this in so holy a cause, for so notable an advancement of the church's power? He commanded the treasure to be brought to Rome, and the monks obeyed with tears. But he could not keep it. He was consumed with self-reproach. St. Benedict himself seemed to protest against the sacrilege, and he finally sent back the whole.

The German court was anxious and angry at the election of Frederick without reference to the imperial authority. Stephen sent Hildebrand to the Empress, and he found no difficulty in justifying to her the resumption by the Romans of the right of free election. During Hildebrand's absence, Stephen, desiring to visit Tuscany, being in feeble health, and possibly having some premonition of his approaching death, before his departure enjoined the bishops, nobles, and priests, under penalty of anathema, in case he should die during his absence, to nominate no successor before Hildebrand's return. He had scarcely arrived at Florence when he died, on the 29th of March, 1058. With him ended the succession of five German popes who had filled the chair from Clement II.

The imperial party at Rome at once sent to the Empress, placing the nomination in her hands; but the Emperor's minority offered to the Roman barons, who had been compelled to disgorge some of the church's stolen wealth, an opportunity for getting the papal election into their hands. The Tusculan party and all the factions created by the severity of the foreign popes combined for this purpose with the enemies of Hildebrand among the married and simoniacal clergy. They constituted a secret assembly by night and chose John Mincius, Cardinal Bishop of Velletri, one of the five named by Frederick on the death of Victor II. Several priests were intimidated into giving their consent, and John was privately inaugurated as Benedict X. Rome resounded with the tumult of arms, and the populace, made happy for the hour with the gold stolen from St. Peter's, once more gave their allegiance to a Tuscan-noble Pope.

Benedict occupied the Lateran as Pope during the

rest of the year 1058. Meanwhile Hildebrand in Germany had received the news of the outrage. As the nomination had been offered to the Empress, he obtained authority from her to proceed to a new election, and was sent as her plenipotentiary to Florence, where he succeeded in enlisting the coöperation of Godfrey of Lorraine. Though the rival of the Empress, Godfrey had a common interest with her in wresting the Papacy from the lawless Romans. A large number of bishops joined Hildebrand at Florence, and by their assembly, Gerard, Archbishop of Florence, a Burgundian, was chosen as Pope under the name of Nicholas II. His Burgundian origin made him more agreeable to the Germans than an Italian would have been, and Godfrey heartily concurred in the choice.

The Empress gave her confirmation on a secret stipulation that her son should be crowned Emperor. Nicholas at once proceeded to Rome, backed by Godfrey and his troops. Hildebrand found means to bribe a part of the Romans and some of the counts, and before Godfrey's army arrived the Roman factions were furiously fighting among themselves. The Trasteverines opened the gate; Godfrey's troops poured in, occupied the Leonina[1] and the Tiber

[1] The Trastevere was in the only division of the city on the right or Tuscan side of the Tiber. This division comprised also the Janiculum and the Vatican. The Leonina was the section occupied by the Vatican. It had not been included within the wall of Aurelian, and remained outside even after the erection of St. Peter's. The work of enclosure was begun by Leo IV., in 848, and completed in 852. The whole Vatican region was surrounded with a thick wall like a horseshoe in outline, nearly forty feet high and protected by twenty-four strong towers. The region thus enclosed was known as *Civitas Leonina*.

Preliminary Treaty with the Normans. 45

Island, and stormed the Lateran. Benedict fled, and Nicholas entered the city with Godfrey and Hildebrand.

By this vigorous stroke the nomination of the Pope was transferred from the German sovereign to the princes of Tuscany. The imperialists were not deceived either as to the intent or the author of this movement. They recognized the hand of Hildebrand, and reproached him for conspiring with Beatrix " to set up a new idol false and frivolous," without the knowledge of the Romans. Quite as important for the future development of the Papacy was the alliance with the Normans. Immediately after Nicholas's inauguration Hildebrand concluded a preliminary treaty with them in Campania, and took back with him to Rome three hundred Norman horsemen, who besieged Benedict in the fortress of Galeria, about fifteen miles from the city. Benedict appeared upon the wall, and began to curse the Roman people who had made him Pope against his will; but he finally consented to abdicate on a pledge of security for his life, which was given by thirty Roman nobles. He took refuge near the church of Santa Maria Maggiore; but thirty days later Hildebrand seized him and had him carried before Nicholas and a council in the Lateran. Here the pontifical robes were put upon him and then stripped off before the altar, and he was forced to subscribe a confession of numerous sins, drawn up by Hildebrand, after which he was formally deposed from all spiritual dignities. (He lived for twenty years afterwards, in the monastery of St. Agnes, closely watched by his enemies.)

The temporary success of the Roman nobility in the election of Benedict stimulated the reform-party to new energy under Hildebrand's leadership. They were determined to free the papal election from the interference alike of the Roman nobles and of the German throne. A council was convoked by Nicholas in Rome (April, 1059), in which Benedict X. was condemned, and the prohibitions of simony and priestly marriage were renewed. Berengar of Tours appeared, and was forced to burn his books in the council-chamber. But the most significant act of the council was the passage of a decree concerning the papal election. It was the greatest revolution attempted in the hierarchy since the days of the apostles. The council enacted that on the death of a Pope the cardinal bishops should first assemble and nominate a successor; they should then summon the cardinal priests to vote upon their choice; and finally the people should be consulted and give their assent. The authority of the German Emperor was vaguely recognized; but the terms were adroitly framed to express the supremacy of the Pope over the Emperor, rather than the right of the Emperor over the papal election; and they reduced the right to a personal privilege accorded by the Roman Church itself. The actual election was vested in the higher clergy. The lower clergy and the people were simply to assent. The college of the Roman cardinals was thus erected into an ecclesiastical senate, from which alone, in time, the popes must proceed.[1] Finally, in order to with-

---

[1] See Peter Damiani's "Epist. ad Card. Episcopos," in which the cardinal bishops are styled "spiritual senators of the universal church."

draw the elections from the violence of city revolutions, it was decreed that they should no longer be locally confined to Rome, but that even a minority of cardinals should be competent to choose a Pope canonically in another place. Moreover, the candidate need not belong to one of the Roman churches. This decree, accompanied by a fearful anathema,[1] was ratified by general consent, and the signatures of a hundred and thirteen bishops and of many other ecclesiastics were attached to it. The name of Hildebrand appears with the simple title " monk and sub-deacon of the Roman Church."

Menaced by a life-and-death struggle with the German empire, by the Roman patricians and the German nobles, the hopes of Nicholas were directed to the Normans, who were still under the ban of the church. Hildebrand's keen eye foresaw that the Normans would found a dynasty in Italy, and that, by recognizing it, a vassal state and a powerful protection against the city of Rome and the German empire would be secured to the church.

The Normans, since their victory over Leo IX., had acquired nearly the whole of Apulia and Calabria. The disturbances in the Papacy had favored the attempts of Robert Guiscard, who since 1056 had ruled the Norman military republic in Apulia. The impotence of Constantinople, the weakness of Germany under the regency, the needs of the Papacy, the characteristics of the Normans, all conspired to found a Norman kingdom. In 1058 Richard of Aversa wrested Capua from Landulph V., the last of the

[1] See Milman, " History of Latin Christianity," bk. vi., chap. iii.

Lombard princes. Soon afterwards Guiscard overpowered Troja, to which the Pope laid claim, and was laid under ban by Nicholas as a robber of church property. Under Hildebrand's influence Nicholas now abandoned the belligerent policy of Leo IX., and entered into league with the Normans. At Melfi, in the summer of 1059, Richard of Aversa and Robert Guiscard received from Nicholas their conquests, except Benevento, as fiefs of the Holy See. The rights of the plundered rulers were as little regarded as the so-called supremacy of the German empire. "One legitimacy was seen to vanish and another to emerge out of a robbery." It might well be asked how the Pope had acquired that proprietorship of the whole kingdom of Naples which he now conferred. He based his right, no doubt, on the fabled Donation of Constantine. The Normans took the oath of vassalage to the Pope, engaged to pay an annual tribute, and swore to assist the church in maintaining its possessions, and to aid the popes who should be canonically chosen by the superior cardinals. Thus Rome, at one stroke, acquired control of Byzantine, Saracenic, and imperial Italy, and the election decree of Nicholas II. was committed to the protection of Norman swords.

The election decree and the Norman alliance created dissatisfaction in both Germany and Italy. Many of the Roman nobles were of German descent and held by the Emperor, while others, of Latin origin, no less earnestly contested the sovereignty of the Pope. Rome was divided between a papal and an imperial party. The popes for a long time had not sprung from the great Roman families; consequently they had no secure hold upon the barons, and were compelled to rely for the subjection of the city mainly upon the hated Normans. A Pope lived over a volcano which, in its quietest moments, never failed to remind him of the fires which raged below. The city was studded with the towers and castles of rapacious nobles. Proud families jealous of their ancestral rights; petty princes who subsisted by plunder and struck at any hand which wrested from them their ill-gotten booty; a venal and fickle populace ready to throw itself at a moment's notice upon the side which offered the largest pay; cardinals and clergy deep in plots and conspiracies, and as rapacious and unprincipled as the titled robbers to whom they ministered the sacraments of the church; a soldiery hardened to every horror and sacrilege—furnished the elements of an explosion which might break out at any moment and deluge the city with blood.

The death of Nicholas, on the 27th of July, 1061, threatened to bring on a catastrophe. The enemies of reform held a parliament, resolved to confer the patriciate on the young King Henry, sent him the insignia, and besought him to give Rome a Pope. They were joined by many Lombard bishops and by envoys of Milan, who urged the Empress not to allow her son to be robbed of his imperial rights, but to nominate a Lombard Pope and an enemy of clerical celibacy. Indeed, the agitation created by the reform-movement was nowhere greater than in Milan. The Milanese clergy were rich and numerous; clerical positions were purchased by the sons of the nobility; most of the priests were married, and the reform-decrees accordingly aroused the bitterest opposition. On the other hand, the pride and insubordination of the noble-clergy created among the more democratic portion of the people a popular party fired with zeal for reform. The partisans of the old system rallied round Guido of Valate, who had been archbishop since 1045; while the reform-party, known as the Pataria, and in closest relations with Hildebrand, found their leaders in Landolfo and Erlembaldo, two brothers of noble family, with the fanatical deacon Arialdo, who attached himself to them as preacher.

While the imperialists of Lombardy thus combined with their friends in Rome to elect an anti-Hildebrandian Pope, the Roman reformers sent Cardinal Stephen to the German court, which refused to receive him. Not content with this, the German bishops held a synod, at which they declared void the acts of the Roman council—a proceeding which Peter Damiani, naturally enough, characterized as "a conspiracy against the Roman Church, and a specimen of audacity wholly incredible." Hildebrand thereupon assembled the cardinals, on the 1st of October, 1061, and caused Anselm of Badagio, Bishop of Lucca, a Lombard, to be elected according to the provisions of the new decree under the title of Alexander II. This prelate was the intimate friend of Hildebrand, and one of the founders of the Pataria; and Hildebrand hoped to avail himself of his long and friendly relations with the German court. The newly elected Pope was borne in triumph by a crowd of monks in frocks without sleeves, carrying a gourd on their left side and a sack on the right. Some cries were raised in the crowd: "Away, lepers! bagmen!" but Guiscard, who was present with a strong force of Norman knights, sustained the election, and the imperial partisans did not venture to make any disturbance.

CHAPTER VI.

CADALOUS—BENZO—HENRY IV.—MILAN.

HE election of Alexander was justly regarded by the Germans as an invasion of imperial rights. The Lombard ecclesiastics, especially those who favored the marriage of the clergy, dreaded his elevation as carrying with it the dominating influence of Hildebrand and of the high monastic party. A number of these, along with the German bishops, under the lead of Guibert of Ravenna, the chancellor of the empire and administrator of the imperial interests in Italy, assembled, in October, at Basle, where the Roman envoys had already invested the ten-year-old Henry IV. with the patriciate, and elected as Pope Cadalous, Bishop of Parma, who assumed the name of Honorius II. It was a mistake, since Cadalous had neither the genius nor the power to fight Hildebrand. Damiani represented him as without character or learning, and declared that if he should prove himself able to explain a single verse of a psalm or a homily he would submit to him as an apostle. The election was no more irregular than other pontifical elections held in Germany under Henry III. and peaceably accepted by

the Romans; but Hildebrand's persistent assertion of the independence of the Roman Church had produced its effect, and made Cadalous's election appear a profanation, even to those who did not overlook the power of Germany. Two hostile popes now confronted each other; the one in Rome, the other beyond the Alps, where he was preparing, with the aid of the Lombard bishops, to descend upon Rome and drive his rival from the Lateran. Rarely has the world regarded a similar conflict with equal interest; for the two popes represented, not two factions, but two powers, the Roman Church and the Roman Empire.

Alexander, weak and dependent, leaned upon Hildebrand, whom he at once appointed chancellor. At his side stood Damiani, whose trenchant pen he set in motion, and who vigorously pelted the antipope with the names of "the devil's preacher," "the apostle of Antichrist," "food for hell-fire," and similar elegant and Christian epithets. Cadalous, on the other hand, formerly the imperial chancellor of Henry III., and a courtier of high standing, found no reason for viewing himself as a usurper, but sufficient reason for calling his opponent such. Not so strong as Hildebrand, he had abundant wealth, and he founded large expectations on the well-known mercenariness of the Romans. In the spring of 1062 he entered Italy, was conducted by the imperialists from city to city in spite of the obstacles interposed by Beatrix, and halted at Parma in order to perfect his arrangements for an advance upon Rome.

In the meantime a contest was going on in Rome

itself. Benzo, the Bishop of Albi in Piedmont, a man of coarse eloquence and popular humor, was the commissioner of the Empress to the Romans. He was a bitter enemy of Hildebrand and his Pope, against whom he launched furious invectives, while he impressed the Italians by his boldness and coarse wit, and especially by his promises to reward their adherence to Honorius with "mountains of gold." Having formed an Honorian party in Tuscany, he went to Rome, where he was received by the German courtiers. The nobles assembled in the Circus Maximus, which had lain in ruins ever since a Gothic king had held there the last chariot-race. Its two obelisks lay upon the ground, its triumphal arches were in fragments, and its arena was overgrown with grass and weeds. But its tiers of seats could still afford sitting for an assembly. Benzo adroitly gave the meeting the character of a Roman popular assembly. Alexander found himself compelled to appear in person. As he rode into the arena, surrounded with cardinals and armed retainers, he was received with a popular tumult and a thundering harangue from Benzo. Benzo denounced him as a perjured traitor to the German court, who had abandoned his see of Lucca and had usurped that of Rome; as an intruder who had obtained his election by bribery and the aid of Norman robbers. He proclaimed Hildebrand as the prime mover in this business, for which they both had incurred damnation. He bade him, in the king's name, to abdicate the chair of St. Peter and to seek forgiveness of Henry.

After a brief denial of these charges Alexander rode

off amid the hootings of the populace. Benzo, on his return to his residence, assembled the imperial partisans, and a deputation was sent by them to Honorius, urging him to hasten to Rome and occupy the apostolic chair.

Honorius, accompanied by Guibert, advanced to Rome and encamped at Monte Mario.[1] His force was attacked by the Hildebrandians, and a bloody fight ensued; but Honorius entered the Leonina as victor on the 14th of April. Hundreds of slain covered the Neronian field at the foot of Monte Mario, and many Romans were drowned in the river. Honorius, however, was unable to pass into the city proper, nor did he dare remain in the Leonina, but returned to his camp in the Neronian field. Though he heard that Godfrey was on the march, his hopes were fostered by the arrival of an embassy from the Greek Emperor, who acknowledged him, and eagerly seized upon the Roman schism as an opportunity for driving the Normans from Apulia by the help of Alexander's enemies. But all negotiations were broken off by the appearance of Godfrey, who assumed the rôle of mediator. He required both parties to lay aside their arms and both popes to retire to their bishoprics, while he himself would go to Germany and let the question be decided there. Honorius withdrew to Parma and Alexander to Lucca; but events in Germany, in which Hildebrand had a hand, decided the contest in favor of Alexander.

The death of Henry III., leaving as his heir a son

[1] Monte Mario rises over the Ponte Molle, and is reached by the Via di Porta Angelica, which issues from the Piazza of St. Peter.

only five years old, gave an opportunity to the lords, who had long suffered from Henry's oppressions, to free themselves; and on every side parties were formed against the young prince. Agnes had chosen as her principal counsellor Henry, Bishop of Augsburg, a man of large experience and weighty character; but the confidence which she reposed in him at once aroused the jealousy of other bishops who were candidates for the favor of the Empress. They were indignant that one woman should control so many princes and bishops through a man concerning whose relations with her they did not hesitate to circulate the most scandalous reports. They also declared that the young prince was being educated entirely under female influence, and was not instructed in manly studies or chivalrous sports; and that he ought to be made to grow up outside of the palace walls, amid assemblies of nobles and the cares of state and war.

Accordingly, Hanno and Siegfried, the Archbishops of Cologne and Metz, with Otho of Bavaria and Count Ecbert, contrived a plan for his abduction. During a banquet at Kaiserswerth Hanno took occasion in the prince's presence to praise the beauty of his own barge, which was lying in the stream, and invited Henry to go on board and inspect it. No sooner had he mounted the deck, however, than the oarsmen rowed away. Henry threw himself into the river, but was rescued and taken to Cologne, where Hanno was absolute master. The Empress's efforts to rouse the people for the recovery of her son were ineffectual, and Hanno convened at Cologne a council of lords and bishops, who formally approved his act and placed the administration of the empire in his hands, thus taking the regency from the Empress.

This was followed by a complete revolution in the attitude of the empire towards the Papacy. A council was summoned at Augsburg by the false and avaricious Hanno to consider the papal schism. Damiani appeared as the representative of the Hildebrandian party, and Alexander was acknowledged as Pope. The victory of the Hildebrandians was complete, since Guibert, the very soul of the imperialists, was displaced, and the chancellorship of Italy was bestowed upon Bishop Gregory of Vercelli. Alexander was joyfully received by his partisans in January, 1063. Godfrey's troops, united with the Norman forces, held possession of Rome, though they could not drive their opponents from the Leonina; and Alexander, holding only the city proper, tremblingly took up his residence in the Lateran.

Meanwhile the Empress Agnes, disgusted with Germany, repaired to Rome, where she recognized Alexander as Pope. Twelve years before, she had been crowned at her husband's side in St. Peter's amid a throng of princes and knights. She now entered Rome as a penitent, clad in a black woollen robe, and mounted upon an insignificant steed; but she possessed large wealth and costly ornaments, which were lavishly bestowed upon the Roman churches as votive offerings, or consecrated to the service of their altars. She embraced the religious life after a public confession to Damiani, and lived thenceforth austerely at Rome under the ministrations of Hildebrand, who gained over her a power which he afterwards used in his dealings with her son.

Though the Germans had abandoned Honorius, a large part of the Italian clergy adhered to him. He maintained a correspondence with the Empress and with her partisans in Germany, and devoted his wealth to the increase of his military strength. The barons of his faction in and near Rome held the castle of St. Angelo, and kept the city in constant alarm. Archbishop Hanno, beset with the jealousies of his episcopal brethren, and with a rising enemy in the young king, was at length supplanted by Adalbert, Archbishop of Bremen, a man eloquent, dignified, and munificent, who became the guardian and counsellor of Henry. He was a sturdy imperialist, and exhorted his party in Rome to hold out, Cadalous to repossess the papal chair, and Benzo to bring him once more to Rome. His free expenditure of money at Parma for a new expedition to Rome, the support of many Lombard troops, the reaction in the German court, the preoccupation of Guiscard and Richard of Capua in southern Italy, and the lukewarmness of Godfrey enabled him to appear before Rome with his army on the 4th of April, 1063. He obtained possession of St. Peter's by night, and made his headquarters at St. Angelo. Two attempts of his troops to reach the Lateran were repulsed. The conflict raged endlessly. No other city in the world had such facilities for a city-war, since the numerous monuments and public works furnished so many points for fortification. Rome was a forest of towers. The Romans endured this state of affairs for more than a year, while the two popes, the one in the Lateran and the other in St. Angelo, sang masses, hurled bulls and decrees, and vigorously cursed each other.

The death-blow to the hopes of Cadalous was the fall of Adalbert. This prelate, with all his fine qualities, was tainted with the rapacious instincts which characterized so many of his metropolitan brethren who ruthlessly plundered the property of the abbeys. The young king, moreover, was left to devote himself to idle sports. These things caused a combination against him of secular princes, led by Hanno of Cologne and supported by Godfrey. His palace was surrounded, and he was compelled to fly for his life to a distant estate, where he made terms by the sacrifice of the larger portion of his vast property. The Romans had become tired of Cadalous. After more than a year in St. Angelo he purchased for three hundred pounds of silver the privilege of flight to northern Italy. Hanno now summoned, in the emperor's name, a council at Mantua to decide the question of the pontificate. This assembled on the 31st of May, 1064, and declared Alexander to be the lawful Pope. Cadalous retired to his bishopric at Parma, where he lived for several years, never renouncing the papal title. Alexander went to Rome under Godfrey's protection, and the opposing party, for the time being, submitted to the regimen of Hildebrand.

Hildebrand had thus accomplished his purpose. With the recognition of Alexander the feeble efforts of the German regency to assume the patriciate were futile, and the claim of the crown to interfere in papal elections could now be more effectively met. The church was at his beck. Never had such activity pervaded the Lateran, which was thronged with the most distinguished representatives of all Christendom. Rome, through Hildebrand, had again become the metropolitan city. Every attempt at insurrection was held in check by the fear of Godfrey and the Normans.

But in Milan the reform battle was violently renewed. Milan had long occupied an independent attitude towards Rome. Its position had early threatened the universal pretensions of the Roman bishop. The fact of its having been at times the seat of the imperial residence, the prominence given to its archbishopric by the disorders which followed the time of Charlemagne, its conspicuous position as the centre of resistance to the Lombard conquest, its firm stand for Catholic orthodoxy against Lombard Arianism, the popular agitations growing out of the relations between archbishop and emperor—all had tended to develop a spirit of independence and to make the Milanese a distinct people, with a municipal life of their own.

The independent attitude of the city towards Rome in the present contest was favored by distance and by Rome's preoccupation with German affairs; but in Hildebrand's scheme the domination of Milan by Rome was a necessity. Marriage at this time was the universal privilege of the Milanese clergy. Celibacy excited suspicion, and concubinage was regarded as a heinous offence and a bar to ecclesiastical promotion. When, therefore, Anselm, a native of Milan, was made Pope by the Hildebrandian and celibate party, Milan embraced the cause of Cadalous

The crusade against clerical marriage had already been begun by Landolfo, Erlembaldo, and Arialdo, supported by the Pataria, and had resulted in a general raid on the clergy, who had been forced to purchase immunity by subscribing an obligation to celibacy. A papal legation, consisting of Anselm and Damiani, had been sent in 1059 to enforce the submission of the clergy, and their efforts had resulted in an outbreak in which Damiani and Landolfo were in great peril. Landolfo was now dead, but his place had been taken by Erlembaldo, a man valiant, sagacious, and of commanding presence. Alexander, at Hildebrand's suggestion, selected him as military leader in the war against sacerdotal marriage. A series of riots followed, and Guido, the archbishop, after vain attempts to sustain and protect the clergy, was driven from the city, and the preacher Arialdo obtained his excommunication by Alexander in 1066. Returning some time after to the city, and attempting, in disregard of the excommunication, to officiate, he was nearly beaten to death by the followers of Erlembaldo and Arialdo. This outrage caused a reaction which compelled the flight of the fanatical Arialdo, who was betrayed by a priest and cruelly murdered. Erlembaldo, however, soon got the upper hand again, and the contest was carried on with varying fortune until, in 1067, a legation sent by Alexander issued a constitution which protected the clergy from persecution, but decreed suspension for married and concubinary priests.

The reform-movement kept Alexander in constant agitation. The condition of Rome remained insecure, and he was glad to be absent when he could. His secular power was at the lowest ebb, and was a subject of jeering among the great Roman families. His part in the civil administration was an empty form. Both the civil and the criminal jurisdiction were chiefly in the hands of the city prefect, and the strife for this office filled Rome with tumult. The Roman Cencius, the son of a prefect, disappointed in obtaining the office after his father, barred the bridge of Hadrian on the city side with a tower, where he placed watchmen to exact toll from passengers. When a Roman noble could thus control the entrance to St. Peter's it may be judged how small was the Pope's power in the city. Rome was divided into two great camps. The Pope could command no soldiers, the military bands being independent and in the pay of different nobles. His only adherents were those whom he could procure by bribery, or vassals to whom he had granted church property in fief; and as the patrimony of St. Peter was nearly exhausted, the number of these was not large.

Hildebrand would gladly have brought the prefecture into the hands of the reformists; but Cencius's successful rival, Cinthius, who was on intimate terms with Hildebrand, the Pope, and the Milanese reformers, and who was expected to unite nobles, people, and soldiers in the reform-movement, took to preaching in St. Peter's instead of attending to his proper business. "Nothing better illustrates the condition of Rome at that time than the spectacle of Cencius in a tower at the bridge of St. Angelo, robbing and murdering wayfarers, and Cinthius forsaking the civil administration and haranguing in St. Peter's." [1]

The close of Alexander's pontificate was marked by the death of Godfrey in 1069. His son and successor, Godfrey, married Beatrix, the only daughter of Mathilde; so that the Roman see, which was wise enough to recognize the principle of inheritance in the female line, continued to enjoy the protection and support of both mother and daughter. Peter Damiani also died in 1072. Shortly before his death he participated in perhaps the most brilliant church festival ever celebrated in Italy—the consecration of the new basilica of Monte Cassino.[2] The great age of this abbey, its wealth and numbers, and the distinguished men who had issued from it, made it the grandest monastic establishment in Italy. A vast assemblage gathered on this occasion, including the Pope, Hildebrand, the Norman counts, and the Lombard princes. The festival lasted for eight days. It had a political no less than a devotional object. It celebrated the alliance of Rome with the Normans. It was a national Italian festival, and therein a great demonstration against the German empire.

The death of Alexander followed soon after, on the 21st of April, 1073, after a pontificate of nearly twelve years.

---

[1] Gregorovius.
[2] Monte Cassino is fifty-five miles northwest of Naples. See Gregorovius, vol. iv., p. 154.

CHAPTER VII.

HILDEBRAND POPE—GREGORY AND HENRY IV.—THE REFORM SYNOD.

HERE could be no doubt as to Alexander's successor. Hildebrand had been virtually Pope during two pontificates. The efforts of the Clugny party against simony and clerical marriage had been inspired by him, though he had begun his career as the chaplain of a simoniacal Pope. On him who had given the watchword for the fight with the empire the conduct of that struggle now devolved.

On the death of Alexander, Hildebrand, without delay, arranged for the funeral services on the next day. Ancient usage prescribed that a Pope's successor should not be chosen until the third day after the burial. The clergy were assembled in the Lateran [1] church to celebrate the obsequies, and Hilde-

---

[1] The Lateran church derived its name from the senator Plautius Lateranus, on the site of whose house it stood. The Lateran house was given in the fourth century to the Bishop of Rome as his residence; and the church was founded by Constantine. The original church was replaced by another in the beginning of the tenth century. The name of St. John the Baptist was given to it in the sixth century, but it was also known as the Basilica of Constantine, and as the Golden Basilica, from its rich ornaments. The church was nearly destroyed by fire during the pontificate of Clement V. (1305-14), but was rebuilt by him, and subsequently enlarged and remodelled by

brand as archdeacon was conducting the services, when a simultaneous cry arose from clergy and people: "Hildebrand is Pope! St. Peter chooses the archdeacon Hildebrand!" The archdeacon strove to allay the tumult, but the cardinal Hugo Candidus addressed them, saying, "Ye know well that, since the days of the blessed Leo, this tried and prudent archdeacon has exalted the Roman see and delivered this city from many perils; wherefore, since we cannot find any one better qualified for the government of the church or the protection of the city, we, the bishops and cardinals, with one voice elect him as the pastor and bishop of your souls." The people responded with shouts, and Hildebrand was immediately borne to the church St. Peter ad Vincula,[1] and enthroned with the usual ceremonies. The decree of election describes him as a lover of justice and equity, brave in misfortune, moderate in prosperity, and adorned with good morals, chaste, modest, temperate, hospitable, knowing how to rule his own household well, nobly educated, and instructed from infancy in the bosom of the church.[2]

It is interesting to compare this document with the many of his successors. It was regarded as supreme over all the churches of the world.

[1] Known as S. Pietro in Vincoli, on the Esquiline, not far from the baths of Titus. It was built in 442 by Eudoxia, the wife of Valentinian III. The name is derived from the legend that the mother of the Empress brought from Jerusalem the chain of Peter, giving half to Constantinople and the other half to her daughter. The chain which the apostle had worn before his death was also preserved in Rome, and as Pope Leo held the two in his hands, the ends miraculously united. The church was rebuilt in the eighth century and altered into its present form in 1705. It contains the "Moses" of Michelangelo.

[2] For the entire document, see Baronius, "Annales Ecclesiastici."

election decree adopted by the council of 1059, the special programme of the Hildebrandian party. In the former the Emperor is not mentioned. According to the latter the choice was to be made first by the cardinal bishops, after which the clergy were to be called in. The Roman clergy of all grades appear as special electors of Hildebrand, while the bishops, abbots, and cardinals are mentioned only as being present. The method of Hildebrand's election is thus carried back of the terms of the decree of 1059 to the old practice of election by the Roman clergy, with the consent of the neighboring bishops and of the people.

That Hildebrand may have been surprised by the manner of his election is not improbable. That the election itself was a surprise is incredible. He must have known that his name would be the first to be suggested by his party, as it had been on the death of Leo IX.[1]

Messengers were sent to Henry IV. to apprise him of the election. It is not likely that Hildebrand cared much about the assent or dissent of the King, but he had himself drawn or inspired the election de-

---

[1] See Langen, "Geschichte der Römischen Kirche von Gregor VII. bis Innocenz III.," p. 3 ff., and Carl Mirbt, "Die Wahl Gregors VII." Langen thinks that the election was not improvised, and that the election document was already drawn up in expectation of it. Mirbt holds that it was unexpected, and that the election document is not to be regarded as an official announcement of an election consummated by the competent bodies. The register of election and Gregory's own representations agree as to the *time* of the election, and differ as to the *motive* and *mode*. According to the register it was designed; according to Gregory it was unexpected. The register says that the cardinals acted as electors, and says nothing of irregularity. Gregory ascribes the initiative to the people.

cree of 1059, which, though it was one factor of the movement to free the papal election from the interference of the German throne, had recognized, however vaguely, the authority of the German sovereign in the election; and the omission to notify him would have precipitated an untimely conflict with the German court. Hildebrand also sent letters to various dignitaries, in which he styled himself "Bishop Elect of Rome," related the circumstances of his election, and asked their prayers for his protection against the danger which he could not escape. He did not wait for Henry's recognition to begin his official duties,[1] but plunged into them at once. He struck the keynote of his policy with no gentle or uncertain hand. The tone of his deliverances is that of one who has hitherto held himself in check for prudential reasons, but who now feels free to assert himself without restraint. He had reached the point where he could formulate in the roundest terms his theory of papal sovereignty, and he at once gave voice to his claim to the right of dominion over all worldly powers. He had known how to wait and how to gain his ends by roundabout ways. He at once became imperious, dictatorial, and insolent.

From a nineteenth-century point of view it is difficult to understand such assumption. The idea of the

[1] The question whether he sought and obtained the imperial consent has been hotly discussed. His enemies claim that he did not, and that his election was therefore illegal. They claim further that the royal assent was necessary to his being a candidate. The subject is exhaustively treated by Mirbt, "Die Wahl Gregors VII." He concludes that the royal assent was not obtained before the election, but that Gregory sought and received it afterwards. Compare Langen, "Geschichte," etc., pp. 6, 7, notes.

secular sovereignty of the church is one which this age neither comprehends nor tolerates; but the sentiment and the conditions of the eleventh century made both Hildebrand and his monstrous assumptions possible. The mediæval mind knew the powers of the unseen world only through the Roman Church, and did not dream of challenging its right to represent, interpret, and enforce them. Hildebrand's conception appealed to it none the less powerfully because it was chimerical. His radical, stupendous mistake, which the society of his age had not been educated to detect, was the belief that he could realize an ideal so divinely spiritual as that of the kingdom of God by external forces and secular methods; that he could carve out with the sword and shape with the deft fingers of ecclesiastical diplomacy that kingdom which is not of this world, and which is righteousness and joy and peace. The political no less than the moral and intellectual conditions of his time favored his attempt. The manifold divisions of the old empire of Charlemagne and Otto, the presence of the Islamites in Spain, the feeble sovereignty of Germany, the recent Norman conquests in Italy, and the transfer of England to the Normans, all invited the grasp of a master hand.

He put forth that hand at once. While still awaiting his formal inauguration as Pope, a legate was despatched to France to inform the legates there of his election, and to protect the rights of St. Peter in Spain, "whose land from of old belongs to that saint." Henry IV. was not left for a moment in doubt as to the range and absoluteness of the Pope's intent.

Hildebrand at once presented the alternative of submission or the sword. Commissioners were promptly sent to him to come to an understanding as to what was for the advantage of the church and the honor of the empire. If the King shall refuse to listen, Hildebrand will guard himself against the menace of the prophet Jeremiah: "Cursed be he that doeth the work of the Lord deceitfully, and cursed be he that keepeth his hand from blood." He will conclude an agreement with Henry which shall guarantee the rights of the church *as he understands them*. In case Henry shall not submit, which he thinks probable, he will gird himself for a decisive battle.

Meanwhile his own election was under discussion at the German court. A strong party of German and Lombard bishops urged Henry to cancel a papal election made without his authority, and warned him that if he did not promptly nip the violence of Hildebrand in the bud he himself would be the principal sufferer. The King hesitated, but finally sent Count Ebrard to call Hildebrand to account. Hildebrand replied that the position had been forced upon him by the Romans, but that he had delayed his inauguration until the King and the German princes should have been informed. Henry, who was really powerless to change the situation of affairs, accepted the explanation, and appointed Gregory of Vercelli, the chancellor of the Italian kingdom, to act as commissioner at the Pope's formal installation. An immediate and open conflict was thus avoided, but no friendly relation for the future was established; for, only a few days before his installation, Hildebrand, in a letter to Beatrix and Mathilde, expressed himself more threateningly than before concerning the King. He declared that he intended to send messengers to Henry to summon him back to his love for the Roman Church, and to represent to him the becoming mode of assuming the imperial dignity; and that he would resist him to blood rather than perish through participation in his wickedness.

On the 30th of June, 1073, Hildebrand was inaugurated under the title of Gregory VII., in the presence of Agnes and Beatrix, and with Gregory of Vercelli as royal commissioner. The name Gregory was assumed in remembrance of Gregory VI., and the number seven was a side stroke at the empire, since it recognized as a legitimate Pope one whose pontificate had been annulled by imperial authority.

Foreseeing that a conflict with Germany was imminent, Gregory at once took measures, by a journey to southern Italy, to secure the aid of the Normans. He obtained a renewed pledge of fealty from Guiscard, and appointed a meeting with him. He corresponded with the Emperor Michael of Constantinople as to the reinstatement of friendly relations between Rome and Byzantium, but was particular to designate the church of Constantinople as the daughter of the Roman Church. Much to his disgust, Guiscard failed to meet him, as agreed, at Monte Cassino; but he concluded an agreement with Prince Landolfo for the protection of papal rights over Benevento, and received the oath of fealty from Richard of Capua, who also engaged to give the same oath to Henry IV., if he should be requested to do so by the Pope, but without detriment to his fidelity to the Roman Church.

Immediately after Gregory's inauguration the Saxons broke out in revolt. Adalbert, Henry's guardian, had made enemies of the Saxon nobles and had aroused against them the suspicions of the King, who, with a view to holding them in check, had erected fortresses in their territory, the garrisons of which committed many depredations. By these proceedings the whole body of the Saxons was embittered, and took part in the insurrection under the leadership of Otto of Nordheim. The contest assumed the character of a religious war, and the three prelates who were friendly to Henry were forced to flee from the country. Thuringia was also in arms. Henry's castles were besieged and his revenues intercepted, and his chief vassals refused to aid him.

In these straits he wrote to Gregory, who was still in the south of Italy, a humble letter, confessing his guilt in failing to show due honor to the priesthood and to use his sword for the punishment of evil-doers, and entreating the Pope's pardon for having laid hands on church property and for having sold episcopal positions to the unworthy and simoniacal. Gregory forthwith took advantage of this to extend his own power. He commanded Henry to conclude a truce with the Saxons and to submit the decision of the contest to the papal legates. Henry had taken care not to request the Pope's mediation in the Saxon affair. He was anxious only to prevent a rupture at a time when he was weakened by the revolt; and distrusting the fidelity of his great vassals, and perceiving that his troops were not well disposed towards him, he resolved to treat with the Saxons himself.

Fifteen bishops and several princes repaired, on the King's behalf, to the Saxon camp, and a treaty was subscribed of which the principal feature was Henry's agreement to withdraw the garrisons from the castles erected by him in Saxony. The order to this effect was issued on the spot, but was slowly executed. Henry was especially reluctant to relinquish Hartzburg, built upon a height which commanded an important territory, and very strongly fortified. The officers of the fortress refused to open its gates, and Henry, glad of an excuse to prolong the delay, proposed a diet of all the princes of Germany to adjust this and similar questions. The diet was summoned for the 10th of March, 1074, but too late to prevent the uprising of the Saxons, provoked by the delay, to enforce the fulfilment of the pledge. Henry gave orders to dismantle the fortresses, only stipulating that the palace and church erected by him at Hartzburg should be unmolested; but on the 24th of February the insurgents, eighty thousand strong, destroyed not only the military works, but the church also, plundered the treasures, and even dug up the bones of Henry's brother and son.

The King sent a deputation to Rome to expose the cruelty and sacrilege of the Saxons, and to demand the Pope's censure; but Gregory did not care to interfere just then. It was rumored that the Saxon revolt had been fomented by emissaries from Rome, and that the rebels had justified themselves by the Pope's authority. Gregory was in no haste to condemn those who seemed to be armed in the interest of the church, and he was not sorry for anything which kept Henry on the other side of the Alps. Moreover, he was now preparing his decisive blow at simony and the secularization of the bishops. Fully aware of the perils of his undertaking, he neglected no source which seemed to promise material aid. He reminded Count William of Burgundy how, in the presence of Alexander II., and at the tomb of Peter, he had vowed to be ever ready for the defence of the church. He should therefore hold his army in readiness to come to Rome, and should exert himself to enlist the aid of other princes. He is seeking, he continues, to collect a great army, not in order to shed the blood of Christians, but to overawe them, that they may the sooner submit themselves to righteousness. Perhaps William can, after appeasing the Normans, lead his army to Constantinople, to deliver the Christians there from the Saracens.

That Gregory seriously contemplated this object soon appeared, when news came that the Saracens had advanced almost to the walls of Constantinople; and he issued, on the 1st of March, 1074, a formal summons to Christians to deliver the brethren in the East from the hands of the infidels. The call did not issue in a crusade, but the idea of a crusade was broached in the word "brethren." The deliverance of Oriental Christians from the Saracen yoke was indeed contemplated, but with it their subjection to the papal authority; for it was not a Gregorian idea to rescue from the infidels Greeks who were under ban, only to leave them in their insubordination to

Rome. It will soon appear from Gregory's own words that he entertained the thought of going in person to the East with an army, "in order to strengthen the Christians there in their faith."

On the 13th of March, 1074, Gregory opened at Rome the first great reform synod. The official records are wanting. The German and Lombard bishops were absent. The synod enacted that simoniacally consecrated priests should not officiate; that those who had obtained their churches by simony should surrender them; that clergy living in "fornication," under which term marriage was included as well as concubinage, should not perform clerical functions, and that laymen should not avail themselves of them, since their blessing changes into a curse and their prayer into sin. Here is to be observed the Gregorian doctrine that sacramental efficacy depends on the worthiness of the ministrant. Robert Guiscard, who at that moment was besieging Benevento, was anathematized, with all his followers, and Philip I. of France was threatened with excommunication unless he should justify himself before the apostolic nuncios against the charge of simony. The council closed with the excommunication of five German princes for simony.

Excommunication, ban, and anathema were used as practically synonymous terms. It is hardly necessary to remind the reader of the popular conviction that in the clergy was vested the destiny of each soul, and the power of admission to heaven and of exclusion from eternal life; and that without the reception of the sacraments salvation was impossible. This

Ban and Interdict. 75

conviction was the fulcrum of the great lever which Gregory and his successors applied with such power. Excommunication did not confine its operation to delinquencies in faith or morals, but extended to purely secular transgressions. The ban deprived its victim of the sacraments, and extended to all who might have intercourse with him. Hence it practically released all the subjects of an excommunicated sovereign from their allegiance to him. No Christian might speak or eat with the excommunicate. He must live hated and alone in this world and be prepared for damnation in the next. Interdict was an extension of excommunication to a whole district or kingdom. Under interdict the nation was deprived of all exterior exercise of its religion. The altars were despoiled, the crosses, relics, and images laid on the ground and covered, the bells were removed from their towers, mass was celebrated with closed doors, and none but priests were admitted. No religious rite was allowed to the laity except the baptism of new-born infants and communion to the dying. The dead, refused burial in consecrated ground, were thrown into ditches, or buried in common fields without funeral rites. Marriages were celebrated in the churchyards, the use of meat was prohibited, and people were forbidden to salute each other, to shave their beards, or to care for their dress.

The decrees of the council were not favorably received in France, Germany, England, and Lombardy. Opposition was increased by Gregory's reckless violence in attempting to enforce them. Murmurs began to be heard that the Pope was a heretic, setting up an insane dogma against St. Paul's permission to marry, endeavoring to compel men to live like angels, and thereby leading them to lasciviousness. If he should persist it would be seen where he would find his angels for the service of the church. The German priests, among whom celibacy was rare, scouted the edict. The Archbishop of Mainz, on attempting to announce it to his clergy, was greeted with an explosion of cries and threats which made him tremble for his life. In Lombardy the spirit of resistance was furious. In France the Archbishop of Rouen was driven from his pulpit with stones.

The Germans were the thorn in Gregory's flesh. Henry, indeed, by his compliance with the Pope's demand for the dismissal of sundry simoniacal officials, appeared to be wholly submissive to his will; but his apparent submission was only the result of temporary necessity, and the reaction was not long in coming. The captains of Milan, who derived their profit from simony, conspired with the King, and engaged to destroy the Pataria and to kill Erlembaldo. Guibert, the Archbishop of Ravenna, immediately after the synod, had begun his intrigues in Rome, seeking conspirators against the Pope, and joining forces with Cencius, the partisan of Cadalous. Elements favorable to Guibert's plots were not wanting in Rome. The Pope had submitted to the Roman clergy the alternative of living in common in apostolic poverty, or returning to private life and renouncing all churchly emoluments. Many preferred the latter, and were consequently embittered against Gregory. Hundreds of clergy were living in concubinage, and their children and nephews were accustomed to inherit their livings. In St. Peter's more than sixty married wardens, wearing mitres, announced themselves as priests, said masses, promised prayers for money, and appropriated the offerings brought for the pardon of sins. They held orgies by night in the church, and the steps of the altar were polluted with fornication and murder. Gregory made bad blood by stopping these performances and forbidding all celebrations in the church before nine in the morning. Guibert, having rallied these disaffected elements, now returned to Ravenna, and Henry found in Italy, and in St. Peter's itself, as much inflammable material as he could desire.

CHAPTER VIII.

THE INVESTITURE DECREE—CENCIUS ATTACKS THE POPE—THE SYNOD OF WORMS—GREGORY'S ABDICATION DEMANDED.

HE effect of all this appeared when the Pope, towards the middle of June, undertook, with the promised help of Beatrix and Godfrey, his expedition against the Normans. Guibert had by this time excited an uprising in Lombardy, which made it impossible for Mathilde and Beatrix to fulfil their promise of aid, and Gregory was obliged to return to Rome. A fresh instance of his audacity was given by his memorial addressed, in September, to the entire French episcopate, based upon exaggerated reports of the general prevalence of crime and licentiousness. Gregory declared that the King was mainly responsible for this state of things; that he had spent his whole life in crime, and had thus by his example plunged his people into ruin; that only lately he had perpetrated a flagrant act of extortion upon some merchants. The bishops were to blame for not rebuking him. They must urge him to mend his ways under threat of papal penalties; and if he remained obstinate they were to suspend intercourse with him and

to lay France under interdict. This failing, the country must be wrested from him by any means. A little later, in a letter to the Bishop of Rheims, he described the King as a plundering wolf, an unrighteous tyrant, and an enemy of God and religion. To the clergy of Germany he addressed a letter demanding open resistance to all bishops who should refuse the decrees against simony and concubinage, and forbidding the reception of any ministries from simoniacal or concubinary priests. To Henry he complained of the attempts of self-seeking men to create distrust between himself and the King, and announced his intention of summoning the Christians of the West to a crusade on behalf of the Eastern Christians. Already, he said, fifty thousand men were ready to follow him. The church of Constantinople was striving after harmony with the papal see. He would follow the example of former popes who had journeyed to the East to strengthen the faith of Christians, and during this expedition he would intrust the Roman Church to the care of the King. The general summons to the crusade was issued in December, 1074.

Gregory now addressed himself to the task of bringing the north of Europe under papal control; to which end he wrote to Swen, the King of Denmark, reminding him of his duties as a sovereign, and expressing his expectation of receiving delegates from the King for the adjustment of certain ecclesiastical matters, especially the establishment of a metropolitan see in Denmark. This measure was a politic scheme in the papal interest, since, if successful, it would take the Danish sees out of the jurisdiction of the refractory Bishop of Hamburg and Bremen, separate them from direct German influence, and thus render them more manageable by the papal legates. The Pope further wrote that he would be pleased to know to what extent the King would be willing to place his army at the service of the Roman Church, and that he hoped yet to see his son at the head of affairs in Apulia as the defender of the apostolic throne. Truly a far-reaching and ingenious plan— to separate the ecclesiastical jurisdiction of Denmark from Germany, to enlist the power of a Scandinavian prince, and to provide for a Scandinavian sovereignty in southern Italy.

The second great Roman synod was held in the Lateran on the 24th of February, 1075, and was numerously attended. The principal subject of consideration was lay investiture.

This practice rested on the principle that the ruler of a realm had the right to appoint bishops. It was strongly maintained in Germany because the bishoprics and abbeys there had become, to all intents and purposes, political organizations, with rights of coinage, toll, and civil jurisdiction, and with corresponding military duties. On the death of a bishop his ring and staff were brought to the King; and when the King had chosen a successor he put the new bishop or abbot into possession of the temporalities of his fief by "investing" him with the staff and ring and receiving his oath of fealty. This ceremony preceded his consecration. As the bishops and abbots were accustomed to give large presents to the King, this practice of investiture naturally allied itself with simony.

The decree of the synod entirely abrogated the right of investiture by the temporal sovereign. It deposed every bishop or abbot who should receive it from any layman, interdicting him from all communion with the church until he should have abandoned the benefice thus obtained. If any emperor or other secular potentate should grant investiture of a bishopric or other inferior dignity he should suffer the same penalty.

In this decree Gregory gave the watchword for a war of a hundred years between the church and the secular power. This statute made a revolution of the whole feudal system throughout Europe, as regarded the relation of the church, now dominant, to the state. In the empire it annulled the precarious power of the sovereign over almost half his subjects. All the great prelates and abbots, who were at the same time the princes, the nobles, the counsellors, the leaders in the diets and national assemblies, became, to a great degree, independent of the crown; the Emperor had no concern, unless indirectly, in their promotion, no power over their degradation. Their lands and estates were as inviolable as their persons. Every benefice, on the other hand, thus dissevered from the crown, was held, if not directly, yet at the pleasure of the Pope. For as with him was the sole judgment (the laity being excluded) as to the validity of the election, with him was the decision by what offences the dignity might be forfeited; and as the estates and endowments were now inalienable and were withdrawn from the national property and became that of the church and of God, the Pope might be, in fact, liege lord, temporal and spiritual, of half the world."[1]

For some time after the synod Gregory was occupied in carrying out its decrees, in attempting to establish the papal supremacy in Hungary under the guise of mediating between King Solomon and his rival Gensa, and in the effort to become the political and ecclesiastical ruler of Russia. He also renewed his efforts to acquire for himself a new support in the kingdom of Denmark. Henry, meanwhile, had begun to act with great vigor. He threw himself into the movement of the German cities against the pretensions and oppressions of the higher nobility, and displayed real skill and energy in attaching them to himself. The Archbishop of Mainz and the Dukes of Lorraine, Bohemia, and Bavaria joined him, with Rudolph of Suabia. The Saxons had broken with the South-German princes, and Henry had not forgotten the desecration of Hartzburg. In June, 1075, he marched against them with a splendid army, fell upon them at Langensalza, near Hohenburg, and utterly routed them. The victory became a massacre. It was said that scarcely any escaped of the sixty thousand infantry which formed the bulk of the Saxon army.

This victory, which made Henry master of all Germany, braced his courage for the encounter with the Pope. The second Roman synod had put an end to every pretence of friendly relations. The investiture decree bore very hardly upon Henry, whose predecessors from the time of Henry II. had found their

[1] Milman, "History of Latin Christianity," bk. vii., chap. ii.

principal strength in the episcopacy. The possessions of the clergy comprised a considerable part of the soil of the empire, and so long as the King nominated the bishops he held in his hands the control of these territories and of their revenues. The decree, as we have seen, withdrew at one stroke all these estates from the national property and placed them at the command of the Pope.

Any lingering hope which Gregory might have entertained of peaceable relations with Henry was soon dissipated. Erlembaldo had been killed at Milan shortly before the victory of Langensalza, and the Milanese had at once sent a deputation to Henry asking for the appointment of an archbishop, as the chair had been practically vacant since the resignation of the aged Guido di Valate in 1069. Henry nominated Tedaldo, the leader of the disaffected bishops, who a year later excommunicated Gregory himself. Gregory forbade Tedaldo to accept consecration, and addressed a peremptory letter to Henry charging him to confess to a bishop and to submit to penance for having held intercourse with the excommunicate and simoniacal, and defending at length the grounds of the investiture decree. Henry, elated with his victory over the Saxons, was in no mood to submit to papal dictation. The Pope's letter reached him at Goslar at Christmas, and was so ungraciously received that the legates, according to their instructions, summoned the King to appear before the next synod at Rome. Meanwhile the storm had broken at Rome. The plots of Guibert and Hugo Candidus came to a head at the same time that the Pope's letter was received at Goslar. Cencius, the head of the malcontents in the city, and master of St. Angelo, being suspected of dealings with Guibert, was attacked, seized, and narrowly escaped with his life through the intercession of Mathilde. He gave hostages and remained quiet for a time, but was all the while secretly plotting revenge and devising a plan for Gregory's destruction, possibly with Henry's connivance.

The Christmas-eve scene of 1075 is one of the most striking in the history of mediæval Rome. The rain fell in torrents, and the Romans were mostly within doors. The Pope, with a few priests, was celebrating midnight mass at the altar of the manger in Santa Maria Maggiore, one of the most popular churches in Rome, but situated on the Esquiline, a quarter with a bad reputation and frequented by the vagabond shepherds of the Campagna. Suddenly a fierce cry and the clash of arms were heard, and Cencius and his soldiers burst into the church and rushed with drawn swords to the altar. Cencius seized the Pope by the hair, dragged him from the building, and, placing him on a horse behind a soldier, conveyed him to one of his strongholds in the region Parione. The city was aroused, and resounded with the peal of trumpets and the booming of bells. The people flew to arms at the appeal of the clergy; the gates were barred, and the streets were aglare with the red light of torches. The Pope was thrown into a chamber of Cencius's castle, where a man and a woman who had in some way managed to enter with the crowd kindly covered him from the cold and dressed his wounds. Cencius, with drawn sword and fearful imprecations, appeared before the Pope and demanded of him an order for the delivery of his treasure and castles, which Gregory refused. The male and female attendants assailed the prisoner with a storm of abuse, in which the name of Mathilde was frequently heard.

Thus passed the night. The morning saw the people, still ignorant of the Pope's fate, thronging to the Capitol. The report of his imprisonment in the tower of Cencius was the signal for a general rush to that point and a furious assault. The cowardly bravo, seeing himself lost, threw himself at Gregory's feet, imploring mercy. Gregory appears at his best in this crisis. He declared that he freely forgave his personal injuries, but that Cencius's sins against God and the church must be expiated by a pilgrimage to Jerusalem. Cencius managed to escape. His penitence lasted only as long as his danger, and he was soon at his old work of pillaging the domains of the church. The Pope was brought out, stained with blood, and was carried back to Santa Maria, where he completed the mass which the brigands had interrupted, and then returned to the Lateran.

Gregory now determined to proceed to extremes. Henry was already under summons to appear at the Easter synod. Gregory demanded that he should restore the imprisoned Saxon bishops and call a council at which the Pope should appear, so that the bishops might be canonically judged and the excommunicated counsellors dismissed. He declared that if the King should refuse he would cut him off like a rotten branch.

The answer to this insolent demand was the German national synod at Worms on the 24th of January, 1076. Hugo Candidus, the cardinal who, on the occasion of Hildebrand's election, had extolled his virtues to the Roman people, appeared with a biography of the Pope, arraigning him as the worst of men, charging him with having obtained the papal office by bribery and violence, and with licentiousness and necromancy. He also presented a forged letter from the Roman senate, clergy, and people, demanding Gregory's deposition. The King was present, with nearly all the German bishops. Only two had the courage to declare uncanonical the condemnation of an absentee, particularly the Pope, against whom no bishop could prefer charges; but William of Utrecht submitted to these the alternative of affixing their signatures or renouncing their allegiance to the King, and they yielded. A decree was passed containing a long list of charges against Gregory, among which were committing ecclesiastical administration to the hands of the people (referring to the Pataria), breaking his oath not to assume the papal chair, his uncanonical election, and his intimate relations with Beatrix, "so that it is common report that papal decisions and decrees are framed by certain women and that the church is governed by a female saint." On these grounds the council declared that they renounced their allegiance to Gregory and no longer recognized him as Pope.

For his fight with Gregory, Henry sought confederates in Italy. He sent two bishops to Lombardy, where a synod at Piacenza adopted the Worms decree.

The time had now arrived when he had been cited to appear before the Roman synod, which assembled in the Lateran on the 22d of February. The reverend fathers were at first occupied in discussing the good omen conveyed by a remarkable egg, on the shell of which appeared serpents erecting themselves and falling down again. While they were examining this marvel, Roland of Parma, the royal messenger, entered the assembly. When the opening hymn was finished, Roland, without waiting for the Pope to speak, addressed him with the words: "The King, with all German and Italian bishops, commands thee to descend from the usurped chair of St. Peter; for only by their will and the imperial grant can any one attain this dignity." He then proceeded to summon the Roman clergy to meet the King at Whitsuntide in order to receive a new Pope from him; at the same time delivering a letter of the King to the clergy and people of Rome, in which "the monk Hildebrand" was designated as "the usurper of the papal chair," and the Romans were summoned to expel him, and, with the King and all the bishops, to elect a new Pope.[1] To this was appended a letter to Gregory himself, commanding him, on the ground of the decree of Worms and on the authority of the Patrician of the Romans, to renounce the pontificate. Still another letter was addressed by the King to the Roman synod, superscribed: "Henry, King not by usurpation but by divine ordainment, to Hildebrand, no more Pope, but false monk," and concluding with: "Step down! Step down, thou eternally damned!"

[1] See Mirbt, "Die Wahl Gregors VII.," p. 11.

Bishop John of Porto sprang up, shouting "Seize him!" and the city prefect and the civil officers and soldiers, with drawn swords, fell upon Roland and would have slain him but for the protection of the Pope, who covered him with his own person.

The synod, restored at last to order, proceeded to vigorous measures. The Lombard and Roman bishops who had subscribed the Worms decree were promptly excommunicated. Gregory issued the following edict: "I forbid King Henry the rule of the whole German and Italian kingdom, and release all Christians from pledges given or to be given to him, and forbid any one to serve him as King; ... and because he was disobedient as a Christian, companying with excommunicated persons and committing many transgressions, I anathematize him."[1]

This declaration is noteworthy as carrying the Gregorian doctrine of the Papacy. It is an advance on that of Nicholas I., the first Pope who attempted to apply ecclesiastical jurisdiction to monarchs. Nicholas declared that princes, with all believers, are committed to the church for the care of their souls, and are therefore subject to its penalties. Gregory excommunicated Henry not merely as a Christian

---

[1] Langen holds that in this utterance the deposition and not merely the suspension of the King is proclaimed. So Giesebrecht, "Geschichte der deutschen Kaiserzeit." The opposite view is held by Martens in Dove's "Zeitschrift f. Kirchenrecht" (1882). Mirbt exhaustively discusses the question in his careful monograph, "Die Absetzung Heinrichs IV. durch Gregor VII. in der Publicistik jener Zeit" (Leipzig, 1890). Langen's view appears to be justified by Gregory's own words at the synod of February 11, 1079. The majority of authorities recognize no difference between this declaration and that of March 7, 1080.

prelate, but as king of kings. He was not satisfied with the ecclesiastical punishment of excommunication, but claimed dethronement as his special prerogative. Dethronement was not to be regarded as a consequence of excommunication, but as a distinct punishment.

CHAPTER IX.

CANOSA—RUDOLPH OF SUABIA—GREGORY AND WILLIAM THE CONQUEROR.

ALL previous papal bans were feeble in comparison with this thunderbolt. With all the popular recognition of the Pope's power of blessing and cursing, the audacity of this proclamation, depriving of his crown the head of an empire and releasing his subjects from their allegiance, filled European Christendom with amazement, if not with terror.

Gregory followed up the ban of Henry with the deposition of the Bishop of Worms and the excommunication of those who took part in the synod at Piacenza. The sentence of Henry was published in an encyclical addressed "to all who desire to belong to the sheep of St. Peter." Unable to foresee the consequences of his act, Gregory hastened to make overtures to Robert Guiscard. Meanwhile a reaction had begun in Germany, and recantations began to flow in from the subscribers of the Worms decree. The Lombard bishops were less pliable, and at the instigation of Guibert they assembled at Pavia immediately after Easter, and formally laid Gregory under ban. Henry, immediately after the Worms

The Oath to the Empress Disregarded. 91

synod, increased his severity towards the Saxons, rebuilt his castles, and erected some new ones; and by garrisons and extortionate levies endeavored to bend the stubborn spirit of that people. From Saxony he passed to Cologne, and thence to Utrecht, where he first learned of the sentence of excommunication. William, the Bishop of Utrecht, encouraged him to treat it with contempt, and spoke of it to the congregation, after mass, in terms of ridicule. William's sudden death soon after was interpreted by popular superstition as a divine judgment upon his presumption. The King summoned a new synod at Worms to appoint a successor to Gregory; but several of his friendly bishops unexpectedly died; Godfrey of Lorraine was murdered at Antwerp, a new uprising in Saxony was threatened, and the synod did not take place.

In September Gregory summoned Germany to prepare for the choice of a King according to his pleasure. Concerning the oath given to the Empress in case her son should die before her, he declared that she was to be consulted after Henry's deposition, and that if her consent should not be given to the papal plan, the apostolic chair would dissolve all impeding bonds. Evidently the Pope did not yet know how Agnes would regard Henry's deposition; but he was resolved to carry out his policy in any case, and so trifling a thing as a solemn oath to a sovereign was not to be allowed to stand in the way.

Henry's following constantly diminished. Many of the German princes saw in the Pope's decree an opportunity of freeing themselves from a King whom they detested. A formidable conspiracy was already on foot, led by the Dukes Rudolph of Suabia, Welf of Bavaria, and Berthold of Carinthia, with the Bishops of Würzburg and Metz. On the 16th of October, 1076, the Diet of Tribur was convened, which resolved to acknowledge the deposition and to proceed to a new election. The diet sat for seven days. Henry, close by at Oppenheim, negotiated with the assembly in vain, succeeding only in obtaining the appointment of a diet at Augsburg in February, at which the Pope was to appear and decide on the succession to the throne. It was, however, provided that if the King should remain for a year without obtaining absolution from the ban, he should unconditionally forfeit the crown. Henry engaged to confine himself to the administration of public business, and not to set foot in a church; and the princes swore that, if he should keep his oath, they would escort him to Rome to receive the imperial crown, and afterwards join him in expelling the Normans from Apulia and Calabria. Henry issued an edict to the German nation recalling the decree of Worms, and in a letter to the Pope promised him obedience and satisfaction.

Gregory announced to the German bishops and princes his intention of being present at Augsburg in February; but Henry determined to forestall his journey by going to Rome himself. In some way his intention became known, and the papal dukes guarded the Alpine passes in order to prevent his journey. The King accordingly set out from Spires before Christmas, accompanied by his wife and son, and thence travelled by way of Burgundy to the foot of Mount Cenis. Here his mother-in-law, the Marchioness of Susa, and her son Amadeus demanded the cession of five rich bishoprics as the price of his passage through their territory. The passage of the mountain was terrible. The winter was unusually severe; the mountain gorges were choked with snow, and the summits and slopes coated with ice. The horses could not keep their feet. The Queen and her young son, with the women of the cortége, were placed in extemporized drags of skins, and were thus drawn down by the guides.

In the meantime the Pope had set out for Germany, and, having crossed the Apennines on his way to Mantua, was met by the news of Henry's arrival in Italy. Uncertain whether he came as a suppliant or at the head of an army, Gregory turned aside to Canosa, a strong fortress of Mathilde on the right bank of the Ofanto, about fifteen miles from the Adriatic.[1] The castle crowned a commanding height, and was surrounded by three walls. Gregory could not have chosen a more secure asylum at the very gates of a hostile country. He feared the union of the King with the Lombards, and was distressed by the thought of the horrors of war which Henry might bring into Italy.

[1] Canosa is now reached from Reggio in eight hours. This castle was destroyed in 1255. Mathilde had four castles in the neighborhood, which are now pointed out at Quattrocastella. The height commands a magnificent view of the Apennines and of the Lombard plain from Lucca to Modena. Dean Stanley gives an interesting account of his visit in 1863 (" Life and Letters," vol. ii., p. 137). A rough but graphic picture may be found in " Italy from the Alps to Etna," by Stieler, Paulus, and Caden (trans. by F. E. Trollope).

The King was met at Turin by the excommunicated bishops. He could not disguise the weakness of his escort, but pretended that he had come only for their sakes, to demand of the Pope the reasons for his sentence. The bishops entreated him not to acknowledge the power of Gregory; yet they found his position so weak that they resolved to submit for the time, in the hope that, after his interview with Gregory, he might be able to join them again and free himself and his kingdom from the papal hands. The excommunicated prelates of Germany also made their way to Canosa, and presented themselves at the gates, barefoot and in woollen shirts, asking to be received to penitence. The Pope, after admitting them, had them shut up in separate cells, with only bread and water until evening. After several days he received them, imposed rigorous penances, and finally released them from excommunication and dismissed them with the charge to render no aid or homage to Henry until he should have satisfied the church.

Henry, having reached Canosa, obtained an interview with Mathilde, and sent through her a request to the Pope to be released from the ban, which was refused; the Pope insisting that Henry should acknowledge his deposition and declare himself unworthy to reign. While these negotiations were still in progress, Henry suddenly appeared at the castle gate on the 25th of January, 1077, with the excommunicated members of his suite. He was admitted only as far as the second enceinte. He wore the garb of a penitent, and with bare feet stood in the snow, fasting, and shivering in the icy wind until evening. Thus he stood for three days, a spectacle to move all hearts save that of the representative of Jesus Christ. Mathilde entreated for him in vain. At last Henry, worn out, retired to the Chapel of St. Nicholas, where he sought the intercession of Hugo, the Abbot of Clugny. Hugo declared that only Mathilde could prevail with the Pope; and the countess, exchanging tears for reproaches, finally obtained a reluctant consent to Henry's admission. The King knelt in tears, implored forgiveness, and received the terms of submission. He was to appear at the place and time appointed by the Pope, to answer the charges of his subjects. He must guarantee the Pope safe-conduct thither. If he should be found guilty he should resign his kingdom and pledge himself not to seek revenge for his deposition. Until that time he was not to assume the insignia of royalty, nor appropriate any part of the royal revenue except what might be necessary for the maintenance of himself and his attendants. All his subjects were to be released from their oath of allegiance, and, if restored, he was to rule the kingdom according to the Pope's dictation.[1]

On his return from Canosa, Henry was met by the Lombard bishops, who were enraged at him no less than at the Pope, and who reproached him for his pusillanimity in return for all that they had done for him. There was a general demand that he should

---

[1] The story that the Pope endeavored, in the sacrament which followed, to make Henry appeal to Heaven for the sincerity of his confession and the sanction of Gregory's brutality, lacks confirmation.

abdicate in favor of his son Conrad, and that they should march to Rome and elect another Pope who should crown the young Emperor. The state of affairs was so threatening that Gregory, who had left Canosa, thought it most prudent to return. Henry was coldly received in the Lombard cities. He sent to the Pope from Monza, asking to be crowned King of Italy by certain bishops not under interdict; but the Pope refused.

Gregory had overreached himself. The Papacy was not strong enough to bear such a strain. The sentiment of humanity was not dead nor entirely overpowered by superstition. Gregory had given his enemies a point of attack upon his personal character by an act more worthy of a follower of Attila or Genseric than of the disciple of the gentle Christ. He might be the Vicegerent of God, but he had none the less written himself down a brute. The monarchical sentiment was not extinguished in Germany. Henry began to recover strength and to throw off the appearance of submission. He openly reinstated his old counsellors and resumed communication with the Pope's enemies. He was in Italy with leaders who were ready to risk everything against Gregory.

The revolted German princes had gone too far to retreat, and were compelled to proceed to the King's deposition. The place of the diet was changed from Augsburg to Forchheim, and the time to the 13th of March, 1077. The Pope promised to appear, and sent to Henry requiring his attendance, a requisition which Henry evaded. The Pope, however, was detained, and the assembly met in the presence of the papal legates, and elected Rudolph of Suabia as German King. The conditions imposed were that the King should employ no simony in filling the bishops' chairs, and that the German throne should no longer be hereditary—a provision which would give the Pope a decisive voice in its occupation. On the 26th of March Rudolph was anointed at Mainz.

A civil war was thus begun in Germany which lasted for seventeen years. A bloody riot took place at Mainz on the very day of the coronation. Worms closed its gates against the new King; the Bishop of Augsburg returned to Henry's party; at Zurich Rudolph was greeted with a rising of the populace excited by the simoniacal clergy; and at St. Gall, where he had appointed an abbot, the monks broke out in revolt and compelled the abbot to flee for his life.

Henry now resolved to return to Germany and fight. He was joined by reinforcements as he advanced, by many lay lords, and by many towns which sent him troops. A large party of the clergy even in Suabia, Rudolph's province, adhered to him. The loyal sentiment was reviving; not only the personal sentiment towards Henry, but the idea that the royal no less than the papal authority was of God. The Pope was forced to leave Rudolph in the strait into which he had brought him. Rudolph was received in Saxony, and Henry marched into Bavaria and confiscated the domains of Welf. Some of Rudolph's vassals deserted to him, and some others were lukewarm. The war went on—a war of castle against castle, borough against borough, a chaos of murders, conflagrations, and robberies. Agriculture declined, famine extended into the fertile cantons of Bavaria and Suabia, and the borders of the Rhine were laid waste.

Amid these bloody disorders Gregory never ceased to claim that the questions in dispute should be referred to him. In May he wrote for a safe-conduct across the Alps that he might summon the two Kings to submit to his arbitration. Whichever should submit was to be recognized as King at an assembly of laity and clergy in the Pope's commission. All this was the more strange as he had already sent to Rudolph, with his benediction, a crown with the inscription, "Petra dedit Petro, Petrus diadema Rodolpho." The Saxons did not relish this proposal, since it placed Rudolph on the same ground with the excommunicated Henry, before the same tribunal.

Henry now marched to Franconia, and Rudolph to Würzburg, which had declared for Henry, and which he proceeded to besiege. The two armies faced each other with the Neckar between. An agreement was made for a conference of the dignitaries of the empire at Augsburg for the purpose of settling the whole question, and a commission for this conference was issued by the papal legates. Rudolph thereupon abandoned the siege of Würzburg and returned to Saxony, and Henry went to Suabia and occupied himself with burning castles and churches and other depredations. This state of affairs did not consist with Gregory's proposed visit to Germany, for which his safe-conduct had not arrived; besides which he began the year 1078 with the burial of his friend, the Empress Agnes, who, since Henry's deposition, had continued to lead an austere religious life at Rome. Her zeal against simoniacs and married priests, and her sacrifice of maternal tenderness to the interests of the church, were subjects of boasting at the Lateran. By her death Gregory lost his most efficient instrument for conciliating Henry, an ardent admirer, and an active promoter of his plans. About the same time he was also deprived of one of his most faithful adherents in Rome by the assassination of the prefect Cinthius, a bold defender of the church against the Roman barons. All these causes kept him in Italy, where he was busily occupied with his efforts to extend his power in Spain and Corsica. He consoled himself for his failure to reach Germany with the expectation of terminating the German contest at the approaching Roman synod.

This assembly was convoked on the 25th of February, 1078. Both Henry and Rudolph were present by their deputies. Henry's envoys affirmed his submission to the Pope, and declared that his deference to the Pope's impending decision was the only reason why he had not suppressed Rudolph by force of arms. A disposition to condemn Rudolph at once was manifested by some of the delegates, but Gregory deferred his decision until Saturday, when he decreed that an assembly should be held in Germany, under his personal direction or that of his legate, to decide the contest for the throne. Rudolph received the Pope's blessing, but was treated as helpless and without special respect. The synod also renewed the excommunication of the Normans for attacking papal territory, and that of Tedaldo of Milan and Guibert of Ravenna.

Rudolph was naturally irritated at the Pope's inconsistency in acknowledging him as King and renewing Henry's excommunication and deposition, and yet treating both Kings as parties to an undecided contest. Rudolph's followers did not hesitate to represent this inconsistency to Gregory, to his serious embarrassment, since he could not gainsay the facts. It was evident that, since the power was now on Henry's side, the Pope preferred reconciliation with him, and was quite ready to leave Rudolph in the lurch and to keep him merely as a menace to Henry. Rudolph was compelled to seek the alliance of France and of Hungary without waiting for the diet. The Pope again endeavored to enlist the aid of the Normans; but on the 7th of August Henry and Rudolph joined battle at Melrichstadt, in Franconia, without a decisive result. Both Kings sent messengers to Rome, each hoping to convince the Pope that he had been victorious, and on that ground to obtain a declaration in his favor. For the representatives of Rudolph, Gregory, not yet knowing how far he might succeed in his attempts against Henry, had only bombastic words on the greatness of St. Peter's authority, vague promises, and exhortations to hope for the best.

On the 11th of February, 1079, another synod was held at the Lateran, by which the case of Berengar of Tours was finally disposed of. Gregory himself would have been satisfied with Berengar's general declaration that the bread and wine, when consecrated, are the body and blood of Christ; but hints began to circulate that the Pope was compromising with a heretic. A declaration was submitted to Berengar that the bread and wine are not merely consecrated symbols, but the true body and blood of Christ in sensible wise (*sensualiter*), veritably grasped by the hands of the priest and manducated by the teeth of the believing recipient. The Pope at once demanded Berengar's subscription to this. Berengar submitted, and retired with a letter of protection from Gregory.[1] The German question then came up. Rudolph's commissioners complained bitterly of Henry's misdeeds and presented a letter addressed to the synod. In this it was charged that at the last Roman council it had been questioned whether Henry should be excommunicated, while in fact he had been already several times excommunicated. Three years before, he had been excommunicated by the synod and had not improved since that time. Being conditionally absolved, he had not kept his promises, but, on the contrary, had abused the papal legates. His excommunication and Rudolph's recognition followed; notwithstanding which he had desolated Germany and had laid violent hands upon church property especially. The Pope ought at least to keep the excommunication binding until he should have given satisfaction. After Henry's commissioners had been heard in his defence, the opinions of the synod were divided; but the Pope pronounced Henry's

---

[1] Gregory was charged with being secretly in sympathy with Berengar's views. See Langen, p. 103, note, and Jacobi, art. "Berengar von Tours" in Herzog's "Real Encyklopädie."

statements false and declared that he had deposed and had never restored him. An oath was exacted from the commissioners of both parties to give the Pope a safe-conduct to the assembly in Germany, and Gregory wrote encouragingly to Rudolph and the Saxons, summoning them to fight.

In his efforts to extend the authority of the Roman see, Gregory did not overlook England. But he found himself confronted there with a King of larger mould than Henry. William the Conqueror was brave, enterprising, and ambitious, vehement though politic and artful, severe though not ungenerous, a man fully able to measure swords with Gregory, with an equal force of will, equally alive to his own interests, and not likely to brook tamely the imperious insolence of the Italian monk. Gregory demanded of William, through Lanfranc, the Archbishop of Canterbury, the payment of Peter's pence,[1] which he had pledged to Alexander II., and the profession of fealty to the Holy See. As Lanfranc did not exhibit as much zeal in the matter as the Pope thought he should, he received a sharp reminder of his duty; to which he replied that he had advised the King to comply with the Pope's demand, and for further information referred him to William's letter. In this letter William refused the profession of obedience to Rome. The

---

[1] The origin of this annual tribute to the Roman see is uncertain, though it is traced back to Saxon England. It consisted of the payment of a silver penny by every family possessing land or cattle of the yearly value of thirty pence. Ranke ascribes its introduction to King Offa (755–794), for the purpose of paying for the education of the clergy and of aiding pilgrims. This, however, is very doubtful. Lingard thinks it is not earlier than the time of Alfred.

Peter's pence he would pay, because his predecessors had paid it; but they had never bound themselves to obey the Roman see. It was a manly and dignified utterance. Gregory had found his match. The Conqueror kept his promise, but he was not disposed to favor a close intimacy between the Primate of England and the Pope. Gregory's complaints grew louder, until at last Hubert, his legate in England, was commanded to admonish William and to threaten him with the anger of Peter. It may be imagined how much effect this stage-thunder produced upon the stalwart Norman.

CHAPTER X.

HENRY BESIEGES ROME—GREGORY'S FATAL TRIUMPH—HIS DEATH.

THREE legates had been selected by Gregory to decide finally the contest for the German throne. One of these, the Patriarch of Aquileia, turned traitor to the Pope and detained the others in Italy, so that May was well advanced when they reached Germany. It was arranged that the business should be transacted at Würzburg, and that a truce should be observed until after the meeting. But Henry came to the assembly accompanied by troops in order to force the condemnation of Rudolph, and Rudolph remained away and prepared for battle, so that the legates accomplished nothing. One of them, Bishop Ulrich of Padua, hastened to Rome before his colleagues in order to plead the cause of Henry; but besides being already suspected by the Pope, he was publicly contradicted by a monk, an emissary of Rudolph, who accused Henry of perjury, and was confirmed by the third legate, Peter of Albano. Gregory wrote to Rudolph, assuring him of his neutrality and justice, and urging him to patience.

At the beginning of 1080 the two rivals again tried

conclusions. At Flurchheim in Thuringia, Henry was defeated, his camp was abandoned, and he and his Bavarian troops took to flight. Again both parties sent messengers to Rome. Rudolph announced his victory and Henry's flight, and demanded that the Pope should no more flatter Henry, to the contempt of his holy name. Henry threatened the Pope that if the ban were not laid upon Rudolph a new Pope would be elected. These envoys waited in Rome for the synod of March, 1080. Then, although his representatives did not have a fair hearing, Henry was again deposed and Rudolph was acknowledged. The Pope interdicted Henry from the government of all Italy and Germany, and deprived him of all royal power and dignity. His decree concluded thus: "And now, ye apostolic princes, let the whole world know that if it is in your power to bind and loose in heaven, ye can also on earth, from empire and kingdom, from duchies, principalities, countships, and all human possessions, according to their deserts, from each and every one take, and to them give. If you can rule over the spiritual, so, surely, can you rule over the secular. Exercise your judgment on Henry so boldly that all may know that he falls, not by accident, but by your power, in order that he be brought to repentance, and his soul be saved in the day of judgment." A sharper definition of Gregory's theocracy was impossible.

With all the anxiety attendant upon the German disturbances, Gregory was unremitting in his attention to foreign nations and their relations to the Roman see. He caused young foreigners to be sent to Rome to be educated in the Roman faith and polity, that they might return as apostles to their countrymen. Norway, Denmark, Bohemia, Poland, England, occupied him in turn. But the storm which his violence towards Henry had raised was now about to break on his own head. On Whitsunday, 1080, there assembled at Mainz nineteen bishops, who renounced their allegiance to Gregory and adjourned, after inviting the Lombard bishops to a synod at Brixen, which met on the 25th of June. With Henry himself there were present many German and Lombard lords attached to his party, the cardinal Hugo Candidus, and thirty bishops. The Pope was formally charged with irreligious conduct, simony, and preaching sacrilege and incendiarism; with being a defender of perjurers and homicides, a sharer in Berengar's heresy, a necromancer, and possessed with a demon. "For these reasons," the document concluded, "we judge him canonically worthy of deposition and expulsion."

The assembly at once proceeded to the election of a new Pope, and their choice fell upon Guibert of Ravenna, who was present—an old enemy of Gregory, of high birth, learned, skilled in politics, and far more dangerous than Cadalous had been. Henry knelt and paid him homage before the assembly.

The Pope, meanwhile, had gone to Lower Italy in order to form a league with Robert Guiscard. Robert was released from ban, took the oath of fealty to the Pope, and was invested as, "by the grace of God, Duke of Apulia, Calabria, and Sicily." He promised to aid the Pope in the maintenance of the papal prerogatives, to protect him in the possession of papal authority, and, after the Pope's death, to assist, on requisition, the cardinals, clergy, and laity in the choice and inauguration of a successor. The terrible consequences of this compact will soon appear.

In view of the situation of affairs, it seems strange that Gregory should have required the Bishops of Calabria and Apulia, just about this time, to send troops to the aid of the deposed Emperor Michael of Constantinople, who had taken refuge in Italy. The requisition was plainly a consequence of the agreement with Guiscard. Nothing came of the attempt to aid Michael, but the expedition to the East prevented Guiscard from sending troops to the Pope's assistance against Guibert. His inclination to do so in any event may well be doubted, and, to all appearance, the crafty Norman was contemplating this withdrawal of troops from Italy at the very time of his treaty with the Pope. The absolution from ban was very desirable, both to consecrate the expedition to the East and to secure the possessions in Italy which Robert would be compelled to leave without the protection of his own sword.

Henry, feeling that he could not settle matters with Rome until he had finally disposed of Rudolph, undertook, in the beginning of autumn, a new invasion of Saxony. The armies met, on the 13th of October, about three leagues from Leipzig. The Saxons were victorious, but Rudolph was slain.

At the synod of 1081 the ban against Henry was renewed; but the news of Rudolph's death and of greatest agitation. He demanded immediate help from his supporters in Germany, and began to think of the choice of a new anti-king. He also applied to the Normans, and requested Abbot Desiderius, of Monte Cassino, to ascertain Guiscard's disposition towards the Roman Church—a strange request, when he had so recently invested Guiscard as the protector of the papal interests. He desired to know if, after Easter, Robert would come to his assistance with an army, and how many soldiers he could place at his disposal. Henry meanwhile had reached Italy and had pushed forward to Ravenna, and on Friday, the 21st of May, stood with Guibert before the gates of Rome.

His army was small. He had hoped to increase it in Ravenna, and to win the support of Guiscard; but the cunning duke, deaf to Henry's as to Gregory's appeal, sailed after Easter for Durazzo. Henry, however, received the crown of Italy, and caused Guibert to be acknowledged as Clement III. by the Lombards at Pavia. He endeavored in vain to win over the Roman clergy. As the Romans, contrary to his expectation, refused to open their gates to him, he had himself crowned with the imperial crown by Guibert in the royal tent. The heat of the summer and the exhalations from the Campagna soon began to tell upon his forces, and after forty days he withdrew into Tuscany, made an ineffectual attempt against Florence, arrived in Lombardy in August, and attacked the garrisons of Mathilde. Guiscard answered the Pope's entreaties for aid by pleading the demands of his expedition to the East. Meanwhile the Saxons, on the 9th of August, chose Hermann, Count of Luxembourg, as King of Germany; but the other German provinces remained faithful to Henry, and a strong force was raised against Hermann.

Guiscard's enterprise was, ostensibly, against Alexius Comnenus, who had supplanted Michael Ducas on the throne of Constantinople. This usurpation involved a personal disappointment to Guiscard, since his daughter had been betrothed at a tender age to Constantine, Michael's son and heir. With a powerful force he attacked Durazzo,[1] on the coast of Illyria. While Durazzo was thus threatened, Alexius applied to Henry, congratulating him on his success in a pious and just war, complaining that his own empire was disturbed by Guiscard, and asking his alliance. The message was accompanied with a large sum of money and valuable presents, with a promise of more; and Henry at once formed a league with Alexius against Guiscard. His motive was twofold—he needed the money, and the prolongation of the war in the East would keep Guiscard from coming to Gregory's assistance.

In the beginning of 1082 Henry again appeared before Rome and besieged it for forty days; but the Leonina held out, and an attempt of confederates within the walls to fire the buildings adjoining St. Peter's failed. After capturing some friends of the Pope, among them the Bishops of Sutri and Ostia, he sent one division of his troops to Tivoli and another to Tuscany, where he again endeavored to secure the

---

[1] See Gibbon, " Decline and Fall," chap. lvi.

alliance of Mathilde, who, in Guiscard's absence, appeared to be Gregory's only support in Italy. Mathilde, however, remained firm. Animated by the bishops and clergy of Gregory's party, she fought, negotiated, won over several Italian lords by means of presents, burned the castles of others, and sent sums of money to Rome, to raise which she did not hesitate to despoil the church at Canosa of its golden vases and silver candelabra. A third part of Henry's army was sent to Apulia to join the Norman forces of Jordan of Capua, Guiscard's nephew, who had pledged his services to the German King. This last movement decided Guiscard to return, and put an end to Henry's attempts to strengthen himself in southern Italy.

Rome itself now began to show signs of discontent at the stubborn resistance of Gregory. An assembly of bishops, abbots, cardinals, and archpriests was held on the 4th of May, 1082, to consider whether the church treasures could be applied to military expenses. The decision was "No!" An encyclical followed from Gregory, addressed to all Christendom, and intended to stir up the zeal of the faithful for the restoration of the church to her former glory. By November Henry was back again at Rome. Seven months later the Milanese troops of Tedaldo, and the Saxons under Wigbert of Thuringia, scaled the walls, threw down the sleepy sentinels, got possession of a tower, and Henry's soldiers poured into the Leonina. A bloody fight raged round St. Peter's. The Romans intrenched themselves in the portico, but were driven out. The besiegers endeavored to capture the Pope, but he escaped to St. Angelo, through the loopholes of which he could look down upon the penitent of Canosa with the antipope at his side, surrounded with knights, bishops, and Roman nobles, and moving triumphantly towards St. Peter's.

Henry thus held the key to the whole city. The people were growing weary of the siege, and provisions were becoming scarce. He endeavored to win over the Romans by a public appeal. He declared that his refusal to submit to the Roman Church was Gregory's own fault. Gregory had brought the church to the verge of destruction. He had claimed that he was subject to no one's judgment, and had forgotten that Christ says, "Whosoever will be great among you shall be your servant." He who styles himself "the servant of servants" must not subdue the servants of God by force.

At this juncture ambassadors from Alexius of Constantinople arrived to demand Henry's promised expedition into Apulia, where Jordan of Capua was now fighting the returned Guiscard. Jordan compelled Desiderius, the Abbot of Monte Cassino, to accompany him to Rome in order to mediate a peace between the King and the Pope. He rendered homage to Henry, and, upon a large payment, received Capua as an imperial fief; though the brave abbot assured him that the investiture would be valid only after Henry should have been crowned Emperor. At Jordan's request the King confirmed to Desiderius the possession of his noble abbey; but the orthodox abbot writhed under the necessity which detained him for days in such a nest of heretics and compelled him to discuss the burning questions of the day with the " Antichrist " Guibert.

It was finally agreed by the representatives of the Romans, the Pope, and Henry, that the Pope should summon in November a synod to decide upon the King's claims. Henry swore to prevent no bishop from being present; but in a secret article the Romans pledged themselves to help him to his coronation within a given time, whether Gregory should be dead or should have escaped. In the former case a new Pope should be chosen, who would crown him, and the Roman people would swear fealty to him.

At this synod only a few bishops, mostly from Lower Italy, appeared. Those who had committed themselves to Guibert could not obey Gregory's summons, and Henry, in violation of his agreement, had prevented some of Gregory's partisans from approaching Rome. Gregory wished to renew the ban against the King, but was restrained by the synod and obliged to content himself with a general excommunication of those who had hindered the prelates from attending the council.

But Guiscard had finally sent a supply of money, the judicious distribution of which by the Pope among the Roman nobility quickly changed the current of affairs. The promise of Henry's coronation was evaded by the miserable subterfuge that they had promised that the Pope should *give the crown*—not that he should anoint and crown the King. If he should be truly penitent—that is to say, if he would resign his authority into the Pope's hands—he should receive the crown with the Pope's blessing; if not, he

A Venal and Fickle City. 113

should still receive the crown let down to him from St. Angelo at the end of a rod. Indeed, it was wholly a question of money. The Romans were for sale to the highest bidder, and if Henry had had more money he could quickly have gained possession of the city. There was nothing for him but to resume the siege. The Romans had destroyed the fortress which he had thrown up near St. Peter's. He made some incursions into the Campagna, and then started upon an expedition to Apulia; but he had scarcely entered the Norman territory when he was summoned back to Rome by the news that the city had again fallen away from Gregory. The change had come through the people, who were tired of the conflict, rather than through the nobles. The Romans had fought for the Pope, but the representative of the Prince of Peace would give them no hope of peace.

Henry arrived at Rome on the 21st of March, 1084, accompanied by his wife and several German and Italian bishops and nobles. Gregory would sooner die than yield to the King. He still held St. Angelo, a great part of the nobility adhered to him, and the stronger positions in the city were still in the power of his partisans. His nephew, Rusticus, occupied the Cœlian and the Palatine, the Corsi the Capitol, and the Pierleoni the Tiber Island. Henry summoned Gregory before a parliament of the Romans, the nobles, and the bishops of his camp; and on his failure to appear he was declared deposed and Guibert was acknowledged as Pope. On that Palm Sunday Gregory might see Henry and Guibert entering, through the Lateran Gate, into St. Peter's, where Guibert was enthroned as Clement III. At the Easter celebration Guibert crowned Henry and his wife with the imperial diadem, and the Romans conferred on him the patriciate.

Making the Capitol his headquarters, Henry proceeded to storm the fortresses of Rome, especially St. Angelo, while Gregory's messengers hastened to Guiscard to summon him to the rescue. Guiscard resolved to comply, since he knew that Gregory's fall meant the turning of Henry's arms against himself. He broke camp in May with six thousand horse and thirty thousand foot, among whom were large numbers of Saracens, now hastening to the succor of the church which had branded and fought them as infidels. Henry's force had been weakened by his dismissal of the greater part of the Lombard troops, and he could neither resist the Normans nor maintain himself in the city against the fickle Romans. Leaving orders for the demolition of the towers on the Capitol and the walls of the Leonina, he withdrew to Civita Castellana. Three days after his departure the Norman horsemen were thundering at the Lateran Gate.

Guiscard, uncertain whether Henry's withdrawal was not a ruse to fall upon his rear, remained for three days encamped before the city. The Romans kept the gates closed. Their Emperor had forsaken them, and they were confronted with the torments of a siege by the Normans and the ferocious Saracens, whom the Pope had summoned. On the evening of the 28th of May Guiscard's troops carried the Tower of St. Lorenzo and forced an entrance. The

Romans fought desperately, but Guiscard forced his way over the bridge to St. Angelo, freed the Pope, and conducted him to the Lateran. The imperial party rallied and threw themselves upon the invaders; but Guiscard's son, Roger, hastened to the relief of his father with a thousand horse, and Guiscard, in order to save himself, caused a part of the city to be set on fire. The days of Alaric seemed to have returned. Rome lay sacked and in ruins before Gregory's eyes. The burned churches, the outraged maids and matrons, the corpses of the Romans, the bands of citizens led away with ropes into slavery, the children and youth sold like cattle, cried to Heaven against him. Leo the Great had protected the city from Attila, and had mitigated its fate at the hands of Genseric; but it was Gregory, the vicegerent of God on earth, the representative of Jesus Christ, who had invited to their hellish work those fiends against whom he had launched so many curses. It is open to doubt whether the burning of Rome in 64 was the act of Nero; but history does not hesitate to lay the burning and sack of Rome in 1084 to Gregory VII.

The Romans were compelled to renew their oath to Gregory, but it availed little. His career ended amid the ruin and misery which his arrogance and obstinacy had brought upon Rome. Guiscard took hostages and left a garrison in St. Angelo, and, under the escort of his Norman and Saracen friends, Gregory left Rome, never to return, and went to Salerno.

Here he uttered once more the now impotent ban against Henry and Guibert, and issued a last encyclical, depicting in the darkest colors the condition of the church. The news which he received was not of a character to raise his spirits. Guibert was back in Rome. Henry had gone to Germany, and Gregory's most faithful partisans there had been deposed and banished. Mathilde was in peril in Lombardy; he himself was separated from her, in a strange city, surrounded by the Normans, whom he had so often accused of gross manners and rapacious instincts. He was dependent on their chief, whom he could not trust. The infirmities of age were upon him, and he was seized with a fatal sickness. When the cardinals and bishops who surrounded his couch praised him for his labors, he replied, "I put my trust only in this, that I have loved righteousness and hated iniquity." When they expressed their fears as to what might befall them after his death, he said, "I will go thither and commend you with earnest prayer to the God of pity." Being asked to name his successor, he suggested three names—Desiderius of Monte Cassino, Otto of Ostia, and Hugo of Lyons. In reply to the question whether he gave remission to those whom he had excommunicated, he declared that, with the exception of Henry, Guibert, and the other leaders of the uprising against him, he absolved all *who certainly believed that he possessed the power of the apostolic princes, Peter and Paul!* His last words were, "I have loved righteousness and hated iniquity." Did he believe it? It is not for us to say. There is no delusion like moral delusion. If he was sincere, we can only pray to be delivered from the righteousness which Hildebrand loved.

He died on the 25th of May, 1085, probably over seventy years of age. He had occupied the papal chair for twelve years and some months. He was buried at Salerno, in the church of St. Matthew, and a sumptuous chapel was erected over his tomb four centuries later. Rome has no memorial of him except a single inscription on a stone buried in the wall of a chapel in Santa Prudentiana.[1]

[1] " Tempore Gregorii Septeni Praesulis Almi
Presbiter Eximius Praeclarus Vir Benedictus
Moribus Ecclesiam Renovavit Funditus Istam. . . ."

See Gregorovius, vol. iv., p. 246, note.

CHAPTER XI.

CHARACTER AND POLICY OF GREGORY VII.

THE severest critic of Hildebrand is compelled to concede his greatness. He was the creator of the political Papacy of the middle ages; the man who grasped the opportunity presented by the political disintegration of Europe, and who strove to realize, through the church alone, that unity which the church and the empire together had accomplished, after a fashion, in former days. It has been justly said that the Gregorian ideas were not invented nor first propounded by Hildebrand; that "they had been long before a part of mediæval Christianity, interwoven with its most vital doctrines; but he was the first who dared to apply them to the world as he found it. His was that rarest and grandest of gifts, an intellectual courage and power of imaginative belief which, when it has convinced itself of aught, accepts it fully with all its consequences and shrinks not from acting at once upon it."[1] No one before him had so clearly perceived the full logical consequences of the fundamental and universally accepted positions of the Roman Church, and no one had

[1] Bryce, "The Holy Roman Empire," chap. x., p. 160.

made the attempt on such a scale to translate the logic into fact in the polity of the church.

Nature endowed him with an indomitable will, a restless energy, a dauntless courage, a clear perception, an imperious temper, an instinct of leadership, and an intellect of superior power and grasp. His education intensified his native powers by narrowing their range. He was trained to rule in the school of implicit obedience. He was the child of the Roman Church, inspired from childhood with the highest ideas of its prerogative, and reared under conditions which developed knowledge of men, self-restraint, persistence, and diplomatic subtlety. The discipline of a monk taught him to subordinate all personal affections, opinions, and interests to the one object of advancing the power of the church. He rose above the moral level of his age only on the side of the grosser vices. He was untainted with the licentiousness which characterized his time and, to a large extent, the members of his profession. On the other hand, his ideals of veracity, justice, and charity were those of a secular mediæval despot. If it be deemed too severe to say that in him principle was habitually subordinated to policy, it must nevertheless be admitted that his controlling principle included most phases of policy. No conflict between principle and policy emerged where his ecclesiastical ideal was in question. If he did not formally adopt, his course nevertheless ran dangerously close to the edge of the principle that the end justifies the means.

His natural disposition was stern and inflexible, and his bearing haughty and insolent. Those tender sensibilities which the austerities of the cloister never stifled in Bernard of Clairvaux had no place in Hildebrand. The man was merged in the ecclesiastic. If he ever seemed to conciliate or yield, it was only the momentary relaxation of the hand in order to take a firmer grip. Europe was a chess-board on which he played kings, knights, and bishops, and his combinations and moves revealed the genius of a statesman. In the execution of his schemes, his prodigious force of will, his courage which rose with danger, his deftness in handling the factors of his complex problems, the momentum under which he drove forward to his ends, extort admiration from those who most severely censure his aims and methods.

His theocratic conception was magnificent though essentially impracticable. The best proof of its impracticableness was his own inability to realize it. A theorist or a dreamer might have evolved it, but only the audacity of genius would deliberately have undertaken to carry it out. Nor were the results of his attempt by any means insignificant. They cannot be better stated than by Sir James Stephen: "He found the Papacy dependent on the empire; he sustained it by alliances almost commensurate with the Italian peninsula. He found the Papacy electoral by the Roman people and clergy; he left it electoral by a college of papal nomination. He found the Emperor the virtual patron of the Holy See; he wrested that power from his hands. He found the secular clergy the allies and dependents of the secular power; he converted them into the inalienable auxiliaries of his own. He found the higher ecclesiastics in servitude to the temporal sovereigns; he delivered them from that yoke to subjugate them to the Roman tiara. He found the patronage of the church the mere desecrated spoil and merchandise of princes; he reduced it within the dominion of the supreme pontiff."

He was a politician rather than a theologian. His type of Christianity was shaped by church tradition and not by the New Testament. His ecclesiastical claims were founded largely upon the fabled Donation of Constantine and the forged Isidorian Decretals. It is only just to say that these claims were made for the church and not for himself. He struck at real and flagrant abuses in the church, but it is not easy to decide whether or not the principal motive for these attacks lay in his sense of the moral enormity of simony and priestly concubinage and marriage. Both were incompatible with his ideal of a centralized organization, detached from all social ties, and wielded solely in the interests of the absolute and universal supremacy of the Roman see. While his sincerity may be freely conceded and due allowance made for the conditions of his age and training, it is also to be remembered that the same age and the same training produced better men than himself, and that his sincerity deluged a century with blood and tears. With him the church became a secular power which could maintain itself in the competition with other secular powers only by the employment of secular methods. The consequences were appalling, and did not cease with his death.[1]

---

[1] A valuable collection of modern opinions of Hildebrand is contained in the forthcoming volume of the late Dr. Schaff's " History of

Gregory's policy exhibits a development and enlargement of the aims of his predecessors. The tendency of his legislation was to extend the power of the Papacy over the bishops. His policy may be characterized in a word as that of intense centralization. He aimed especially to break down the power of the metropolitans, since there was danger of the metropolitan sees assuming the character of provincial papacies. He arrogated to himself the right to nominate the metropolitans, and also the ancient metropolitan rights in the choice of bishops. He laid down the principle that only the Pope or his legates could depose and reinstate bishops; and by confirming the general right of appeal to Rome he interfered with the bishops' power of judgment. Great stress was laid on the institution of legates, who were empowered to call synods, carry out decrees, exercise judgment upon refractory bishops, and especially break the resistance of the metropolitans. These officials travelled from place to place, secure of the Pope's support, and made themselves infamous by their extortions, demanding their maintenance from the church, and receiving it according to an arbitrary assessment.[1]

On the authority of the Isidorian Decretals, Gregory also struck at the synods of the larger ecclesiastical communities, and, with these, at the national development of the church; claiming that every synod

---

the Christian Church." I am under obligation to his son, the Rev. David Schley Schaff, for furnishing me with the advance sheets.

[1] Some complaints of contemporaries on this subject may be found collected in Gieseler's "Ecclesiastical History," H. B. Smith's ed., vol. ii., p. 374.

required papal confirmation to make its decrees valid. Church property was to be entirely freed from lay control. Though church officers received their temporal possessions from the crown, they were not to receive their investiture with these from the royal giver, but from the Pope. This is the capstone of his polity—the centralization of all church property in the papal see.

The empire was treated as a fief of St. Peter, and the right of confirming or rejecting the future King was demanded of the German princes by the Pope; while of the King himself was required the oath of personal homage and obedience to the Pope in all things. The Emperor's first duty was the service of St. Peter. Besides Germany, Gregory claimed, on the ground of the Donation of Constantine, Sardinia, Corsica, a great part of Middle Italy, Spain, Hungary, and Saxony, as the property of the Roman Church. He demanded the oath of fealty from William of England, from the King of Denmark, and from the Count of Provence, and assumed the authority to make the Prince of Dalmatia King. Wherever his claim was resisted, he urged the duty of princes to obey the Pope and to regard themselves, before all, as the servants of the church. The Pope is the lord of kingdoms and princedoms, and can give and take them at his pleasure. Accordingly, as we have seen, he threatened Philip of France with deposition and actually deposed Henry IV.

His policy embraced all Christendom. He maintained relations with Africa and Armenia, and the ulterior purpose of the crusades was the subjection of the schismatic Greek Church to the Roman see. He claimed the disposal of all ecclesiastical and of all secular power. He claimed the right to judge every one and to be judged by none; and while appealing for the justification of this right to the forged Decretals, he likewise asserted the right of the Pope to create new privileges as circumstances might require.

CHAPTER XII.

URBAN II.—MATHILDE—CONRAD'S TREACHERY—
SYNOD OF PIACENZA—THE FIRST CRUSADE.

REGORY had nominated as his successor, among others, Desiderius, the Abbot of Monte Cassino, a man of high birth and liberal education, but far advanced in years. When summoned to the chair, Desiderius manifested the greatest reluctance. His age made the retirement of his monastery grateful, and he shrank from involving himself, especially as a leader, in the formidable complications which Gregory had bequeathed to his successor. Guibert, or Clement III., was acting as Pope at Ravenna. Desiderius was at last persuaded to go to Rome, and after many remonstrances and refusals was inaugurated as Victor III., on the 9th of May, 1086. He was but the shadow of a Pope. The single year of his pontificate was largely spent in journeys between Rome and Monte Cassino, that peaceful and beloved retreat to which the poor old man's heart was always turning. His principal and almost his only official act was to anathematize Guibert at a council in Benevento, after which he hurried back, sick, to Monte Cassino, and, after charging the bishops and pres-

byters who were present to choose as his successor Otto of Ostia, expired on the 16th of September, 1087.

The year passed without a Pope. On the 8th of March, 1088, the council assembled and elected Otto of Ostia as Urban II. He was a Frenchman from Châtillon, near Rheims, and had been reared under the monastic discipline of Clugny. He was an accomplished orator and diplomatist, with a stronger understanding than Desiderius, and the Gregorians thought that they saw in him one who would carry out Gregory's policy, as he publicly announced his intention of doing. His position was difficult. In Germany, Hermann, after his overthrow by the Emperor, had died not long before Urban's accession, and the Saxons, with nearly all the papal bishops, were inclining to Henry. Conrad, Henry's son, had been for nearly a year in Lombardy, and the Emperor was threatening to come thither himself, to destroy Mathilde and to establish Guibert in Rome. Rome itself was a scene of anarchy, distracted by street fights, baronial tyranny, and the misery of the poverty-stricken populace.

Urban, after spending nearly a year in Sicily, returned to Rome under a Norman escort and took up his residence on the Tiber Island, so poor that the Roman matrons gave him alms. Guibert commanded the greater part of the city. Henry, who was weary of the strife, was inclined to give up Guibert (Clement III.), but was dissuaded by the excommunicated bishops, who stood or fell with the antipope. But Clement could not long maintain himself in Rome, and in the course of the year 1089 he was expelled, and required to swear that he would not return.

Urban meanwhile was delighted by receiving from Sancho of Aragon submission and pledge of tribute, and also a very submissive letter from the French King. Knowing that the enfeebled party of Mathilde was inclined to come to terms with Henry, he conceived the idea of bringing about her marriage with a view of securing thereby a helper for the church. Accordingly, Mathilde, then forty years old, was persuaded to give her hand to the seventeen-year-old Duke Welf of Bavaria. This alliance so strengthened the papal party that Henry was compelled to return to Italy in the spring of 1090, and began after Easter the siege of Mantua, Mathilde's stronghold. Urban was again forced to quit Rome by the increasing power of the imperial party and the defection of the Roman people. Henry's advance moved them to turn again to their Emperor, and in 1091 they possessed themselves of St. Angelo and called back Clement.

The fall of Mantua and other cities in that same year, the discouragement of Mathilde's party, and the defection of Rome frightened the Gregorians. The cunning of the priests, aided by the greed of the elder Welf and the fanaticism of Mathilde, framed an infamous plot to alienate Henry's eldest son from his father. Conrad was Henry's representative in Italy. He inherited his father's vacillating temperament without his passionate energy, was attractive in person and inclined to peaceful pursuits. Mathilde and her clergy held out to him the immediate possession of the kingdom of Italy; and his treachery to his father was explained and justified by a hideous slander to the effect that the Emperor had attempted to make him commit incest with the Empress. Mathilde's complicity in this unnatural act is a blot upon her fame, and, with her absurd marriage, attests the baneful character of the influences invited by her devotion to the Gregorian policy. She sent Conrad to the Pope, who absolved him from his obligations to his father. The most sacred natural ties counted for nothing against papal ambitions. This act of treachery was followed by Milan's defection from Henry, with Lodi, Piacenza, and Cremona. The four cities concluded a twenty years' treaty with Mathilde and her husband, and Conrad was crowned King of Italy at Milan, in 1093. Henry was driven to desperation by his son's ingratitude. He shut himself up and seriously meditated suicide.[1]

Though the Guibertists occupied the Lateran, St. Angelo, and other strong points, Urban was nevertheless able to return to Rome after an absence of nearly two years. His condition was pitiable. The Abbot Godfrey of Vendôme sold his own possessions and furnished him with money with which he bribed the guardian of the Lateran, and on Easter, 1094, he, for the first time, took his seat on the Lateran throne. It is a sorry spectacle—a poor old man, who, with the money of a foreign abbot, has purchased the papal residence, looking out from the

---

[1] See his piteous letters to Louis of France and to Abbot Hugo of Clugny, in Villemain, "Histoire de Grégoire VII.," vol. ii., pp. 390, 399.

The Synod of Piacenza and Praxedis. 129

desolate Lateran upon the ruined churches and the silent, filthy streets patrolled by assassins and vagabonds, and the Emperor shut up in a Lombard city and contemplating self-murder, while round him the provinces are being desolated with fire and sword; it all was a bitter reminder of Hildebrand, who had "loved righteousness and hated iniquity."

On the 1st of March, 1095, Urban held the great Synod of Piacenza, at which four thousand clergy and nearly thirty thousand laymen assembled. The business had to be transacted for the most part in the open air. Here appeared Praxedis or Adelais of Russia, Henry's second wife, and shamelessly detailed to the council certain alleged monstrosities of the Emperor's domestic life, among which were his urging her to incest with Conrad, and compelling her to submit to promiscuous violation by his court and camp. Even with our knowledge of the license of that age it is impossible to credit a bestiality so horrible. The most meagre charity is content to ascribe such a story to diabolical malice voiced by an infamous woman. Not so the papal council. Without waiting for any defence from Henry, the charges were indorsed by the synod, *and the Empress was excused from penitential discipline as an unassenting victim!* With their holy zeal thus kindled, the councillors were now prepared to give a warm reception to the embassy from Constantinople, which presented a plea for aid against the Saracens. Assurances of help were given, and many pledged themselves under oath.

This synod struck the last blow at Henry's fame

and popularity. Its reception of the charges of Praxedis almost totally ruined the imperial party in Lombardy. Some of Henry's most faithful partisans deserted to Conrad and Mathilde. A treaty was concluded between Urban and Conrad, according to which Conrad guaranteed to the Pope personal security, papal dignity, and the prerogative of St. Peter both in and outside of Rome; while the Pope adopted Conrad as the son of the Roman Church, agreed to help him to the German crown, and, on his arrival at Rome, to crown him Emperor. He also gave his support to Conrad's request for the hand of the daughter of Roger of Sicily, who was still a child.

The project of the crusade ripened fast. Latin Christendom was in some measure prepared for this movement. It had floated through the mind of Gregory VII., though his immediate object was not the recovery of the Holy Land, but the defence of the Greek empire against the Seljuks, in return for which it was to render submission to the Pope. Peter of Amiens, better known as Peter the Hermit, who had himself visited Palestine and witnessed the sufferings of the Christians, received from Urban, on his return to Rome, permission to announce the full deliverance of Jerusalem. He traversed Italy and crossed the Alps, barefoot and bareheaded, riding upon a mule and bearing a crucifix, and preaching in pulpits, on the roads, and in the market-places. His influence was extraordinary. France especially was prepared by his appeals to break out into a flame of religious zeal.

From the 18th to the 28th of November, 1095,

was held the great Synod of Clermont, composed of about two hundred bishops and abbots, mostly French, but with a sprinkling of Italians and Spaniards. Urban himself, at whose side stood Peter, addressed the people in the public square, and depicted impressively the atrocities of the Saracens, the downfall of the Greek empire, and the defilement of the Holy Sepulchre, and summoned his hearers to enlist for the work of rescue. He was answered by a tremendous shout, "Deus vult!" and the Pope at once declared that those words should be the battle-cry of the crusade. Every volunteer must first receive the priestly blessing, and then fasten the cross upon his breast. The next day Urban appointed Adhemar, the Bishop of Puy, to represent him in leading the crusade. The general enthusiasm was increased by the announcement that Count Raymond of Toulouse, with his entire force, had taken the cross.

The call to the crusade did not receive an enthusiastic response in Rome. Little zeal was evoked for the rescue of a city which a Roman Emperor had once destroyed, and of the destruction of which the Romans were daily reminded by the Arch of Titus and by the despised population of the Ghetto. The Romans were not slow to perceive that the crusade would divert funds which otherwise would come to Rome. To the Normans, who had tried their spear-points on the Moslems in Sicily, the summons was welcome. Norman Italy ruled the first crusade through Bohemond and Tancred. Germany was cold, and was distracted, besides, by its own civil troubles. The weakness of the imperial idea was disclosed by the failure of the secular head of Christendom to unfurl the banner of the crusade. The Papacy assumed the office which belonged to the empire; and as the movement which united Christendom proceeded from the church, it proved that the church and not the empire was the uniting force of European society. In England the Normans were occupied with securing their possessions, and Spain was busy with a crusade in her own kingdom. The romantic narrative of this expedition belongs to another volume of this series.

The marriage of Mathilde had been, as every one knew, only a political device. Mathilde did not want a husband, but a helper in the fight with Henry. Welf, on the other hand, who wanted to possess and govern her territories, was treated by her as a presumptuous boy. The fact now appeared, which had been concealed from the Welfs, that her property was already formally bequeathed to the church by the deed given to Gregory. Welf, after the Council of Piacenza, separated from Mathilde, feeling himself defrauded in his bargain; and the sagacious Urban lent his aid to the separation as readily as he had promoted the marriage, since he had reaped the advantage of the alliance and was now glad to get out of the way any pretender to Mathilde's property. The grounds publicly alleged for the separation were perhaps better suited to an eleventh-century audience than to decent readers of the present day. The relations of Welf with the saintly Mathilde had no doubt been of a platonic character; but the old Welf was ablaze with wrath when he found that his son had been used only as a papal puppet, and that the vast estates of the countess were out of his reach. He at once betook himself to Henry, his excommunicated enemy, who came out of his retirement, while the Welfs hastened to Germany to strengthen the imperial party, and Henry followed them, leaving northern Italy to Mathilde.

The resistance of Clement's partisans at Rome was feeble, and Urban, through the treachery of the garrison, gained possession of St. Angelo, and, being thus able to call himself master of Rome, returned to southern Italy to strengthen his alliance with the Normans. On the 24th of April, 1099, at a council in St. Peter's, he renewed all his own and Gregory's decrees, and "enthroned," to use his own term, the vile Praxedis, who had ended her life in an Italian cloister, ordering that the day of her death and that of her canonization should both be celebrated in future. On the 29th of July he died at Rome, in the castle of the Pierleoni, too soon to rejoice over the capture of Jerusalem by the crusaders. He lives in history as the inspirer of the first crusade. He had not maintained the Papacy at the high level of the Gregorian ideal. While fully committed to Gregory's policy, he was a man of smaller mould than Hildebrand, more pliable, and more cautious. In his effort to maintain himself against Henry, some of his measures drew upon him the reproaches of the strong Gregorians: and in dogmatic decisions, in which he occasionally contradicted himself, he sometimes made concessions which menaced the integrity of the Gregorian system and arrayed against him the powerful party of Clugny.

CHAPTER XIII.

PASCHAL II.—DEATH OF HENRY IV.—HENRY V.—
THE INVESTITURE CONTEST.

HE line of the history for the next twenty-three years is woven of many strands, but one thread runs continuously through the whole—the investiture contest. The beginning of this fight was the famous decree of the synod of 1075, afterwards ratified by Urban in 1099.

The Papacy remained in the hands of the Gregorians. Rainer, a monk of Clugny and Abbot of St. Laurentius, was installed on the 14th of August, 1099, as Paschal II. Clement did not hesitate to renew the struggle with him, but the struggle was brief. Paschal's first act was to drive him, with the aid of Count Roger, out of Albano, where he had put himself under the protection of the Campagna counts. He retired to Civita Castellana, and suddenly died there in the autumn of 1100. As his followers boasted of the numerous miracles wrought at his tomb in Ravenna, Paschal caused his corpse to be exhumed and thrown into the river. The Pope had already interested himself in the crusade, issuing a call to the bishops and abbots of France to send troops to the East; and on hearing of the capture of Jerusalem he addressed a congratulatory letter to the crusaders, expressing his joy at the discovery of the holy lance and of a portion of the cross. In his summons to France he declared the object of the crusade to be to bring the Eastern Church "into the condition in which it ought to be"; and in his letter to the crusaders he again voices Gregory's idea of the chief object of a crusade—to subject the Eastern Church to Rome—since he commands obedience to his legate, "in order to regulate everything in the church, delivered from the Saracens, according to the canons."

The Guibertists took advantage of his absence in Melfi, at his first synod, to set up a new antipope, Theodoric of St. Rufina, who was enthroned by night in St. Peter's, but never enjoyed his new dignity, since he was at once compelled to flee, and was soon after arrested and imprisoned. The irrepressible Guibertists immediately elected another Pope, Albert of Sabina, whose term of office was a trifle longer than his predecessor's, and who enjoyed besides the honor of a public appearance in Rome. Paschal's followers stripped him of his pallium and led him through the streets seated on a horse with his face to the tail.

The efforts to establish the papal supremacy in England have already been noticed. The Norman kings did not prove to be docile subjects of the Pope. Lanfranc, the Archbishop of Canterbury, had recognized the sovereign's right of investiture, and Gregory VII. had not ventured beyond threats to William I.

William Rufus maintained the right of royal investiture, and after a long delay selected Anselm for the chair of Canterbury, made vacant by the death of Lanfranc. Anselm, who belonged to the Gregorian party, at first refused the honor, but finally consented on condition that he should be recognized by Urban, and asked permission to go to Rome and receive the pallium [1] from him. William refused on the ground that England was still undecided between Urban and Clement, but sent privately to Rome and obtained the pallium for Anselm, which was brought to England by a papal legate, and Urban was acknowledged. But a new quarrel soon broke out, which resulted in Anselm's exile. He retired to Rome and was honorably received by Urban as a martyr to the cause of religion, though neither Urban nor Paschal ventured upon strong measures against the King. Anselm, during his residence at Rome, became strongly imbued with the Gregorian ideas concerning investiture. On his return to England under Henry I., trouble broke out again. Henry urged him to receive the archbishopric of Canterbury again by royal investiture; but Anselm was under instructions from Rome to carry out the decrees of 1099 in England, where they had been ungraciously received. His attempt to enforce them was met by the opposition and threats of King, priests, bishops, and clergy. Refus-

---

[1] The pallium was a white woollen scarf of a handbreadth, adorned with six black crosses, and worn by the highest dignitaries of the church on the most solemn occasions. From the sixth century the popes claimed that every metropolitan or archbishop must obtain the pallium from Rome, before which he was not in possession of his title of archbishop or of his full authority.

ing to receive the see of Canterbury by royal investiture, the King finally requested him to go himself to Rome and ask for his sovereign the privilege of investiture, threatening that England would break with Rome if the request should be refused. He then purposely delayed Anselm's return. Anselm had secretly given instructions that such a permission, if granted, should not come into the hands of the papal legate in England; but Paschal refused. "The King," he said, "wants to appoint bishops himself; but a man cannot make a god, and priests are called in Scripture representatives of God."

Henry IV., as we have seen, had returned to Germany in 1097. His presence created a revolution in his favor; and at a diet at Mainz he took the opportunity to urge the princes and bishops to pass over the succession of his ungrateful son Conrad, and devolve it on his second son Henry. This was done about a year later at the Diet of Cologne, and Henry was anointed at Aix-la-Chapelle, under oath that, during his father's life and without his permission, he would neither claim the government of the empire nor even of the patrimonial territories. All fear of a contention between the brothers was removed by the death of Conrad at Florence in July, 1101, despised and forsaken. A season of peace seemed to be dawning for Henry. The princes of Saxony, Bohemia, and other parts of Germany attached themselves to him; religious animosities abated, and even ecclesiastics of the papal party accepted promotions at his hands. He proclaimed a peace of four years, exacting of the princes a solemn oath to maintain it under the heaviest penalties. Commerce and agriculture revived, and all classes and conditions rejoiced and throve in the genial atmosphere of peace.

But the excommunication was still in force, and Henry desired to be reconciled to the church. The death of Guibert had afforded an opportunity for an adjustment with Paschal on more favorable terms, but Henry had not availed himself of it. He was urged, and possibly was disposed, to recognize Paschal, and proposed to visit Rome and submit the dispute to a general council; but this design was not carried out, and at a synod of Italian and foreign bishops in March, 1102, Paschal renewed the excommunication in the following terms: "Because the King Henry has never ceased to rend the vesture of Christ—that is, to lay waste the church by plunder and conflagration, to defile it by his sensualities, his perjuries, and his homicides—and hath, therefore, first by Pope Gregory of blessed memory, afterwards by the most holy Urban, my predecessor, on account of his contumacy, been excommunicated and condemned, we also, in this our synod, by the judgment of the whole church, deliver him up to a perpetual anathema."

This act did not immediately affect Henry's relations to Germany, nor provoke him to hostilities. He seems not to have abandoned the hope of reconciliation with the Pope, and publicly announced his intention, as soon as that should have been effected, to make over the empire to young Henry and to go on a crusade to Palestine.

That passive submission to papal claims was not

universal may be seen from the Pope's experience in Belgium. In January, 1102, he issued a summons to Count Robert of Flanders, just returned from Jerusalem, to oppose the adherents of Henry in Liége, and to follow up Henry himself, "that chief of heretics," with all his might. He could offer no more acceptable sacrifice to God than to fight him who would assume the sovereignty of the church and introduce simony. The Liégers replied that, with all respect to the papal authority, they were inclined to found their right against the Pope on the ancient episcopal constitution. "According to the ancient tradition," they said, "we have our bishop, archbishop, and provincial synod; and whatever is decided at this synod according to Holy Scripture is not to be referred to Rome. Such reference is proper only in weightier matters on which Scripture does not pronounce. We reject those Roman legates who run about only to enrich themselves. They may be known by their fruits, which are not improvement of life and morals, but murder and sacrilege. We are excommunicated because we hold by the old rules and are not carried about by every wind of teaching." They go on to recall the atrocities which, from Silvester to Gregory VII., have resulted from the avarice of the Roman see, and how the imperial power has proved mightier than the bans of the last three popes. They appeal to Gregory the Great, according to whom only secular princes are to bear the sword, even against heretics. Hildebrand had been the first to lift himself against the royal crown and to gird himself with the sword of war against the Emperor.

Henry I. of England was not satisfied with the Pope's answer on the investiture question. He declared that he would lay Anselm under royal ban if he should refuse to consecrate bishops or abbots nominated by himself. Another embassy to the Pope was equally unsuccessful. The Pope exhorted Anselm to stand firm, confirmed him in the primacy of England, and thus made him responsible, not to the legate, but only to the Roman see itself. He informed him that at the late Lateran synod he had emphasized the decree that no cleric is to be the vassal of a layman or to receive from a lay hand a church or church property. The Pope sought to appease Henry by ascribing to him personally a most compliant disposition towards the see, and his resistance to the curia to the influence of evil advisers. He praised him for his respect to the clergy, and would only warn him against those who would persuade him to the act of investiture.

At Benevento, in August, the Pope was visited by an English commissioner with the report that Henry's commissioners to Rome had announced that Paschal had orally confirmed Henry's investitures. As this statement had been contradicted by Anselm's commissioners, a new delegation had been sent to ascertain the facts. The Pope roundly denied the report, and banned the commissioners who had announced it, and all who, by reason of it, had given or received investiture or consecration. In the spring of 1103 Henry again sent Anselm to Rome with his decided refusal to renounce investiture, even if it should cost him his crown. Paschal replied that he would not grant it, if it should cost him his head, and forbade Anselm all intercourse with those invested by the King. The question came up again at the Lateran synod of 1105, but without any result beyond the excommunication of the King's counsellors, and of all who had allowed themselves to be invested by him.

Paschal's attention was now occupied by a contest nearer home. The family of Colonna possessed a castle among the Latian hills, which overhung the Labican road five miles from Tusculum, together with the villages of Monte Porzio and Zagorolo. Peter Colonna was a nephew of Benedict IX. These places were papal territory, and Paschal was determined to maintain his right over them. He was opposed in Rome by the Corsi, whose stronghold was on the Capitol. When Paschal caused their fortifications to be destroyed, Stephen Corso obtained possession of a fortress near St. Paul's, and from this carried on marauding expeditions against Rome. Being at last driven out, he intrenched himself in the Maritima, where he seized some papal towns. This uprising of the Corsi was connected with a third attempt of the imperialists to install an antipope. The Corsi selected for this purpose one Maginolf, and elected him on the 18th of November as Silvester IV. For their support they had summoned to the city Werner of Ancona, a Suabian who had served under Leo IX. in his disastrous Norman expedition. Paschal took refuge in the Tiber Island. He could not prevent Maginolf's enthronement in the Lateran; but Maginolf had no money, and in a few days was obliged to leave the city and to betake himself to

Werner's camp at Tivoli. Paschal returned to the Lateran, but found his condition intolerable. Only a part of the nobility was on his side, and he finally abandoned the city and put himself under the protection of Mathilde, in order to call a council.

The downfall of Henry IV. was now close at hand. At the end of the year 1104 he was compelled a second time to mourn the treachery of a son. Accompanied by young Henry, he had set out upon a military expedition and had reached Fritzlar, when the prince suddenly left his father's camp and went to Ratisbon, where he was joined by many of the younger nobles and princes and raised the standard of revolt. The movement was instigated by the older papal nobles of the Emperor's court; and the reason assigned for it was his excommunication. Young Henry applied to the Pope to be released from the oath given to his father at his coronation. Paschal promised him divine pardon on condition of his fidelity to the Roman Church, and released him from the ban incurred by intercourse with his excommunicated father, blasphemously ascribing the breach between the father and the son to the inspiration of God. By this alliance with the Pope Henry soon gained a powerful following. He rejected all overtures from his father on the ground that he was still under ban, and finally had him imprisoned at Bechelheim, near Kreuznach. Here the Emperor was treated with neglect and cruelty until he was taken to Ingelheim, to a diet composed wholly of his enemies, where, under the alternative of perpetual imprisonment, he resigned his crown, his castles, his treasures, and his patrimony.

The diet adjourned to Mainz and elected and invested Henry V. as King.

The English investiture question emerged again at the beginning of 1106, and was finally decided. The demands of the King were now supported by both Anselm and Hugo of Lyons. Paschal, beset on all sides, and having his eye upon Germany, yielded. Anselm's support had been gained by the King's withdrawal of a part of his claims, while Paschal also made concessions. Henry surrendered the right of investing with ring and staff, and Paschal consented that the bishops should do homage to the King for their temporal properties and privileges. The King thus renounced the claim to confer the spiritual office, while the temporal allegiance of the prelates was secured by their homage to the crown. The struggle resulted essentially to the King's advantage, since, by dispensing with the form of granting the ring and staff, he retained the power of nomination to the wealthy ecclesiastical positions of the realm.

On the 7th of August, 1106, Henry IV. closed his sorrowful life after a reign of nearly fifty years. Papal malignity vented its impotent spite upon the dead. The dying request of the aged Emperor to be buried with his ancestors in the cathedral of Spires was refused. His body was conveyed to the church of St. Lambert in Liége, and buried; but the Bishop Othbert was compelled to disinter it, and it was laid in an unconsecrated building on an island in the Moselle, where a single monk chanted psalms beside it. Finally, by Henry's permission, it was removed to the cathedral at Spires; but the bishop, fired with saintly indignation, imposed penance upon those who joined in the funeral procession, and had the body placed in an unconsecrated chapel. Five years elapsed before the Emperor was permitted to rest in the cathedral vault with his kindred.

The investiture question was now revived in Germany by Henry V. At the beginning of 1107 Paschal received at Châlons commissioners from the German King, with Archbishop Benno, of Treves, as their speaker. The archbishop in his address assumed that, as an ancient right, the choice of bishops must be ratified by the Emperor, the clergy, and the people, and that the person elected must be invested with ring and staff by the Emperor, to whom he must then swear fealty. The Emperor is entitled to this because the temporal privileges connected with the episcopal chairs can be granted by him alone. The answer was the old commonplace that thus the church becomes the King's servant; that ring and staff belong to the altar; that the holy consecration is invalidated by the subordination of clerical hands to the blood-stained hands of laymen. The commissioners replied that the matter would be decided in Rome, and no doubt with the sword. Paschal quashed the discussion, and went to Troyes to open a great synod on the 23d of May.

Here the German King's claim to the right of investiture was discussed. The King's commissioners claimed that the privilege of nominating bishops had been granted by the Pope to Charlemagne, and protested against the adjudication of the German King's rights in a foreign country. A year's delay was granted, to allow the King to appear at Rome, and the synod ordained the deposition of those invested by the laity and of those who had consecrated them.

Henry's request for the imperial crown called forth from Paschal another prohibition of lay investiture, and of the conferring of church property by laymen, at the synod of March, 1110. Henry, at the Diet of Ratisbon a little later, announced his intention of going to Rome to receive the imperial crown, to establish order in Italy, and to take measures for the protection of the church in obedience to the Pope. He waited only to celebrate his betrothal to Matilda, the infant daughter of Henry I. of England, and then set out for Rome with thirty thousand knights and a body of the most learned transalpine scholars. The cities of Lombardy looked with hatred on the foreign host. Novara resisted and was laid in ashes, while the other cities, with the exception of Milan, appalled by this fearful example, hastened to send contributions of money to the King. The united forces assembled at Roncaglia, near Piacenza. Even Mathilde was too politic to offend an Emperor backed by such an army. She did not appear before him, but remained at Canosa, and communicated with him through commissioners. She swore allegiance to him, and promised fealty against all enemies but the Pope, in return for which Henry confirmed her in all her possessions and privileges. The army advanced, suffering heavy losses from the rains in the Apennine passes. Pontremoli suffered the fate of Novara. Henry kept Christmas at Florence, compelled Pisa and Lucca to conclude a treaty of peace, and levelled the fortifications of Arezzo and destroyed a great part of the city itself.

The Pope was in severe straits. He had no longer to deal with an aged and wearied monarch with his own realm in arms against him, but with a young and vigorous prince, who, with far greater force of will, inherited his father's craftiness; with a burning ambition, a recognized authority over the nobles of his land, an empire far more formidable than in Hildebrand's day, and a determination to enforce the rights of the crown, which, as his father's fate had shown him, was the sole condition of the continued existence of his empire. He was resolved to maintain with the sword the right of investiture, and to demolish the pretentious structure of Gregory VII. Paschal's condition was worse than Gregory's, for the Normans were embarrassed by internal weakness, Mathilde was old and neutral, the religious passions were chilled, and Christendom was longing for the settlement of the dispute on any terms.

The issue was sharp. Henry stood by the right of investiture, and the Pope by the deliverances of his predecessors, which he himself had solemnly confirmed. The solution was simple enough if the church would only adopt it. The knot of the case lay in the temporal possessions of the clergy, by which they were continually embroiled in secular strifes and compelled to assume the prerogatives of secular powers. Because of their vast territorial domains, bishops and abbots were constantly under the necessity of attending civil courts, and even of engaging in military service. The bishops had only to

A Great Papal Concession. 147

renounce this secular power and position and to return to their purely ecclesiastical estate and functions. The church had only to agree to be content with such revenue as was derived from tithes and offerings. From that moment the strife would cease; the consecration of bishops would be the prerogative of the church, with which the state would have no right to interfere. The clergy once desecularized, the interference of the secular power with church affairs would be a palpable invasion of ecclesiastical right.

It was a tremendous concession, but it was demanded of a helpless Pope, and the demand was backed by an army which could not be safely trifled with. Paschal acquiesced and proposed the following basis: The bishops should surrender to the empire all the possessions and royalties which they had received of the empire and of the kingdom of Italy from the days of Charlemagne, Louis the Pious, and Henry I.—all the cities, duchies, marquisates, countships, rights of coinage, customs, tolls, rights of raising troops, all castles and courts. The church should henceforth live by its tithes. The King, on his part, should surrender the right of investiture. The King was to guarantee to the Roman see all its possessions, the patrimony of St. Peter as granted by Pepin, Charlemagne, and Louis, and to the Pope personal security by oath and hostages. A second document was prepared in which it was promised that when the King should have fulfilled the pledges given, the Pope, on the day of the coronation, would command the German prelates to restore the imperial properties, would forbid his successor to revoke this decree under penalty of anathema, and would crown the King and support him with his authority in the maintenance of his empire. All the great princes of the empire were to guarantee the treaty by oath.

Henry agreed, under the proviso that he held himself bound only in case the German prelates, in obedience to the Pope's command, should surrender the imperial properties.

CHAPTER XIV.

THE CORONATION RIOT—PASCHAL'S BROKEN OATH—DEATH OF MATHILDE—GELASIUS II.—CALIXTUS II.

N the 12th of February, 1111, Henry V. made his entry into Rome. Having sworn before the gate of St. Peter to protect the privileges of the Pope and of the Roman Church, the solemnities of the imperial coronation began. On arriving at the church, the Pope demanded of the King the renunciation of the right of investiture. The King replied with a formal declaration that he did not intend to take the church properties given by former emperors, but demanded that the Pope should now fulfil his promise of the renunciation by the clergy of imperial property. The Pope had already drawn up an edict to this effect, which he submitted. Henry then demanded the renunciation by the German bishops according to the proposed agreement. They decidedly refused. Henry saw in the proceeding only a device of the Pope to get possession of his renunciation, and then leave him to encounter the resistance of the bishops and princes. The Pope refused to receive the King's renunciation of the right of invest-

iture so long as the bishops persisted in their refusal. Henry withdrew for consultation with his bishops, who declined to recognize the treaty. Night was approaching, and Paschal demanded that the long consultation should be terminated. The bishops cried out that the treaty could not be fulfilled. The King demanded the imperial crown, and the Pope refused. A knight sprang up, angrily shouting, "What need of so many words? My master will receive the crown as it was received by Pepin, by Charlemagne, and by Louis."

Some cardinals proposed that the coronation should proceed and the discussion be postponed until the next day; some of the bishops urged Henry to seize the Pope's person. Armed men surrounded Paschal and the high altar, and compelled the Pope to place himself in the tribune under the swords of the knights. The shouts of priests and nobles, the clash of arms, cries for help, maltreatment of trembling clerics, made the dark cathedral a veritable storm-centre. While the Pope and the cardinals huddled together under the halberds of the mercenaries, fresh bodies of troops thronged the church, and the whole city on that side of the Tiber was in an uproar. Paschal and his cortége were finally conveyed to one of the buildings of St. Peter's and placed under guard. This put an end to all discipline; priests and laymen alike were robbed and struck down with swords, and a raid was made upon the treasures of the church.

Two cardinal bishops succeeded in escaping over the bridge of St. Angelo, and a furious uprising of the people ensued. At dawn they broke into the Leonina to rescue the Pope. The King sprang bare-

The Right of Investiture Conceded. 151

foot upon his horse and rode into the atrium of the basilica, dashed down the steps, and threw himself into the fight. Five Romans were struck down by his lance, but he himself fell wounded from his horse. Otto of Milan, in his attempt to rescue him, was torn in pieces. The Romans were at last driven back over the bridge, and the Pope was taken in charge by the royal troops.

Henry withdrew from the Leonina under cover of the night, and remained for two days in camp under arms, while the Romans, thirsting for revenge, again assembled and swore battle to the death; but on the night of the 15th of February Henry broke camp and withdrew to the Sabina, taking with him as prisoners the Pope and sixteen cardinals, while the soldiers dragged in his train Roman consuls and priests with ropes. At Fiano the army crossed the Tiber, and encamped near Tivoli. It was Henry's purpose to form a league with the Tusculan counts, and to cut off any aid which the Normans might bring. He left the Pope in the castle of Trevi.

On the 2d of April he was again before Rome with the Pope in his camp. He finally agreed to release the prisoners on condition that the Pope would take no more measures against him and would grant him the crown-right of investiture, which should signify, not the conferring of church offices, but only of the imperial fiefs connected with them. Paschal at last yielded, saying, "For the deliverance and peace of the church I am forced to consent to what for my life's sake I would not have granted." It was agreed that Henry should have the right to invest with staff and ring bishops and abbots chosen without simony and violence. If any one should be chosen without his consent, he was not to be consecrated without royal investiture. Possible strifes in the choice of bishops should be restrained by royal authority. The Pope took an oath not to disturb the King, either on account of the indignities he had suffered, or about the matter of investiture; never to lay him under ban, and to crown him and maintain his authority in his empire. The King agreed to release the Pope, never to seize him again, not to disturb the Roman people, to guarantee the property of the Roman see, and to obey the Pope without detriment to the honor of the empire.

On the 13th of April the coronation ceremonies began again and proceeded in the usual way, except that, after the coronation and during the mass, the Pope handed to the Emperor the right of investiture.[1] The peace between the Pope and the Emperor compelled Maginolf to make a formal declaration in Henry's camp, promising to render obedience to the Pope, and confessing that he had wrongfully assumed the papal office.

The Roman clergy were displeased at Paschal's concession. The Gregorians were indignant. They saw Gregory's work undone by Paschal's weakness. The cardinals who had not been imprisoned with him professed to despise him for not having preferred a martyr's death to submission. They denounced him as a betrayer of the Lord, and the unhappy pontiff hid himself in Terracina and in the island of Ponza. They took the opportunity of his absence to

[1] The document is given by Gregorovius, vol. iv., p. 330.

hold a council and condemn the treaty. The Pope wrote to them in July, saying that he would make good again what he had done. He soon took a decisive step. He wrote to Archbishop Guido of Vienne asserting that the treaty obtained from him by force was invalid throughout and null and void; that he condemned it eternally, and newly confirmed whatever the apostolic canons, the councils, and the popes, especially Gregory VII. and Urban II., had established. In March, 1112, at a synod in Rome, he related his imprisonment by the King, and declared that he would be true to his oath, but that he was not bound by written documents framed under compulsion. He also repeated the declaration that he held by the decrees of the popes, especially Gregory and Urban.

The synod cancelled and declared void the privilege extorted by the violence of Henry. Paschal thus succeeded in throwing upon the synod what he feared to do himself, and extricated himself by getting the investiture concession repudiated, but refusing, at the same time, to break his oath not to disturb the King by church censures. Thus if Henry should continue to invest, his acts would be irregular and sinful, but would be endured as an unavoidable evil. Naturally this cowardly evasion satisfied neither party. The French church, dissatisfied with the relations between Henry and the Pope, at a great synod in September, 1112, reaffirmed the canonical requirements concerning investiture, repudiated the Pope's concession to the German Emperor, and declared Henry excommunicated. These deliverances were sent to Rome with the threat that Paschal's refusal to confirm them would create a schism. The Pope succumbed, and confirmed the decrees. Some quiet years ensued for him, during which he went to and fro between Rome and southern Italy, seeking to perpetuate and strengthen the Norman alliance.

On the 24th of July, 1115, Mathilde died. She had borne a prominent part in the ecclesiastical struggles of nearly forty years, during which she had been the active and devoted friend of the Roman see and of the Gregorian party. She commanded the admiration of her contemporaries by her beauty and accomplishments, as well as by her energy and boldness. Her vast possessions and personal influence made her an ally whose aid was courted by both parties in the strife. Both her marriages were for political ends, and the history of neither enhances her reputation for the domestic virtues, while the last is a reproach to her womanhood. Her reputation for piety is stained by her encouragement of the treachery of Conrad. Dante is supposed by many to have immortalized her in his exquisite picture of the earthly paradise in the twenty-eighth canto of the "Purgatorio." But this is more than doubtful. There are seven Mathildes for whom this honor is claimed. It is more than improbable that the Ghibelline Dante should have so exalted a pronounced Guelf who made continual war on the empire; and the characteristic traits of the Countess Mathilde do not at all answer to those of Dante's lovely portrait.[1]

[1] The subject is exhaustively discussed by Scartazzini in his "Excursus on the Twenty-eighth Purgatorio," and his decision is very emphatic against the Countess of Tuscany.

At the Lateran synod of March Paschal repeated the story of the extorted treaty, confessed his error, and condemned with eternal anathema the privilege granted to Henry. He evaded the demand for the excommunication of the Emperor, but declared the excommunication pronounced by the Synod of Vienne to be legitimate.

Henry's situation in Germany was not comfortable. His most faithful followers were threatening to desert him. He had attempted a reconciliation with the friends of his father, and he at last obtained the reluctant consent of the Pope to the Emperor's interment in the ancestral tomb at Spires, and performed his obsequies with great splendor. In 1114 he celebrated his marriage with Matilda of England at Mainz. The Saxons were restless. An insurrection broke out in Cologne with which the princes of the Lower Rhine were in league; and in his attempt to reduce the city he was repulsed with heavy loss. Lewis of Thuringia, whom he had formerly imprisoned, headed a new insurrection of Saxon and Thuringian nobles, who succeeded in defeating the Emperor in a battle near Mansfeld in 1115. All North Germany and nearly the whole German church deserted him.

The death of Mathilde determined him to go to Italy. The Pope must be prevented, if possible, from obtaining possession of that vast inheritance which she had made over to the Roman see; for this would make him a king in Italy. Henry arrived in Rome about Easter, 1117, and on his approach Paschal fled to Lower Italy. The Emperor was cordially received by the Roman people, but not by the higher clergy. He freely distributed money to the nobles, took the city prefect into his pay, reinstated Ptolemæus, the Count of Tusculum, in his possessions, and gave him his natural daughter in marriage, thus securing in the city a powerful partisan. Attempts at negotiation with the cardinals failed, and he finally withdrew. Paschal returned to find the Roman factions furiously fighting each other. His reappearance created a movement in his favor. He was engaged in besieging St. Peter's, when he died on the 21st of January, 1118. The papal see had suffered greatly from his weakness and indecision. He had not only brought the city into collision with the Emperor, but into a condition of constant internal tumult, so that he was continually being forced to leave it and to make journeys into Italy.

A monk succeeded to the apostolic chair, John of Gaeta, chancellor under Urban II. and archdeacon under Paschal, of whom he was the most faithful supporter and the sharer of his imprisonment. He was unanimously elected on the 24th of January, 1118, as Gelasius II.

The election was secret. No notice was taken of the Emperor's right to confirm. The old man resisted his elevation to a position so dangerous. Being only a deacon, it was necessary for him to be ordained presbyter before he could be installed as Pope, and this could not be done until March. In the meantime he had a foretaste of what awaited him. His monastery was in the district commanded by the towers of the Frangipani. During the election proceedings the doors of the conclave were burst open, and furious Romans dashed in with drawn swords. The newly elected Pope was seized by the throat, beaten with fists and kicks, dragged from the church to the house of Cencius Frangipani, and thrown into chains. Similar outrages were inflicted on the electors, and many of them reached their homes half dead. The city prefect, the Norman Stephen, and others hastened to the rescue with troops and a multitude of the populace, set the Pope on a white horse, and escorted him to the Lateran.

The Frangipani hastened to inform Henry of the election of a Pope without his consent, and another catastrophe awaited Gelasius before his consecration. Henry had armed for an attack on Rome and the enforcement of the concessions of 1111. On the night of the 2d of March the Pope was awakened by the announcement that Henry was already in the porch of the Vatican. He fled with his entire following, and the party embarked in two vessels on the Tiber for Gaeta. A storm prevented them from reaching the sea, and the Germans, following up the vessels as they labored amid the tawny waters, kept them under the fire of their arrows, while the thunder bellowed and the lightning flared, screaming their threats to set them on fire with pitched hoops if the Pope were not surrendered to them. The fugitives at last succeeded in landing unobserved. A broad-shouldered cardinal bore Gelasius on his back to the fortress of St. Paul at Ardea, from which, by the way of Terracina, the drenched and seasick company finally reached Gaeta, where Gelasius received priestly ordination and was installed on the next day.

In March Henry set up an antipope in the person of a Portuguese archbishop, Maurice of Braga, otherwise known as Maurice Burdinus, who was installed as Gregory VIII. Gelasius at Gaeta of course excommunicated this interloper, and at Capua, in April, laid Henry under ban, and busied himself in arming against him with the assistance of the Norman barons.

Henry, recrowned by his Pope, left Rome to return to Germany by the way of Lombardy. Gelasius returned and began to concoct plans with the Norman princes to relieve himself of Burdinus; but an attack by the Frangipani, while he was celebrating mass, compelled him again to flee. He reached France, and died at Clugny about a month after his arrival. He was the last sacrifice of the investiture struggle.

By six cardinals, who were the companions of Gelasius in his exile, and a few other Romans a foreigner was elected in a foreign land to the chair of St. Peter. Guido, Archbishop of Vienne, was chosen at Clugny on the 2d of February, 1119, on the ground of his hostile attitude towards investiture. He refused to assume the office until his election should be confirmed by the cardinals at Rome. A commission was at once sent to Rome, which assembled the Romans at St. John's, on the Tiber Island, and afterwards at the Capitol, where the election was ratified by the nobles of the Catholic party, the city prefect, the clergy, and the people. Guido was installed in February, at Vienne, as Calixtus II.

A Frenchman, elected and enthroned in France, and on such an issue, could not think of entering Rome. In France, on the contrary, no opposition was offered. The Pope soon began to prepare for the synod at Rheims, where the issue between the see and the empire was to be decided. The Bishop of Ostia and the Roman presbyter Gregory were sent by him to Henry, whom they met between Verdun and Metz. Two documents were drawn up, in which the Emperor and the Pope respectively engaged to make peace with the opposite party, and to restore the property lost in the contest. The Emperor renounced the right of investiture; he made peace with all who had been involved in war for the cause of the church; he promised to restore all the churches in his possession, and to procure the restoration of those which had been granted to others. Ecclesiastical disputes were to be settled by ecclesiastical laws, temporal disputes by civil judges. The Pope pledged himself to restore everything gained in the war.

The Synod of Rheims was opened with great state on the 20th of October, 1119, and, after disposing of several items of business, took a recess of a few days, in order that the Pope and the Emperor might meet at Moisson and ratify the treaty already drawn up. Some suspicions of Henry's good faith deterred the Pope from appearing in person, and he remained in the castle of Moisson and carried on the negotiation through his commissioners. A more careful scrutiny of the treaty had awakened doubts on the part of the papal counsellors as to the exact purport of Henry's concession. They assumed that the imperial fiefs remained attached to the prelacies, while the Emperor held that no fief could be bestowed without final investiture, and that the treaty left him full power over the fiefs of the church in the empire. So certain had Henry been of the conclusion of the treaty and his consequent absolution that he had already stipulated as to the form of his absolution, that he was not to appear before the Pope barefoot, as a penitent. But the negotiations were broken off, and Calixtus returned to Rheims, where he solemnly pronounced the excommunication of the Emperor.

CHAPTER XV.

THE CISTERCIANS — TREATY OF WORMS — THE FRANGIPANI AND PIERLEONI—HONORIUS II.

N the 23d of December, 1119, the Pope gave his formal approval to a movement of the greatest importance to the Papacy, though its full significance was not apparent at the time. This was the Benedictine reform of Abbot Stephen of Citeaux, the first attempt to organize an order of monks wholly independent of the episcopal power and directly under the control of the Pope. The movement was on the line of Gregory's policy of curtailing the power of the bishops, and resulted in the formation of an international army in the service of the Roman see.

The abbey of Citeaux was founded in 1098, by Robert, the Abbot of Molesme. It was named after its original home, the forest of Cistercium or Citeaux, about fourteen miles northeast of Beaune, in Burgundy. By a special edict, Paschal II., in 1100, placed it under the immediate authority of the Pope. Its rule was that of Benedict. The monastery of Citeaux was founded as a kind of protest against Clugny. Clugny was wealthy and magnificent, while at Citeaux every kind of display was banished. The crucifix was of wood, the candelabra of iron, and the censers of copper. The ascetic discipline and the admission of Bernard of Clairvaux, in 1113, drew to it such crowds of devotees that it became necessary, within two years after Bernard's entrance, to found four new monasteries—La Ferté, Pontigny, Clairvaux, and Morimond. In 1119 the number of Cistercian abbeys had increased to thirteen; in 1151 to five hundred; and in the middle of the thirteenth century to eighteen hundred. In 1119 the constitution of the order, the "Charta Caritatis," was issued by Stephen Harding, the abbot, and confirmed, as already noted, by Calixtus II. Led by Bernard, the order occupied one of the foremost positions in Christendom. It crushed Abélard, Arnold of Brescia, and the Cathari; it preached the second crusade; it called into life the great military orders of the Templars, Calatrava,*Alcantara, and Montesa. We shall have numerous occasions of noting its influence in the subsequent history.

On Calixtus's return to Rome in June, 1120, he took possession of the Lateran, and later of St. Peter's, received the oaths of the entire Roman nobility, and commenced an attack on the antipope Burdinus, whom he besieged in Sutri, and who was surrendered by the inhabitants of that town and very roughly treated. Calixtus, in a letter to France, declared that he had gotten into his power that idol of the German Emperor who had built a "devil's nest" in Sutri, and that he would be brought to Rome a prisoner, bound upon a camel. This actually took place. Burdinus, clad in a shaggy goat's hide and mounted backwards on a camel, was led through Rome like a beast amid blows of whips and showers of stones. He was imprisoned, condemned to banishment, and, after being removed from one castle of Campania to another, died in a monastery. His fall hastened the end of the investiture contest.

Steps were being taken in Germany towards a settlement with the Pope. At the end of September, 1121, the Emperor, at Würzburg, submitted to a number of princes selected as arbitrators, the draft of a treaty according to which the Emperor was to submit to the Pope, and the question of investiture was to be referred to the papal synod. In the meantime peace should be maintained. The treaty was finally framed at Mainz in the presence of the papal legates, and was sealed with the imperial seal by the chancellor, the Archbishop of Cologne, and subscribed by a number of archbishops, bishops, and princes, and by the Abbot of Fulda.

On the 23d of September, 1122, a great popular assembly gathered at Worms in the open air. The two documents were made public. That of the Emperor declared his willingness to surrender investiture by ring and staff, so that the bishops could be chosen according to the canons and freely consecrated; in other words, the clergy throughout the empire should have the right of free election without imperial interference. The Emperor would restore to the Church of Rome and to all other churches, and to nobles, the possessions and feudal sovereignties which had been seized in his father's and in his own times. He would grant peace to the Pope and to all his partisans, and, when summoned, would protect the church in all things. The Pope's document declared that all elections of bishops and abbots should take place in the presence of the Emperor or of his commissioners, without bribery or violence, and with an appeal in contested elections to the metropolitan and provincial bishops. After his election the bishop elect was to receive by the touch of the sceptre all the temporal rights, principalities, and possessions of his see, except those held immediately by the see of Rome, and was faithfully to discharge to the Emperor all duties attaching to those principalities. The Pope would grant peace to the Emperor and his followers, and would assist him on all lawful occasions.

This treaty was ratified by the most solemn ceremonies. The papal legate celebrated mass, gave the Eucharist to the Emperor, pronounced him reconciled to the Holy See, and received him and all his partisans with the kiss of peace into the bosom of the church. The consummation of the treaty was hailed with universal joy. Not less moving than the spectacle of the multitudes at Clermont, glowing with enthusiasm for the first crusade under the eloquence of Urban, is that of those thousands of Germans at Worms, rejoicing over the compact which terminated a bloody strife of fifty years.

Out of this contest, thus happily ended, much more accrued to Europe than the settlement of the paltry formality of ring and staff. As in many other great conflicts, the ostensible and trifling cause involved great and antagonistic principles. The church had been fighting for complete independence and the subjugation of the empire. The empire aimed to bring the spiritual power back to its old position under Constantine and Justinian. Both parties receded from their extremes. The church relinquished the attempt to hold great temporal possessions without secular obligations, and the Emperor surrendered the claim to fill ecclesiastical benefices with his own partisans in return for money or other considerations. It was a movement towards the anti-Gregorian policy of rendering unto Cæsar the things which are Cæsar's, and unto God the things which are God's. The long struggle was not without its wholesome results. The very passions and conflicts of opinion which it evoked shook Europe out of its lethargy. Its influence was soon apparent in the essays of philosophic thought and theological protest. It stimulated the study of jurisprudence and the spirit of republican freedom and civic fellowship. It diverted business and exchange into the hands of laymen and led to the formation of the great commercial guilds. It proved that the programme of Gregory VII. could not be carried out against the stand of the great political powers for their ancient national rights and for the claims on the church which attached to these.

The results of the Treaty of Worms were different in different parts of the empire. In Germany Henry was able to unite the secular princes unanimously, and mostly the spiritual lords, against the Papacy. In Lombardy, on the other hand, the Pataria prevailed in most of the principal cities, and broke the power of the imperial party, while in other cities a continual war was waged with the bishops. In the latter part of the eleventh century, in those cities where the upper burgher population had the control, nobles and merchants combined in the civic administration without drawing their support from the empire. In Burgundy and Middle Italy the custody and guardianship of vacant benefices [1] were principally in the hands of counts and lords, or of the cities. In southern Italy the Norman power was steadily growing, and neither the papal nor the imperial power asserted itself decisively.

By the Treaty of Worms the Emperor renounced investiture for the whole empire. In future both that and the conferring of ecclesiastical positions resided in the church; but in Germany the Emperor, after all, retained the controlling influence in ecclesiastical appointments. He could introduce a candidate at the elections; he retained the proprietorship and the disposal of most of the church property, and conveyed its possession by the sceptre. As the royal investiture must precede the clerical, it followed that the Emperor could exclude a candidate whom he did not approve, and that the imperial church property was no longer granted as church property, but independently by the Emperor. The possible misunderstanding was carefully guarded that church investiture carried with it imperial church property. The reference of contested elections to the metropolitans was a blow at the Hildebrandian policy of weakening their influence, and restored the provincial associations and their connection with the throne, which it had been Hildebrand's object to destroy.

[1] Technically known as "regale."

On the 18th of March, 1122, the great Lateran synod was opened by the Pope. Over three hundred bishops were in attendance. The Treaty of Worms was formally sanctioned. After the synod Calixtus gave his attention to the improvement of the Lateran palace, which had been almost entirely neglected by the popes since Leo IV. in the ninth century. He began by erecting a new chapel to St. Nicholas of Bari, in the tribune of which were painted the likenesses of his famous predecessors from Alexander II. The chapel might serve as a monument of all the popes who had waged the battle with the empire. But Calixtus also had the triumph of the church painted in a new audience-hall, where Gelasius II., Paschal II., Urban II., Victor III., Gregory VII., Alexander II., and himself were depicted with the antipopes beneath their feet as footstools, and the Treaty of Worms was inscribed on the walls.

After a military expedition to Lower Italy, Calixtus returned to Rome, where he died of a fever on the 14th of December, 1124. His death introduces a new contest for the papal throne, in which the unity of the Papacy and of the Western Church was menaced by two prominent Roman families.

The name of the Frangipani first appears in the year 1014 in their ancestor Leo. Their name ("bread-breakers") was explained by a tradition that at some remote date one of their ancestors had distributed bread to the poor during a famine; and the family arms exhibited two lions confronting each other on a red field, and holding loaves in their claws. Leo's son Cencius was, in the time of Gregory VII., an influential consul, and his son John, the father of that Cencius who assaulted Gelasius, married the sister of Stephen the Norman. Their towers and palaces were near the Arch of Titus and at the Coliseum.[1]

The family of the Pierleoni was of Jewish descent. Few historical studies are more interesting than that of the Jews under the Roman empire. The irrepressible vitality of this race is a source of constant amazement. Their native pliancy took advantage of disaster, and calamities which would have exterminated any other people became to them sources of power and growth. Conquered and dispersed by Rome, they formed in every Roman province and city an element which it was impossible to overlook. They obtained not only the right of citizenship, but also concessions which were refused to native citizens. Clinging tenaciously to their ancient law, they nevertheless entered freely into the broader life of the Gentile world. At once fanatical and complaisant, they found means to break down every barrier which their law and tradition opposed to Gentile intercourse. Fascinated by the power and beauty of Greek culture, they turned it successfully to the uses of proselytism. They held in their hands the world's commerce and a large share of its wealth, and thus made themselves indispensable. Scattered over the world, they preserved their national unity, and, by the constant communication of each of their communities with all the rest, controlled vast interests. They were the standing jest of Roman literature, the butt of Roman wits, yet their faith became a fashion

[1] The name of the amphitheatre is used of a region.

among the fops of Nero's court, and dandies and royal courtesans affected enthusiasm for the sacred books of Moses.

A Jewish community had existed since the time of Pompey in the Trastevere and around the bridges of the Tiber Island. They numbered only a few hundreds, and maintained themselves against their persecutors by their talent, cunning, and secretly hoarded gold. The best physicians and the richest money-changers of Rome were Jews.

The grandfather of that Peter Leonis who, during the investiture struggle, played so distinguished a part in Rome, was a Trasteverine Jew, who had often assisted the papal court with funds in its financial straits, and who finally received Christian baptism and the Christian name of Benedictus Christianus. His son Leo, who received his baptismal name from Leo IX., allied himself by marriage with the Roman nobility, and attached himself to the party of Gregory VII.; and his son Pierleone became a man of large political influence in Rome. From his castle he commanded the Tiber Island, and Urban II. intrusted St. Angelo to him and died in his palace. The people treated him as a usurer, and the nobility as an upstart; but the friendship of the popes, the family alliances, the money and the influence so quickly covered the Jewish lineage that the Pierleoni were soon renowned as the most distinguished princely family of Rome. They were in feud with the Frangipani, who were imperialists.

Peter Leonis had destined his son Peter for the priesthood. The young man went to Paris and probably listened to Abélard, and finally took the cowl at Clugny. Paschal brought him to Rome and made him deacon. He accompanied Gelasius to France, and in 1120 was made cardinal priest of Santa Maria in Trastevere by Calixtus.

On the death of Calixtus the Frangipani came forward with their candidate for the vacant chair, and in order to gain time contrived that there should be no discussion of the matter until the third day. Their object was to elect a Pope friendly to the Emperor; and their candidate was Lambert of Ostia, while the people's candidate was Cardinal Saxo of Anagni, and that of the Pierleoni the presbyter Theobald. On the 16th of December an assembly for election was convened, and Theobald was invested with the papal mantle as Cœlestine II.; but Robert Frangipani at once proclaimed Lambert as Honorius II., and after some disturbance this was agreed to and Theobald was set aside. Lambert was of humble origin, from the neighborhood of Bologna, but was well educated. He had received from Paschal the diocese of Ostia and Velletri, and was one of those who had concluded the Treaty of Worms. The Abbot of Monte Cassino, when informed of the election, remarked, "I don't know whose son his Holiness is; I only know that he is chock-full of literature from head to foot."

CHAPTER XVI.

LOTHAIR THE SAXON—THE SOUTH-ITALIAN KINGDOM—INNOCENT AND ANACLETUS—BERNARD OF CLAIRVAUX.

ENRY V. died childless, in May, 1125, and with him closed the Franconian line of German emperors. His natural heirs were his two nephews, the brothers Conrad and Frederick of Hohenstaufen. The Hohenstaufen, by their fidelity to Henry IV., had first established his power. Their family name was derived from the hill Staufen, in Suabia, which overlooked the valley of the Rems. Frederick was Duke of Suabia, and Conrad Duke of the Franks. The nobles, however, desired an Emperor who would not prove too powerful, and who would not be disposed to attack the Pope or the independence of the feudal lords. They turned, therefore, to the Saxons, and selected Lothair, the champion for a long time of the nobles and of the church against the Emperor. He was elected as Lothair III. in August, 1125, at the old election field of Kamba, by an assembly of nearly sixty thousand, representing the whole German people.

The Gregorian Papacy could never long remain

reconciled to any measure which tended to thwart its greed for secular power or to allow it less than absolute control in temporalities; whence it may be supposed that it would not frown upon any plausible pretext for evading certain provisions of the Treaty of Worms. Most welcome to the Pope, therefore, was the concession volunteered by Lothair in his gratitude for his election, by which he renounced the right to the homage of the clergy for their imperial fiefs, along with the right to have the bishops elected in his presence, thus forfeiting the control over the elections secured to him by the Treaty of Worms. He consented that the ecclesiastical consecration should precede the investiture by sceptre, and that the invested party should give only an oath of allegiance to the sovereign, without detriment to the spiritual obligations of his office, and not a "hominium" or fief-oath.

But the papal sky was by no means unclouded in other quarters. Trouble had arisen between the Pope and Monte Cassino. One of Honorius's first acts after his consecration was to administer a severe rebuke to the Abbot Oderisius for certain errors of administration, and to remove the imprisoned antipope Burdinus out of his jurisdiction. Honorius now charged that Oderisius was plotting to unseat him and to secure the papal office for himself, and summoned him to answer at Rome. On his refusal the Pope deposed him, and, on his persisting in officiating, excommunicated him. The brethren of the abbey chose one Nicholas as his successor, but the Pope was determined to force another candidate upon them. When, however, he demanded of this candidate the oath of fealty to himself, it was refused on the ground that Monte Cassino had never been heretical or schismatic.

Roger of Sicily, too, brought down the ban upon himself by claiming the succession of William, Duke of Apulia, who had died without children. He affirmed that William had acknowledged him as his heir, and seized the opportunity to unite all southern Italy; for of all the states only Capua and Naples remained independent. He made himself master of Salerno and Amalfi, and received the homage of many cities. Honorius was resolved to prevent the establishment of a south-Italian monarchy, and treated Roger's act as sacrilegious. He declared that William's lands reverted to the papal see, and hastened to Benevento, where Roger, enraged at his refusal to invest him with Apulia as a feudary of the church, laid waste the Beneventine territory. The Pope retired to Capua and summoned it to aid in the war against the Sicilian. Robert of Capua mobilized his troops, but Roger quietly waited until the summer heat dissolved them, and the experience of Leo IX. was then repeated. Honorius found himself obliged to come to terms. When Roger followed him to Benevento, the forsaken Pope asked for peace, and the Sicilian compelled the Holy Father to come out of the city, and on the bridge of the river Calore, under the broiling August sun, to give him the investiture of the dukedom of Apulia and Calabria. The church could not prevent the founding of the Neapolitan monarchy. This important event changed the politics of Italy and of the popes. Honorius's temporary advantage consisted in his obtaining the feudal sovereignty of southern Italy.

These matters kept the Pope in continual movement between Rome and Apulia. The Frangipani protected Rome in his interest, and furnished him with the means of carrying on his petty wars with the captains of the Campagna. In his last sickness he was carried to the fortified monastery of St. Gregory, where he looked from a window upon the furious crowd, which believed him already dead, fighting for the papal crown. He died on the 14th of February, 1130.

The new election could not legally take place until after his burial; but the papal party could not wait for this. They hurried his body into an open pit in the monastery in order that their faction might proceed at once to an election. The letter of the requirement having thus been observed, the corpse was taken back to the Lateran, and the dead Pope and his newly chosen successor entered it together.

It was at first agreed to leave the choice to eight cardinals, among whom was Peter Leonis; but Honorius was hardly dead when five of the electors, in the monastery where he had expired, and where the proximity of the Frangipani's castles afforded security, proclaimed the cardinal Gregory of St. Angelo as Innocent II. The other party, much the more numerous, and supported by the Roman nobility and people, hastened to the church of San Marco, near the fortified quarter of the Pierleoni, and elected Peter, the son of Peter Leonis, as Anacletus II.

Both elections took place on the same day, the 14th of February. Anacletus at once proceeded to storm and despoil St. Peter's and other churches of the city, and two days after his election took possession of the Lateran. He then attempted to seize Innocent, but he had escaped to the protection of the Frangipani. Lothair promptly received from him an invitation to come to Rome the next winter for his imperial coronation, and to bring with him such a force as would enable him to overthrow the enemies of the church and of the empire.

But a fortnight had not passed before Innocent was reminded of the saying, "Put not your trust in princes." The Frangipani, probably on account of bribes, deserted him, and he sought refuge in the Trastevere, and then secretly made his escape to France. Anacletus made use even of the ceremonies of Passion Week to win Lothair. He proclaimed on the 27th of March the ban against Conrad of Hohenstaufen, who had assumed the royal title in opposition to Lothair a little more than a year before; and on Good Friday made a public intercession for Lothair. Many of Innocent's partisans were gained by threats or bribes, and Anacletus conferred privileges and issued canonical decisions as if he were in undisputed possession.

But declarations in favor of Innocent began to make themselves heard. The Archbishop of Ravenna affirmed that Innocent was legally elected; that Pierleone, who had long desired the office, had obtained it by bloodshed and simony; and that all Italy acknowledged Innocent, and condemned Pierleone as not an apostle, but an apostate; not Catholic, but heretic; not consecrated, but execrated. The Bishop of Lucca expressed himself to the same effect. Louis of France, through the influence of Bernard of Clairvaux, acknowledged him. Then the voices of the great synods began to be heard. The Synod of Clermont uttered its recognition in October. Here appeared commissioners from Lothair to announce that the assembly at Würzburg, in that same month, had acknowledged Innocent as lawful Pope and had pronounced the ban upon Anacletus. Henry of England, also through Bernard's influence, gave his adherence to Innocent, and had a personal interview with him at Chartres. Innocent and Lothair met at Liége in March, and the synod held at that time, at which ninety bishops and abbots and thirteen cardinals were present, pronounced Innocent Pope and banned Anacletus, Conrad, and Frederick. The Synod of Rheims followed in October, and commissioners to that body from England and from Castile and Aragon presented the homage of those kingdoms to Innocent. Thus, soon after his expulsion from Rome, he was acknowledged by Germany, England, France, a great part of Italy, and all the monastic orders.

The name of Bernard of Clairvaux now claims special attention.

Though the reform-movement of the eleventh century had not accomplished all that its promoters had hoped for, though much violence, luxury, and immorality still characterized the clergy and monks, the movement had nevertheless created a strong party against such abuses. This party was not, as in Leo IX.'s time, allied with the Papacy. It assumed, rather, a critical attitude towards the Papacy; but it developed men of great personal force, who, more than institutions, contributed to the work of reform; men who exercised for the time an almost unlimited control over the people and the churches, and who compelled even the Papacy to follow them. Such was Bernard of Clairvaux, the central figure of the period with which we now have to deal; its most powerful and impressive personality. During half of the twelfth century he is the head of Christendom, and his life, as Dean Milman remarks, is the history of the Western Church. More than any other he represents the new piety of the time, and is the decisive factor in all the great transactions of the age.

He was born in Burgundy near Dijon, in 1091. His father, Tescelin, was a distinguished knight, and his mother a noble lady of the ducal house of Burgundy, deeply pious, and devoted to charitable works and to the education of her children. Bernard was elegant in person, graceful in manners, and early distinguished for his literary proficiency. At the age of twenty-two he embraced the monastic life, entering the abbey of Citeaux, which at that time was undistinguished, poor, and unpopular, by reason of the severity of its discipline. For Citeaux, as has already been said, was a protest against Clugny. Clugny, though it had once stood at the head of the reform-movement, had been corrupted by its great wealth, and had not contributed to the removal of the current monastic abuses. Bernard's presence at

Citeaux attracted such numbers that it became necessary to colonize, and in 1115, a year after his profession, he was sent out to found a new monastery. He selected the site at Clairvaux,[1] in a valley covered with forest, known as "the Valley of Wormwood," and a notorious haunt of robbers. The Cistercian order was severely ascetic. The Benedictine rule was its foundation, but without the modifications with respect to food and clothing which had been introduced at Clugny. The sites selected for its houses were usually in wild regions, far from human intercourse. The Cistercians gave themselves to prayer, ascetic practice, and agricultural labor, in the prosecution of which last they developed the order of lay brothers. Their severity of discipline brought to them large gifts, and numerous members of all conditions, so that they were abundantly supplied with the best workmen; and the surplus of such ability compelled them to enter more and more into business intercourse. As the Cistercians chose unopened territory for cultivation, their real estate rapidly increased in value. Intelligence, experience, and the interchange of all fresh knowledge at the annual meetings of the general chapter raised their institutions to the character of model farms. With the magnificence of Clugny they renounced most of the literary work.

While Clugny had completed itself by the annexation of older monasteries, or by instituting depend-

---

[1] Clairvaux is about one hundred and thirty-seven miles from Paris, on the road to Basle by Troyes. It is in the department of Aube, and the river Aube runs not far from it. The monastery is in ruins.

ent priories, Citeaux developed by sending out independent colonies. The Abbot of Citeaux was general abbot, but his power was limited, not only by the general chapter of all the abbots and a standing committee, but also by the inner independence of each monastery. The individual monk was not bound to the Abbot of Citeaux, but to the abbot of his own monastery, until the orders of his abbot should send him elsewhere. The extension under this system was remarkable. Clugny never really extended beyond France; but Citeaux spread over all the lands of the Western Church. By its general chapter it maintained a living interchange between its individual parts, created a uniform policy, and thus, within a short time, became an ecclesiastical power of the first rank.

CHAPTER XVII.

MYSTICAL PIETY—BERNARD AND HUGO OF ST. VICTOR—NORBERT AND THE PRÆMONSTRANTS.

ERNARD represented not only a new type of monastic organization, but a distinct type of religious life. The development of mediæval piety followed, on the one hand, the line of externalism—salvation by works, penance, pilgrimage, sacraments, fastings, offerings, seclusion—every outward appliance by which the flesh could be mortified and the Deity propitiated. On the other hand, it pursued the track marked out by Augustine in the cultivation of a type of religiousness which emphasized the Christian consciousness and regarded faith as a principle of life rather than as a mere assent to dogma; a principle which presupposed the direct contact of the soul with God, and a divine operation in the soul. According to Augustine, love, joy, trust, and strength to overcome the world and the flesh are the elements of religion and spring from the soul's actual possession of God in Christ. John Scotus Erigena, who began to teach in Paris about the middle of the ninth century, translated certain works falsely attributed to Dionysius the Areopagite, Paul's convert at Athens,[1]

---

[1] Acts xvii. 34.

Scholasticism of Erigena. 181

and popularly identified with Dionysius or St. Denys, the apostle of France and the first Bishop of Paris. The object of these mystical writings was to show how man might attain to perfect communion with God. They taught that the influences continually emanating from God proceed downwards to man through successive "hierarchies" or ranks of beings which reflect the divine loveliness; and that thus man is drawn to God.[1]

Erigena carried out the Dionysian system, and endeavored to expound it by the aid of Aristotle. His work attracted comparatively little attention, however, until, in the eleventh century, after the attempt of Gregory VII. to subjugate western Europe to the Roman hierarchy, the movings of an independent spiritual life began to be felt. In place of a theology propagated by tradition and received on priestly authority, there emerged a science founded on the writings of Aristotle, which endeavored to submit the traditional doctrines of the church to the test of reason, and to show that they answered to reason. This science was especially cultivated in France and dominated the French schools; but it threatened, on the one hand, to make the natural reason the arbiter of the church's faith, while, on the other hand, by reason of its rigid formalism, it failed to appeal to the heart. For the heart-life had been mightily stirred in the Gregorian fight, as was shown by the crusading enthusiasm, by the rise of new and

---

[1] See B. F. Westcott, "Religious Thought in the West;" Robert A. Vaughan, "Hours with the Mystics;" Preger, art. "Theologie, mystische," in Herzog's "Real Encyklopädie."

multiform monastic orders, and by the mysticism which developed over against the scholasticism of Erigena, and which was especially fostered in the school of St. Victor in Paris.

This mysticism was related to the Augustinian teaching, but it was far more than a revival of Augustinian thought. "The chords of Christic mysticism, which Augustine had struck with an uncertain hand, grew into a rapturous melody."[1] The pietism of the twelfth century followed two lines—that of the Dionysian mysticism and that of the passionate love of Jesus. The former was represented by Hugo and Richard of St. Victor, the latter by Bernard. With both the ultimate object was the spiritual vision and enjoyment of God, and the ethical and religious purification and power which flowed from these. Hugo's process was logical, Bernard's ethical, intuitional, and emotional. Hugo laid out the path by which the soul ascends to God. He traced the rational process by which it mounts through the kingdom of this world, from the manifoldness of visible things to the oneness of God, by the successive steps of cogitation, meditation, and speculation, to contemplation, and so to the heavenly sphere and the vision of the divine.[2] Then the soul beholds in

---

[1] Harnack, "Dogmengeschichte."
[2] Compare the beautiful words which Dante puts into the mouth of Bernard:

> "Or questi, che dall' infima lacuna
> Dell' universo insin qui ha vedute
> Le vite spiritali ad una ad una,
> Supplica a te, per grazia, di virtute
> Tanto, che possa con gli occhi levarsi
> Più alto verso l' ultima salute."
>
> *Paradiso*, xxxiii., 22–27.

Christ God and man united—the full manifestation of divine love, wisdom, and power, both in creation and in redemption, and all designed for its spiritual enjoyment and holiness. Then first, under the power of this revelation, enters the passionate tumult of feeling, the emotional love of God as manifest in Christ.

Bernard, like Hugo, sought the revelation of the divine in Christ—in the image of the personal, historical, human Jesus; but practically he ignored the successive rational steps prescribed by Hugo for the attainment of the divine ecstasy. He rather aspired to scale the heights of heavenly communion by ravishment. Love, springing from faith, bears the soul upwards, and love is begotten in the contemplation of Jesus. He is the image of God. Whoso beholds him beholds God. Contemplation concentrates itself upon him. The spectacle of his humiliation and suffering takes possession of the heart and overpowers it. In this contemplation of Christ the soul communes with God as friend with friend, as bride with bridegroom; and often it is carried above the vision of the suffering One to the vision of the glorified One who inflames the heart with the intensest ardor of love. The result of this vision and rapturous communion is humiliation for sin and intenser striving after likeness to the divine.

It is interesting to see how the metaphysical element thus intertwines itself with the ecstatic, the combination retaining traces of the intellectual Neoplatonism in which the roots of mysticism were embedded. More than a hint of this appears in Hugo's rational cognition of the successive steps by which the spirit mounts to its celestial goal; in the metaphysical contemplation of the world and of the soul; in the weighing of the evidences of divine love which convince the soul that it belongs wholly to God. Even the emotional intercourse with Christ is a stage to something beyond. The spiritual vision aspires to overpass the historical and to attain the calm, passionless contemplation of the timeless Logos of the Trinity, the creator and maintainer of the world. Thus the mystical merges ultimately into the metaphysical; experience into ontological and cosmological theology; Hugo and Bernard into Anselm. This side of the matter, however, is not emphasized by Bernard. Although he and his followers turn to account and apply the Victorine theory, although the two conceptions of the mystical life and communion do not exclude each other, yet the peculiar, vital element of the Bernardine pietism is the contemplation of the historical, suffering Jesus.

The mysticism of this age, however, did not detach itself from the church. The rather it emphasized the sacraments and all holy ordinances, and the practice of discipline and works, as media of grace for the enjoyment of the ecstatic communion, and the church as the teacher of truths inaccessible to the unaided reason. It intensified the sense of sin; and this feature, of which Anselm was the principal exponent, appeared in the significance attaching to penitential discipline, which was regarded as expiation, and in the emphasis upon the idea that contemplation was possible only through continual penitence and purification.

Mysticism fell into the life of the twelfth century as a prolific seed. Many influences conspired to lead pious spirits into its paths, such as the secularization of the clergy, the barrenness of the rationalistic theology, and the strife between the ecclesiastical and the secular powers. It found a congenial soil in the female convents, such as those of the Beguines and Beghards. In certain prominent women, as Hildegard of Bingen and Elizabeth of Schönau, it assumed a prophetic character, and rebuked the vices of the day. In the thirteenth and fourteenth centuries the mystical life, especially in the female convents, revealed itself in numerous ecstatic phenomena, which are recorded in the diaries of the nun Gertrude, of Mechthild of Hackeborn, of Margaret and Christina Ebner, of Angela of Foligni, Brigitta of Sweden, and Catherine of Siena, and which furnish psychological studies of great interest.

The mystical theory was fostered by the scholastics, Bonaventura, Thomas Aquinas, and Albertus Magnus, and through Albertus found footing in Germany, where its first important representative was David of Augsburg. Extending itself in the forms of preaching, proverb, song, and allegorical poetry, it finally dominated the religious life, while the influence of the scholastic theology, extant only in the Latin language, was confined to a class.

Nearly two hundred years after Bernard the celestial hierarchies of Dionysius reappear in the circles of Dante's "Paradiso," along with the mystical theology of St. Victor and Bonaventura and the philosophic theology of Aquinas. In his portrait of Bernard, Dante, with consummate art, has ignored the monk, and seized upon that chivalrous quality which, sublimed by the spirit of worship, spent itself upon the Virgin Mother. He appears as "her faithful Bernard," at whose intercession she will grant to the poet the beatific vision; and there, with the holy rose unfolding its petals of light, there rises from his lips, like an incense cloud from a silver censer, that wondrous blending of hymn and prayer than which the literature of the world has nothing more exquisite:

"Vergine madre, figlia del tuo figlio,
Umile ed alta più che creatura," etc. [1]

The effect of this conception of Christian life upon Bernard appeared in a character of singular purity and refinement. His high ideal of personal purity led him into such severe physical discipline that his health was permanently weakened, and he remained an invalid to his dying day. His energy was restless and untiring, his courage indomitable, his tact and persuasiveness irresistible. The absence of self-consciousness, his spiritual insight, his fervent zeal, his high intellectuality, the fine play of his imagination, and his intensity of conviction made him a preacher on whose words thousands hung, and to whose power they willingly yielded. He had full command of the forces which were behind the principal movements of the age, yet his personal qualities were the secret of his power and gave him access to all classes alike. He was the vigorous champion of clerical reform,

[1] "Paradiso," xxxi., 100; xxxiii., 1-27.

but at the same time of the conscience of the age against the secular development of the Papacy and of the church. His conception of the church was far more spiritual than Hildebrand's. He was a loyal churchman, but he held no doctrine of papal infallibility which blinded him to errors in pontifical decisions. He has nowhere defined the limits of the papal rights. He held as strongly as Hildebrand or Urban to the immediate divine origin of the Papacy; but he found limits for its exercise in the popes themselves.[1]

Before leaving this subject, mention should be made of one who has been called the "second saint" of this age—Norbert of Xanthen. At the beginning of the twelfth century loud complaints were current against the canons or prebendaries of the collegiate churches. The reform-movement of the previous century seemed to have passed over their heads without leaving any trace. They lived in concubinage in their own houses, held private property, consumed church revenues in luxury, and rebelled, sometimes with arms, against their bishops, especially those of the reform-party. Against this abuse arose the canon-foundations of St. Victor in Paris, an institution which exerted the greatest influence throughout France, as well as in England, Italy, and Germany. There soon grew out of it a kind of "congregation," after the model of Clugny, whose

---

[1] It is, perhaps, hardly necessary to refer the reader, who may desire to know more of the life and character of Bernard, to the brilliant and delightful volume by Dr. R. S. Storrs, "Bernard of Clairvaux" (Scribners, 1893).

most prominent personality was Hugo of St. Victor. Norbert entered into the work of this order, and brought to it the organization of Citeaux; and in 1120 founded the order of the Præmonstrants or Præmonstratensians, a name derived from Prémontré, between Rheims and Laon. The order had at one time a thousand male and five hundred female abbeys. The rules were those of Augustine.[1] No meat was allowed, and the regimen included scourging.

For several centuries this order was the rival of the Cistercians, though the Cistercian order was, in almost all particulars, its model. Each order formed an independent fellowship. All their property was in their own hands and at their own disposal. Norbert stood by Bernard in the fight for reform, in politics, and in theology, though his influence over the masses was not equal to Bernard's. As Archbishop of Magdeburg, he exercised great influence over Lothair III. He is, so far as is known, the first who adopted the idea of preaching in the itinerant fashion of Jesus and the apostles as described in Matthew x., and that of the forest life which was afterwards carried out by Francis of Assisi. Both he and Bernard, while they stand on the ground of the eleventh-century reform, exhibit the fuller individualizing which underlies the advancing culture.

[1] So called. They did not originate with the Bishop of Hippo.

CHAPTER XVIII.

THE PAPACY AND ROGER OF SICILY—INNOCENT AND ANACLETUS—SCHOLASTICISM.

INNOCENT, leaving Rheims early in November, 1131, passed the rest of the year in France. He issued the decree of privilege to the Cistercian order and gave a charter to the abbey of Clairvaux. Then, crossing the Alps into Lombardy, he met Lothair at Roncaglia, after which he went to Pisa, where he succeeded in concluding a peace between that city and Genoa. At Calcinajo, in the Pisan territory, he again met Lothair and arranged with him to go at once to Rome, the King by land and the Pope by sea.

Innocent entered the city in April and occupied the Lateran, while Lothair remained encamped on the Aventine. Anacletus was in St. Peter's. A fleet of Genoans and Pisans soon appeared to support Innocent. On the 4th of June, 1133, Lothair, with his wife, Richinza, received the imperial crown in the Lateran. Safe in St. Angelo, on the other side of the Tiber, Anacletus could enjoy his laugh at seeing the gates of St. Peter once more closed against an imperial coronation. Four days after the coronation

Innocent gave to the royal pair the possessions of Mathilde in fief, and at the same time a document formally attesting the imperial coronation and pledging all rights attaching thereunto. Anacletus attempted to open negotiations with Lothair and Innocent, but was repulsed and publicly condemned by the German princes of the Emperor's retinue. The effect of this action was strengthened by the arrival of Robert of Capua with the papal legate of Benevento. Anacletus, however, had the long purse which was the supreme power in Rome, and employed it so successfully among the Romans that Lothair was compelled to leave the city before the middle of June. This proceeding was the signal for bloodshed between the two Roman parties, and forced Innocent soon to follow the Emperor and to repair to Pisa, where he did not find the assistance which he expected, owing to Pisa's jealousy of the growing naval power of Sicily. Roger of Sicily had been victorious in Apulia — a success which went to strengthen Anacletus; and the Pisans refused to take the field against him without the aid of the Genoese.

Bernard was indignant at the Emperor's delay, and wrote to him rebuking his ingratitude to Pisa, which had always been the most powerful ally of the empire. Meanwhile Anacletus had obtained possession of the Lateran, from which he wrote to the Archbishop of Compostella, whom he was vainly seeking to win over to his side, that Lothair had been forced to leave the city, that Innocent had fled to Pisa, that he had celebrated Easter in the Lateran and had wrested from his enemies the churches of St. John

Bernard Ends the Milan Schism. 191

and St. Paul, with several fortified positions, and that with the help of his friends, especially Roger of Sicily, he would destroy his opposers.

At the Pisan council in May, 1135, the principal matter was the deposition and anathematizing of Anacletus. If anathemas had been stones, Anacletus would long before have shared the fate of the martyr Stephen. Roger of Sicily was also anathematized; traffic with Sicily and Apulia and service under Roger were prohibited; and the same indulgence was pledged to all who should enlist against Pierleone or Roger as to the crusaders at Clermont. Bernard, with several cardinals, went to Milan in the commission of the Pope, to try to put an end to the schism which had existed there ever since the coronation of Conrad and the election of Anacletus. The Milanese archbishop Anselm, who had crowned Conrad in 1129, and who was Anacletus's chief supporter in Upper Italy, had been displaced by the Pisan council. Under Bernard's influence, Roboald, the former vicar, was chosen as Anselm's successor. The Milanese abjured Anacletus and acknowledged Lothair as their King and Emperor. Roboald at once took the oath of allegiance, and Bernard's intercession with the Emperor procured mild treatment for the Milanese.

This was one of Bernard's proudest triumphs. All Italy as far as the Tiber now paid homage to Innocent II. Only the city of Rome, the Campagna, and southern Italy held by Anacletus. The hope of unseating Anacletus lay in breaking the power of Roger. The Pisans carried on a brief contest with him, but without any decisive result except the overthrow of Amalfi in 1136; and Anacletus bestowed on him the titles of "Advocate of the Church" and "Patrician of the Romans," and granted him certain privileges which menaced the independence of the Papacy.

At Bamberg, in March, 1135, Frederick of Suabia submitted to the Emperor, and a new expedition to Rome was determined upon, to which Frederick promised to lend his aid. A special impulse to this expedition was given by the Pope's sending to Lothair a cardinal with Robert of Capua, who had been expelled by Roger and who now demanded that Lothair should free Sicily from Roger, who was in league with Anacletus.

Lothair set out for Italy from Würzburg in August, 1136, with the intention of driving Roger from Sicily. He passed through the marches along the coast, while his son-in-law Henry, with a smaller force, went by way of Florence to Viterbo. These two armies moved through Italy like a whirlwind, desolating the country with fire and sword. The whole of Apulia was subjected as far as Bari. Henry the Proud, Duke of Tuscany, laid waste those districts in Latium which acknowledged Anacletus. The fall of Bari was decisive. Roger sued for peace, with the condition that Lothair should give Apulia to his son. This Lothair refused. Roger escaped to Sicily, and the Emperor and Innocent went to Melfi.

Here a dispute arose between them over the Abbot of Monte Cassino, who appeared at the Emperor's command. The Pope demanded that he should appear barefoot and as a penitent, because of his part in the schism; that he should swear unconditional obedience to him, and curse Anacletus and all his following. A double problem was concealed in these demands—the independent relation of the abbey to the Pope, and to the Emperor and the empire. The abbot appealed to the Emperor, who decided in his favor and requested the Pope to pardon him and remit the oath. The Pope refused, and the Emperor assumed the secular right over the abbey. After much haggling the Pope yielded, renounced the oath of fidelity to himself, and received the abbey again into favor. The dispute was subsequently renewed, however, on the point that Raynal, the abbot, had been consecrated as deacon by Anacletus, had taken part in the schism, and was suspected of being in league with Roger. Lothair arranged that the settlement should be left to the Pope, the Emperor, and the princes. Raynal's election was declared void, and a new strife broke out between the cardinals and the monks about a new election. It was finally settled that the Emperor should nominate, the monks elect, and the Pope consecrate.

When Innocent, in October, appeared again in Roman territory, the party of Anacletus was fast collapsing. Their only support was Roger of Sicily, who, as soon as the Emperor had left southern Italy, returned and recovered his position. Salerno, Benevento, and Monte Cassino were soon in his hands. Bernard now endeavored to prevail on Roger to acknowledge Innocent. He induced him to consent to hear three cardinals from each side; and Roger, in

November, underwent the penance of listening for four days to the contestants—Bernard for Innocent, and the learned and eloquent Peter of Pisa for Anacletus. An amusing feature of the affair was that Bernard converted Peter. Roger then asked that a cardinal from each side should accompany him to Sicily and present the case before the ecclesiastics there. The proposition was accepted, but Roger stubbornly adhered to Anacletus. In the meantime Lothair, worn out with the hardships of war, died on the 4th of December, 1137. Anacletus followed him a year later, having for eight years maintained the struggle as antipope.

His college of cardinals immediately applied to Roger for permission to elect a new Pope, and in March, 1138, Cardinal Gregory was chosen as Victor IV. The election, however, only served the Romans as a means for obtaining more favorable terms of peace. Innocent, by means of bribes, won over most of the cardinals of Victor's party, and he was forced, in May, to lay his insignia at the Pope's feet. The Pierleoni took the oath to Innocent, and the schismatic clergy pledged him obedience. All Rome rejoiced and showered praises upon Bernard.

At the great synod in April of the following year the triumph of the Pope and the zeal of the western churches were duly set forth; but Innocent was not noble enough to forego the expression of his revengeful feeling. Anacletus was denounced; his present adherents were named and angrily rebuked, and stripped of their pallia and staves; a bishop was sent to France to overthrow all altars consecrated by the schismatics; Roger was excommunicated, and the Pope determined to undertake another expedition against him. In carrying out this enterprise the Pope suffered a defeat and was taken prisoner; but Roger desired peace, and at last received from the Pope the kingdom of Sicily as a fief.

In announcing this transaction the Pope exhibited a marked lack of candor. As Anacletus had made Roger King, Innocent ascribed that act to his predecessor, Honorius II., in order to conceal the humiliation of having ratified the act of an antipope. Honorius had really recognized Roger only as Duke of Apulia. Innocent, however, recognized him as King in consideration of six hundred gold pieces as an annual tribute, according to Roger's agreement with Anacletus. On Innocent's return to Rome the Romans demanded that he should break this treaty, and a feeling was created against him which threatened trouble for the future.

But a conflict more serious than any political struggle, both in its origin and in its tendencies, was now to engage the attention of the Roman see, which, up to this time, had never been called to deal on any very large scale with developments in the world of thought. The rise of the scholastic philosophy and theology inaugurates one of the great intellectual movements of this century. Fully to treat this subject requires far more space than the limits of this volume allow; and the attempt would carry the reader into a jungle of metaphysical subtleties which would yield neither interest nor profit. A few general outlines and leading facts will be necessary in order to follow intelligently the course of our history.

Ancient philosophy disappeared about the beginning of the sixth century. Its last representative was Boethius, who died in 525. Four years later Justinian closed the Athenian schools. The Christian fathers did not deal with theology on a philosophical basis, but simply as churchmen. They formulated and fixed their dogmas by the decisions of the great church councils. With the close of the sixth century theological production ceased. All the materials for the formation of a doctrinal system of Christianity were at hand. From the seventh to the eleventh century, theological writers, as Cassiodorus, Bede, Alcuin, were merely compilers of extracts and writers of glosses. They wove together extracts from different fathers, occasionally adding a few words of their own. Even the glosses were compilations, masses of literal, moral, and mystical fragments intermingled with a few crude grammatical observations. We have a high Roman Catholic authority for the statement that about the sixth or seventh century "the oral or traditionary teaching, which allowed scope to the individual teacher, had hardened into a written tradition."[1] The patristic dogmas were passively accepted. They were not only not controverted, but not even treated.

Intimations of a more independent spirit began to appear early in the eleventh century as the result of intercourse and disputes with the Greek Church and growing familiarity with such writings of Aristotle as

[1] Cardinal Newman.

had been translated by Boethius. Greek monks, driven from their homes by the iconoclastic controversy, had introduced the Greek language, learning, dialectics, and theology into the monasteries. John Scotus Erigena translated the works of Dionysius the Areopagite, and thus brought Neoplatonism into western Europe. He applied philosophy to the study of theology, and refused to recognize the absolute authority of church tradition, asserting that reason equally with authority proceeds from God, and therefore that the two cannot contradict each other. In short, there was arising a tendency to apply the reason to theological dogma, and the dialectic methods of Aristotle to its exposition. It would be wrong, however, to regard scholasticism as a protest against dogmatic theology. On the contrary, it assumed that each single dogma is absolute divine truth, and undertook both to trace and to expound it by its dialectical processes. It assumed that all things must be understood from theology and must therefore be traced back to theology. It assumed the piety of the thinker, and has been defined as "piety become conscious and manifest," so that its roots were interlaced with those of mysticism; scholasticism endeavoring to attain by logical demonstration what mysticism sought through intuition and inward experience. Mysticism was the subjective side of scholasticism.

Scholasticism therefore went beyond the preservation, arrangement, and application of dogma. It added no new dogmas, neither did it alter the essential contents of the old ones; but it sought to give them a rational basis, and thus to elevate them from matters of faith to matters of science, and to form the whole mass into a consistent system; "to create the philosophy of Christianity; to demonstrate Christianity as rational, and the rational as Christian; to fuse faith and science, theology and philosophy, into a perfect unity."

The principle of scholasticism was first clearly set forth and successfully employed by Anselm of Canterbury (1033–1109), who is known as "the second Augustine." He was a strict holder of church tradition, regarding the dogmas of the church as identical with revelation itself, and not to be rejected even if they were unintelligible. His formula was, "I believe in order that I may understand; I do not seek to understand in order that I may believe." The whole circumference of dogma was not only to be grounded by rational methods in such a way as to be conceived, but so as that, by means of these methods, even one unacquainted with Christianity might be forced to acknowledge its truth. Thus his "Cur Deus Homo" is an exposition of the metaphysical necessity of the incarnation and death of Christ for human sin; and his "Proslogion" develops the ontological argument for the existence of God from the idea of a perfect being as it resides in the human mind.

The scholastic giants were divided into two parties —the Nominalists and the Realists. The philosophic question in dispute was the nature of universals. To illustrate: A man sees a trolley and a telephone. He says these are phenomena of a common archetypal reality known as electricity. He sees that a rose is red and a sunflower yellow. He says these two hues are phenomena of a common antecedent fact which he calls color. So a man implies the antecedent fact of humanity. A good man is the expression of an eternal, general reality of righteousness. These archetypes have a real, objective existence; they are not mere names for collective aggregates of particulars. Righteousness is as truly a fact as a righteous man. The red of the rose and the yellow of the sunflower are different expressions of generic color. Electricity is a force existing antecedently, independently, and outside of its phenomena. These archetypes are the invariable element which, in each case, is the basis of the varying phenomena and constitutes their essence; and they are called universals as including their special manifestations. The man who holds that these universals are *real*, objective existences is called a realist.

Another, however, denies this and affirms that these universals have no real existence. They are, he says, merely convenient methods by which the mind groups classes of facts. They are abstractions, fictions. Only individual things have a real existence. Universals are only *names, nomina.* This man is a nominalist. The formula of the realist is, " Universalia ante rem " (" Universals are before the thing "). The formula of the nominalist is, " Universalia post rem " (" Universals are subsequent to the thing "). Anselm and Bernard and William of Champeaux were realists. Nominalism was represented by Roscelin, canon of Compiègne, whose position was vigorously assailed by Anselm. It is not difficult to see how radically theological conceptions, such as the nature of Christ's humanity and of sin, were affected according as they rested upon the one or the other of these theories.

CHAPTER XIX.

ABÉLARD—LAST DAYS OF INNOCENT II.—TIVOLI—
THE ROMANS PROCLAIM A REPUBLIC.

ALL France was now agitated by a new champion in the scholastic arena, who appeared in the person of Abélard. He was born in 1079, and his Christian name was Pierre de Palais. His first teacher in philosophy was the celebrated Roscelin, who had already provoked the opposition of Anselm by his nominalism and the tritheistic doctrine of the Trinity which he founded upon it. He came to Paris about 1100, and became a pupil of William of Champeaux, the president of the cathedral school of that city. His powers of argument and of easy and graceful expression quickly awakened attention, and his influence over his fellow-students alienated them from William and drew upon him the dislike of his teacher.

After some time spent at Laon he returned to Paris and entered upon a brilliant career as a lecturer. Here began his unfortunate and criminal relation with Héloïse, with its train of calamities, which finally incapacitated him for ecclesiastical honors. He retired to the monastery of St. Denys, became a severe reformer, and opened a school which was attended by large crowds. Here he composed a book on the Trinity, which caused him to be condemned by the Council of Soissons in 1121. He was compelled to burn his book and to recite the Athanasian Creed, and was imprisoned in the convent of St. Médard. Returning after a short time to St. Denys, he ventured to question the identity of St. Denys and Dionysius the Areopagite, was again obliged to leave, and betook himself to a wild district near Troyes, where he once more attracted throngs of students. The monastery there was called the "Paraclete." Its inmates were bound by no religious vows and governed by no rigid monastic rules; and the time was spent in scholastic discussion of the profoundest mysteries of religion.

The Paraclete was not far from Clairvaux, and Abélard's proceedings attracted the attention and provoked the animosity of Bernard, and of Norbert, then Bishop of Magkeburg. Under these circumstances he accepted, in 1125, an invitation to become abbot of the monastery of St. Gildas in Brittany, where his life was in constant danger from his efforts to bring the dissolute and lawless monks into order. In the interval between his retiring from St. Gildas and the year 1136 his principal works were composed.[1] About 1136 he opened a school at Mount St. Geneviève, where he taught for a short time. Here we

[1] A complete edition of Abélard's works and letters was published by Victor Cousin, Paris, 1849, 1859. They may also be found, with the exception of the "Dialectica" and the "Sic et Non," in Migne's "Patrologia," vol. clxxviii. Biography, Charles de Rémusat, "Abélard" (Paris, 1845); I. L. Jacobi, "Abälard und Heloise"

reach the point where he falls into the regular course of our narrative.

Between the mystic and the rationalist, between Bernard's genuine humility, settled faith in tradition, and mystical intuitionalism, and Abélard's vanity, self-assertiveness, intellectual pugnacity, and critical temper, there could be little affiliation. In philosophy the difference between them is not easy to define. Bernard was a realist, and Abélard held a kind of *via media* between nominalism and realism as it was commonly understood. He was what is termed in modern metaphysics a "conceptualist." He detected in realism possibilities of pantheism; and while denying the nominalist doctrine that universals are only abstractions or fictions, and holding that they have a real existence, he maintained that they do not exist substantially but conceptually. In other words, they are cognizable by the individual only as mental conceptions. Such general ideas as humanity and righteousness are not substances, but they may be formed by the faculty of pure thought, thought which does not act through the senses or the imagination, and the ideas thus formed are conceptual entities.

The philosophical divergence, however, produced no collision between Abélard and Bernard. This came with the emergence of Abélard's philosophy into the region of theology. No doubt his teachings were often misunderstood, misrepresented, and exaggerated. His conception of Biblical inspiration was

(Berlin, 1850). See also Bonnier, "Abélard et St. Bernard" (Paris, 1862); Bornemann, "Anselmus et Abelardus, sive initia scholasticismi" (Copenhagen, 1840); Hayd, "Abelard und seine Lehre" (Regensburg, 1863).

indeed loose according to the churchly standard; but he was not a denier of revelation. He grounded piety in the human manifestation of Jesus and God's revelation in it; though the whole motive was essentially ethical. He did not summarily reject the authorities of the church; he even ascribed to the fathers a certain measure of inspiration; but he desired to know why he believed; he challenged the infallibility of tradition; he claimed the right of subjecting it to scientific proof against mere dogmatic assertion. Nevertheless he made the boundaries of human knowledge narrower than most strong traditionalists; he detected the danger of pantheism in realism, and compelled William of Champeaux to acknowledge it and to modify his views. His philosophy contemplated the vindication of the distinct personality of God as against the pantheistic identification of God with the world; but his whole attitude towards a system which had much to lose by the prevalence of free inquiry, and the life and power of which depended largely upon an atmosphere of passive faith and acquiescent ignorance, was adapted to awaken the utmost terror and animosity among orthodox churchmen.

The theological difference between Bernard and himself was pronounced. Faith, which in Bernard was a calm and settled assurance, directly wrought by divine grace accompanied by the testimony of Scripture and experience, was to Abélard an intellectual conviction starting in doubt, and wrought out by the critical study of conflicting opinions. Biblical inspiration stood upon the same level with the inspiration of the church fathers and the greater Greek philosophers. He delighted in showing how the fathers contradicted themselves.[1] Original sin was only a punishment; redemption the substitution of the law of love for the law of fear; atonement merely a moral force to kindle love to God. The quality of sin was conditioned by a man's own view of the will of God, and sin consisted in refusing to perform that will as the man himself conceived it. Thus even the perpetrators of cruel martyrdoms and the crucifiers of Christ and the murderers of Stephen were excused. The Trinity was a necessary idea of the reason; its persons were merely phases of the one divine personality.

The clash was inevitable. William of Thierry, Bernard's intimate friend, on reading two of Abélard's books, wrote to Bernard and to the Bishop of Chartres stating his objections and calling upon them to withstand the heresy. Bernard, after reading the books, had an interview with Abélard, who promised to amend whatever might be amiss in his writings, but continued nevertheless to defend his opinions. Bernard then began to warn people against him and to suppress the circulation of his works, and wrote to the Pope and the cardinals urging them to interpose authoritatively for the arrest of these dangerous doctrines. He also wrote to the Archbishop of Rheims and other prelates, and, somewhat later, went to Rome himself in order to hasten the Pope's decision.

In July, 1141, the Pope issued a rescript to Bernard and to the Archbishops of Sens and Rheims,

[1] As in the "Sic et Non."

condemning the teachings of Abélard, imposing silence on him as a heretic, excommunicating his followers, and ordering his confinement in a monastery and the burning of his books. Abélard claimed the privilege of appearing before the synod which was about to assemble at Sens, where the King and a large concourse of nobles and prelates were to be present, and to vindicate his opinions there. Consent was given. The synod, which met in June, 1140, was a splendid assemblage of rank and learning. Bernard appeared and presented passages from Abélard's writings as the ground of the charge of heresy. The reading of these passages was interrupted by Abélard, who took an appeal to the Pope and immediately left the council. The examination of his opinions was continued, and of the seventeen passages submitted fourteen were condemned. The controversy was soon settled, however, by the death of Abélard at the priory of St. Marcel, near Châlons on the Saône, on the 21st of April, 1142.

His influence survived him; survives, in some sense, to this day. He met the fate which always attends the inroad of thought and learning into the snug retreats of fixed belief and accepted tradition. His disaster was due, largely, to his own unrestrained passion and arrogance; but he carries with him the sympathy of all open-eyed and fair-minded men by his courage in the fight against a bloated ecclesiastical conservatism, and a lethargic submission to authority in matters of faith; and, as in all such cases, the result, though late, is on the side of the thinker, even though some of his positions may be disproved by later and calmer thought. The gain is not only in the residuum of truth which goes over from such a man into succeeding generations. It lies in the break into the popular conviction that whatever is is right; in the opening of men's eyes to the fact that every question has two sides; in the awakening of the salutary doubt of the authority of bare assertion; in demonstrating that the established is not beyond challenge; that there is a principle of expansion in truth; that " God fulfils himself in many ways," and not only in the ways laid down by fathers and priests.

Notwithstanding the well-grounded charges against Abélard personally, notwithstanding the vast interests involved in the existing ecclesiastical system, he " laid the foundation," to quote the words of Harnack, "for the classical expression of mediæval conservative theology." Aristotle wrought through him to formulate the new religious ideas in theology. Much of what provoked opposition in his own time, subsequently came to be regarded as orthodox. He was the first who abandoned the method of treating theology in its separate parts, and undertook to reduce it to a complete course in more or less systematic form. He thus opened the way for his successors to attempt the solution of all theological problems. Among his pupils were Peter the Lombard, the collector and expositor of the patristic statements, the framer of axioms and definitions on which later theologians built their superstructures, and two popes, Cœlestine II. and Alexander III.

The latter days of Innocent's pontificate were darkened by the storm which for several years had been gathering in Rome. The little city of Tivoli has become renowned in history and poetry for its natural beauty. The Tivolese boasted that their quarries had furnished the stone for the buildings of imperial and papal Rome. Its villas bore the names of Horace, Cicero, Brutus, Sallust, and the Pisos. Its beautiful gorges, through which the Anio poured its waters, were the fabled haunts of the sirens and of Neptune, and the ruins of its temples recalled the names of Hercules, Vesta, and the Albunean sibyl.[1] It furnished statues, mosaics, and precious marbles for the adornment of Rome.[2] Goths, Lombards, and Arabs had laid it waste. Ruins of walls and temples and of the Claudian aqueduct, an amphitheatre, and numerous fountains still remained. The streets bore the old names, and churches, monasteries, and mediæval towers had arisen on the ancient sites of temples.

Although papal officers had protected in Tivoli the rights of the Roman Church, the citizens displayed a peculiarly independent spirit, and the city enjoyed a freer municipal existence than other Roman towns. The peculiar exemptions enjoyed by it had relaxed the allegiance of other cities, which began to assert their individuality, and Rome found itself compelled to carry on war with a number of petty princes. When Otto III.'s governor, Mazzolinus, was slain by

---

[1] Horace, bk. i., ode vii., 12.
[2] "The Flora, the Antinous of the Capitol, the Faunus, the Centaurs, the Ceres, the Isis, the Harpocrates, Sosus's mosaic of doves, and the various other works which now fill the museums of Rome and other cities, must have lain in the ruins of splendid porticoes, buried in dust and forgotten by mankind." (Gregorovius.)

the Tivolese in 1001, the Emperor threatened to destroy the city, but was propitiated by the humble submission of the citizens, and merely razed a portion of the walls. During the investiture contest Tivoli was on the side of the antipopes. Paschal II. had subjected it with difficulty, and Innocent II., probably with the aid of Lothair, had wrested it from Anacletus; but it had recovered itself. When the sons of Roger of Sicily came in 1140 and subdued the border cities on the Liris, the Tivolese fortified their territory; and though Innocent was appeased for the time by Roger, the city in 1141 rose against the Pope, and a furious war with Rome ensued, in which the Tivolese, successful at first, finally yielded, not to the Romans but to the Pope. The Romans were displeased with the terms of surrender, since the Pope refused to destroy the city. A revolution was the result, in which the secular power of the Pope was sacrificed.

It is greatly to be regretted that almost no sources of information remain concerning so important a crisis. The Romans assembled at the Capitol, proclaimed a republic, restored the senate, threatened to withdraw all allegiance from the Pope, and again took the field against Tivoli. In the midst of this tempest, and probably because of it, Innocent died on the 24th of September, 1143. He had passed half of his pontificate in exile or as a commander of military expeditions. With him closed the Gregorian period of the city's history, and his death inaugurates the deliverance of Rome from the papal domination.

CHAPTER XX.

EUGENIUS III.—ARNOLD OF BRESCIA—BERNARD'S CRUSADE.

AN undisturbed and apparently unanimous election followed on the third day after Innocent's death. Guido di Castello, a pupil of Abélard, was chosen as Cœlestine II. His one notable act was the repeal of the interdict which Innocent had laid upon France. In less than six months he died, and was succeeded by Gerard of Bologna as Lucius II.

Roger of Sicily endeavored to get himself acknowledged again as a papal feudary by Lucius, but the two could not agree upon terms. According to some accounts—for our information is defective—a treaty was at last arranged by which Roger agreed to support the Pope against the Romans. But worse troubles soon confronted Lucius. The Romans chose Jordanes of the Pierleoni, a brother of Anacletus II., as their Patrician, and a second time established the senate at the Capitol. Almost all the consuls were on the Pope's side, and he hoped with these, and possibly with the help of Roger, to defeat the Roman Commune. The patrician nobles and even the Frangipani were with him. The first city constitution was adopted in 1144, and the senatorial epoch was reckoned from the Jewish Jordanes Pierleone. The Commune now proposed to deprive the Pope of his temporal power. His appeal to the German Emperor, Conrad III., was disregarded. He made a desperate effort to recover his ground, and personally joined in the storming of the Capitol, where a stone felled him to the ground. He died a few days after, on the 15th of February, 1145.

Because of the dangers of the crisis, an election was held on the day of the Pope's death, and Bernard of St. Anastasius, sometimes known as Bernard of Pisa, a pupil of Bernard of Clairvaux, was chosen. He was a man of no genius. Bernard himself was at first ashamed of him, and expressed to the cardinals his surprise and distress at his election. "May God be gracious to you!" he writes to them. "What have you done? Have you raised a dead man? Could he who had escaped the hands of the devil, the seductions of the flesh, and the honors of the world, not escape you?" His soft character, accustomed to leisure and repose, awakened Bernard's fears; but he wrote an encouraging letter to the new Pope, calling him his "joy and crown," and exhorting him to serve the church according to the teaching of Christ and the examples of Paul and Peter, and not to desire to lord it over God's heritage. Let him imitate Peter in keeping his hands free from gifts, so that he can say, "Silver and gold have I none." "Who will grant me," he continues, "before I die, to see the church as she was in the olden days, when the apostles cast their nets, not to catch silver and gold, but souls?"

Bernard, however, was agreeably disappointed by the vigor of the Pope's conduct. He was refused by the senators the road to St. Peter's, where he was to be installed. They demanded his renunciation of the civil power and his recognition of the Republic. Rome was in arms. The Pope fled on the third day after his election to the Sabine fortress of Montecelli, and thence to Farfa, where he was installed on the 18th of February, 1145, as Eugenius III.

Bernard's influence over Eugenius was such that it was whispered in some quarters that not Eugenius but Bernard was Pope. He urged the cardinals to support Eugenius with all their power. Conrad was again besought to come to the rescue, but replied only with promises. Meanwhile confusion reigned in Rome. Palaces and towers of cardinals were stormed, sacked, and destroyed. The people gave themselves up to wild excesses. St. Peter's was surrounded with storming-engines. The city prefecture was abolished; the Patrician alone was to represent the majority of the Roman people, and all who refused to recognize him were banished. Eugenius nevertheless assembled the vassals of the church at Viterbo, and was soon able to send a force to the assistance of the papal party in its fight against the senate; and the wearied people at last demanded his return. He resolved to acknowledge the Republic under the authority of the papal chair before the Emperor should place it under that of the empire. The Romans dismissed the Patrician, restored the prefect, and paid homage to the Pope, while the Pope, in turn, approved the continuation of the Commune under his investiture.

The Commune thus won its recognition from the Pope, and the senate was also invested by him. Only the name was Roman; the character was new. The senate had at first a plebeian quality, although many of the nobles had joined the Commune. The full senate of fifty-six formed the Great Council or Consistory, and at its head was a committee of Procurators of the Republic, chosen from the senate itself, possessing both legislative and executive authority, and changed several times each year. The coins bore the old inscription, " Senatus Populusque Romanus," but also the figure of an apostle, with the words, " Roman. Principe."

Eugenius was again in the Lateran before Christmas, but the city and the surrounding country were still unsettled. Nobles and clergy looked with rage at the senate, which was endeavoring to extend its power over the whole Campagna. Tivoli began again to create disturbance. The Romans once more demanded its destruction, and were not satisfied with Eugenius's consent to the demolition of its walls. The Pope withdrew to St. Angelo, which was still in the possession of the Pierleoni; then left the city, and, after a year spent in Viterbo, Pisa, and Lombardy, went to France, where Louis VII. was arming for the second crusade.

During his two years' absence the Romans continued to regard the senate as invested by him, yet they now felt themselves entirely free. Tivoli was punished by the execution of many of its citizens. The contest went on with the Tuscan and Latin cities; the nobles seized many of the church patrimonies;

robbery prevailed, and the ecclesiastical state was lost in little baronial despotisms, hostile alike to the senate and to the Pope.

It was now that Arnold of Brescia, who had for some time been lost in exile, appeared in Rome as a popular leader. He had been reared amid the growing republicanism of the Lombard cities, and, like so many others, had been drawn to France by the eloquence of Abélard. He was not attracted by the religious philosophy, but by the political, practical, and social bearings of Abélard's teaching. His orthodoxy was unimpeachable, and his moral life pure and severe. The Gregorian Papacy, with its large landed estates and its judicial and military functions, first called out his hostility. He desired to reduce the clergy to primitive, apostolic poverty, to confiscate their wealth, and to deprive them of their secular power. They should be only ministers of religion and subject to the civil authority. He aimed also at a reform of the civil power. His ideal was a great Christian republic governed by a popular assembly. He first advocated these views in his native town, Brescia, in the contest with the Bishop Manfred, whose overbearing assertion of temporal power, together with his assault upon the vices of the clergy, caused the expulsion of himself and his friends.

Arnold became a monk of the most austere type. He summoned the people to compel the clergy to renounce all secular power and all property. His doctrines spread throughout Lombardy, and the bishops and a majority of the nobles accused him at the Lateran council of 1139, when he was expelled from Italy. He found refuge in Zurich, and Bernard urged the Pope to secure his person and to burn his books. The Pope issued orders to this effect, but Arnold found a protector in the person of Guido di Castello, afterwards Cœlestine II. For some years all traces of him are lost; but after the death of Innocent II. he returned to Italy and was released from the ban by Eugenius, on promise of submission. He lived for some time in concealment at Rome, until, after Eugenius's flight to France, he openly appeared and proclaimed his doctrines to the citizens. Nothing could rejoice him more than the foundation of the Roman Republic.

The religious sect which he had founded in Brescia, known as Lombards or Arnoldists, revived at Rome; for his doctrines of apostolic poverty and moral purity secured him numerous adherents, including many women. His political teaching found a ready response in the Roman senate. His glowing declamation in the *lingua rustica*, that corrupt Latin which would have set the teeth of Cicero or Varro on edge, stirred the hearts of the legislators as he stood, pale and worn, on the ruins of the Capitol. He pictured the pride, avarice, and hypocrisy of the cardinals; declared that their college was an exchange-bank and a den of thieves; and asserted that the Pope was not a successor of the apostles and a shepherd of souls, but a man of blood, an incendiary, a hangman of the churches, and a destroyer of innocence, who did nothing but fatten his flesh and fill his coffers with stolen property. As he imitated neither the doctrine nor the life of the apostles, neither obedience nor reverence was due to him. Arnold was the man of the hour in Rome. The Republic formally took him into its protection and service, and the lower clergy and nobles eagerly embraced his democratic principles. The Gregorian hierarchy was assailed from all sides. The clergy of the smaller churches leagued themselves against the cardinal aristocracy, who already possessed fortified palaces in the city and were living like princes.

Responding to the desire of Louis of France, Eugenius about this time summoned him and his subjects to a new crusade. The Holy See had strong motives for this act. The evidences of an awakening independence, both in the theological and the political circles of the West—evidences such as Abélard's heresies and Arnold's popular influence—threatened both the power of the popes and the doctrines of the church. Already the talk was rife about rebuilding the Capitol and substituting for the pontifical authority that of the consuls and tribunes of ancient Rome. A crusade would be a timely diversion, turning men's minds from dangerous novelties and rallying them round the earliest sanctuaries of the Christian faith. Eugenius congratulated the French King on his pious resolve, and by letters exhorted all Christians to assume the cross. He regretted that he could not personally animate the souls of the faithful as Urban had done, but he confided to Bernard the mission of preaching the crusade in France and Germany.

At the call of Urban the faithful had rallied for the rescue of the Holy Sepulchre. The object now presented was the deliverance of Edessa, in northwestern Mesopotamia, where the bishop, with many clergy, had been murdered by the pagans. Edessa was one of the oldest cities of the East, being identified by one tradition with Ur of the Chaldees. The beginnings of the Christian faith there went back at least to the former half of the second century, possibly earlier. Tradition even related that one of its early kings, Abgarus, had a personal correspondence with Christ.

One assembly had already been convoked at Bourges by King Louis, where his project was made known; but Bernard had advised the King to defer further measures until he should have consulted the Pope. Eugenius's approbation having been signified, a second assembly was held at Vèzelai, in Burgundy, where Bernard, from a hillside just outside the gates, addressed the immense throng with moving effect, and was followed by the King. The air resounded with cries of "Deus vult! The cross!" The crosses which Bernard had brought were not sufficient, and he and several others tore their garments into strips to satisfy the zeal of the faithful. After the assembly of Vèzelai he continued to preach in the cities and their adjoining territories, and acquitted himself so successfully that he could write to Eugenius, "The villages and the castles are deserted, and there are none left but widows and orphans whose husbands and parents are still living."

In 1149 the Pope prepared to crush the insurrection in Rome and to establish his power there by force of arms. He placed Cardinal Guido at the head of the enterprise, and Roger sent him auxiliaries; but, in spite of all the expenditure of French money, the effort failed. Negotiations with the Roman senators under the lead of Jordanes came to nothing. The republicans would only promise to furnish the revenues of St. Peter if the church would sustain the senators and assume the public burdens. A complete understanding with Roger was never reached. He allowed several bishops of his kingdom to be consecrated by the Pope, but repeated embassies could not bring him to a decisive treaty. An accommodation with the Romans was reached in November, and the Pope again took up his residence in Rome. He was to receive his former revenues, but only on condition that he would tolerate the continuance of the senate and the presence of Arnold of Brescia.

The republicans were looking with new interest towards Germany. There was a rumor of an impending league between Conrad and the Emperor of Constantinople against the Pope, and of a counter-alliance between the French King and Roger. The republicans addressed a letter to Conrad expressing their surprise that he had left their former letters unanswered. They desired, they said, nothing else than the restoration of the empire as it was when it ruled the world through the senate and people of Rome, and to beat down those who until now had disgraced it. They had already taken the towers and houses which, with the Pope and the King of Sicily, were hostile to the empire. The Pope, the Frangipani, the Pierleoni, the Sicilians, desired to prevent their bestowal of the imperial crown upon him. They were busy restoring the Milvian bridge, and walling it so as to afford a passage for the army to St. Angelo, where the Pierleoni and their allies were plotting the Emperor's destruction. If Conrad would but come to Rome, he would be able, after removing all clerical obstacles, to rule from Rome more freely than his predecessors. Many letters of individual senators and Arnoldists were added to this.

Conrad, occupied with affairs at home, and without any real insight into the condition of things at Rome, disregarded this appeal. The influence of the friends of Roman freedom at his court was counteracted by the Abbot Wibald of Stablo, who was moved by Guido to keep the German King from hostile measures against the Pope. Conrad had also declared, as the Pope knew, that he did not recognize Roger as King, and that he rejected all that Bernard and others had said in his favor. In order to hinder the league between Conrad and the Greek Emperor, and to obliterate the effects of his unfortunate crusade, which had resulted in the destruction of both the French and the German army, Bernard planned a new expedition to the East, but without success. About this time also he addressed to the Pope his treatise " De Consideratione," the composition of which had employed him at intervals from 1149 to 1152, and may have helped to divert his mind amid his personal sorrow and the popular exasperation at the disastrous issue of the crusade. In this work, which is the best exhibition of Bernard's spirit, he presented his ideal of a true Christian pastor, an ideal which was in painful contrast with many of the pastoral types furnished by the apostolic see; and in it he admonished Eugenius to cultivate the qualities becoming a minister of Jesus Christ, reminding him that he must soon render his account to God for his administration of the vast trust committed to him. Bernard died in 1153, about a year after sending this book to the Pope.

Eugenius left Rome in June, not to return until 1152. Conrad finally decided upon an expedition to Rome in order to receive the imperial crown; but his plans were cut short by his death in February, 1152. He was the only German sovereign since Otto I. who had not been crowned Emperor—a fact which in no wise impaired his power. Every imperial coronation had brought bloodshed in its train; but if patriotic Romans might congratulate themselves that they had not been visited by a German expedition for fifteen years, they were yet obliged to confess that never, as during those fifteen years, had Italy been so disunited and so harassed with civil wars.

CHAPTER XXI.

BARBAROSSA—HADRIAN IV.—WILLIAM OF SICILY—BARBAROSSA AND THE ROMANS—THE GAUNTLET THROWN DOWN TO THE POPE.

ONRAD'S successor was his nephew, the Hohenstaufen Frederick I. or Barbarossa, who was elected by the princes at Frankfort, in March, 1152, and was crowned at Aix. In him the empire found a ruler worthy to be named with Charlemagne or Otto the Great. He was but thirty-one years old, but was already famous for his achievements, and his election was approved by all Germany. He aimed at something higher than the reconciliation of family quarrels. He was determined to restore to the empire the power of Charlemagne. He was prepared to assert in the strongest terms, not only in Germany but in Italy, the imperial prerogative as derived from God and not from the Pope, and his absolute independence of the chair of St. Peter.

Immediately upon his election he sent to the Pope requesting him to participate in his coronation. He promised obedience to the Roman Church, and the fulfilment of Conrad's promise to free the papal chair. The Republic looked askance at an imperial message addressed to the Pope alone. At once the old investiture question began to emerge. Wichmann, the Bishop of Zeitz, had received the investiture of the archbishopric of Magdeburg from Frederick; and Eugenius at once warned the cathedral chapter of Magdeburg against receiving him, and rebuked several bishops who had approved Frederick's act. He also charged his legate to inform the new King that the prerogative of the church had been invaded by a decision of a recent imperial diet at Ulm to the effect that robbers and incendiaries who had injured church property were to be excommunicated only after their sentence by a civil court.

Three legates were sent to Germany to negotiate terms with the Emperor. The terms proposed by the Pope were that Frederick should swear not to conclude peace with either the Romans or Roger of Sicily without the Pope's approval; that he should endeavor to subject the Romans to the Pope, and to maintain the secular rights of St. Peter; that he was to give the Greek Emperor no territory west of the Adriatic. In return, the Pope would engage to crown Frederick as Emperor, to exalt his empire, and to proceed against his enemies with canonical measures, and against the Greek Emperor if he should attempt to occupy land west of the sea.

Frederick accepted the terms at Constance, but the agreement caused great excitement in Rome. The democrats and Arnoldists were determined to know nothing more of either Pope or Emperor. They demanded the appointment of a hundred senators and two annual consuls. It seemed as though the Romans were ready to reject the German emperorship as a usurpation. How dependent the Papacy was on Germany appeared soon after, when the legates, Bernard and Gregory, did not hesitate to approve Frederick's separation from his wife, Adelheid of Vohburg, ostensibly on the ground of relationship within forbidden limits. But when, in accordance with Eugenius's orders, they refused to confirm Wichmann, Frederick bade them leave the country. Eugenius, however, was not destined to breast the storm which was already gathering. He died at Tivoli on the 29th of June, 1153. By means of money he had almost wholly broken the power of the senate.

He was succeeded, the next month, by a Roman, Conrad, Bishop of Sabina, very old, but well versed in the business of the papal court, who took the name of Anastasius IV. He sent a cardinal to Germany with instructions to refuse the elevation of Wichmann to the see of Magdeburg, and the legate experienced the same treatment as Bernard and Gregory. In order to bring the matter to an end, Frederick sent Wichmann to Rome to receive the pallium. The Pope hit upon the clumsy and transparent evasion of allowing Wichmann to take the pallium himself from the altar, if he was conscious of having been canonically chosen; and Wichmann was induced to give a reluctant consent to this piece of foolery. Having signalized his pontificate by this brilliant stroke of ecclesiastical diplomacy, Anastasius died in December, 1154.

Nicholas of Albano was elected the next day, and installed in St. Peter's as Hadrian IV. He was an

Englishman by birth, whose only inheritance from his father was the name of Brakspeare. He had left his own country in the pursuit of learning, had been received into a monastery at Arles, and had risen to the abbacy. At Rome he won the confidence of Eugenius, who made him cardinal and sent him as his legate to Norway. He was learned, eloquent, and of blameless morals.

The senate refused to recognize him, and he refused to recognize the senate. He vainly demanded the expulsion of Arnold. He could not get possession of the Lateran, but remained within St. Peter's, which was fortified. The growing hatred towards the priests soon resulted in an attack upon a cardinal, who was stabbed on his way to visit the Pope. Hadrian met this act with a unique proceeding. He laid the metropolitan city of Christendom under interdict. Finally, at the instance of the clergy and people, the senators elect volunteered a pledge under oath to expel Arnold and his followers from the city; and under this pledge the interdict was removed.

A second contest soon followed with William of Sicily, the successor of Roger, who, immediately after Hadrian's accession, made him proffers of peace. The Pope sent legates to him at Salerno, but they were refused audience because the Pope's letter was addressed, not to "the King," but to "the Lord" of Sicily. William at once struck at the apple of the papal eye, Benevento, and then moved into Latium, where he burned several towns. As a matter of course he was laid under ban; but he was much less disturbed by this than by the approach of Barbarossa, who had entered Lombardy in the beginning of May with a considerable force, and was now in Tuscany. His uncommonly rapid march to Lombardy made the Pope anxious. He hardly knew whether he was to receive a friend or an enemy.

Frederick found in Italy a condition of affairs far different from that which his predecessors had known. The Normans were now wholly independent of the empire; the great manufacturing and commercial cities of Lombardy had grown into strong, independent communities, indisposed to submit to any foreign master, and choosing their own burgomasters and consuls, their senates and their administrative officers. Arnold of Brescia had fallen, not long before, into the power of Cardinal Oddo at Bricola, but had been taken in charge by the Viscount of Campiglia, and conveyed to his castle for safety. The Pope, as a pretext for ascertaining Frederick's real attitude, sent to him asking for instructions how to dispose of Arnold; and his messengers were crossed by deputies from Frederick to the Pope to treat about the imperial coronation. After considerable hesitation Hadrian agreed to the coronation, and went to Nepi in June, where he met the King.

At this meeting Barbarossa flatly refused to render the Pope the "groom service," or, in other words, to hold his stirrup. Accordingly, when the King approached and knelt at his feet, the Pope refused him the kiss of peace. The highest dignitaries of Christendom were in perturbation over a stirrup, and Barbarossa was at last persuaded to concede this childish demand.

The Romans, meanwhile, had not delayed to send commissioners to Frederick, asking him to recognize the senate and to renew the old Roman autonomy. They congratulated him on his arrival, if he came in peace and with the intention of delivering them from the yoke of the clergy. Thus, they proceeded, the splendor of ancient times, the supremacy of Rome over the world, may return, and her ruler succeed to the name and fame of Augustus. Rome, through the wisdom of its senate and the boldness of its knights, extended its authority to the world's end, but has lost its renown and power. The Romans have arisen to renew the glory of the Emperor and of the divine Republic, have restored the senate and the knightly estate. Should Frederick not rejoice thereat? Should he not regard a work so glorious and so necessary to his own dignity as worthy of reward? "Once thou wert our guest-friend, now we have made thee a citizen. We have given thee what was rightfully ours. Thou art bound to maintain our old customs and our old charters. Thou shalt pay us five thousand pounds of silver for proclaiming thee on the Capitol, and shalt swear to maintain the Republic even unto blood, and to confirm our privileges by oath under the imperial signature."

Frederick's reply to this mixture of bombast, insolence, and greed was haughty and contemptuous. He related at length the conveyance of the empire to Charlemagne and his descendants. They had now summoned him, the new Emperor, in their distress. It was an appeal with tears—the appeal of misery to fortune, of weakness to power. So he had come.

They are to-day his subjects. He is rightful possessor. Who dares to wrest the club from Hercules? They demand three oaths. Their demand is just or it is not. If not, they must not make it nor he grant it. If it is, he freely concedes it. What need of an oath? How should he withhold from them the right which he would grant to the least? They demand money. Is not Rome ashamed to treat with its Emperor as with a broker? "These German nobles are my patricians—the true Romans. This is the senate clothed with perpetual authority. Here are your legions; you will obey such laws as I shall enact."

The Romans retired crestfallen. Frederick, by the Pope's advice, sent on a part of his army in advance, under the charge of Cardinal Octavian, to occupy the Leonina which was in Hadrian's hands. Octavian was the Pope's bitterest enemy and a friend of the German empire; and this commission was a device of Hadrian's to get him away as soon as possible from Frederick's camp, where he had already shown a disposition to make trouble. The advance accomplished its entrance early on the morning of the 18th of June, and was followed on the same day by Frederick. The coronation was at once performed in St. Peter's; but Rome refused to acknowledge the Emperor, and the people gathered in arms at the Capitol.

The Emperor, still wearing the crown, retired to his camp with a few followers. Soon after midnight the Romans broke over the Tiber bridge into the Leonina, stormed the Vatican, where the Pope was, and attacked Frederick's camp. Henry of Saxony, "the Lion," passed through the breach made by

Henry V. into the Leonina, and fell upon the rear of the Romans. The fight raged on the bridge of St. Angelo and around the ancient fish-ponds until night, when the Romans yielded, having lost about a thousand men, killed or drowned in the river. About two hundred were taken prisoners, and the rest fled to St. Angelo or to the city. At the Pope's request the Emperor delivered the prisoners to the city prefect, and along with them Arnold of Brescia, who was hanged and burned, and his ashes were thrown into the Tiber. The Pope and the Emperor retired to the Sabina.[1] The city of Tivoli delivered its keys to the Emperor, and in return Frederick released the citizens from allegiance to himself and exhorted them to obey the Pope without detriment to the imperial rights.

The reservation of imperial rights was a pregnant phrase according to Barbarossa's interpretation. The actual renewal of the old Roman empire, the supreme domination of the world, the church, and the Pope by the Emperor, was the vision which had passed before his mind from the beginning of his reign, and the realization of which Hadrian feared. A new conflict between the empire and the Papacy was inevitable.

So much the more important did it appear to Hadrian, after Frederick's coronation, to strengthen his power in Italy. Accordingly in September he led an expedition against William of Sicily at the summons of the barons and cities of Apulia. Neces-

---

[1] The Sabina adjoined Roman Tuscany, Campania, and Umbria, being separated from them by the Tiber, the Anio, and the Nar respectively.

sity compelled William to seek the Pope's favor. The Byzantine Emperor had agreed, on condition of receiving from Hadrian three cities of Apulia, to furnish him auxiliaries against the King of Sicily, and to pay five thousand pounds of gold into the papal exchequer. On the other hand, a union of the Byzantine and Western empires against common enemies, especially Sicily, had long been in contemplation. In view of these dangers William asked for absolution, promising the oath of fealty and the surrender of the churches in his territory, demanding as indemnity three townships and five thousand pounds of gold, and holding out a hope of subjecting Rome to the apostolic see. In the meantime he conquered Apulia and Magna Græcia. Hadrian sent the greater part of his cardinals to meet the victor in Campania, while he himself remained in Benevento. When the King appeared, his subjection to the Roman Church was demanded, which William after some hesitation promised. The Pope then gave him three banners, and invested him in fief with the kingdom of Sicily, the duchy of Apulia, and the principality of Capua. Elections to ecclesiastical positions were to be free, but were to have the royal confirmation, and a yearly tribute in money was to be paid to the Pope.

The tension between the Pope and the Emperor steadily increased. Hadrian's reconciliation with William made Frederick uneasy. Several barons who were injured by that treaty repaired to him in Lombardy, and he now contracted a second marriage with Beatrix of Burgundy, which signified a great increase of the imperial power. Although in 1153 two papal legates had sanctioned the dissolution of his first marriage, the Pope now strongly remonstrated against that separation, in consequence of which the Emperor forbade the cardinals to set foot in Germany. In October appeared a deputation from the Pope to Frederick with a formal complaint against this act, which, Hadrian said, appeared to him strange in view of the favor shown the Emperor in conferring the imperial crown.

Frederick received this complaint at the Diet of Besançon. It was remarked that the dependence of the imperial dignity on the Pope assumed in this document was expressed in the Lateran by pictures and inscriptions, especially in the words applied to Lothair to the effect that he had received the imperial crown as the gift of the Pope.[1] Hadrian had promised the removal of this at Frederick's coronation. One of the legates was imprudent enough to ask from whom the Emperor held the empire, if not from the Pope; whereupon Otto of Bavaria drew his sword. Frederick prevented bloodshed and commanded the legates to leave early the next day and to return to Rome by the shortest route. He furthermore issued a vigorous proclamation to the whole empire, declaring that, while he will hold the empire from God and protect the peace of the church with the imperial arms, there proceeds from the head of the church, on which Christ has stamped the character of peace and love, discord, the poison of death and disease. He fears schism between the worldly

---

[1] " Rex stetit ante fores, jurans prius Urbis honores,
Post homo fit Papae, sumit quo dante coronam."

and the spiritual powers—a contamination of the whole church. The legates, puffed up with the mammon of unrighteousness, have presented a papal letter full of arrogance and execrable boasting. He (the Emperor) has saved both the evil priests from the judgment of death which menaced them; but because they led others to publish letters in order to spirt the poison of their wickedness into the German churches, he has commanded them to return to Rome. Since he holds the imperial dignity from God alone, through the choice of the princes, and since St. Peter enjoined to fear God and honor the King, *every one who says that he holds the imperial crown as a gift (beneficium) from the Pope is an adversary of the divine order and of the teaching of St. Peter, and therefore guilty of a lie. He will rather die than allow such unheard-of arrogance to contaminate the imperial office.*

Ringing words these. The issue was sharply stated, the gauntlet thrown down. The Pope issued a letter to the German bishops, complaining of the treatment of his legates, and enjoining them to exert themselves to change the Emperor's mind. Frederick replied that he had no thought of encroaching on the province of the church, but that for the imperial crown he had only the divine goodness to thank. He had not forbidden his country to the legates, but only their travelling about with the letters which they brought. He had not barred the way for pilgrims to Rome, but had only opposed the abuses of travel thither by which the churches of Germany were burdened. The church desired to bury the empire. It had begun with a picture, had added an inscription, and out of these presently a law would arise. That picture, with the inscription, must be destroyed. He also expressed his indignation at the treaty between the Pope and William of Sicily.

The bishops, in relating their interview with the Emperor, informed the Pope that the significant and unexampled expressions in the papal letter were generally disapproved; that an expedition into Italy was in preparation, and that the Emperor might be appeased by a new letter. Accordingly Hadrian, who was in great danger from the hostility of the Normans, wrote to Frederick explaining that he had used the term *beneficium* in the sense of an *act of kindness*, a *benefit*, and not of an *enfeoffment*. The *conveying* of the crown meant only placing it on the Emperor's head. Two cardinals were sent with this letter, and at Modena met Chancellor Rainald and the Palgrave Otto, who were arranging for the new Italian expedition. These two, in reporting the interview to Frederick, told him that the Pope had at the same time sent legates to William of Sicily, who had dismissed them with the words, "You are sent to us with hostile intent against the Emperor, and two others have been sent to the Emperor in order to win his favor and dishonor us. Out then quickly! or we will punish you as traitors." They also advised the Emperor to accept the explanations in the Pope's letter, but to make no further concessions. It was now in his power, they said, to destroy Rome and to deal with Pope and cardinals as he pleased.

CHAPTER XXII.

RONCAGLIA—HADRIAN AND FREDERICK AT ISSUE—TWO POPES IN THE FIELD.

HE Emperor arrived in Italy in July with a powerful army, and in September compelled the submission of proud Milan. From the 11th to the 25th of September he held a great assembly in the plain of Roncaglia, where the full imperial power was confirmed as against the claims of the cities and of the Pope, and the prerogatives of the empire were defined in the terms of the civil law. The civil law had never perished from Gaul and Italy, and in the twelfth century its study was vigorously prosecuted in Italy, in Paris, and in Oxford, where the Pandects of Justinian were commented upon and expounded. The most renowned jurists of Bologna, full of enthusiasm for the old Roman imperial law, invested the Hohenstaufen with all the absolutism of Justinian, styling him "lord of the world," "sole fountain of legislation," the absolute master of the lives and property of all his subjects, and the embodiment of right and justice. "Do and ordain what thou wilt," said the Archbishop of Milan, speaking for the assembled magnates of Lombardy. "Thy will is law,

as it is written: ' Whatever pleases the prince has the force of law, since the people have transferred to him all their own sovereignty and power.' "

Such utterances voiced the dream of empire which had beckoned Frederick into Italy; and men are ever but too ready to believe that which formulates their fondest hope; but Frederick did not see that the empire of Charlemagne and of Justinian was now impossible. Lombardy was the place where, with a finer sense, he might have caught the first breaths of the new democratic spirit which was stirring in Europe.

The gap was thus opened between the Papacy and the empire because of the gap opened between the empire and the cities. The Papacy must take sides with one or the other of these, and there could be little doubt that it would range itself with the cities. For investiture, which, since the Treaty of Worms, had slumbered, or at most only turned in its sleep, would either be the link between the cities and the Emperor, or would come to the front again as a civic question. It was the interest of the cities to withdraw from the Emperor the crown-right, the courts, and the magistracies; and what was against the Emperor was for the interest of the Papacy. The Lombard republics and churches won their independence at last out of the fight on investiture as a civil question.

Irritation between the Pope and the Emperor was inflamed by several minor matters. The Pope refused to appoint Frederick's candidate to the see of Ravenna; he despatched a letter to the Emperor by the hands of a low ragamuffin; and the Emperor ordained that, in imperial communications to the Pope, the Emperor's name should precede the Pope's. At last Hadrian summoned Milan and other Lombard cities to revolt, and sent four cardinals to Bologna in April, 1159, where they ventilated the grievance that the Emperor had violated the Treaty of Constance concluded in 1153 with Eugenius. Frederick declared that the Pope himself had first violated this treaty by the peace with the Normans at Benevento, but professed his readiness to submit the matter to arbitration. Hadrian rejected this suggestion, and sent back the two cardinals with imperative demands, which were laid before a great assembly of the princes in June.

The principal subject was the renewal of the Treaty of Constance. The Pope demanded that the Emperor should not send messengers to Rome without his previous knowledge, because at Rome all secular power resides in the Pope. No requisitions were to be made on papal property, and no forage was to be taken from papal territory, except on the occasion of an imperial coronation. This would prevent the imperial forces from crossing the papal frontier. The Italian bishops were to swear allegiance, but not a fief-oath, to the Emperor, and were not to receive imperial messengers. The Roman Church was to be restored to the possession of the Mathilde property, the duchy of Spoleto, Corsica, and Sardinia.

Frederick complained of broken agreements; of the understanding, without his knowledge, with the Sicilian King, the Romans, and the Greeks; of the circulation of cardinal legates without his permission, their entrance into royal and episcopal palaces, and their fleecing of the churches. He declared that he would demand no homage of the Italian bishops if they, on their part, would renounce the fiefs which they held of the empire. If they chose to listen to the Pope when he asked what they had to do with the Emperor, they must submit to the Emperor's commands, else what had they to do with the estates of the empire? He would not require that imperial ambassadors should be lodged in episcopal palaces when those palaces were situated on episcopal ground. If they stood on the lands of the empire they were imperial and not episcopal palaces. As to the admission of his envoys to Rome, if he is really Emperor and not such merely in appearance, Rome cannot withdraw itself from his authority. He received very graciously a deputation of the Romans who expressed their regret for the attack at the time of his coronation; and he intimated that if he could not make terms with the Pope, he might do so with the senate and people of Rome.

This manly and sensible attitude of the Emperor seemed to render peace impossible, and Hadrian, dreading another imperial invasion, departed to Tusculum. Frederick's ambassadors in the meantime were exercising imperial rights on papal territory, which called out a sharp letter from the Pope, holding up to the Emperor his lack of piety towards "his father and mother—St. Peter and the Roman Church." The Emperor's reply was characteristic: "Frederick, by the grace of God Emperor of the Romans, desires Hadrian, the highest bishop of the

Catholic Church, to confine himself to all that Jesus began both to do and to teach." He went on to say that before Constantine the church had no worldly possessions, and that what she now has she owes to the gifts of the princes. For this reason he places his own name before the Pope's. Why should he not demand homage from those who are gods by adoption and hold their feudal property as such, since the Founder of the secular and spiritual power, who asks nothing of human sovereigns, but gives all to all, and pays tithe to the Emperor for himself and St. Peter, gives to the Pope the command: "Learn of me; for I am meek and lowly in heart"? Either bishops should renounce their worldly possessions, or, if they hold them, should render to God what is God's and to Cæsar what is Cæsar's. The churches and cities are closed to the cardinal legates because they are not preachers, but plunderers; not mediators, but robbers; not maintainers of the empire, but insatiable money-makers. He cannot but return the Pope such an answer when he sees how the beast of pride has crept into the chair of St. Peter.

In this critical state of affairs the Papacy again obtained allies in Sicily, and in the Lombard cities, Milan, Brescia, and Piacenza, who sent commissioners to the Pope and urged him to pronounce the ban against the Emperor; promising to enter into no treaty with him without the Pope's permission. Before Hadrian could carry out this request, he died at Anagni in September, 1159.

The next day the cardinals began to busy themselves about the choice of a successor, and after three days reached a divided result. The division was between the papal and the imperial candidate. By the majority Roland of Siena was chosen—the leader of papal politics against the Emperor. He had long served in Bologna as professor of canon law, was brought to Rome by Eugenius, and was finally made chancellor of the Roman Church. He was chosen as Alexander III. Two cardinals, secretly supported by imperial deputies, had, from the first, fixed upon Cardinal Octavian, an imperialist. The electors of Roland were in the act of investing him with the papal mantle, when Octavian tore it from his shoulders. A senator sprang up and recovered it. Octavian, in anticipation of some such proceeding, had brought a mantle with him, and now called for it and had it placed upon himself, which was done in such haste that it was reversed; and in his confusion he fastened the lower end about his neck. At this point the doors of the church were opened, and the imperial troops thronged in with drawn swords, and carried forth Octavian in state. Alexander, with his followers, fled to a fortress near St. Peter's, called the "munitio ecclesiæ Sancti Petri," where they remained for nine days, besieged by Octavian, who, in the meantime, assumed the name of Victor IV.

The party of Octavian claimed that the cardinals had agreed not to proceed to the election without unanimous consent, but that, in a secret synod at Anagni during Hadrian's life, the anti-imperialist cardinals had sworn to select one of their own party. This conspiracy was organized by the money of William of Sicily. The Octavians acknowledged that they were in the minority, but asserted that Roland's election had been forced in violation of the compact. In the representations addressed by them to different parties, much stress was laid on the understanding with William of Sicily. Roland, after remaining in the Trastevere until the 17th of September, was set free by one of the Frangipani and some other nobles hostile to Octavian, and was installed as Alexander III. three days after.

Octavian was obliged to leave Rome after a vain attempt to obtain recognition, and one of Alexander's first official acts was the usual excommunication of his rival. But Octavian had found three bishops who declared their readiness to inaugurate him, and he was accordingly enthroned at Farfa on the 4th of October as Victor IV.

Alexander's commissioners to Frederick met with a very cool reception, and the Emperor sent a letter addressed "to the Chancellor Roland and the other cardinals who chose him as Pope." He announced that, in order to avoid the threatened schism, he had called a general council at Pavia for the 13th of January, at which the bishops of his empire, with others from England, France, Hungary, and Dacia, would appear; and he summoned Alexander to be present and submit to the decision of this assembly. Victor soon after appeared at the Emperor's court, and tried to induce him to come at once to the assistance of the church. He declared that he had been elected by the bishops, the cardinal presbyters, and the Roman clergy, and according to the wish of the people. He emphasized Alexander's compact with

William of Sicily, and denounced him and his party as liars, heretics, and schismatics. A circular letter from the Bishop of Tusculum, about the same time, ascribed the division in the electoral college to the league of Hadrian with William, and declared that the papal party had sworn at Anagni to procure the Emperor's excommunication, and, in case of the Pope's death, to choose one of their own number. The affair is a very dark one, but William of Sicily was evidently somewhere near the bottom of it. Gerhoch of Reichersperg, a stiff, conservative churchman, allied with the reform-party, declared that the two cardinals on Victor's side confessed that they themselves had been parties to the conspiracy, in the hope of escaping punishment by their confession, and that they pronounced Alexander's election invalid because it had been effected by a conspiracy of twelve bribed cardinals.

Alexander was naturally indignant at the letter "to the Chancellor Roland," and in his answer denounced the Emperor's proposal to call a council without his consent, and his summons to the Pope to appear thereat. The Pope was subject to no tribunal and would not appear. The breach between Alexander and Frederick was thus confirmed. Alexander must now work the harder for recognition in other countries. He wrote to the French Queen, Constantia; he sent cardinals to France and England to work for his recognition; he addressed himself to the Lombard bishops; his legate went to Milan, and with the sanction of the archbishop published the excommunication of "Octavian the antipope and Frederick the Emperor"; and a few days later the ban was proclaimed against the consuls of all the cities in league with Frederick. Clugny was against him, and the abbot Hugo had already acknowledged Victor. On the other hand, the Carthusians and Cistercians were actively enlisted in his cause. Victor, on his part, issued an encyclical setting forth the depraved condition of the Roman see; declaring that those who had recourse to the tribunal of Roland escaped as from a prison, naked and plundered; that ecclesiastical offices were sold like cattle, and that the clergy was the scoff of the world because of its robbery and simony.

The Emperor opened the council at Pavia on the 11th of February, 1160. Prelates of both parties were present, with commissioners from the kings of England, Denmark, and France, and numerous abbots ·and provosts. Alexander refused to appear, but Victor came with testimonials of his election from the canons of St. Peter and many Roman clergy. A letter was laid before the assembly from the Chapter of St. Peter, in which the proceedings of the election were detailed from the Octavian point of view. According to this, the delay of the election was owing to an intrigue of the Rolandists. The main points urged were that Roland, by his own admission, had never been invested with the papal mantle; that the election of Octavian had been initiated by the whole clergy and people of Rome; and that Roland had appeared after the election without the papal insignia.[1]

The council acknowledged Octavian, and issued an encyclical to all western Christendom, relating its

[1] The entire contents of the document are given by Langen, p. 451.

decisions and their grounds, and declaring that Roland had circulated falsehoods concerning the election proceedings. Victor IV. was now called in to be enthroned. The Emperor himself led his horse. Between the Emperor and the Patriarch of Aquileia the Pope advanced to the altar, where the Emperor and the princes kissed his feet and presented gifts. The usual excommunication of the other Pope followed, and Victor summoned William of Sicily and the Milanese to answer for the injury inflicted on the empire and the church. Frederick, in a letter to the Archbishop of Salzburg, related the transactions of the council, and again emphasized the conspiracy of Roland and his cardinals with William, Milan, Brescia, and Piacenza. This emphasis was due in part to the fact that letters of Alexander to the insurgent Lombard cities had been intercepted and were in the Emperor's hands.

The decisions of Pavia gave Alexander the opportunity for pronouncing the ban upon Frederick and the release of his subjects from their allegiance. He actively prosecuted his efforts for recognition by other powers, even the Byzantine Emperor. The English and French bishops decided in his favor. The two kings, Henry II. and Louis VII., refused to commit themselves, and pronounced the decision of the bishops to be contrary to their will. The great council at Toulouse in the autumn of 1160, at which both those monarchs were present, with representatives of the German Emperor and of both popes, took up the question again. Frederick consented to its being reopened because the decisions of Pavia had met with little approbation, and it was most desirable to secure the approval of Henry and Louis. The council decided for Alexander on the ground that his investiture with the papal mantle had been prevented by force, and that Octavian had preceded him only for that reason, and, further, that his installation had been regular, which was not the case with Octavian's.

Many thought that it would be best to await the death of one of the popes, and to let the church be governed in the meantime by the bishops. Henry was won over to this opinion, and was induced to change his mind only by a disgraceful intrigue of Alexander's legates. His son of seven years was already betrothed to the infant daughter of Louis. In order to put the English King at once in possession of certain strongholds in France, the legates issued a dispensation for the immediate conclusion of the marriage. The feeling of Louis, who, on the question of acknowledgment, sided with Henry without knowing his motive, and who had accordingly endeavored to persuade the Byzantine Emperor to acknowledge Alexander, was that of one doubly betrayed. He immediately banished the papal legates from the country. Thus, while the danger to the Papacy was temporarily arrested by the Council of Toulouse, Alexander's victory was converted into a partial defeat.

The Council of Toulouse was followed by similar assemblies in Spain, Ireland, and Norway. Alexander sent the Scotch Bishop of Moray as his legate to Scotland, commissioned to consecrate the new

Bishop of St. Andrews, and, in contradiction of his predecessors, recognized Scotland's independence of the Archbishop of York. By this means he hoped to win the adherence of Scotland. He succeeded in effecting an outward reconciliation with Louis of France, so that the expelled legates were present at the coronation of the new Queen, Alice; and he sought to bind the King of England more closely to himself by the canonization of Edward the Confessor.

The German Emperor and Victor sought to reverse the decision at Toulouse by a new general council, which was opened at Cremona in May, 1161, and was continued at Neulodi in June. The Emperor and Victor were present, with a large number of prelates, five metropolitans, five Roman senators, and commissioners from England, France, Poland, and Bohemia. Victor's recognition was reaffirmed, and excommunication was pronounced upon the Emperor's Lombard enemies. Alexander, meanwhile, had determined to go to Rome. He had subjected Latium with the aid of the Sicilians; his interest was growing in Rome through the absence of the antipope; the newly elected senators had declared for him; and so, by the influence of the Frangipani, he was able to enter the city on the 16th of June. But the Emperor's forces were approaching, and in less than a fortnight he was compelled to retire, and for the next ten months was itinerating in Italy, until in April, 1162, he found refuge in France, the old-time resort of papal fugitives. On his arrival at Montpellier he asked the protection of the French King, and was received by the church dignitaries with respect.

Frederick, meanwhile, was carrying matters with a high hand in Lombardy. The walls of Milan were destroyed and its citizens dispersed. Italy trembled at its fall. Rome, in its terror, acknowledged Victor, and Frederick withdrew by way of Turin to Burgundy, leaving behind him a desolated country.

CHAPTER XXIII.

THOMAS À BECKET—PASCHAL III.—ALEXANDER, BECKET, AND HENRY II.

N February, 1163, Alexander came to reside in Paris. He prevailed upon Louis to hold a great synod at Tours, in which Henry of England agreed to participate on condition that the rights of his crown should not be impaired, and that no innovations should be introduced into England. The Pope assented to these conditions, though they pointed very distinctly to the restoration of the old English church-right, against which Anselm of Canterbury had so long fought and which was soon to be again assailed.

The council, composed mostly of French prelates and clergy, was opened on the 19th of May. The first place next to the Pope was occupied by Thomas à Becket, the successor of Theobald in the see of Canterbury.

Under the patronage of Henry, Becket had been advanced to the chancellorship of England, and had been made Provost of Beverley, Dean of Hastings, and Constable of the Tower, besides being put in possession of certain large baronies which had escheated to the crown. He maintained a luxurious state which no English subject had ever before displayed. He was the intimate friend and companion of his sovereign. His retinue was large, his house was a place of education for the sons of the proudest nobles, and the greatest barons and the King himself delighted to be received at his table. His leisure was employed in field-sports, and he rendered important military service to the King in his French campaigns. As he had never interfered with the King's policy in ecclesiastical matters, Henry was surprised by his new attitude immediately upon his appointment to the see of Canterbury. Not only did he personally assume the character of sanctity and practise the severest austerities, while he maintained the splendor of his former estate, but he appeared as the representative of the Gregorian ecclesiasticism. This was the man who now came to Tours at the head of all the English bishops, and who, by the Pope's command, was escorted into the city by the whole concourse of cardinals.

The opening speech of the Bishop of Lisieux was aimed directly at Frederick, and the ban was pronounced upon Victor and his defenders, among whom was the Abbot of Clugny. Sundry canons were adopted, against the Albigenses, against simony, against the teaching of natural philosophy and secular jurisprudence by monks, against the validity of consecrations by Victor and other schismatics, and against the holding of church property by laymen. Becket introduced a proposal for the canonization of Anselm of Canterbury—a proposal which Henry did not approve, and which was ingeniously evaded by Alexander. He did not wish to offend the English King by approving it, while he had the strongest reasons for not offending Becket and his party. He accordingly refused the canonization at the synod, but empowered Becket to investigate through a synod the miracles ascribed to Anselm, and to decide the matter of canonization as he might see fit.

The Pope endeavored to annoy Frederick in every way. Hearing that the Emperor was about to undertake an expedition to Hungary, he took measures for the obstruction of his passage. Ambassadors came to him from Manuel, the Emperor of Constantinople, who had been won over by the French King, to pay homage and to solicit alliance; and their negotiations with the Pope and Louis, while they promised little, helped to keep up courage for the fight with Frederick. The Pope urged Louis to advise the King of Sicily, through the Byzantine ambassadors, to arm against Frederick and his allies, since they had designs on his territory. To Becket, who had sent a special messenger to communicate his sufferings and fears in the contest with Henry, he replied that he would have to bear his troubles as a penance for his conduct as Chancellor of England, but assured him of the protection of the papal chair so far as should be consistent with justice and reason. The Pope evidently saw the wisdom of being on his guard with a man whose imperious and headstrong temper was likely to involve him in difficulties at a point where his relations with Frederick called for extreme caution.

Henry requested Alexander to name Roger of

"Constitutions of Clarendon."

York as papal legate for England—a proposal very annoying to Becket, but urged by Henry because Becket would thus be rendered harmless, and the supreme authority of the English church would be in the hands of Roger, who was in sympathy with himself. The Pope was afraid of estranging Henry and unwilling to abandon Becket; but he finally made Roger legate, promising Becket that the see of Canterbury should never be subject to any authority but his own.

In January, 1164, the famous "Constitutions of Clarendon" were adopted, the tendency of which was to subject ecclesiastical appointment and conduct to the authority of the crown. The revenues of vacant archbishoprics, bishoprics, and abbeys were to come into the King's hands. Electors for their occupants were to be summoned by the King, and the elections were to take place in his presence. The prelate elect was to do homage to the sovereign for life, limb, and worldly honors, excepting his order. Archbishops, bishops, and all beneficiaries were to be regarded as barons of the realm, and to be subject to the burdens attaching to that rank, and were to assist other barons at all trials except capital cases. No one was to quit the realm without the royal permission. The royal courts were to decide whether the offences of the clergy were cases for civil or ecclesiastical jurisdiction, and a verdict of "guilty" removed the offender from ecclesiastical protection. Disputes concerning presentations or rights of presentation to benefices were to be decided in the royal courts, and the King's consent was necessary to the appointment to a benefice. Appeals to Rome were limited by the provision that no appeal could be taken from the archbishop's court under the royal supervision without the King's consent. The King's tenants-in-chief and officers of his household were exempt from excommunication, and their lands from interdict, until information had been laid before the King.

Becket took the oath, with the lay barons and bishops, to maintain these Constitutions; but when they were finally drawn up and presented to him, he refused his subscription and immediately wrote to the Pope for absolution from his oath, which was granted. Alexander, when asked by the King to confirm the articles, told Becket to concede what was consistent with the honor of the clerical estate, at the same time admonishing him to yield to the King wherever he could do so without detriment to his clerical rights. But he soon began to take a decided attitude against the Clarendon articles, and forbade the English bishops to surrender any portion of church freedom or to take a new oath. If they had already given improper promises, they were not to fulfil them. Becket, meanwhile, was inflicting penance on himself for his oath to sustain the articles, and was refraining from mass, until the Pope commanded him to resume his clerical duties and told him that if he felt oppressed in his conscience he might confess to a priest.

On the 20th of April, 1164, Victor died at Lucca, and the imperial party, without waiting for an expression from the Emperor, elected Guido of Cremera as Paschal III. The Emperor yielded a grudging confirmation, and Paschal found himself opposed by some of the German bishops of the Victorine faction who did not care to prolong the schism, and also by Clugny and the episcopate of Burgundy, both of which had supported Victor.

Becket was cited in October before a council of the realm at Northampton, on a charge of withholding justice from a royal officer who claimed an estate from the see of Canterbury. The council pronounced him guilty of perjury and treason, and declared all his property confiscate. His appeal to the Pope, and his prohibition of his suffragans from sitting in judgment in a secular council—two direct violations of the Clarendon articles—led some of the bishops to ask the King to exempt them from concurring in the sentence, they promising to unite in a request to the Pope to depose Becket. A deputation led by Roger of York and Gilbert of London accordingly waited upon the Pope, complained of Becket as a disturber of the peace, and submitted for his confirmation the sentence pronounced at Northampton. Alexander was much embarrassed. He promised to send legates to England to investigate the case, but did not bind himself not to confer personally with Becket. Becket, who had taken refuge in Flanders, came in person to the Pope, and laid before him the articles of Clarendon. Alexander at first blamed him for betraying his office by recognizing these articles.[1] Becket con-

---

[1] Froude justly observes that the story that the Pope and cardinals had never seen the "Constitutions" is incredible. ("Life and Times of Thomas à Becket.")

fessed, declaring that he had been placed in the see of Canterbury by secular power, and had accepted it uncanonically. He now relinquished it, to be restored or not, as the Pope might determine. It was a rare opportunity for Alexander, but he did not use it. Becket was too important an agent in the contest with the King of England to be sacrificed. The Pope reinstated him. He was assigned a residence near Sens, and was bidden to remain quiet and to avoid irritating Henry for the present.

During Alexander's absence from Rome the city had been quietly governed by the senate, which, in its acts, took no cognizance of the Pope. Judicial documents of this period are dated in the era of Victor IV. Alexander's representative in Rome, Julius of Palestrina, died, and his successor prevailed upon the Romans to take the oath to Alexander, and to constitute the senate according to the papal sense. A deputation was sent to Alexander urging him to return. The efforts in his favor were assisted by the bitterness created by the operations of Christian of Mainz, the soldier-bishop and the faithful warrior of Frederick. Paschal had taken up his residence in Viterbo, which was Frederick's basis of all expeditions against Rome. Christian and the Count Gotelin were in command of the imperialists there, and they penetrated into Latium and pressed the Romans so hard that they finally purchased a truce and declared themselves ready to acknowledge Paschal if Alexander should refuse to return.

In the meantime a marriage contract had been

arranged between Henry's daughter and a son of Barbarossa, and Henry agreed to send commissioners to a diet at Würzburg, at which Paschal should be acknowledged. The diet was opened on the 22d of May, and the presence of Henry's commissioners and the exertions of Bishop Rainald of Dassel turned the scale against Alexander. The Emperor asserted the canonical election of Paschal and swore to remain true to him and never to acknowledge Alexander. The diet enacted that an oath abjuring Alexander should be taken by every male in the empire over twelve years old. Constrained by necessity and conditionally, the German bishops and princes pledged themselves to the Würzburg decisions, and the English deputies, in the King's name, likewise swore adherence to Paschal.

Henry, however, failed in gaining the English bishops for Paschal at the Synod of London, and found himself compelled to ask the Pope's pardon for his compact with the Emperor. This fiasco encouraged Alexander to attempt the restoration of Becket, and also to prevail on Henry not to insist on the Clarendon articles, especially *to allow no transgressions growing out of the violation of oaths and out of contests over church affairs to be brought before secular tribunals.* He exhorted Becket to endeavor to conciliate the King, and declared invalid the sentence of confiscation pronounced upon him at Northampton. But the Pope did not find Henry at all tractable in the matter of Becket's restoration. The King, moreover, wrote to the cardinals, roundly asserting the independence and sovereignty of his crown; and Alexander thought it most expedient to let Becket remain for the time being in France, and requested Louis to give him a bishopric or an abbacy somewhere.

Alexander embarked for Rome in August, 1165. His galley escaped the pirates and the Pisans, and William of Sicily escorted him from Messina to Rome, where he arrived in November. He was burdened with debt, and the gifts and loans from France were insufficient to maintain him in Rome among a people who, as he himself said, even in the midst of peace looked only to the hands of the Pope. He thought, however, that he could now take more stringent measures with Henry of England, and accordingly exhorted the monks of Canterbury to support Becket. In his financial distress he wrote to the Archbishop of Rheims for aid, and urged him to sustain Becket, who was still in France, and soon after admonished the English bishops and the church of Canterbury to do nothing without Becket's consent. Especially, in the event of Henry's death, they were not to anoint and crown his successor without Becket's approval. His next step was to name Becket legate for all England except the see of York, which was the most high-handed measure he had yet taken in opposition to Henry—to set up over his realm an archbishop whom he had deposed. He directed Becket to go forward in all that concerned the property or the rights of the church. He next commanded the bishops of the province of Canterbury to see that all benefices taken from Becket's clergy by the orders of the King were restored to them, and finally directed the Archbishop of Rouen to urge the King to recall Becket.

Henry had taken sides with Paschal. He welcomed an opportunity of falling out with Alexander and his cardinals who had supported Becket against him. Rainald of Dassel wrote that the King purposed to send a strong deputation to Rome to demand of the Pope that he abandon Becket, invalidate his acts, and swear to maintain the English church-right. In case of his refusal, he will cut loose from him with all his kingdom, fight him, and ban every one in England who shall acknowledge him. Frederick indorsed this plan, and, in expectation of Henry's aid, armed for a new Roman expedition to expel Alexander. But in May, 1166, William of Sicily died and left the Pope sixty thousand florins, to which his son and successor, William II., added a like sum, besides contemplating a marriage with the daughter of the Greek Emperor. Under such circumstances it behoved Barbarossa to make his attack powerful and decisive.

But the dangers which menaced Alexander from England and Germany forced him to make concessions. Against Becket's protest he consented to send legates to England. To the appeal of the English bishops against Becket he replied that his legates were invested with full powers. He informed Henry that he had forbidden Becket to annoy him or his realm before the decision of the legates. If he should issue any offensive sentence before that time, it would be invalid. The legates were to absolve the royal counsellors excommunicated by Becket. To Becket he wrote that he had exhorted the King to restore him to favor. He must forbear all measures against Henry and his kingdom. If the King shall refuse to listen to the legates, Alexander will know how to maintain Becket's rights. He is to keep this letter secret.

CHAPTER XXIV.

BATTLE OF MONTE PORZIO—BARBAROSSA'S DISASTERS—BECKET.

LATE in 1166 Barbarossa went to Italy. Lombardy was boiling with hatred towards him, and the Emperor did not suspect the extent or the intensity of the opposition which he was to encounter. The Pope found his allies in the subjected cities, which united in a league for life and death. The Greek Emperor Manuel also came to his assistance. He sent ships to Ancona, and agreed to subject the Greek Church to the Papacy if Alexander would acknowledge him as Emperor of the West. This was not to be thought of; but Alexander meant to keep his hand on Manuel as a convenience in case of emergency. He treated his messengers respectfully, and sent legates to Constantinople, promising to continue the ban on Frederick and to decree his deposition. Frederick's plan was to drive the Greeks from Ancona and the Pope from Rome, and to install Paschal III. in St. Peter's; while Rainald of Cologne, with a small force, was to make a way for Paschal from Tuscany.

Rainald accordingly approached Rome while Barbarossa was still before Ancona. Almost all the fortified places turned against Alexander. His exhortations and his money alike failed to prevent the secession of a part of the people to Frederick and Paschal. Still the majority of the Romans adhered to him because of their childish hatred of some little neighboring cities like Albano, Tivoli, and Tusculum, which refused to acknowledge the senate and united with the imperialists. It was this which brought on a catastrophe.

Over Tusculum the Pope had obtained rights by Eugenius's purchase of Oddo Frangipani's share in the city. Hadrian IV. had given the papal share in fief to the elder son of Ptolemæus II., and had made him his vassal. The senate, however, was unwilling that the church should appear as the protectress of this city which refused the state obedience and tribute. Rainald, with his Cologne troops, entered Tusculum, where the enraged Romans besieged him. He sent for help to Ancona, and Christian of Mainz, with thirteen hundred Germans and savage Brabantines, came at once. Christian encamped at Monte Porzio, near Tusculum, and sent messengers to Rome, who were received with scorn. On the 29th of May, 1167, the Romans attacked him with nearly forty thousand men, the largest force which they had sent into the field for centuries. The Germans animated their courage with the battle-song, " Christus der du geboren warst." The Brabantines were driven back; but the compact little body of the Cologne cavalry opportunely appeared from Tusculum, a troop of Christian's took the Romans on the flank, and an irresistible charge cut their army in two. Horse and foot fled while the broadswords of the Brabantines mowed through the struggling masses. Scarcely a third of the Roman army reached the city, and only the walls of Aurelian and the approaching night stayed the pursuit. The fields and roads were strewn with dead and wounded, and thousands were carried prisoners to Viterbo.

The panic in the city equalled that in the field. The Pope wept, and committed himself to the protection of the Frangipani at the Coliseum. The Germans encamped before Rome, strengthened by recruits from the towns of the Campagna. Christian sent word to the Emperor to come and complete the work; and Barbarossa, after receiving the capitulation of Ancona, hastened to the city and appeared at Monte Mario on the 22d of July. A Sicilian force sent against him was repulsed, and he stormed and captured the Leonina, which was occupied by the adherents of the Pope, who still held St. Peter's. The church was barricaded on every side; its roof was covered with catapults, and the interior, even the tomb of the apostle, bristled with arms. The city held out for eight days. Walls and towers and the portico erected by Innocent II. were destroyed, and the whole Leonina was a heap of rubbish. The church alone resisted; fire was thrown into the court, and a splendid mosaic was destroyed which adorned the wall above, while the Viterbese lifted from their hinges the bronze gates, to convey them to their own city as a memorial of the siege. Frederick of Rotenburg, the son of the Emperor Conrad, had the doors of the cathedral broken open with axes. When at last St. Peter's itself was in danger of being destroyed by fire, the garrison laid down their arms. The church was polluted with blood and with dead bodies.

The cathedral was carried on the 29th. The next day Paschal was installed there, and on the 1st of August Beatrix, the wife of Barbarossa, was crowned Empress by the antipope. Though surrounded by the Roman imperialists, the Emperor's forces were confined to the Leonina, and the Romans, furious at their defeat, kept possession of the city. Alexander remained in the stronghold of the Frangipani. Two Sicilian galleys came up the river to take him away if he should desire to escape; but he distributed the money which they brought him to the Frangipani and Pierleoni, and to the guards at the gates, and sent the vessels back.

At last Conrad, Archbishop of Mainz, who had gone over to Alexander and had thereby lost his benefice, was sent to Frederick's camp. He represented that the Pope was the only obstacle to peace, and proposed that both popes should abdicate and that a third should be canonically chosen. The proposition was rejected by Alexander and his cardinals, but the wearied Romans agreed to it, and a popular uprising took place which drove Alexander from the city. Three days after, he was sitting in pilgrim's garb at a fountain near Cape Circello, sharing his meal with his companions. At Terracina he resumed the papal robes, and reached Benevento in August.

His flight defeated the Emperor's hopes of coming to an agreement with the church, but facilitated peace with the city. Just about this time the Pisans entered the Tiber with eight galleys, and destroyed the country-seats on the banks; and one of the vessels advanced as far as the Ripa Romea.[1] The courage of the Romans failed, and Frederick, who could not hope to take by storm the towers of the nobles, even if Rome should open its gates, was disposed to make reasonable terms. Peace was concluded on the following conditions: Senate and people swore fidelity to the Emperor and to defend the crown-rights within and without the city. The Emperor recognized the senate with its existing powers, but as invested by him, confirmed the validity of all Roman wills and contracts, and granted exemption from all taxes and duties. He restored the prefecture as an imperial office, caused a new common council to be chosen, and took four hundred hostages from the Romans.

But just here, at the height of his power, with his imperial rights restored in Rome, his Pope in St. Peter's, the Gregorian hierarchy overthrown, and the reëstablishment of the universal empire of Rome apparently within his grasp, a new enemy appeared. A tremendous rain-storm burst upon the city on the 2d of August, followed by intense heat and an outbreak of the Roman fever, which made fearful havoc among the citizens and destroyed the flower of his army. Thousands died, and their corpses were thrown into the river; and the Emperor, with the remnant of his forces, withdrew on the 6th of August, left Paschal and the hostages at Viterbo, and went on to Pisa and thence to Pavia, losing more than two thousand men on the way.

[1] Now the port of Ripa Grande.

Close upon this disaster followed the revolt of the Lombard cities. Venice, Verona and her dependencies, Vicenza, Padua, Treviso, Ferrara, Brescia, Bergamo, Cremona, Milan, Lodi, Piacenza, Parma, Mantua, Modena, and Bologna entered into league to throw off the imperial yoke; and in the spring of 1168 Frederick left Italy and made his way to Germany in disguise. This democratic uprising worked for the advantage of the Papacy. The Pope became in Lombardy the protector of the democracy which he was fighting at Rome; and the freedom of the church became identified, for the time being, with the freedom of the Republic. "The moral power of the church enhanced or sanctified the energy of the cities, and the triumph of the democracy delivered the Papacy from the schism and from the imperial dictation."

The Romans meanwhile continued their battles with the little neighboring cities. They destroyed Albano in 1168, assisted by Christian of Mainz and the imperial prefect who led the German party in Rome. Paschal had returned, and the senators had taken him up in order to obtain the freedom of the Roman hostages; but they would not allow him to enter the city. On the other side of the Tiber, under the protection of Stephen Tebaldi, he was tremblingly awaiting the change of the senate by the new election in November, when, on the 20th of September, 1168, he died in the Vatican, and his place was filled by John, Abbot of Struma, with the title of Calixtus III.

Alexander, at Benevento, was still annoyed with the quarrel between Becket and Henry II. At the request of the English bishops, in 1166, he had appointed two cardinals, Otho, and William of Pavia, as legates to England with full powers. War had broken out between England and France, and Alexander determined to use these legates to restore peace, and instructed them accordingly. He also directed them not to consecrate a bishop until Becket should have been restored. Becket was very angry, not only at the appointment of legates, but also at the selection of Otho and William, whom he charged with craftiness, falsehood, and avarice. He declared that he would never submit to their arbitration. He intended to anathematize the King and to declare an interdict, but learned, to his consternation, of the Pope's letter to the King invalidating all sentences of his issued before the decision of the legates.

A meeting of the cardinals with Becket was finally arranged at Gisors, at which the alternative was submitted to him of recognizing the Clarendon articles or abdicating, both of which he refused. It was agreed between the legates, the King, and the bishops that the bishops should appeal to the Pope against Becket; and the legates suspended him until the Pope's answer should be received. To Becket's great indignation, the suspension was confirmed. Alexander still preserved a friendly tone in his letters to Henry; but as the King's obstinacy seemed to be only confirmed by these attempts at conciliation, a new papal deputation was sent to him, urging him to restore Becket, and reminding him how often the Pope had restrained the archbishop from pronouncing sentence against him.

But the vacillation of the Roman see during this

tedious contest was too patent to be covered by such pettifogging. Alexander has, not too severely, been called a chameleon. Another change now developed in the opposite direction. The Pope dropped the tone of entreaty, declaring that he could no longer tolerate Henry's stubbornness; that he would no longer close Becket's mouth, and that the sword of St. Peter was not so rusted that it could not be drawn. At the end of 1168 he removed Becket's suspension, recalled the legates, and resolved to make another attempt at reconciliation, now that peace had been arranged between France and England.

At an assembly at Montmirail, convened on the 7th of January, 1169, to witness the formal reconciliation of the two kings, Becket appeared, and professed his readiness to submit the whole case to the judgment of the kings and of the assembly, but added, "saving the honor of God;" whereupon Henry abruptly broke off the negotiation. Becket's obstinacy at first disgusted Louis, but he soon took him into favor again. Henry sent to Alexander, offering him large sums and free disposal of the chair of Canterbury if he would keep Becket away. Alexander refused, but agreed to send two new deputies for further negotiation, and forbade Becket to take any measures against Henry until after the departure of the delegates; but before he received these instructions, Becket at Clairvaux banned Gilbert of London and other followers of the King. Alexander was greatly embarrassed, and evaded and shuffled in the hope that time would bring about a solution. The two new deputies, Gratian and Vivian, were sent, not cardinals, but ecclesiastical lawyers. The Pope reproved Becket for the excommunication of Gilbert, and commanded him to suspend the sentence.

At a second conference at Montmartre between Henry and Louis, Becket consented not to usurp the functions of the civil power on condition of the restoration of his estates and the payment of the arrears of rent. To this, notwithstanding the objections of Louis, Henry assented. But Becket's concession was only in order to gain time. He urged the Pope to lay Normandy under interdict as the surest means of enforcing Henry's submission. The Pope replied by recommending Becket to humble himself before the King, and by instructing the Archbishop of Rouen and the Bishop of Nevers to absolve Gilbert of London and the others whom Becket had excommunicated at Clairvaux. He also gave those prelates authority to lay under interdict all Henry's territory on the Continent if he should not yield within forty days.

Exasperating as was the absolution of the bishops of London and Salisbury to Becket, a harder blow was in store. Henry's feeble health made him anxious to settle the succession by the coronation of his son, and he had invited the Pope to perform the ceremony. The coronation was the recognized prerogative of the Archbishop of Canterbury; but the uncertainty as to the duration of Becket's exile and the state of the King's health made it unwise to delay. It soon came out that the Archbishop of York had received a commission from the Pope to crown the prince. Becket was furious, and declared that in the court of Rome, now as ever, Christ was crucified and Barabbas released; but he set himself to work upon the weak and vacillating Pope to get the commission annulled, and succeeded in persuading him to issue an order to Roger not to officiate. This order Roger, for some unknown reason, never received, and accordingly crowned Prince Henry at Westminster on the 14th of June, 1170, assisted by the bishops of London, Salisbury, Durham, and Rochester.

Becket spared no effort to create the impression that the coronation was illegal and the title invalid. Henry, anxious to escape the threatened interdict, attempted once more to compose the quarrel, and at Frêteval, in July, a formal reconciliation with Becket took place on the terms proposed at Montmartre. The questions of the Clarendon articles and the coronation were evaded. Becket at once secretly obtained from the Pope letters of suspension against the Archbishop of York and the bishops who had officiated at the coronation. Alexander informed these prelates of their suspension, and declared that they had infringed Becket's rights by participating in the coronation, and that Roger had intruded himself into the see of Canterbury, and had performed an act which did not belong to him. This was followed by a general order to the English bishops to remove from their benefices all clergy who had disregarded ban or interdict, to excommunicate them if obstinate, and if they should officiate after excommunication to commit them permanently to monasteries. He instructed the Archbishops of Sens and Rouen to demand of Henry the renunciation of the Clarendon articles *as agreed upon in the reconciliation with Becket*, and the compensation of Becket for his financial losses; and if he should not comply with these requisitions in thirty days to lay his territory on the Continent under interdict. The bishops of the English territory on the Continent were authorized to lay that territory under interdict if the King should not fully restore Becket, and a direct demand was made upon Henry to reinstate him and to exact an oath from his son to protect the franchises of the Church of Canterbury.

Four months after the Treaty of Fréteval the King recalled Becket to England. Two strong parties were hostile to him—the bishops, with a considerable part of the clergy, and certain nobles and royal officers who occupied property claimed by the see of Canterbury, or held estates of the see in sequestration. On his arrival at Sandwich he was met by a party of his enemies, who searched his baggage and demanded that he should absolve the bishops. They were answered by a volley from that well-stocked arsenal of abuse which was always at Becket's command. The bishops in question were described as archdevils, priests of Baal, standard-bearers of the Balaamites, and children of perdition. By a secret messenger, a nun disguised as a boy, he sent to Roger of York the letter of suspension, and to the Bishops of London and Salisbury the decree of excommunication. He entered Canterbury amid enthusiastic demonstrations from the populace; but his triumph was brief. Certain knights of Henry's court, acting upon a hasty and angry expression of the

King, took matters into their own hands, and on the evening of the 29th of December, 1170, hewed Becket down with their swords in the north transept of Canterbury Cathedral.

Becket, ecclesiastically, was a lineal descendant of Hildebrand. He represented the Gregorian idea of the complete subordination of the secular to the ecclesiastical power. This was the real issue behind the fight on the Clarendon articles and the whole quarrel with Henry II. Personally, it is as wide of the mark to characterize him summarily as an unscrupulous traitor as it is to write him down a saint. We must not expect too much. With all his versatility and force of will, he was not an original man and did not rise above the level of his age. His character was thoroughly secular. The act of Henry which converted into an archbishop a soldier, a courtier, a statesman, and a man of pleasure, did not change the man himself, any more than a similar act by Barbarossa changed Christian of Mainz. The man remained the same at the core, though charity may set down his suddenly assumed austerities to a sincere determination to conform himself to a position for which his previous training and associations had unfitted him. It is evident that the saintly side of his life was perfunctory and unnatural. "An artificial and conscious striving after saintship," to use the words of Mr. Freeman, "was something very unlike the natural and inevitable saintship of Anselm." His general sincerity may be granted, but he could not always be trusted to keep faith. He was obstinate and intractable, haughty and imperious; his temper was furious, and his language on occasion violent and abusive. His courage was magnificent, his energy indomitable. He had somehow won the heart of the common people, and was hailed by them as the father of the orphans and the judge of the widows; and his morals were chaste amid strong temptations.

CHAPTER XXV.

PAPAL TRANSACTIONS IN FRANCE AND ENGLAND —BARBAROSSA IN LOMBARDY—BATTLE OF LEGNANO—TREATY OF VENICE—CLOSE OF ALEXANDER'S PONTIFICATE.

HE antipope Calixtus III. was acknowledged in Germany at the Diet of Bamberg in June, 1169; and on the 15th of August, Philip, the Archbishop of Cologne, who had received the pallium from another antipope, Paschal III., crowned Henry, the four-year-old son of Barbarossa, as King at Aachen. Frederick, in the following year, attempted negotiations with Alexander, who was now at the head of the Lombard league; but as he refused definitely to recognize Alexander as rightful Pope, nothing resulted but the renewal and confirmation of the compact between the Pope and the Lombards.

Frederick continued his efforts to form an alliance with Louis of France. He contemplated a marriage between his son and the daughter of Louis. A personal interview of the two monarchs greatly disturbed the Pope, and he bade Henry, the Archbishop of Rheims, and Louis's brother, to try to find out what had passed between them and to inform him. He warned Louis against the proposed marriage, charged Henry of Rheims to hinder it in every way possible, and urged instead a marriage with the son of the Byzantine Emperor, which, he said, would secure for the French kingdom and for the maiden's relatives an inexhaustible fund of money.

Alexander now hoped to be received in Rome, and in October, 1170, entered Tusculum with an armed force; but the Romans refused to admit him to the city, and he was forced to remain in Tusculum for more than two years, in sight of Rome, and abandoned it in 1173 only to continue his exile in Segni.

Hadrian IV., in 1156, had given Ireland to Henry II. Hadrian's appropriation of the island was simply a gigantic and audacious theft, justified by his own assertion that Ireland and all islands to which the light of Christianity had come belonged indubitably to the Holy See. Now, after fifteen years, Henry took possession of Ireland and put the Irish church wholly under the control of the Pope. Henry's hasty words about Becket—" What cowards have I about me that no one will deliver me from this low-born priest?"—were already being used against him by the clergy. The murder of the "martyr and saint" was laid at his door. This was a most effective lever which enabled Alexander to take a high tone of moral indignation towards the King. It began to be rumored that the Pope intended to excommunicate Henry and to lay all his dominions both in England and on the Continent under interdict. Superstition and remorse did their part in bending the stubborn King. At last, on the 27th of September, 1172, in the cathedral of Avranches, in Normandy, the following terms were arranged between Henry and the papal legates: The King was to disclaim under oath the guilt of Becket's murder, but was to give satisfaction because his words had moved the murderers to the act. These murderers must undertake a crusade. The King must renounce the Clarendon articles, give the free right of appeal to Rome, receive the kingdom for himself and his successors from the Pope, and he and they were to regard themselves as rightful kings only if acknowledged by the Pope. He was to restore the property of the Church of Canterbury and to show favor to both clergy and laity who had favored Becket. He should, if required, undertake a penitential pilgrimage to Jerusalem, Rome, or Compostella. He must kneel to the legates as a penitent and receive absolution, but without disrobing or blows.

The absolution document of the cardinals, in which the King's promises were registered, did not contain the provisions respecting the feudal relation of England to the Pope. The greater part of the Constitutions of Clarendon remained in force; the King continued to fill the episcopal chairs, and the clergy did not leave the country without his permission. Only the right of appeal to Rome was assured.

But Henry soon drew upon himself again the threats of the Pope. The young prince Henry, brave, ambitious, and liberal, began to aspire to independence. According to his father's promise to the Pope and Louis, he was recrowned by the Archbishop of Rouen, and his wife, Margaret, with him.

While visiting his father-in-law in Paris, Louis took the opportunity to persuade him that by his coronation he had acquired the right to sovereignty, and was entitled to the immediate possession of a part if not the whole, of his dominions. Accordingly, on his return to England, he requested his father to resign to him either the crown of England or the duchy of Normandy; and, on the King's refusal, made his escape to Paris, where he was protected and supported by Louis. To add to King Henry's misfortunes, his Queen, Eleanor, betrayed extreme jealousy and discontent, and persuaded her two younger sons, Geoffrey and Richard, that they also were entitled to the immediate possession of the territories assigned to them. She engaged them to fly secretly to France, and had disguised herself in male attire to follow them, when she was seized by the King's order, and thrown into prison with two daughters of the King of France, the one Henry's daughter-in-law and the other about to become such.

In this dangerous situation Henry applied to the Pope to excommunicate his enemies and to compel the obedience of his children. Alexander, the Archbishop of Tarantaise, the Bishop of Clermont, and the Prior of Chartreuse were instructed to demand the release of Louis's children within forty days, under penalty of ban and interdict; but the spiritual weapons did not prove effective, and the Pope found it prudent to fall back upon the rôle of mediator, which, however, proved equally impotent.

Naturally war followed between England and France. Many of the Norman nobility deserted to

Prince Henry, and the Breton and Gascon barons inclined to the cause of Geoffrey and Richard. Disaffection had crept in among the English, and the Earls of Leicester and Chester had openly declared against the King. Louis had formally engaged the chief vassals of the crown on the side of his son-in-law. Prince Henry had actually assumed the functions of sovereignty by distributing portions of his father's territories among these, and the Counts of Flanders, Boulogne, Blois, and Eu had openly enlisted under his banner. William of Scotland had joined the confederacy, and a plan had been concerted for a simultaneous invasion of different parts of Henry's domain.

The war between England and France was far from agreeable to the Pope, since it interfered with his plans in the East. He, however, renewed the unsuccessful attempt of four years before to inaugurate a crusade, declaring that such an enterprise would work to allay the hostility between the French and the English, which was so injurious to the interests of all Christendom as well as to those of the Holy Land. The bugbear which haunted him, a family alliance between Louis and Barbarossa, moved him to appeal again to Henry of Rheims, without whose aid, he imagined, the project could not be carried out. He bade the archbishop to endeavor to convince Louis that he should seek help against his enemies, not from a man, but from God; which, translated into papal terms, meant that he should marry his daughter to the son of the Byzantine Emperor, and not to the son of Barbarossa. That he might omit no means of conciliating Louis, he canonized Bernard of Clairvaux.

With a view to effect a peace between Henry and Louis, he sent Cardinal Hugo to England in October, 1175. Louis was complaining of Henry's delay of the marriage of his daughter, who was betrothed to Louis's son, Duke Richard of Aquitaine. Alexander instructed the legate to require Henry to have the marriage ceremony performed within two months, under penalty of an interdict upon the province of Canterbury. The legate did not carry out this order, and every semblance of peace between the two kings soon disappeared.

In the meantime the contest between Alexander and Barbarossa was drawing to a close. In the autumn of 1174, the Emperor, on the invitation of the Roman senate, again crossed the Alps with the intention of humbling the Pope and the Lombards. Christian of Mainz preceded him, but was checked by the desperate resistance of Ancona, while the Emperor laid siege to Alessandria, the fortress erected and named in honor of the Pope. The stubborn defence of both Ancona and Alessandria stimulated the courage of the burghers, and forced Barbarossa to treat for peace with the Pope. Alexander sent three cardinals into Lombardy; but Barbarossa's attempt to separate the Lombards from the Pope terminated the negotiations amid the reproaches of the cardinals that the Emperor alone was responsible for protracting the schism.

The issue was fought out at Legnano on the 29th of May, 1176. Here the long-cherished fiction of the Holy Roman Empire—the domination of Christendom on the basis of the unity of faith—and the idea of national right and national independence met face to face and tried conclusions. Barbarossa's persistent effort of twenty-five years to destroy the freedom of the Italian cities was hopelessly defeated. Legnano was "the Marathon of the Lombard republics."

New negotiations followed. While the Emperor still hoped to separate the Pope from his Lombard allies, the Pope desired only a peace which should include the King of Sicily with the Lombards; and as the report had been circulated in Lombardy that he had made peace with the Emperor for himself alone, he announced that he was coming to Lombardy in person, and that he would agree to no terms which should not include the Lombards, the King of Sicily, and other helpers of the church.

The terms proposed in the conference at Anagni in the beginning of November were that Barbarossa should acknowledge Alexander as lawful Pope, surrender to him the prefecture of the city of Rome, and renounce imperial rights over it, and give up the Mathilde property and other church fiefs with the "regalia" of St. Peter's and other church property. Pope and Emperor should support each other as father and son. The Emperor should also conclude peace with the Lombards on terms framed by arbitrators appointed by himself, the Pope, and the Lombards; and likewise with the King of Sicily, the Emperor of Constantinople, and all who had assisted the Roman Church. The conflicts of the Emperor with the church which had arisen before the time of Hadrian IV., and those with the King of Sicily,

The Peace of Venice. 277

should be adjusted by a court of arbitration constituted by the Pope and the Emperor. The antipope Calixtus was to receive an abbacy. The Emperor, the Empress, and their son Henry were to be regarded by the Holy See as "Catholic, and in good and regular standing."

Venice was selected as the place for the confirmation of the treaty, and in May, 1177,[1] a congress assembled, where, for the first time, deputies of free cities appeared, independent of Pope or Emperor. The terms arranged at Anagni were ratified. The Emperor was to insure the King of Sicily and the Emperor of Constantinople a peace of fifteen years, and to promise peace to the other helpers of the church, and was also to agree, under oath, to a six years' peace with the Lombards; while the Pope, at a general council, was to threaten with the ban every one who should disturb the peace between the empire and the church.

The Emperor, with the special permission of the Pope, made his formal entrance into Venice on the 24th of July. Early in the morning the Pope sent out to him seven cardinals, to whom Barbarossa abjured the three antipopes and pledged obedience to Alexander. Having received absolution, he entered the city, where, in front of St. Mark's, he kissed the Pope's feet and received from him in return the kiss of peace. Alexander led the Emperor by the hand into the church and gave him his blessing. The next day, at mass, Barbarossa and the princes again kissed the Pope's feet and handed him a present of

[1] Authorities differ as to the month. I follow Langen.

money; and on leaving the church, the Emperor held the Pope's stirrup. On the 1st of August the peace was solemnly ratified in public. The Pope opened the proceedings with an address in which Barbarossa figured as the returned prodigal. The Emperor acknowledged his fault in rejecting Alexander, repeated his oaths of peace and truce, and again received absolution. On the 14th of August the promised synod was held in St. Mark's, and the anathema pronounced upon all who should break the peace just concluded. Calixtus III. was declared deposed, and schismatics who should continue obstinate were banned.

The Peace of Venice was an important epoch in the history of Italy. The impression, upon Rome especially, was profound. The relations which it instituted between the city and the Pope and Emperor placed it upon less favorable ground than the Lombards. While all Italy was rejoicing, the Romans lost the courage to prolong the contest with the Pope, whom the Emperor acknowledged as the ruler of Rome. Alexander knew that his exile was at an end. Seven Roman nobles brought him letters from the senate, the clergy, and the people, inviting him to return. Still mistrustful, he sent cardinals to Rome to negotiate with the people. After some delay an agreement was reached. The new senators took the oath of fealty to the Pope; St. Peter's and all its revenues were restored to him, and security was pledged to all travellers to Rome.

After a banishment of ten years, the Pope advanced by way of Tusculum to Rome, and made his entry on the 12th of March, 1178, the festival of St.

Gregory. He was received with great pomp by the senate and the magistrates; the knights and soldiers greeted him with sound of trumpets, and the people bore olive-branches and chanted triumphal hymns. His tent would not hold the throngs which crowded to kiss his feet, and it was evening before he could reach the gate of the Lateran, where, from the ancient dwelling of the popes, he gave the people his benediction.

But settled peace seemed impossible. The elements of discord were too many and too powerful to be permanently composed by treaties and foot-kissing and stirrup-holding. Foreshadowings of a new division between the Pope and the Emperor soon made their appearance. The Pope found it necessary to complain that the March, which belonged to the empire only in part and mostly to the church, had been assigned at Venice under his very eyes, and without asking his consent, to "some one" (Conrad of Lützelhard). Nor were the Pope's relations with the Romans by any means happy. People and senate had acknowledged him under constraint, and the strife continued between the Republic and the Pope. The papal power was hated without being feared. Murmurs were heard, and there were signs of an eruption, not only in the city but in the entire territory. Every place in Roman territory emulated the Lombards. Every one had its own municipality, with its consuls or other magistrates at its head. Many barons in Tuscany refused alike to acknowledge the Pope and to submit to the Roman senate. Schisms were inaugurated on every side. Calixtus, the antipope, refused to obey the decisions of Venice, and Viterbo served him as a residence, where he was supported by the lords of Vico, among whom was the city prefect John.

Out of hatred to Viterbo, the Romans resisted the imperial troops, led by Christian of Mainz, the Emperor's plenipotentiary. Alexander was compelled by the strained relations between Christian and the Romans to retire again to Tusculum, where he had the gratification of receiving the submission of Calixtus. The Pope treated him kindly, and, later, made him rector of Benevento. Notwithstanding this, the imperialists, contrary to Frederick's wish, chose another antipope in September, 1178—Lando of Sezza, a Frangipani, under the title of Innocent III. He found little support, and in January, 1180, was seized and confined for life in the monastery of Cava.

Alexander's eventful life was now drawing to a close. He held a general synod at the Lateran in March, 1179, where the Peace of Venice was sanctioned, the consecrations of schismatic popes and their followers were declared invalid, and it was decreed that, in future, the lawful Pope should be only he upon whom two parties of the cardinals against one should agree. Alexander then retired from Rome to his old haunts, Anagni, Segni, and Velletri. On the 18th of September, 1181, occurred the death of Louis of France, who was succeeded by his son Philip Augustus, Philip II.

From Tusculum Alexander issued a new and unavailing summons to a crusade. He died on the 30th of August, 1181. So many bitter enemies had he among the Romans that his bier, as it was borne to the Lateran, was pelted with stones and mud. No Pope since Hadrian I. had occupied the chair so long; but during eighteen of the twenty-two years he had presided over a divided church, and he had spent more than half of his pontificate in exile. He represented the aims and the general policy of Hildebrand. He was energetic, but politic and vacillating. He united the training of a lawyer with that of a theologian. With all his weakness and vacillation, he extended the conquests of Gregory VII. and of Calixtus II. He seriously weakened the imperial power, and his pontificate will be remembered, if for nothing else, as marking the successful assertion of their freedom by the Italian cities—a result which, as has been justly remarked, was his good fortune and not his merit.

His interest in learning was shown by repeated decrees in favor of professors, especially in France, and by his promotion of free education. His own literary work was considerable, and a part of it has only recently come to light.

CHAPTER XXVI.

FIVE POPES IN TEN YEARS—THIRD CRUSADE—THE NEW ROMAN CONSTITUTION—DEATH OF BARBAROSSA—HENRY VI. EMPEROR.

IN September, 1181, Hubald, Bishop of Ostia and Velletri, a Cistercian, was elected Pope and enthroned at Velletri as Lucius III. He went to Rome after two months, but was compelled to leave it before four months had elapsed. A new issue had arisen between the Pope and the Romans. The Romans, in 1170, in violation of their agreement with Alexander, had entirely demolished the walls of Tusculum. The Tusculans now began to restore them, but the Romans interfered; and the Pope, whose relations with Barbarossa were friendly, appealed to Christian of Mainz, who was in Tuscany. He came at once, and attacked and plundered Rome as a punishment for expelling the Pope and for repeated invasions of his territory. The August fever proved fatal to him. He was one of the greatest princes of his age, and, while bearing the office of an archbishop, never laid aside the characteristics of a warrior, but remained till his death a lusty knight, devoted to war and to beauty.

His death was a serious blow to the Pope. The Romans now boldly attacked the towns of the Campagna which still adhered to him. Again they laid waste the territory of Tusculum and penetrated far into Latium. Their hatred of the clergy was intense, and they inflicted on them the greatest cruelties. Having on one occasion seized a party of priests on the Campagna, they blinded all but one of them, set them on asses, put upon their heads parchment mitres on which the names of cardinals were displayed, and forced the one whose eyes they had spared to conduct this ghastly procession to the Pope.

The Pope moved about between Velletri, Segni, and Anagni; and in July, 1184, went to Verona and met Barbarossa, who, not long before, had concluded a definite peace with the Lombard cities.[1] The negotiations between them occupied more than three months, but the Pope could obtain from the Emperor no binding promise to assist him against the Romans, nor come to any understanding concerning the Mathilde property. He proposed to Barbarossa to crown his son Henry at once as Emperor. A few bulls, decrees, and canonistic decisions issued from Verona in 1184 and 1185 complete the record of Lucius's pontificate. He died on the 25th of November, 1185.

Humbert of Crivellis succeeded as Urban III., one of Barbarossa's bitterest enemies. The hostility soon broke out, the immediate causes being the marriage of Barbarossa's son, Henry VI., with Constantia, the

---

[1] At Constance, 1183, by which the autonomy of the Lombard cities was substantially conceded, with the right to fortify themselves, levy armies, and extend the bounds of their confederacy.

heiress of Sicily, and Urban's refusal to crown him. The Roman see was disconcerted by the splendid result which German statecraft had extracted from Sicily. The dynasty of Roger was well-nigh extinct; William II. remained childless, and therefore favored the union of Roger's daughter with the heir to the German crown. Sicily, the anxiously guarded fief of the papal see, and which had so often served it against the German throne, would, after William's death, fall to the German empire. Without regard to the Pope, the feudal lord of Sicily, and in spite of his protest, the marriage was celebrated at Milan in January, 1186. At the same time Frederick had Henry crowned Emperor. As the Pope refused the imperial crown, and, as Bishop of Milan, the Lombard crown also, the coronation was performed by the Patriarch of Aquileia and several Italian bishops, who were, of course, rewarded for their participation with suspension by Urban.

On his return from Italy, Frederick, irritated by the Pope, carried his hostility so far as to commission his son for an inroad into the papal territory, and to close the Alpine passes, so as to render all intercourse with the Pope impossible. The Romans willingly aided Henry; the districts of Latium, which still adhered to the Pope, were laid waste, and all hope of his return to Rome was cut off.

Urban resolved on extreme measures, and forbade imperial messengers sent to treat about conditions of peace to enter Verona, where he himself was forced to remain. He was disposed to pronounce the ban upon the Emperor, but the Veronese declared that this should not be done in their city. He then thought of going to Venice and issuing the ban there, and set out for that purpose in the autumn, but only reached Ferrara, where he died in October, 1187, without having set foot in Rome during his pontificate. His death was ascribed to his grief at the news of the capture of Jerusalem by Saladin, an event which shook Europe with surprise and consternation. Political complications and private afflictions were alike forgotten. Superstition saw the eyes of the images of Christ and of the saints drop bloody tears. Every one accused himself of having brought down the vengeance of Heaven upon the Holy City by his own offences, and sought to appease divine justice by penitence. Luxury was banished, injuries were forgotten, alms were lavishly distributed, and Christians gave themselves to fasting and mortification.

Albert of Benevento, an imperialist, succeeded Urban in October, 1187, as Gregory VIII. He was a man of mild disposition, and his two chief wishes were peace with the empire and a crusade to Jerusalem. The Papacy was exhausted by the contest under Alexander III.; the Peace of Venice and the Treaty of Constance had ended the war with the cities, and the marriage alliance with Sicily had strengthened the imperial throne. Gregory hastened to come to an agreement with Frederick. He engaged not to interfere with his claims upon Sicily, and to acknowledge all imperial rights in Italy. He issued letters to Christendom touching the fall of Jerusalem, and set out for Pisa for the purpose of reconciling it with Genoa, so that the two might combine to reconquer Palestine. In October he summoned the Emperor and the German princes to equip a crusade. Next to the religious and moral reform of the church this was the ruling idea of his brief pontificate. In church politics he seemed disposed to sink the Gregorian ideal, to appear only as the first of bishops, and to restore all secular power to the Emperor's hands. He died at Pisa in December, 1187.

Paul of Palestrina followed, a Roman by birth, as Clement III. He set himself to promote the crusade inaugurated by Gregory VIII. He accomplished the peace between Genoa and Pisa, and appointed a legate to preach the crusade in Germany. He sent envoys to Rome to negotiate for his return, and in February, 1188, entered the city, where he was received with great splendor. During the forty-four years of the existence of the Roman senate, the popes, almost continuously, had been sacrificed to this revolution in the city government. Innocent II. died amid the tumult of its first proclamation, and probably because of it; Lucius II. fell by a stone in the attempt to storm the republican intrenchments on the Capitol; Eugenius III., Alexander III., Lucius III., Urban III., and Gregory VIII. had spent their pontificates wholly or partly in exile. Clement III. now at last brought the Papacy back to Rome, concluding a formal treaty with the city as an independent power. The fruit of the Lombard victories and of the vigorous resistance of the Romans to Emperor and Pope had ripened. Rome came into the same relations with the Pope as the Lombard cities with the Emperor.

By the treaty the Pope was recognized as sovereign. He was to invest the senate at the Capitol, and the senate was to swear fealty to him. He regained the right of issuing coins, of which the senate, however, was to retain a third, in order to free the churches from the debts incurred by the war. St. Peter's and all the churches were made over to him, and all the former papal revenues were restored. The senate retained the control of the Lucanian bridge over the Anio on account of the feud with Tivoli. The Pope was to indemnify the Romans for the losses by the war, and agreed to give a hundred pounds annually for the restoration of the city walls. He was to have the right to summon the Roman militia, at his own cost, to defend his patrimony. Tusculum was to belong to the Roman see in perpetuity, and its walls and fortifications were to be destroyed by the beginning of 1189. The Pope was not to hinder the Romans from prosecuting the war with Tivoli.

The constitution of 1188 was thus a most important advance of the Roman commonwealth. Both the imperial and the patrician power were mastered. The Emperor's right was not considered. It had been practically renounced in the Treaty of Venice. The city had passed out of its old relations. The Pope possessed in it neither ruling nor legislative power.

The third crusade progressed rapidly under the auspices of Germany, England, and France. William, the Archbishop of Tyre, came from the East to solicit the aid of the Christian princes, and was commissioned by the Pope to preach the holy war. From Italy he went to France, and appeared at an assembly convoked by Henry II. and Philip II. near Gisors. On his arrival, the two kings, who were still at war, laid down their arms. William was received with enthusiasm, and proceeded to relate the capture of Jerusalem by Saladin, which moved the assembly to tears. He then exhorted them to take the cross. "The gates of the Holy City are broken, and her guardians are exposed with cattle in the markets of infidel cities. The inhabitants of forty cities have been driven from their homes, and with their weeping families are wandering among the nations of Asia without finding a stone on which to lay their heads. How can you seek any other renown than that of delivering the holy places? Within sight of this assembly I have beheld preparations for war. Why are you armed with these swords? You are fighting here for the banks of a river, for the limits of a province, while infidels trample the banks of Siloa, and the cross of Christ is dragged ignominiously through the streets of Bagdad? The prophets and saints buried at Jerusalem, the churches transformed into mosques, the very stones of the sepulchres, all cry to you to avenge the glory of God and the death of your brethren."

Henry and Philip embraced and were the first to receive the cross. A crowd of nobles and knights, with several bishops of France and England, took the crusading oath. It was resolved that all who did not take the cross should pay a tenth of their revenues and of the value of their property of all kinds, which was to be known as the "Saladin tithe." William then proceeded to Germany, and a general diet was convoked at Mainz, where Frederick descended from his throne and received the cross from William, and was followed by his son Frederick of Suabia and by Leopold of Austria and Berthold of Moravia.

Before Frederick opened the crusade in the spring of 1189, peace was concluded at Hagenau, on the 9th of April, between himself and the Pope. Clement consented to crown Henry VI. as Emperor, but Frederick himself postponed the coronation. In May, Frederick, at the head of thirty thousand men, marched to Constantinople and across the desert highlands of Asia Minor. He captured Iconium, moved on to Cilicia, and arrived at the bank of the river Seleph or Calicadnus, near the Cydnus. The stream was swollen by the rains, and in attempting to cross or to bathe he was drowned on the 10th of June, 1190. Clement recognized Henry, and arranged for his coronation at Easter, 1191; but Clement died in the previous March.

Barbarossa, though hated in Italy, is a magnificent figure in the history of Germany and of the middle ages. To the German mind he is the representative of the returning glory of the fatherland. His ideal of empire was impracticable. He aimed at renewing the universal sovereignty of the Roman Cæsars, and his effort to realize this ideal promoted the cause of popular freedom and hastened the emancipation of the Lombard cities. Haughty and imperious, he was also generous and magnanimous. His solid common sense detected the radical fallacy of the Gregorian papal ideal, and he struck at it with both word and sword. The questions of the proprietorship of church property and of the position and jurisdiction of the metropolitan sees were in the background in his contest with Alexander III. The central point of that contest was the restitution of the imperial sovereignty over the Papacy and its territorial possessions.

He restored in large measure the ancient independence of the German church and its connection with the throne. It occupied again the first position in the empire. Its representatives were thrice as numerous as the secular princes, and were supreme both in the council and in the army of the Emperor. His influence on his people during his latter years was ennobling, and his reign marks the dawn of poetry and culture. A more cosmopolitan spirit pervaded all circles. Germany began to win her share in the world's commerce, and to develop her individual industries. The influence of the ancient models of culture passed on from France into Germany, and is seen in the improved Latinity of her contemporary historians. The division-wall between lay and clerical culture was breached, and the poetic impulse communicated itself to the clergy.

The popular legends say that Barbarossa did not die, but is sleeping in a grotto at Kyffhäuser, whence he will come forth at the appointed hour to renew the ancient glory of the empire.

> "Er ist niemals gestorben,
> Er lebt darin noch jetzt;
> Er hat im Schloss verborgen
> Zum Schlaf sich hingesetzt.
>
> "Er hat hinabgenommen
> Des Reiches Herrlichkeit,
> Und wird einst wiederkommen
> Mit ihr zu seiner Zeit."

Clement's successor was the Cardinal Hyacinth, who took the name of Cœlestine III. He was eighty-five years old. Henry VI. was now approaching Rome with a large force to receive the imperial crown. Easter was drawing near, and the Pope was at first disposed to make difficulties about the coronation, while Henry was eager to hasten it so as to enter at once upon his expedition to Sicily. There were possibilities of trouble, too, in the senate, if it should be inclined to object to the coronation. The Romans availed themselves of these circumstances to get Tusculum finally into their power. That city had for three years been in arms against the combined attacks of the Pope and the senate, and, as a last resource, had turned to Henry and had received from him a German garrison. The Romans declared that they would resist Henry's coronation if he did not deliver Tusculum to them; while, if he should consent, they would compel the Pope to crown him at once. Henry agreed to this act of treachery, but threw the responsibility on the Pope, who had made it a condition of his coronation that he should deliver Tusculum to him.

The King entered the Leonina on the 14th of April, but the Romans closed the gates against his army. His coronation, with his wife's, took place in St. Peter's. The garrison of Tusculum received orders to open their gates, and the Romans glutted their vengeance on the unfortunate city. The principal citizens were either massacred or mutilated. The walls were levelled, and the city which had served the Pope as a check upon the Roman populace, and the Emperor as a stronghold against the Pope, finally disappeared from history. Henry, with his army, went to Apulia to expel Tancred, his wife's natural brother, whom the Normans had set up as King of Sicily, and to claim the kingdom of Naples; but after capturing Salerno he lost nearly his whole army by an epidemic, and was obliged to flee, leaving his wife a prisoner in the hands of Tancred, who made terms with the Pope and received the kingdom as his feudal vassal. The temporary advantage thus gained by the Roman see, in spite of the marriage alliance between Sicily and the Hohenstaufen, widened the breach between the Papacy and the empire.

The hostility increased when the Emperor repossessed himself of Sicily and began to fill the bishoprics in Germany. Matters were brought to an issue in September, 1192, by Henry's placing Lothair of Bonn in the episcopal chair of Liége. The Pope's candidate, Autbert, received consecration by his command, whereupon Henry destroyed the chapter-houses and forbade Autbert to enter Germany. A few days after he caused him to be assassinated. The Pope banned the murderer. Henry prohibited journeys to Rome, and imprisoned at Siena the cardinal bishop Octavian of Ostia, who was returning to France.

Richard I. had succeeded to the English throne in 1189. With Philip of France he had engaged in the crusade, and the two kings were under a mutual pledge not to invade each other's dominions during its continuance. Jealousy, however, arose between them on the way to Constantinople, and at Acre, where both distinguished themselves. Philip, disgusted at Richard's popularity, returned to Europe and began intriguing against England. After the truce with Saladin, Richard set out to return, and, attempting to pass through Germany in disguise, was detected and seized at Vienna by Leopold of Austria, who, enraged at some insult received during the siege of Acre, threw him into prison, and in 1193 handed him over to the Emperor, who confined him in the castle of Tiefels and refused to release him except on the payment of an enormous ransom and the acknowledgment of himself as his feudal lord. Philip had secured the alliance of the Emperor in his war with Richard, and endeavored to persuade Henry to give Richard up to him.

As a crusader, Richard was under the special protection of the Pope; and Cœlestine was at once appealed to by the Archbishop of Rouen and by clergy in Germany to interfere. The queen-mother, Eleanor, addressed to him urgent letters, begging him to send legates and to restore her son. The legates, however, were not forthcoming, and did not appear during Richard's inprisonment, although the Pope threatened both France and Germany with interdict if Richard were not released. Under the influence of this menace and of the protest of the German barons, Henry at last agreed to liberate Richard for an immense sum; but Leopold of Austria, after Richard's release, detained hostages for the payment of the ransom. On Richard's complaint to the Pope, Cœlestine excommunicated Leopold, laid his country under interdict, and commissioned the Bishop of Verona to have the sentence proclaimed, every Sunday and holiday, throughout the duchy.

CHAPTER XXVII.

THE EMPEROR MASTER OF ITALY—PAPAL COMPLICATIONS IN FRANCE AND SPAIN—DEATH OF HENRY VI. AND CŒLESTINE III.—THE GREAT HERESIES.

THE death of Tancred caused Henry to set out again for Italy in the summer of 1194, in order to secure possession of the kingdom of Sicily, for which he greatly desired the Pope's confirmation. His visit to Sicily was signalized by atrocious cruelties. Having caused himself and his wife to be crowned at Palermo, he put out the eyes of Tancred's son, mutilated and tortured many of his partisans, had the corpse of Tancred disinterred and rifled of the royal insignia, and imprisoned his widow. The Emperor was thus master of Italy. Even the papal territory was in his hands, and the Lombards saw themselves in danger of losing their hardly won freedom. He committed the administration of Italy to Germans, created his brother Philip Duke of Tuscany, and enfeoffed him with the Mathilde property, Conrad of Ürslingen with Spoleto, and the general Markwald with Romagna and the Marches. He took possession of the church's patrimony almost to the gates of

Rome, professed to be master even in the Trastevere, and styled himself Duke of the Campagna. He appeared to have revived his father's ideal of universal empire, of the enslavement of Italy, and of the overthrow of the Gregorian Papacy. The city prefect in Rome habitually opposed the Pope, and the Frangipani allied themselves with the Emperor. The feeble Cœlestine was forced not only to abandon to the senate the government of Rome, but also to surrender to the Emperor the Sabina and the Maritima.[1] The secular power of St. Peter seemed to be passing away. The papal finances were in a desperate condition, and simony prevailed in the Curia as never before.

New complications now appeared in France. Philip Augustus since 1193 had been married to Ingeborg, the sister of the King of Denmark, but had separated from her on the pretended ground of blood-relationship with his first wife. On the appeal of Ingeborg and her brother to Rome, the Pope sent two legates to France, who, however, were able to accomplish nothing. He then wrote to the Archbishop of Sens, expressing his regret for the King's conduct, enlarging upon the sacredness of the marriage relation and the care which the church should observe respecting it, declaring the separation invalid, and commanding the archbishop to thwart any possible attempt of the King to contract a new marriage. The same order was given to the Archbishop of Rheims, and Philip was commanded to resume his relation with Ingeborg. But within four weeks Philip married Agnes, the daughter of the Duke of Tyrol.

[1] A strip on the coast from Terracina northward to Toscanella.

Henry VI., in the meantime, endeavored to make peace with the Pope, regardless of consequences. Having become master of Italy, he was infatuated with the idea of seizing the Byzantine throne, and thus uniting East and West under his sceptre. The shortest road to this was a new crusade. Accordingly he wrote to the Pope that the best means of delivering the Holy Land and extirpating prevalent heresies was the reconciliation of the church and the state. He desired Cœlestine to send legates to treat with him concerning peace. At Bari, on Good Friday, 1195, the Emperor privately took the cross, and had the crusade preached at Easter by way of thanksgiving for the divine mercy which had enabled him to overcome Sicily. The Pope returned a conciliatory answer, sent two cardinals to discuss matters with the Emperor, and appointed two others to go to Germany during the summer and preach the crusade, according to Henry's desire. About the same time he charged his legate in England, Archbishop Hubert of Canterbury, with the English bishops, to take part in the enterprise and to induce King Richard to do so. He issued a new bull of privilege to the Latin clergy at the Holy Sepulchre, and took ecclesiastical possession of the island of Cyprus, which had been conquered by Richard of England in 1191, sending two legates to superintend the collection of tithes. He also addressed himself to the suppression of the infidels in the West, enjoining the kings of Spain to take up arms against the Saracens.

King Alfonso of Leon proved refractory. Because of his marriage with the daughter of King Sancho I.

of Portugal, who was related to him by blood, he, with his wife and father-in-law, had been laid under ban. Through the submission of his wife, the Princess Therese, who took the veil and was afterwards honored as a saint, the marriage was dissolved and the ban removed. But the King was in league with the Saracens against Castile, and refused to abandon his alliance; and Cœlestine accordingly renewed the ban, summoned his subjects to fight the Saracens, and commanded the Archbishop of Toledo, in case the King should continue his league with the infidels, to release them from their allegiance in the name of the apostolic see.

The attempt of the Emperor to unite the kingdom of Sicily with the empire had been vigorously opposed in Germany, especially by the bishops. The project of the crusade met with a better reception, and was indorsed by the Diet of Würzburg in March, 1196. At this diet the Emperor also gained the consent of the princes to make the German crown and the imperial dignity hereditary, and therefore independent of the Pope. Even the opposing princes were persuaded to acknowledge, at Frankfort, the three-year-old son of the Emperor, Frederick, as heir to the crown. While Henry was arming for a new expedition to Italy, he continued his negotiations with the Pope. There was an abundance of matter. Letters of Cœlestine to the Byzantine Emperor Alexius had been intercepted by Henry's servants; the Emperor's brother Philip had committed many acts of violence in Italy; and Henry's own outrages in Sicily were regarded by the Curia as crimes.

In the summer of 1196 Henry made his last disastrous expedition to Italy. Some weeks were spent near Tivoli in negotiations with the Pope about anointing young Frederick as King; but nothing was accomplished, and the Emperor moved on to Sicily. His final experience there might easily have been construed as a retribution for his horrible cruelties. A conspiracy was formed against him, in which his own wife, and according to some accounts the Pope, participated, and from which he barely escaped. He sent young Frederick to Germany in charge of his brother Philip to have him crowned there; but before their arrival he died on the 28th of September, 1197. As he was still under excommunication, the Archbishop of Messana went to Rome to obtain permission for his interment, which the Pope granted on condition that Richard of England should receive back the price of his ransom. Frederick's reception of the Sicilian crown he made dependent on the agreement of the cardinals. The Empress must swear that Frederick was the lawful son of the Emperor and herself; and for their consent the Pope and the college of cardinals were to receive a thousand marks of silver.

After the Emperor's death a great part of Tuscany and the kingdom of Sicily returned to the sovereignty of the Pope. Other territories, on the contrary, such as imperial Tuscany, armed themselves against the attempts which were now being begun by the Roman Curia to extend its secular sovereignty beyond any previous limits.

Cœlestine did not long survive the Emperor. His

last sickness attacked him just before Christmas. He assembled the cardinals for consultation about his successor, but they refused to accept his candidate, John of St. Paul, of the house of Colonna, and he died on the 8th of January, 1198. Forsaken by the princes, almost wholly bereft of his secular power, with an empty treasury, he little dreamed that his immediate successor would most fully carry out the Gregorian conception of the church's secular dominion. Eighty-five years old when he assumed the papal chair, Cœlestine could not, especially with such an Emperor as Henry VI., realize this ideal. Mild and yielding by nature, the sharp antagonisms in his administration were owing to his dependence upon their representatives in the college of cardinals—his two immediate successors, Innocent III. and Honorius III. Following the leader of the zealots, Cardinal Lothair, he seemed to desire to be another Alexander III.; but under the counsel of his personal friend Cencius his strenuousness relaxed. Hence he was continually experiencing defeats, was powerless in Rome, and left to his successor numerous unsettled complications in different parts of Europe.

Before going further, our attention must be directed to the principal forms of heresy with which several succeeding pontificates came into conflict.

The heresies of this period may be roughly divided into two classes—the one including those who held all the great essential truths of Christianity, but were opposed to the whole sacerdotal system, and the other those who were tainted with serious doctrinal errors. It should be said in advance that almost our only sources of information are the representations of the persecutors. The literature of the persecuted has well-nigh vanished.

The conditions of society in southern France were favorable to the propagation of heresy. The whole population and civilization were in marked contrast with those of the north. The various elements which, from remote antiquity, had successively occupied the soil—Phœnician, Greek, Gothic, Saracenic—had set a cosmopolitan stamp upon the population. The citizens of Narbonne and Marseilles were of a different type from the citizens of Paris. Culture and luxury had made greater progress than in the north. Chivalry and poetry were assiduously cultivated by the nobles. The people of the commercial cities were enlightened and educated. The clergy were negligent, luxurious, and despised by the people, and the patent derelictions of the church were freely criticised by those who possessed any religious earnestness or positive conviction. Bernard of Clairvaux pathetically described the state of religion in the territories of the Count of Toulouse: " Churches without people, people without priests, priests without the reverence due to them, Christians without Christ, sacraments no longer sacred, the apostolic and prophetic voices silenced by the voice of a single heretic."

It was amid such a population that the first antisacerdotal heresy was preached, in Val Louise, about 1106, by Pierre de Bruys, of Embrun, and forty years later by a monk, Henry of Lausanne. They taught that infant baptism was useless, rejected the Eucharist, declared that churches were unnecessary and should be destroyed, that alms, masses, and prayers for the dead were unavailing, and that the cross, as the instrument on which Christ was tortured, should not be invoked but destroyed.

In the second half of the twelfth century appeared Peter Waldo, a rich merchant of Lyons, who, desiring to know the Scriptures, caused a translation of the New Testament to be made into the Romance language, and a collection of extracts from the fathers, known as "the Sentences." He became filled with zeal to imitate the apostolic life as commanded by Christ, and accordingly sold his property and devoted himself to preaching in the streets and fields. Others associated themselves with him, who were sent to preach in neighboring towns. They assumed a peculiar dress, and a sandal with a plate affixed to it, from which they were called *insabbatati* or *zaptati* ("shoed"). They called themselves *Li Poure de Lyod* (" the Poor of Lyons ").[1] Being forbidden to preach by the Archbishop of Lyons, they disobeyed and were excommunicated. Peter appealed to the Pope, who approved his vow of poverty and authorized him to preach when permitted by the priests.

[1] The attempt has been made to prove for the Waldenses an earlier origin. According to this, the name *Vaudois* is derived from *vaux*, or *Waldenses* from *vallis*. The apostolic church of Italy, it is said, proscribed by the Papacy, withdrew into Upper Italy and found an asylum in the valleys, and the name originally meant "Christians of the valleys." They are primitive Christians, descendants and representatives of the primitive church through Claudius of Turin (820). See Alexis Muston, " L'Israel des Alpes," translated by J. Montgomery; E. Comba, " Waldo and the Waldensians before the Reformation "; and " Storia della Riforma in Italia." Monastier, " Histoire de l'Église Vaudoise"; Dieckhoff, " Die Waldenser im Mittelalter "; Herzog, " Die Romanischen Waldenser "; Henry C. Lea, " A History of the Inquisition in the Middle Ages."

In 1179 they appeared before the Lateran council, submitted their version of the Scriptures, and asked for permission to preach. Lucius III. anathematized them at the Council of Verona in 1184. At Narbonne, in 1190, they publicly discussed in the cathedral with one Raymond of Daventry six propositions: that they refused obedience to Pope and prelates; that all, even laymen, may preach; that God is to be obeyed rather than man; that women may preach; that masses, prayers, and alms for the dead are useless; that prayer in bed or in a stable is as efficacious as in a church. They held that the ministrations of sinful priests were invalid, and that confession to a layman was as good as that to a priest. Their three distinctive rules of morality were: every lie is a mortal sin; every oath, even in court, is unlawful; homicide is never admissible, even in judicial executions or in war. Their persecutors universally testified to their chastity, temperance, truthfulness, and modesty. They revered the Scriptures, and had translations of the whole Bible in the vulgar tongue.

More dangerous to the church was a sect in which, for a time, the Waldenses, by force of circumstances, were partially merged—the Cathari, or "pure." Their doctrine grew out of the dualistic teaching of Manes, who appeared in Persia about the middle of the third century. He taught that the world was the product of two eternal and antagonistic principles, good and evil. Spirit is identified with the good, matter with the evil principle. Every individual man is at once a child of light and darkness—has a good soul and a body substantially evil. The redemption of light from darkness is effected by Christ and by the Holy Ghost; but as matter is essentially evil, the human Christ was only a phantom. The morality of this system was severely ascetic, the great aim being to destroy corporeity and to set the soul free from the fetters of matter.

Manichæism appeared in Europe before the close of the third century, and was everywhere persecuted in the Roman empire. It was especially loathsome to the church, and the object of the active hostility of popes, bishops, and emperors from the time of Leo the Great. From one of its leaders, Paul of Samosata, the system acquired the name of Paulicianism. The Cathari, who sprang from the same Manichæan source, originated in eastern Europe, probably in Bulgaria, and their first traces in the West are found in France and Flanders. Their principal seat was in southern France, where they were known as Albigenses. The basis of their doctrinal system was Manichæan. They rejected all church machinery. The Roman Church was "the synagogue of Satan," in which salvation was impossible. The Catharan church inherited the power to bind and loose. They translated the Scriptures, but retained the Latin prayers. The Eucharist was replaced by the "Benediction of bread," which was performed daily at table. Every act of eating or drinking was preceded by prayer. Confession was general, and was performed monthly by the assembly of the faithful. The principal ceremony was the "Consolamentum," or baptism of the Holy Spirit, which reunited the soul to the Holy Spirit and wrought absolution from sin. It consisted in the imposition of hands, required two ministrants, and could be performed by a woman. Torture at the end of life relieved them of torment in the next world, and suicide was not uncommon.

They were strictly ascetic. Matter was the work of Satan, and the Catharan must be continually warring with the flesh. Hence whatever tended to the reproduction of animal life was avoided. Marriage was prohibited except among a few. Meat, milk, and eggs were forbidden. They fasted three days in the week, and had three annual fasts of forty days each. They were mostly peasants and mechanics; their habits were moral, and their proselytizing zeal extreme. They appeared in France as early as 1017, and in Lombardy a little later. By 1052 their teaching had extended to Germany, and became more widely spread as the twelfth century advanced.

Italy was deeply infected, Milan being the centre. About the middle of the eleventh century, and during the papal attempts to enforce celibacy on the Milanese clergy, there arose there the term "Patarins." This word was derived from *pates*, which in the old Romance dialects meant "old linen." Rag-pickers in Lombardy were known as "Patari," and the quarter in Milan inhabited by them was named "Pataria." From their Bulgarian origin the Patari were also known as "Bulgari," "Bugari," or "Bugres"; and from the number of weavers among them they received in France the name of "Texerant" or "Textores." The name "Albigenses" arose from the district of Albi, where they were numerous, and came into general use during the crusades against Raymond of Toulouse. In Italy the heresy offered the most stubborn resistance to all attempts to extirpate it. The numerous subdivisions of the country and the constant strife between the civic communities rendered any general means of repression impossible. It pervaded all the northern half of the peninsula, and was found as far south as Calabria.

CHAPTER XXVIII.

INNOCENT III.—STEPS TOWARDS PAPAL SUPREMACY IN ITALY—A NEW CRUSADE PROCLAIMED—THE CONTEST FOR THE GERMAN CROWN.

OTHAIR, the son of Count Trasimund of Segni, the nephew of Clement III., and the kinsman of several cardinals, was born at Anagni in 1160 or 1161. He studied theology and jurisprudence at Rome, Paris, and Bologna, was consecrated as subdeacon by Gregory VIII., and was made cardinal deacon by Clement III. He lost his influence on the accession of Cœlestine III., partly through family feuds and partly through the contrast between his character and that of the Pope—between his youthful energy and the Pope's senile weakness. This very contrast, however, together with Cœlestine's numerous defeats and the prospect of the revival of the papal power in Italy, were the reasons why, on the day of Cœlestine's death, he was elected Pope at the age of thirty-seven, as Innocent III.

Without waiting for his installation, he began at once to issue mandates and decisions, and took in hand the work for which he had been specially chosen. As a financial basis of his policy, he proceeded to restore the Roman patrimony. He quashed a treaty with the bishops and city authorities of Tuscany, reclaimed the duchy as the property of the Roman Church, demanded the free canonical right of appointment to church offices in Lower Italy, and put the Maritima and the Sabina under senatorial control. The day after his enthronement he received the oath of fealty from the city prefect, and then sent two cardinals to take the March of Ancona and the duchy of Ravenna from Markwald, who held them as imperial fiefs.

Markwald of Anweiler was a knight of Alsace, the seneschal of Henry VI., and called himself the Duke of Ravenna. He was the most formidable of the German chiefs whom Henry had placed in charge of the Italian cities; and by reason of his valor and cruelty was a favorite of the Emperor, who, on his death-bed, appointed him regent of Sicily. Conscious of his danger from Innocent, he attempted in vain to draw the Pope into an alliance with himself. Italy was restless under the German rule. Numerous cities successively renounced their allegiance to Markwald, and left him only Camerina and Ascoli. Innocent's cardinals banned him, received the oath of fealty from his subjects, and released them from their allegiance; and Markwald, after ravaging the whole territory adjoining Ravenna, retired to southern Italy. The Duke Conrad desired to hold Spoleto as a papal fief, but such was the popular hatred of the Germans that the Pope sent him home, and Tuscany, with the exception of Pisa and Spoleto, entered into a formal league in the papal interest, and bound itself to recognize no one as King or Emperor without the Pope's approval.

The old trouble, the inheritance of the Sicilian kingdom, again came to the front. The widow of Henry VI., immediately after her husband's death, had her son Frederick crowned at Palermo, and sent gifts to the Pope in order to secure his ratification. But Innocent demanded her renunciation of the four privileges granted first by Hadrian IV. and afterwards by Clement III. These were the refusal of the right to appeal to Rome, the visitation of papal legates only by the King's request, the confirmation by the King of all ecclesiastical appointments, and the holding of synods only in places where the King might be residing and with his permission. The Empress yielded, took the oath of fealty to the Pope, promised tribute, and received in return the kingdom of Sicily as a papal fief.

The unexpected death of Henry VI. awakened doubts as to whether the young Frederick would be recognized as heir to the German throne; and on the strength of these doubts, Philip of Suabia, in his anxiety to keep the crown in his own family, consented to his own election, and was crowned by the legate at Worms—a proceeding which was contrary to the Pope's wish, and was the introduction to a new and serious conflict.

By such proceedings Innocent labored to reëstablish the papal domination in Italy, and thereby to obtain the money for a comprehensive ecclesiastical administration. At the same time he aimed at the reformation of the Roman Curia, where bribery and extortion prevailed, and struck vigorously at these and other current abuses. He forbade all officers of the Curia to receive money beyond the prescribed fees for the issuing of bulls and briefs; he prohibited papal notaries from having doorkeepers in the anterooms to receive presents of money; and he banished the exchange-booths from the Lateran palace. He despatched business with great energy and promptness. A consistory was held three times a week, at which he personally dealt with more important matters; and his legal knowledge and administrative ability soon became so famed that legal experts came from far and near to learn of him. The register of his letters, more extensive than that of any of his predecessors, shows both by its contents and by its classical style how carefully and efficiently he administered his office.

He did not delay to take measures for the establishment of his authority in foreign countries. He interposed to prevent the scandalous marriage of the daughter of the King of Castile to her uncle, the King of Leon; and when the latter refused to obey, laid the kingdom under interdict. He also pronounced the ban upon the King of Navarre for his treachery towards the King of Castile, and commanded Cardinal Rainer to undertake a crusade against heretics in France, such as the Waldenses, Cathari, and Patarines. He directed the metropolitans of Aix, Narbonne, and other sees, to proceed against those who should attempt to establish new churches, "synagogues of the devil," to punish with exile and confiscation those who refused to submit, and to proclaim remission of sins to all who should take part in this crusade. The legate was also to demand of the King of Portugal the payment of Peter's pence, which was now ten years in arrear. He endeavored to persuade Philip of France to take back his lawful wife, not omitting to tell the King that he now dispenses justice not merely with princes but over them.

Richard of England received from him special tokens of distinction in memory of his former services and misfortunes, and as an enemy of the Hohenstaufen; but in the contest of the monks of Canterbury with their archbishop, Hubert, he took sides against Hubert and the King.

In the summer of 1198 the Pope addressed himself to the project of a new crusade, which appeared to him one of the most important duties of his pontificate. In a general letter he powerfully depicted the shameful condition of the holy places in the East, and announced that the crusade would take place the next March. Prelates were sent throughout Europe to make peace between princes and to exhort them to unite against the common enemies of God. Boxes were placed in all the churches to receive contributions. Priests were enjoined to command all penitents at the confessionals to support the enterprise, and to declare that no error could find pardon with God without at least the sincere will of participating in the crusade. Innocent ordered his own plate to be melted down, would allow only vessels of clay or wood on his table while the crusade lasted, and contributed a ship-load of provisions.

A five years' truce was effected between England

and France; but Philip persistently refused to separate from Agnes, and France was accordingly laid under interdict. Philip finally yielded; but though Agnes died soon after, he could not be induced to obey the Pope by again receiving Ingeborg. In the communications on this subject even the possibility of witchcraft was discussed. The Pope wrote to Philip that if he thought that the union with Ingeborg was made impossible by the work of the devil, he should nevertheless make the attempt with prayers, alms, and masses. If these should not avail, he would issue further instructions concerning the dissolution of the marriage by reason of the *impedimentum maleficii*. Later, a cardinal received orders to investigate the matter on the spot, and finally to send the Queen to Rome; and much anger was aroused by Innocent's legitimizing the sons of the dismissed wife and declaring them competent to inherit. The King did not resume his relations with Ingeborg until 1213, when, at the Pope's command, he was arming for a war with England, and was anxious to conciliate the people, and especially the King of Denmark.

With the project of the crusade there was bound up, as usual, that of the subjection of the Greek to the Roman Church. To the Byzantine Emperor, Alexius, Innocent wrote, congratulating him on his blessed privilege of defending the holy places, and reminding him that the Greek Church had been unfaithful to the Church of Rome, its rightful superior. He offered him remission of sins if he would participate in the crusade and arrange with the papal officers sent to him what was necessary for the prosperity of the empire and of the church. He also represented to the Patriarch of Constantinople that the Greek Church had withdrawn itself from the teachings of Peter and had broken the unity of the church, and exhorted him to forward the crusade and to see to it that "the daughter return to her mother, and that there be again one flock and one shepherd."

Naturally, Innocent was especially anxious to establish his secular supremacy in Italy. On his return to Rome in October, he exhorted the Tuscan authorities to continue obedient to the Papacy, basing his exhortation on the famous doctrine of the two lights. The papal power resembles the sun, the royal power the moon. The sun is greater than the moon in every respect, and dispenses light to it. The two heads of the two powers have their place in Italy, which, by divine ordainment, holds the primacy over all provinces. Italy, therefore, is the object of the Pope's special care. There lies the foundation of the Christian religion, and through it the primate of the apostolic church rules both kings and the heads of the priesthood.

Even in Italy, however, considerable repugnance to church domination manifested itself in many quarters; and accordingly Innocent sent instructions to Viterbo to regard all favorers of heretics as dishonorable, to prohibit them from holding office and from testifying and inheriting, and to treat their acts as invalid and their goods as confiscate. If through this true believers suffer injury, it is because they are punished for the guilt of their fathers, according to the divine word which declares that the sins of the fathers are visited upon the children. In spite of these brutal measures, Viterbo and Orvieto continued to be the headquarters of heresy in the papal territory, so that, later, new proceedings became necessary. The zeal for heresy-hunting endangered all who belonged to the Waldensians or Patarines; but as Innocent had learned that certain parties accused of heresy in the diocese of Verona had not departed from orthodoxy, he commanded the bishop to examine them, and if he should find them orthodox, to declare them Catholic and permit intercourse with them.

The Empress Constantia died in November, 1198, committing her son to the guardianship of the Pope, with a council of regency consisting of four prelates from southern Italy. Markwald took this opportunity to claim the administration of Sicily and the guardianship of young Frederick, alleging a testament of the Emperor to that effect. He attacked San Germano, and nearly succeeded in capturing Monte Cassino, but was finally compelled to return to Sicily, pursued by the proclamations of Innocent, and died not long after at Palermo.

The contest for the German throne now claimed the Pope's attention. Philip of Suabia, the only surviving son of Barbarossa, had, as already stated, been crowned King at Worms. The enemies of his house, headed by the Archbishops of Cologne and Treves, elected Otto IV., son of Henry the Lion, a Guelf. A weak and contested sovereignty in Germany was an opportunity for the Papacy. A powerful Emperor meant a German expedition into Italy, a struggle with the Pope, and a menace to his secular power in Germany. The Hohenstaufen were the born enemies of the Papacy, and the attempt of Henry VI. to make the crown hereditary in that house had failed, because it interfered with the claim of the see to assign the imperial crown at its pleasure. It was easy to predict, therefore, on which side the Pope's influence would be thrown. Otto of Brunswick, the son of the sworn enemy of the Hohenstaufen and the nephew of Richard of England, was sure to find favor at the papal court. But Innocent craftily kept himself in the background, knowing that the majority of the German princes was with Philip.

The fight broke out in 1198. Otto was crowned, according to custom, by the Archbishop of Cologne at Aachen, and then applied to the Pope for the imperial crown and the ban against those who refused to recognize him. Among other things he promised that he would not collect the revenues of vacant bishoprics—a question which, in Barbarossa's time, had led to repeated conflicts with the Pope. Otto's request was backed by the Archbishop of Cologne and other German princes, and by Richard of England. Philip also had himself crowned at Mainz by the Bishop of Tarantaise, with the participation of the papal legate, the Bishop of Sutri, who acted without commission.

Richard Cœur de Lion died in 1199, and his brother and successor, John, attempted to obtain from the Pope a decision in favor of Otto. Innocent at last informed the Archbishop of Cologne that he was not disinclined to declare for Otto. He exhorted the partisans of Philip not to destroy the unity of the empire, and said that he wished to decide for the one who had the majority and the greater merit. Meanwhile the Bishop of Sutri returned to Rome in Philip's commission, and Philip's friends among the German princes and Philip of France urged the Pope to bestow the imperial crown on him.

The Archbishop of Mainz, acting under the Pope's approval, managed that the contest should be decided by a commission of arbitration under his own presidency at Boppard. Otto repeated his request for the papal ban, and Philip sent commissioners to Rome, to whom Innocent, in full consistory, expounded the relations between the secular and the spiritual powers. The priest is higher than the King, since the priest anoints the King. The Lord in the Old Testament names the priests "gods," the kings only "princes." The priest has power over souls, the King over bodies; and as high as the soul is above the body, so high is the priest above the King. The reader may easily imagine the rest. No doubt the German envoys were greatly edified by this piece of allegorical exposition, of which Innocent appears to have been very fond, and which possessed the advantage of making Scripture prove anything he might desire.

From allegory he proceeded to history, declaring that under Barbarossa the empire was united while the church was divided; but the schism and he who fostered it were stricken to the earth. Now the church is one and the empire is divided. He concluded with the assertion, which had the old Hildebrandian ring, that the empire is granted as an investiture by the Pope. He sent a letter to all the German princes, commanding them to recognize the worthiest as King. He declared that Philip seemed to him to have the majority, but that in Otto's favor was the regularity of the coronation and the fact that the crown was not hereditary.

CHAPTER XXIX.

HERESY ATTACKED IN FRANCE—INNOCENT DECIDES FOR OTTO—THE CRUSADERS AT VENICE—THE NEW LATIN EMPIRE IN THE EAST.

T was not likely that Innocent would long keep his hands off that stronghold of heresy, southern France. Raymond VI. of Toulouse in 1195 succeeded his father in the possession of those vast territories in the south, which made him almost an independent sovereign. He was allied by marriage with the royal houses of Castile, Aragon, Navarre, France, and England, and was personally on friendly terms with the French King. His easy indifference to religious questions encouraged the spread of heresy in his dominions. Most of his barons were either favorably disposed towards the Cathari or belonged to them. Toleration had endured for nearly a generation; the land was prosperous and at peace; but the condition of the church was such as to excite the indignation of the Pope. It had fallen into such disrepute among the people that it seemed likely to disappear altogether. The small number of Catholics in proportion to the entire population indicated the extent

of the ravages of heresy, and the barons were rapidly despoiling the clergy of their possessions.

Among Innocent's first acts was a summons to the Archbishop of Ausch to extirpate heresy by the utmost ecclesiastical rigor, and if necessary by the aid of the secular power. Two commissioners were soon after sent to represent the see in the heretical region, armed with letters to all the princes, nobles, and people of southern France, empowering them to enforce whatever regulations might seem necessary by means of the secular power, by banishment, and by confiscation. For some time these measures only made matters worse; for the local prelates, angry at the special powers conferred upon the legates, and afraid of the exposure of their own evil lives, did not raise a finger to help the papal emissaries. Whenever the legates remonstrated with the heretics, they were answered by allusions to the idleness, licentiousness, and avarice of the clergy.

Innocent therefore took stronger measures. In May, 1204, he put at the head of the movement Arnaud of Citeaux, the superior of the Cistercians, a stern, resolute, and implacable man, and issued a commission with extraordinary powers. Ecclesiastical censures were to be abandoned, and force was to be employed. All impenitent heretics were to be delivered to the secular authority for perpetual proscription and confiscation of property; and remission of sins was to be offered to all who should aid in the holy work of suppressing heresy. A special clause authorized the legates to absolve all who were under excommunication for crimes of violence on condition of their joining in the heresy-hunt. Thus the Brabançons, Hainaulters, Aragonese, Catalans, and other bands of freebooters, idle and dissipated peasants ruined by war, outlaws, escaped criminals, outcast monks—wretches who had been the terror of the country, and who had been anathematized by the Third Lateran Council in 1179—were deliberately let loose by his Holiness, and encouraged by him to new atrocities in the interest of the religion of Christ. Innocent also wrote to Philip Augustus, urging him to draw the sword and "slay the wolves."

This attempt also failed. Again the local clergy refused to second the efforts of the papal legates. Philip held aloof, and even Pedro of Aragon refused the bait of a concession of all the lands and goods which he might acquire from heretics. Pierre de Castelnau, one of the legates, visited Provence and attempted to unite the nobles for the expulsion of heretics. Raymond refused, and the legate anathematized him and laid his territories under interdict, which sentence was confirmed by the Pope, who also wrote to Raymond in abusive style, threatening him with the vengeance of God here and hereafter, and with the division of his territories among the princes of Christendom. Raymond, however, remained indifferent. The Cistercian abbots became discouraged and retired; Raoul the legate died, and Arnaud was summoned elsewhere.

In the meantime Innocent had given his decision in favor of Otto. An obstacle had indeed presented itself in John of England's agreement with Philip of France, with whom he had just concluded peace, not to support Otto with money or troops without his approval; but the Pope disposed of this by the simple process of declaring the agreement invalid. Towards the end of the year 1200 he sent his legate to Germany with a bull awarding the crown to Otto. In this document he appealed to his right to approve the election of the German Emperor, on the ground that the empire had been transferred from the Greeks to the Germans through the Pope. Frederick was yet a child, and would eventually unite the Sicilian with the imperial throne, to the injury of the church. Against Philip was the fact that Cœlestine III. had banned him for occupying and plundering papal provinces, and that he had been absolved against the Pope's command and without giving satisfaction. He himself had also banned him for aiding Markwald. By recognizing Philip the succession would become hereditary, and this would be the more disastrous because his family had been persecutors of the church.

Such a piece of special pleading displayed the consciousness of a weak case. No immediate consequences followed, and Innocent accordingly sent three legates into Germany to exhort the princes to choose him who would best serve the empire and the church, or else to leave the decision to him. On the 1st of March he announced to Otto that, in virtue of his plenary apostolic power, he acknowledged him as King, and was resolved to give him the imperial crown.

Following this declaration a swarm of letters issued from the Pope to dignitaries of all ranks, civil and ecclesiastical, commanding or soliciting their support of Otto. On the 8th of June, 1201, Otto at Neuss took the oath to the Pope, swearing especially to defend his secular dominion and to help him to what was yet missing. He was proclaimed King at Cologne by the papal legate, Guido of Palestrina, in the Pope's name. The concourse of prelates and nobles which the legate had summoned to Cologne did not appear. Some of the bishops closed their doors against his messengers. He summoned them a second time, and began to threaten interdict; but he wrote to the Pope in encouraging terms, declaring that nothing was now heard of Philip and his partisans.

He was soon to hear. Even while he was writing, an assembly was convening at Bamberg—two archbishops, eleven bishops, the King of Bohemia, the Dukes of Saxony, Austria, Steyermark, Meran, Zähringen, the Stadtholder of Burgundy, with a number of other princes, and three abbots. The spirit of Barbarossa spoke out again in their words to the Pope. This language of the legate—surely the Pope has not authorized it! The presumptuousness of it! What ground can be cited for such pretensions? When has it been heard of that a Pope or his legate has dared to take part in the election of a King of the Romans, either as elector or judge? On the contrary, the Pope's election has been dependent upon the Emperor's consent. There is no higher council in a contested election for the empire than the princes of the empire. Let the Pope punish the legate for his presumption, acknowledge Philip, and crown him as is his duty. The King of France also reproached the Pope for becoming the protector of his enemy Otto, and threatened him with hostile measures.

In Innocent's reply, he disclaimed any intention of interfering with the rights of the electors, but reasserted his right and duty to test the fitness of him whom he had to consecrate and crown. He had respected the rights of the electors, and had withheld the imperial dignity from one who regarded it as his inheritance. He commended Guido for his dealing, and exhorted the somewhat timid Otto to be steadfast and to form an alliance with the Roman senate and people, and with the rectors and city authorities in Tuscany. He held that the oath of homage to Philip was invalid because he had rejected him, and peremptorily commanded the Archbishops of Salzburg, Magdeburg, and Bremen, Philip's partisans, to submit to Otto. In a similar tone he wrote to the King of France, representing that Otto had promised never to encroach on French interests, while he had the worst to fear from Philip.

The German bishops, however, were not scared by these pontifical thunders. They cared little or nothing for Innocent's excommunications. The most of them supported Philip during the entire contest. Almost all of them were princes, and related to the noble houses. The Archbishop of Mainz answered Innocent's excommunication by excommunicating him, and sent to Italy to persuade the cities of Romagna to throw off the papal yoke. The Archbishop of Cologne, who had crowned Otto, deserted him for his rival. The Bishops of Bamberg, Halberstadt, Spires, Passau, Eichstadt, and Friesingen openly defied the

Pope. The Archbishops of Salzburg, Magdeburg, Treves, Bremen, and Besançon declared for Philip. Conrad of Rabensberg, a Hohenstaufen and Philip's chancellor, was bought by the Pope with the bishopric of Würzburg. He was murdered soon after, and Philip refused to redress the crime.

Even a pontiff as clear-headed and resolute as Innocent might well be appalled at the problem which Germany thus presented; but these complications did not prevent him from pressing his crusade. The result of the crusades thus far had not been such as to encourage a new enterprise. The fearful waste of life, the countless atrocities, the loss of cities and strongholds won in bloody battle or siege, the failure of the great German expedition, the jealousies and dissensions among the crusaders themselves, the feud between the only real defenders of the Holy Land— the Knights Hospitallers and Templars—and the utterly depraved morals of the Christians in Palestine, were quite sufficient to deter the most ardent enthusiasts from a fourth attempt. Innocent, however, threw himself into the project as one conscious of a divine mission. European Christendom responded languidly. Richard of England and Philip of France were engrossed with their own quarrels, and Germany was torn by the factions of the rival emperors.

Enthusiasm was finally rekindled by the preaching of Fulk of Neuilly, who went forth as another Peter the Hermit under Innocent's commission, proclaiming the crusade in Normandy, Brittany, Burgundy, and Flanders. Through his fervid appeals and Innocent's incessant exhortations, the crusade was at last resolved upon. The fatal experience of the former land-marches through Europe determined the leaders to go by sea from Venice, which alone could furnish a fleet sufficient to transport so large an army. Six ambassadors from France accordingly went to Venice to arrange terms with the Venetian government. After eight days the Doge announced that the Republic would furnish transportation for forty-five hundred horses and nine thousand squires, and ships for forty-five hundred knights and twenty thousand infantry, would provision the fleet for nine months, and would furnish fifty galleys as its own share in the expedition, for the sum of eighty-five thousand marks.

In the spring of 1202 the army marched to Venice. The fleet was ready to set sail on their arrival, but the Venetians demanded payment in advance, and the crusaders were unable to command more than half the sum. Taking advantage of this, the Doge proposed to remit the remainder if the crusaders would assist the Republic in subduing the city of Zara,[1] which had been taken from it by the King of Hungary. The crusaders hesitated at employing their arms against a Christian city under the protection of the Pope, and at assuming the position of hirelings of the Venetian Republic. The Pope sent a special messenger to remonstrate against the undertaking, which he condemned as sacrilegious. The Doge, on his part, maintained that the Pope had no right to restrain the crusaders from a legitimate enter-

---

[1] In Dalmatia, on the Adriatic, one hundred and thirty miles southeast of Trieste. Anciently known as Jadara.

prise, a war against revolted subjects and pirates, who endangered the freedom of the seas and menaced the safety of pilgrims to the Holy Land. In order to remove all scruples he announced his own intention of participating in the crusade. Many of the Venetians pledged themselves to accompany him, and he thus won over the crusaders, and in a manner placed himself at the head of the enterprise.

Just as the host was ready to embark, messengers appeared from Alexius, the son of the dethroned and imprisoned Isaac, Emperor of Constantinople, entreating the aid of the crusaders to replace his father on his throne. Alexius himself made his way to Philip of Suabia, who had married his sister Irene, and who received him kindly, though he was unable to aid him by reason of his contest with Otto. He then applied to Innocent, who paid no attention to him, whereupon he appealed to the crusaders at Venice, where the arrival of his envoys excited great interest and sympathy. As everything was now ready, however, for the movement upon Zara, the consideration of his case was deferred, and the fleet set sail. They arrived before Zara in November, 1202. The city was rich, populous, and well fortified, and was defended by a Hungarian garrison. After five days it surrendered, and was given up to pillage, and the booty was divided between the Venetians and the French. A quarrel among the victors followed, in which more blood was shed than in the siege; and the season being now too far advanced for navigation, the Doge proposed that they should winter at Zara.

The Pope was anxious that the army should set

out for Syria; but messengers arrived from Philip of Suabia, who was desirous of placing his brother-in-law on the Byzantine throne, urging them to proceed to Constantinople. Much discussion followed. The Venetians, who bore a grudge against the Greeks, were far more disposed to make war on them than on the infidels; but it was finally determined to accept Alexius's proposals and to embark for Constantinople at the opening of the spring.

The history of this undertaking belongs to Dr. Ludlow's volume of this series. The Pope's position was embarrassing. The prospect of bringing the Greek Church into line once more was alluring; but, on the other hand, the conquest of Constantinople was directly in the interest of Philip of Suabia. Innocent finally expressed his disapproval of the expedition, but also his hope that terms of accommodation might be agreed upon, and that the debates concerning the Eastern Empire might be referred to him. Upon the crusaders who had embarked in the Byzantine enterprise, he showered reproaches, but to no purpose. Constantinople was taken, Isaac was liberated from prison, and the young Alexius was crowned in St. Sophia as joint Emperor with his father. His triumph was of short duration. Various causes contributed to create a revolution, which resulted in the death of Alexius by poison and strangling, and the crowning of a demagogue named Mourzoufle as Emperor. The crusaders again laid siege to the city, and after a terrible fight captured it, almost as much to their own surprise as to that of the Greeks. They now determined that a Latin Emperor should be placed on the Byzantine throne, and elected Baldwin, the Count of Flanders and Hainault.

Baldwin at once communicated with the Pope, assuring him that this victory was more important than the conquest of Palestine, because Constantinople was now at the service of the Roman Church and of the Holy Land. But he hoped now to accomplish the conquest of Palestine. The Pope might now, by a general letter, summon men of the West of every condition and race to assist him in his new empire. He entreated him especially to send clergy to instruct the Greeks, and to hold a great council in Constantinople in order to unite the new Rome with the old.

Innocent replied, congratulating Baldwin. The subjection of the Greek Church to the apostolic see, the transfer of the Byzantine empire from the hands of schismatics to those of Catholics, is the main feature of the victory. In a letter to the clergy who had taken part in the crusade, he dilated as follows: "In the Gospel narrative, as Mary Magdalene hastened to the sepulchre and told Peter and John that it was empty, Peter signified the Latins, among whom he labored till his death. John, who founded the churches in Asia, signified the Greeks. Mary Magdalene signified the Jews, for whom the Pharisees had buried the Messiah in the Old Testament so that they could not find him. John came more quickly to the tomb, meaning that the Old Testament was known to the Greeks earlier than to the Latins; but he did not enter the tomb, and did not see the Lord's napkin; that is, the Greeks had not acquired the complete understanding of the Old Testament, and especially of the secret of the Godhead. Peter, however, went into the grave, and saw everything; that is, the Latins had the full knowledge of the doctrine of the Trinity and of Christology," etc.

The Pope at once assumed the supervision of the new empire. All western sovereigns and prelates were commanded to maintain friendly relations with the new Latin kingdom. The clergy were exhorted to be active in subjecting the Greeks to the apostolic chair; they should see that the Latin service was celebrated in Constantinople, and should fill with Latins the places vacated by the Greeks, besides electing a bishop, to be installed by the Pope or his legate.

Next in importance to the election of the Emperor was the election of the Patriarch. The Latins in Constantinople undertook this duty, but Innocent formally quashed their action and himself named a candidate. After profuse allegorizing, according to his wont, he proceeded to say that as the Emperor had been selected from the French, the Venetians should be represented by the Patriarch, and they had actually chosen the Roman subdeacon Thomas Morosini. Their act was invalid; but as the subdeacon was worthy and well endowed, and as he, the Pope, desires to show himself gracious towards the Venetians, he nominates Thomas in virtue of his plenary power. By the erection of the church of Constantinople into a patriarchate, the Pope has shown that he is the representative of the God-man, who alone possesses such power.

CHAPTER XXX.

STEPHEN LANGTON—OTTO'S CAUSE WEAKENING—
THE TEMPLARS.

HE years from 1204 to 1207 presented a mesh of political and ecclesiastical affairs which taxed all the resources of the Roman see. Disturbances in Rome caused Innocent to withdraw in the spring of 1203, and he remained absent for nearly a year. From the beginning of his pontificate there had been a party opposed to him and to the establishment of the papal sovereignty. During his absence the malcontents took advantage of the approaching senatorial election to create disturbance, and the city again became a battle-field. The names of Rainer, Pierleone, Poli, Capoccio, Pandolfo, were bandied by the different factions. Where there were no stone towers, wooden ones were erected; ditches were dug, walls were thrown up, old baths and churches were converted into forts, slingers and bowmen were enlisted, and catapults planted. Many were slain, houses were destroyed, and even fire was used. Finally the storm spent itself, and the insurgents once more took the oath to the Pope.

In the East, Baldwin died in prison, and the Pope

recognized his brother Henry as Emperor. Serious complications were arising in England. Though the right of nominating to the bishoprics remained nominally with the chapters, the royal license was necessary before election, and the royal approval before consecration and taking possession of temporalities, so that the King had practically controlled appointments to the greater sees. Some of the English sees, however, which had grown out of monasteries or were connected with them, asserted the rights of chapters. Particularly the monks of Christ Church in Canterbury claimed the right of election to the metropolitan see, and stubbornly maintained the claim against the suffragan prelates.

Hubert, the Archbishop of Canterbury, died in 1205, and some of the junior monks of Christ Church, without waiting for the King's sanction, on the night of Hubert's death, secretly chose Reginald, their superior, installed him before midnight as archbishop, and, under pledge of strict secrecy, sent him to Rome to obtain the confirmation of his election. Reginald's vanity prompted him to disregard the obligation to secrecy, and to travel under the name and with the state of an archbishop; and the object of his journey soon became known in England. The King was enraged at the contempt shown for his authority, and the suffragan bishops at having been excluded from the election. The monks of Christ Church, disgusted with Reginald and repenting their haste, declared the election void, and under the royal sanction elected John de Gray, Bishop of Norwich and a leader in the King's council. He was enthroned in the King's presence, and invested with his temporalities by the King himself.

Innocent decided in favor of the right of the monks, and the papal court annulled the elections of both Reginald and John, and ordered the monks who appeared on behalf of the King and of Norwich to proceed to a new election at Rome, and to choose Stephen Langton, an Englishman by birth, but educated in France. The Pope endeavored to conciliate King John. He sent him four magnificent rings adorned with precious stones, accompanied by a letter in which he explained the moral significance of the jewels.[1] John, however, was very angry, and vowed that he never would acknowledge Langton. He wrote to the Pope, expressing his indignation, reminding him that he drew more wealth from England than from any kingdom beyond the Alps, threatening to forbid all communication between England and Rome, and declaring that Langton would set foot in England at his peril. The Pope responded by laying England under interdict.

In Germany, notwithstanding the efforts of the Pope, Otto's following had considerably diminished. Philip had ventured to approach Innocent with the largest promises—a crusade, restoration of all church property unlawfully acquired, not to appropriate the property of deceased prelates, free election, and reform of the clergy. If he should become lord of the Byzantine empire, he would subject the church of Constantinople to Rome. He would persistently

---

[1] See Richard Thomson, "Historical Essay on the Magna Charta," p. 513.

defend the Roman Church, would promote alliances of his daughters and relatives with relatives of the Pope, and would render satisfaction for former transgressions. All availed nothing. The unfaithfulness of the Archbishop of Cologne called forth from the Pope a menacing monition to obedience; and in order to make sure for the future of the spiritual princes of the empire, he issued an entirely novel mandate that the archbishops, on receiving the pallium, should issue a special document promising to obey the Pope even in affairs of the empire, and declaring that refusal merits punishment by suspension.

Philip's progress in Italy also caused Innocent much uneasiness. Otto's following in Germany had so diminished that Philip could venture to treat his own former coronation as invalid; and on the 1st of January, 1205, he was crowned again at Aachen by the Archbishop of Cologne, who was consequently banned in June following. Cologne was now almost the only community which remained faithful to Otto. By the next year he was so forsaken that he desired to conclude a truce with Philip, and the Pope undertook the office of mediator. Philip consented to submit to the arbitration of a commission of papal representatives and princes of the realm. He maintained his right, and repudiated the charge of having been banned by Cœlestine III. Innocent endeavored to effect a one year's truce; but from his sending the Patriarch of Aquileia to Philip, the rumor arose that he had abandoned Otto and was seeking to make peace with Philip. The truce was not made. Otto and Philip again crossed swords, and Philip succeeded in overpowering Cologne. This was followed by a splendid embassy from Philip to Rome, with promises of submission to the see.

About this time Innocent's attention was drawn to the Templars, against whom serious charges had been preferred. This remarkable order of priestly soldiers originated in Jerusalem in 1118, in the association of nine knights under a vow to the Patriarch of Jerusalem to guard the public roads between Jerusalem and the Jordan for the protection of Christian pilgrims. Baldwin II., the King of Jerusalem, allotted them quarters in his own palace near the site of Solomon's temple, whence their name Templars. He also commended them to Bernard of Clairvaux, from whose influence the order received the impulse to its subsequent wonderful development. The order was formally recognized by the Council of Troyes in 1128. Their original poverty, so great that two of their number had but one horse between them, was commemorated by the device on their seal of a war-horse with two riders.

They speedily became the right arm of the crusades, and their history for a hundred and forty years is the history of the crusades. Clad in armor from head to heel, with their long, naked swords at their sides and their lances in hand, led by their black-and-white banner called *Beauseant*, and which bore the inscription, " Non nobis, Domine, non nobis, sed nomini tuo da gloriam," they were always found where the danger was greatest and the fight hottest; and their close ranks, their lofty stature, and their war-horses in steel mail dispersed or bore down the battalions of the Saracens.

Long before Bernard's death in 1153, their order was established in almost every kingdom in Latin Christendom. The community was half monastic and half military. Its three orders were knights, chaplains, and men at arms. Its three vows were implicit obedience to superiors, chastity, and the renunciation of personal property. Their dress was originally a white mantle with a red cross; but the white was afterwards confined to knights, and the others wore black. Gold and silver ornaments on their arms or horse-trappings were prohibited.

Their devotion to the holy wars was soon rewarded with munificent gifts of land, castles, and wealth of all kinds. In less than a hundred and fifty years from their foundation they numbered twenty thousand knights and nine thousand houses or "commanderies" in Europe and in the East. They were powerful feudal lords in all the kingdoms of Europe; their property was scattered from Denmark to Spain, and from Ireland to Cyprus; they were almoners of kings and godfathers to their children, and both in Paris and in London their houses were used as strongholds for the royal treasure. They were also summoned to the great councils of the church.

When their great charter was issued by Alexander III., they had already ceased to be a lay community. Clergy had been admitted in considerable numbers, so that they administered within themselves all the rites of religion. The popes recognized their services to the crusades by conferring on them the largest privileges and exemptions. Their immunities increased greatly from the time of Alexander III., and were confirmed by Innocent III. Bishops were forbidden to pronounce excommunication or interdict upon them or their churches. All wares and necessaries for their use were exempt from duties. Taxes could be levied upon them only by the Pope. Their churches had the right of asylum; neither from the knights nor the chaplains of the order could the bishops require the oath of fealty; and they were allowed to disregard any official documents which contravened the liberties of the order. Their allegiance was to the Pope and to the Grand Master, whose instructions were absolutely binding on every member.

It would have been strange if an order thus practically independent of both civil and ecclesiastical authority had not developed abuses and corruptions. The actual extent of these will always be a matter of dispute. No doubt their familiar intercourse with Islamite nobles and princes tended to relax the rigidity of their faith; and it was charged that they had so far yielded to such influence as to be guilty, in many cases, of scornful denial of the Saviour. Their reputation for strictness of morals deteriorated. It was said that in their secret conclaves they celebrated blasphemous and obscene rites, idolatries identical with those of the ancient Ophites or serpent-worshippers.[1] To these charges were added those of effem-

---

[1] The subject is discussed by Hallam, "View of the State of Europe During the Middle Ages," in the fifteenth note to chap. i. He refers to an essay in the elaborate work of Von Hammer, " Mines de l'Orient

inacy, haughtiness, falsehood, and avarice. It was asserted that they performed service in churches which were under interdict, that they would attach the sign of the cross to the breast of any vagabond, and that for an annual payment of two or three pence they would guarantee Christian burial even to the excommunicate.

Innocent, who had been their steadfast and powerful friend, was evidently satisfied that there were substantial grounds of complaint. He felt that the order had gone too far in the setting aside of the bishops; and he rebuked them, telling them that many of their members wore the cross but did not follow its teaching; that instead of being a savor of life unto life they were a savor of death unto death. He warned them that abuses like those alleged against them would be followed by withdrawal of their privileges; and he summoned the Grand Master to answer to these charges under penalty of severe measures.

exploitées," which draws its evidence from a comparison of the sculptures extant on certain Gnostic and Ophitic bowls with those in churches built by the Templars. He declares that the images and symbols in some of the churches are extremely obscene. This portion of Von Hammer's work appeared in 1855 under the title "Die Schuld der Templer." The modern literature of the subject is quite extensive. Among the prominent works may be mentioned: Loiseleur, " La Doctrine Secrète des Templiers " (1872); Hans Prutz, " Geheimlehre und Geheimstatuten des Tempelordens " (1879); F. Jacquot, " Défense des Templiers," etc. (1882).

CHAPTER XXXI.

THE ALBIGENSIAN CRUSADE.

E come now to one of the darkest pages in the history of the Papacy, and to the foulest blot on the character and administration of Innocent III.—the crusade against the Albigenses. In the study of this episode, every right-thinking reader rises above theological and ecclesiastical differences into the region of common human rights and natural humane instincts. The movement was the legitimate outcome of the Hildebrandian idea, and was instinct with its spirit.

The essential facts of the case, succinctly stated, are these: A large, peaceful, and prosperous province, governed by a generous and tolerant prince, embraced in its population large numbers of sectaries. Although later Christian thought condemns some of their tenets as erroneous, they were industrious, loyal, and orderly. Their pure morality was in strong contrast with that of the licentious, avaricious, and lazy clergy of the established church, and the fervor of their devotion with the idle and heartless ceremonies of papal worship. Upon this community Innocent fixed his eye, and determined to bring it, by force if necessary, into conformity with Romish dogma and practice. Upon this peaceful and moral population his mandate let loose all the power of the secular arm, and encouraged, by promises of papal indulgence, bands of freebooters—men without conscience and without pity, and stained with every crime—to act as his agents in enforcing submission. The Vicegerent of God, the man who delighted to represent himself as commissioned by the God-man, precipitated upon these unoffending and defenceless people all the horrors of murder, rapine, and unbridled lust, for the glory of God and the honor of the church of Christ.

It has already been noted that Innocent, in May, 1207, confirmed the excommunication pronounced by his legate, Pierre de Castelnau, upon Raymond VI. of Toulouse, and that all his efforts had failed to convince or convert the heretics. Letters representing the alarming growth of heresy caused him, in November of the same year, to proclaim a crusade against the heretical province, offering the same indulgence as to volunteers for Palestine, and engaging to take under the special protection of the church the lands of all who should enlist in the good work. All creditors of crusaders were to postpone their claims without interest, and the lands of heretics were to be abandoned to the spoilers. The proclamation, however, did not meet with an immediate response. To the Pope's appeal to Philip of France for coöperation, the King replied coldly that his relations with England would not allow him to divide his forces, but intimated that he would assist if he could be assured of a two years' truce, and if the

Murder of Pierre de Castelnau.   339

barons and knights of France should be disposed to engage in the crusade.

Matters were brought to a crisis by the murder of Pierre de Castelnau, which the bishops who carried the report to Rome unjustly attributed to the instigation of Raymond. In March, 1208, Innocent issued letters to all prelates in the heretical provinces, commanding them to excommunicate the murderers and abettors, including Raymond, releasing all Raymond's vassals from their allegiance, and declaring his lands to be the lawful prey of any Catholic who might possess himself of them. Letters were also sent to Philip and his chief barons, urging them to take part in the crusade. Commissioners were sent to negotiate a two years' truce between England and France, and Arnaud of Citeaux called a general chapter of his order, at which it was resolved to devote all its energies to preaching the crusade. Many great nobles responded, and contingents came from Germany and Lombardy.

Raymond appealed in vain to both Philip of France and Otto of Germany. He then went to the council held by Arnaud at Aubinas, to prove his innocence and to make peace; but he was refused a hearing, and applied to Rome for terms of submission. Innocent demanded that, as security for his good faith, he should place in his hands his seven most important strongholds, after which he should be heard. Raymond consented, and the two new legates, Milo and Theodisius, treated him with great friendliness. Raymond did not know that they had instructions from Innocent to beguile him with fair promises, detach him from the heretical interest, and, when the heretics should have been disposed of by the crusaders, to deal with him as they pleased. He was played with with the most devilish cruelty and craft. His seven castles were delivered, and his power of resistance was thus weakened; and he was then formally reconciled to the church with the most humiliating ceremonies. All that he gained by his submission was the privilege of joining the crusade and subjugating his own territory; and the excommunication was soon renewed on the flimsy pretext that he had not within sixty days performed the impossible task of expelling all heretics.

The crusaders assembled to the number of twenty thousand horsemen and over two hundred thousand foot at Lyons on the 24th of June, 1207. Raymond Roger of Béziers, the nephew of Raymond of Toulouse, had garrisoned his capital at the approach of the crusaders, but withdrew to Carcassonne. Reginald, the Bishop of Béziers, was with the crusading army, and obtained permission to offer the city of Béziers full exemption if the heretics should be delivered up or expelled. The offer was refused, the city was carried by storm, a horrible massacre followed, and the city was burned. Another detachment of the crusaders overpowered the castle of Chasseneuil, and the inhabitants were given their choice between conversion and the stake. Most of them preferred the latter. Innumerable strongholds were surrendered without resistance, and a mountainous region, bristling with castles, which might have held out for years, was occupied in a month or two.

Surrender of Carcassonne.

The army moved on to Carcassonne, where Raymond Roger had determined to make the last stand. A siege was commenced, and the two outer suburbs were carried and burned. Raymond was offered the privilege of departing with eleven others if he would surrender the city. He refused; but the town was crowded with refugees, the heat was intense, and the water-supply failed, causing pestilence. Raymond Roger was decoyed into the crusaders' camp on pretence of negotiation, was treacherously detained, and died soon after. The city was surrendered, and the people were allowed to depart with barely enough clothing to cover their nakedness.

The siege of Carcassonne introduces two men who played a prominent part in this movement—Simon de Montfort and Pedro of Aragon. Pedro was the suzerain of Béziers. He was regarded as a model of chivalry and religious zeal no less than of licentious gallantry. In 1204 he had taken the oath to Innocent with a pledge to exterminate heresy, had offered his kingdom to the Roman see, and had subjected it to an annual tribute. Montfort was the younger son of the Count of Evreuse, a descendant of Rollo the Norman, and Earl of Leicester by his mother's right. He had served in the crusade of 1201, under Baldwin of Flanders.

After the capture of Carcassonne the conquered territory was bestowed upon Montfort; but the withdrawal of the great body of the crusaders left him with only a small force, consisting mostly of Burgundians and Germans, and the homage which he received from his new vassals was only formal. Notwithstanding this, he succeeded in mastering additional strongholds, and extended his dominion over the Albigeois. He made haste to get into Innocent's good graces, since the Pope's confirmation was necessary to his new dignity, and his assistance important for maintaining it. He offered liberal tribute, which was accepted; but Innocent excused himself from sending military aid on account of complaints from Palestine that forces had been diverted from the rescue of the holy places by the French crusade.

A new campaign was begun in 1210 by Montfort in order to master the castles which still held out; and the reduction of these was attended with the usual atrocities. Arnaud of Citeaux was resolved on Raymond's ruin, and Montfort was eager to extend his own dominion. In 1209 Toulouse had been summoned by the legate to surrender all whom his emissaries might select as heretics. The Toulousans appealed to the Pope, protesting that there were no heretics. Raymond went to Rome and demanded a trial. Innocent declared that the Toulousans had justified themselves, and instructed the Archbishops of Narbonne and Arles to call a council for the trial of Raymond; but a letter of Innocent to Arnaud informed him that the matter had been intrusted to the new legate, Theodisius, merely as a lure for Raymond. To lull Raymond's suspicions, the Pope presented him with a splendid robe and a ring. Arnaud assumed a friendly demeanor. He and Montfort visited Raymond in Toulouse, and were splendidly entertained. Raymond, with his easy, credulous nature, was a puppet in the hands of these two.

"Tra male gatte era venuto 'l sorco."

The offer of the opportunity for purgation was a fraud and a farce. The legates knew that Raymond would clear himself, and the readiest method of eluding this lay in charging him with failure to perform the impossible task of clearing his land of heresy. A day three months distant was appointed for him to appear and purge himself of heresy, and when he presented himself at that time he was informed that his purgation could not be received until he should have suppressed heresy in his territories. Innocent's approbation of this dastardly trick appears in his letter to Raymond in December, 1210, expressing his sorrow that he had not fulfilled his promise, and warning him that his lands would be delivered to the crusaders in case of his failure to do so.

Raymond awoke at last to the fact that his ruin was designed, and began to prepare for war. The siege of Toulouse was determined upon by the crusaders, and the Toulousans were informed that they would not be spared unless they should drive Raymond from the city and renounce their allegiance to him. They refused, and made so heroic a defence that Montfort was forced to retire. This was followed by a fresh excommunication of the city, and Raymond now took the field, but with little success. The crusade was still preached; Montfort's army was renewed by fresh swarms of pilgrims, and the war was prosecuted with savage ferocity. By 1212 Raymond's territories were reduced to Montauban and Toulouse, and Toulouse was practically beleaguered. Innocent now seemed to awake to a sense of his treachery. Raymond's dominions had been seized, yet he himself had had no trial or conviction. On Montfort's applying for confirmation of his conquests, Innocent affected surprise. He said that, though suspected of heresy, Raymond had never been convicted. He did not know why the opportunity for purgation ordered by him had never been afforded! In the absence of formal trial and conviction, his lands could not be assigned to another.

This was followed by a letter to Theodisius and the Bishop of Riez, cautioning them not to be remiss in their duty as they had been. To this Theodisius replied with the transparent falsehood that he had repeatedly summoned Raymond to justify himself, and that Raymond had neglected to make reparation to certain prelates and churches. A council was called at Avignon, to give a pretext for pushing Raymond to the wall; but Avignon was unhealthful, many prelates refused to attend, and Theodisius was sick. Another council was summoned at Lavaur, not far from Toulouse. Pedro of Aragon now appeared as Raymond's protector. He could not be indifferent to the growing power of Montfort. The conquered fiefs were being filled with Frenchmen, and a parliament had just been held to organize the institutions of the country on a French basis. Pedro had already sent to Innocent, complaining of the action of the legates, and he came to Toulouse to intercede for Raymond.

Pedro's envoys secured from Innocent a command to Montfort to surrender all lands taken from those who were not heretics, and instructions to Arnaud not to let the Toulousan war interfere with the crusade against the Saracens. At Lavaur, Pedro produced a general cession to himself, by Raymond, of all his territories, with similar cessions by several other counts. He asked restitution of these lands on condition that their owners should give satisfaction to the church. But the prelates, led by Arnaud, were bent on the destruction of Toulouse, and refused to admit Raymond to purge himself, and even refused him an interview, while they threatened Pedro with excommunication for intercourse with heretics and excommunicates. Theodisius and some bishops were sent to Rome to urge Innocent not to draw back, and hey painted Raymond in the darkest colors. Letters poured in from bishops in every part of southern France, declaring that all that was needed was the destruction of Toulouse, and that if Raymond were allowed to raise his head chaos would come again.

Innocent had solemnly declared that Raymond should have the opportunity of vindicating himself, and should be condemned only after trial; but he yielded to this pressure, and wrote to Pedro to cease protecting heretics under penalty of being himself the object of a new crusade. The orders which had been sent him for the restoration of non-heretical lands were recalled, as having been granted on misrepresentation. Toulouse could obtain reconciliation only by the banishment of those whom its fanatical bishop, Foulques, might designate as heretics.

Meanwhile the crusade had been vigorously preached in France, and Louis, Philip's son, with many barons, had taken the cross, when Philip's preparations to invade England put a stop to the movement. Pedro entered into closer alliance with Raymond, and received the oath of fealty from the inhabitants of Toulouse. He then formally declared war, and besieged Muret, ten miles from Toulouse, where he was utterly defeated by Montfort, and lost his life. In 1214 the Counts of Toulouse, Foix, and Comminges, the Viscount of Narbonne, and the city of Toulouse gave their unqualified submission to the Pope's legate, and engaged to expel heretics; and Raymond placed his dominions in the legate's hands.

But the land did not receive peace with submission. Montfort had been reduced to severe straits. Toulouse had put him on the defensive, and Narbonne had refused him entrance; and the legate was merely playing a game to tide him over the time of his weakness and to divert the provinces until new recruits should join the crusading army. These now poured in in swarms. Their first exploit was the capture of Maurillac, where appears the first distinct reference to the Waldenses in the history of the war. Seven of them were found among the captives and burned. Montfort extended his authority over the Agenois, Quercy, Limousin, Ronergue, and Périgord; and resistance being at an end, the legates, in 1215, assembled a council at Montpellier, where Raymond was deposed and Montfort elected lord over the whole territory. Innocent's confirmation was obtained, together with the declaration that Raymond was deposed for heresy, though he had never had the trial which had been promised him.

By the battle of Bouvines, in 1215, in which Otto

and the King of England were defeated by France, Louis was released for the performance of his crusading vow. The two Raymonds, father and son, had withdrawn to await the great council at which the elder Raymond's fate was to be decided, and which met in St. Peter's in November, 1215. Here it was assumed that Raymond had been found guilty of heresy. He was deprived of his dominions, and sentenced to dwell elsewhere, and all the territories won by the crusaders, along with Toulouse, were assigned to Montfort. The decision was the signal for revolt. The elder Raymond proceeded to Spain to raise troops, and the whole South rose to welcome him. Montfort set fire to Toulouse, but the citizens barricaded the streets and held out until he agreed to spare it for thirty thousand marks. He, however, destroyed what remained of the walls and disarmed the inhabitants.

Innocent died in July, 1216, but Honorius III. prosecuted the crusade. Montfort, having crossed the Rhone, was rapidly subduing the territories left to young Raymond, when he was recalled by the report that Toulouse was in revolt, and that Raymond VI. had been received there with auxiliaries from Spain. He hastened back, and in September, 1217, commenced the second siege, which continued for nine months, and was resisted with desperate courage by the citizens. Montfort was killed by a stone from a mangonel, worked, it was said, by women. He is commemorated in an odd rilievo in the exquisite little church of St. Nazaire, at Carcassonne, representing the assault of Toulouse. The besieged are bringing a mangonel to bear, and some angels are conveying the soul of Montfort into the sky. His death was regarded as the signal of liberation, and wherever the garrisons were not too strong, the people rose, massacred the invaders, and returned to their former lords.

Honorius III. recognized Montfort's son, Amauri, as his successor, banned the two Raymonds, and granted Philip a twentieth of the ecclesiastical revenue for another crusade. Louis led another army against Toulouse, with no better success than before. The heretics reappeared as soon as the invaders had withdrawn, and heresy was openly preached and taught. The church was regarded as the national enemy. Philip refused to renew the crusade, and Raymond VI. died in August, 1222. His body lay unburied for a century and a half in the house of the Hospitallers.

It is needless to follow the history further through the negotiations of Raymond VII., King Louis, Amauri, and Arnaud. Another crusade was organized on a large scale, was led by Louis, and attacked Avignon, which capitulated; but on approaching Toulouse, Louis, for some unknown reason, abandoned the enterprise and returned. Raymond continued the struggle for some time with varying success, until, under Pope Gregory IX., in April, 1229, peace was finally concluded by Raymond's complete submission to the church. Two thirds of his dominions were sacrificed, and the fortifications of Toulouse were destroyed. The church had conquered, but she had only begun. The next stage was the Inquisition.

CHAPTER XXXII.

INNOCENT ABANDONS OTTO—TROUBLES IN THE EAST—MURDER OF PHILIP AND RECOGNITION OF OTTO—A NEW CONTEST BETWEEN INNOCENT AND OTTO—FREDERICK OF HOHENSTAUFEN CROWNED.

URING the year 1207 Philip's cause had prospered in Germany. While waiting for the result of the embassy which he had sent the previous year to Rome, he strove in every way, by alliances, assemblies, and journeys, to extend his influence in the empire, especially in those regions where Otto's friends were most numerous. From Frankfort, early in February, he went to Gelnhausen, where he betrothed his third daughter, Maria, to Henry, the son of Henry of Lower Lorraine. The citizens of Cologne begged him to honor them with a visit, and he entered the city the evening before Easter, and was formally received by the clergy and welcomed with the acclamations of the people.

Innocent had fostered the war in Germany for ten years, only to be defeated. Otto's cause had become desperate, and the Pope, who was not celebrated for keeping faith where his interests were involved, felt compelled to abandon him and to break his pledges of alliance. He arranged to send the cardinals Hugolino and Leo of the Holy Cross to Germany. They were to obtain from Philip a pledge to render the oath to the Pope in respect of all for which he had been banned, and to acknowledge the Pope's commands, in return for which the cardinals had authority to absolve him. They were to insist on his dismissal of the army which he had collected against Otto, and to bring about a meeting of the two rivals, and a truce of a year if peace could not be effected.

Innocent announced this embassy to all the spiritual and secular princes of the realm. Philip's embassy, returning from Rome, preceded them in order to announce their speedy arrival and to procure their safe-conduct. They arrived in August. Philip received them at Speyer, and entertained them splendidly at his own cost. He gave the required oath, and was absolved. As soon as the tidings of this reached the Pope, he sent a special messenger to congratulate Philip on his return to the church, and to assure him of his countenance. The legates then proceeded to negotiations for peace. An assembly was convoked at Nordhausen, and another later at Quedlinburg. The legates proposed that Otto should marry Philip's eldest daughter, Beatrix, and should obtain certain properties with her; should renounce the royal title and recognize his father-in-law as King. Otto, however, was angry at being offered a price for the crown; the attempt at a treaty failed, and the most that could be secured was a truce.

Neither was the state of affairs in the East satisfactory to the Pope. However conciliatory his dealings with the Greeks, the establishment of a Latin empire and the placing of Latins in the episcopal chairs was regarded by them as an intolerable act of violence, against which they were in constant revolt. The energy of the conquerors was enervated by the climate, by the riches of Greece, and by the long sojourn in Constantinople, and corruption was fast creeping into the crusading host. The Greeks, driven at last to desperation, formed a conspiracy under Theodore Lascaris with the Bulgarians under King Joannicius; and the crusaders, who were widely dispersed in Greece and Asia Minor, found themselves assailed by a furious and pitiless enemy. At Adrianople, in Thrace, they suffered a crushing defeat from the united Greeks, Bulgarians, and Tartars, who took possession of the provinces, massacred twenty thousand Armenian allies of the crusaders at Natolia, desolated the shores of the Hellespont, and penetrated into Thessalonica. The Pope's exhortations to the Christians of the West to take up arms for the relief of the Latins in Byzantium fell upon deaf ears or were evaded under various pretexts. The King of Hungary alone raised a force to march to Constantinople. The crusading enthusiasm had cooled under the long succession of disasters, and the warriors whom spear and sword could not frighten shrank from the menaces of pestilence and famine.

Innocent did not relax his efforts. Every new obstacle seemed to stimulate him to bring all his energies and all the influence of his position to bear upon the eastern enterprise. Nor were his efforts wholly unavailing. The German princes agreed to a general crusading tax throughout the empire; the Templars and Hospitallers at Jerusalem obtained authority to devote the contributions of the Cistercians, about a thousand pounds, to this purpose; a cardinal was sent to France, and many French knights were persuaded to enlist; and the Pope's eloquence was expended without stint to induce the faithful in Lombardy and in the March to take up arms.

During the year 1208 affairs in Germany took a tragical turn. Philip, after his reconciliation, had obtained the Pope's recognition, and had good reason to expect the imperial crown. At the beginning of June he was in Bamberg, the appointed rendezvous of his army. He had celebrated the betrothal of his niece, the daughter of Otto, Duke of Burgundy, with the Duke of Meran. Owing to some malady, he had himself bled, and was lying on his bed at midday in a chamber of the episcopal palace, when Otto of Wittelsbach demanded audience on pretended business of importance, and, entering, struck Philip dead with a blow of his sword.

Innocent received the news at Sora, and expressed the strongest abhorrence of the act and of its perpetrator. Otto at once took steps to revive his sunken fortunes. Though he at first entertained thoughts of revenge on those who had resisted his elevation, he yielded to wiser counsels, and agreed to submit his election to an assembly of princes. This moderation won him the support of many of Philip's former partisans. He hastened to address himself to the Pope in order to secure his influence with the princes. The

Pope, who had so recently abandoned him, assured him of his unchanged favor, and accompanied the assurance with sundry pious exhortations. As there was already some talk of the succession of Frederick II., Otto must energetically guard his own rights. At the same time Innocent wrote to the German bishops that, though he abhorred the act of Philip's murder, it was a favorable dispensation of God. He forbade them to crown a new king under penalty of ban. God had visibly confirmed the election of Otto.

An assembly at Arnstädt decided to elect Otto. His formal recognition took place at Frankfort in November, 1208, by a numerously attended diet of princes and other dignitaries. With a view to avoiding new complications, the diet decided that henceforth descent should confer no claim to the crown, and that the election of the German sovereign should be once for all in the hands of the Archbishops of Mainz, Cologne, and Treves, the Palgrave of the Rhine, the Duke of Saxony, and the Count of Brandenburg, to whom the King of Bohemia should subsequently be added.

The Pope was delighted. The cities of Italy paid homage to Otto, and on the 22d of March, 1209, at Speyer, he gave the guarantees required by the Pope —subjection to the papal chair, freedom of episcopal elections and of appeals to Rome, renunciation of episcopal revenues during the vacancy of benefices, persecution of heretics, and maintenance of the Pope's secular power in Italy. In May he celebrated his betrothal to Beatrix, the daughter of Philip, as a means of conciliating the Hohenstaufen, and in October following arrived at Rome. The Saturday after his arrival he went to St. Peter's to offer prayer. He was attended by a brilliant cortége of prelates and princes, and by six thousand men in armor, besides a great number of archers. For some unknown reason a fight took place, in which some of the Germans were killed and the Bishop of Augsburg was roughly handled. The coronation took place on the 24th of October, 1209, with great magnificence, in St. Peter's. The same night the fray broke out again. The Romans made a furious onslaught on the German knights, and a large number of men and horses were killed.

Even at the meeting of the Pope and the Emperor at Viterbo, just before the coronation, a division was foreshadowed by Innocent's demand that Otto should surrender, immediately after his coronation, the lands of the church now occupied by his troops. Irritation was also created by the attack in the city on the German troops. These seeds of strife rapidly fructified. Otto remained in Italy after his coronation in order to secure his imperial rights. He took possession of the cities on the frontier of the Mathilde territory, and consulted the jurists as to his rights over that territory. They replied that the Emperor had surrendered those rights in ignorance, and might resume them. The principal Tuscan cities opened their gates to him. He visited Ferrara, Imola, Piacenza, and Milan, and confirmed to them the franchises granted by former emperors, reconciled their parties, appeased their animosities, and endeavored by every means to bind them to himself.

He then proceeded to attack church territories in Campania. There were not wanting those in Rome who desired his success and the restoration of the former imperial dignity. His proceedings became more and more offensive. He so guarded the cities and strongholds that nobody could come to Rome without his consent. Clergy carrying papal letters from the city were robbed of them, many strangers on their way to the city were forced to return, and even crusaders were set upon and maltreated.

Innocent wrote to the Emperor, bidding him consider how he owed his elevation to the Pope, and acknowledge the Lord of heaven, who thrusts down the mighty from their thrones and uplifts the poor. Otto is not content with the limits which satisfied his predecessors, but is attempting to fall upon the inheritance of St. Peter, which it is his duty to enlarge rather than to diminish. The Pope is sacredly bound to defend the property of the church with the sword of the Spirit. God punishes the great as the small. Let him beware lest God uproot him from the land of the living. If Otto persists in his course he will be compelled to anathematize him.

Otto replied that he had no wish to trespass upon the Pope's spiritual authority, but that the secular power belonged to himself. He intended to subject all Italy. He attempted to seize the Norman territories, the heritage of Frederick of Hohenstaufen, to add Sicily to his dominions, and to expel Frederick. The excommunication was at last launched; all the bishops of Italy were commanded to publish it, and Otto's subjects were released from their allegiance.

The Pope now turned to the King of France, who had persistently opposed Otto's election, and wrote to him that he had been deceived in the Emperor, who was carrying his haughty assumption so far that he desired to subject all the kings of the earth; that Otto had rejected his exhortations to keep peace with France, and had declared that so long as Philip held possession of the territory of his uncle, John of England, on French soil, he could not lift up his eyes for shame. Let Philip therefore remain faithful to the Roman Church. Philip received this communication with great joy, and gave orders to prepare for war with the Emperor.

But Otto's cause was waning in Germany. He had been absent for nearly three years, and the way was prepared for the Hohenstaufen to regain the crown. The publication of the ban was enthusiastically welcomed, especially in Suabia, where Otto's oppressions had created discontent. The bishops saw the danger which threatened the church if some bounds were not set to his pretensions; a dangerous confederacy was rapidly growing, and several cities of Italy were already in declared alliance with Innocent and Frederick. The decision was finally taken at an assembly at Nürnberg to depose Otto and make Frederick King, and two commissioners were sent to invite him to accept the crown.

It was hard for the Pope to take up the cause of the Hohenstaufen, whom he cordially hated and who had brought so many evils upon the church; but Otto's ingratitude rankled in his breast, and he entertained the hope of binding Frederick to himself by his favors. The German embassy appeared at Palermo, and presented to young Frederick, only seventeen years of age, the letter of the princes inviting him to accept the crown. His young wife remonstrated; the nobles of Sicily reminded him of the artfulness of the Germans; but he burned for revenge on Otto, who had menaced his Sicilian kingdom; he was stirred by the prospect of restoring his house to its former dignity; he thought he saw the succession secured in his first-born son; and he turned his back on the sunny skies of the South and on the voluptuous luxury of the Sicilian court, to begin one of the saddest records of mediæval history.

It was too late for Otto to quell the revolt in Germany. Italy was estranged from him. His cruelty and avarice had alienated many of his former friends. He hastened to celebrate his marriage with Beatrix, with the hope of drawing to himself a portion of the Guelfs;[1] but Beatrix died only a few days after the wedding, poisoned, it was rumored, by Otto's Italian mistresses; and the Suabians and Bavarians deserted his camp and went over to Frederick. The Pope was behind Frederick with blessings and gold. The

---

[1] The terms "Guelf" and "Ghibelline" first appear as party names in Germany in 1140, in the forms of "Welf" and "Waiblingen." Both were family names. Henry the Proud was of the house of Welf, and aspired to the succession on the death of Lothair, and consequently hesitated to acknowledge Conrad III., of the house of Hohenstaufen, who was chosen. In the war which followed, Count Welf, the brother of Henry the Proud, was besieged in Weinsberg, and during the siege his followers raised the cry "Welf!" while the besiegers shouted "Waiblingen!" which was the birthplace of Conrad's brother, Frederick of Suabia. The names were converted into "Guelfo" and "Ghibellino" by the Italians, and came to represent respectively the papal and the imperial party.

young prince was welcomed at Rome by the cardinals and the senate. Avoiding the Pass of Trent, which was guarded by Otto's partisans, he made his way by obscure routes to Coire, and occupied Constance a few hours in advance of Otto, who found its gates closed against him. All Germany along the Rhine declared for him, and he became master of South Germany almost without a battle. He was crowned at Aachen on the 25th of July, 1215; and Otto, after one more desperate attempt to recover his power, retired to his paternal estates, and died in poverty and humiliation at the Hartzburg on the 19th of May, 1218.

CHAPTER XXXIII.

INNOCENT AND JOHN OF ENGLAND—THE CHILDREN'S CRUSADE—THE TWELFTH GENERAL COUNCIL—DEATH OF INNOCENT III.

URING the revolution in Germany the contest between King John of England and the papal court had been maturing. Innocent laid England under interdict in the spring of 1208. John uttered dreadful threats against prelates who should dare to proclaim the interdict. The sheriffs were ordered to expel all such from the realm, and the greatest outrages were perpetrated, by the King's orders, upon their persons and property. Langton wrote to John, urging him to submit. John replied that Langton was not canonically chosen, but that if he would renounce his assumed right, the rights of Canterbury should be cared for to the honor of the royal majesty and not to Langton's disadvantage. John, however, did not wish to break absolutely with the Pope, and accordingly sent envoys to say that he would acknowledge Langton out of reverence for the Pope, but would not personally confer upon him the investiture of the archiepiscopal property, since he could not bring

himself to regard him with complacency. That office he would transfer to the Pope.

Innocent accordingly commissioned the Bishops of London, Ely, and Worcester to confer the investiture in his name, though he wrote to John that it would be more creditable if he should perform that office himself. This was soon followed by another letter, rebuking the King and threatening him with excommunication: "See! the bow is bent. Flee from the arrow which has not yet flown, that it wound thee not!"

As this warning produced no effect, Innocent commissioned the Bishops of London, Ely, and Worcester to pronounce the excommunication and to send the sentence for publication to the few prelates still remaining in the kingdom. The three bishops, however, dared not return from Flanders, where they had taken refuge, and the bishops who remained in England had not the courage to obey the Pope's command, so that only a vague rumor of the excommunication was circulated. Geoffrey, Archdeacon of Norwich, who was employed in the royal exchequer, ventured in open council to declare his scruples against intercourse with the excommunicated sovereign, and his courage cost him his life; for the King pursued him to Norwich, threw him into prison, and had him incased in a leaden mantle.

The Pope could not enforce the proclamation of the ban. The people patiently endured the suspension of public worship, and the secular barons regarded with malicious delight the distress of the bishops, and displayed great zeal in the King's service. Innocent also took decisive measures with reference to the property of Berengaria, Richard's widow, which John persisted in withholding from her on one pretence and another. The Pope commanded a settlement within six months. If this should not be made, the estates belonging to the Queen should be put under special interdict until all obligations were discharged. John refused settlement, and soon committed a new outrage by laying a tax on the diocese of York; and when the archbishop proposed to go to Rome and protest, the King seized his property and enjoined his jurisdiction.

Such was the condition of affairs up to 1212, when Innocent formally released John's subjects from their allegiance, and forbade all intercourse with the King under pain of excommunication. Now appeared Pandolfo, the Pope's legate, with a papal embassy, and had an interview with John at Northampton, where he demanded the return of Langton and the restoration of the Archbishop of York. The King replied that if Langton dared to show himself in England he would hang him. A war of words followed. John declared that if Langton would resign he would promise to-acknowledge whomsoever the Pope might nominate in his place, and to give Langton a see, perhaps in England. The legate answered that it was not the church's habit to depose any bishop without sufficient grounds, but that it knew how to cast down refractory kings. "Can you make good your words?" sneered John. "The Pope has pronounced the ban over you, and it is in operation," answered Pandolfo. "Anything more?" "Surely.

From this day all Englishmen who have had communication with you are excluded from the church." "What more?" "Your subjects are released from their allegiance. Your kingdom belongs to any one who will take it." "Anything else?" "In God's name we declare to you that your heir can never be crowned." "My messengers informed me," replied John, " that you were well disposed towards me; but I see that you mean to drive me from my kingdom. If I had known that you came with such views, I would have had you and your fellows set upon asses."

One more step still remained to the Pope—the sentence of deposition. To carry this into effect, he proposed to use the King of France. An assembly was convoked at Soissons in April, 1213, and the Bishops of London and Ely proclaimed the sentence, and exhorted the King of France and all others to take up arms to dethrone the King of England and replace him with a worthier sovereign. Philip at once proceeded to arm an immense force. The fleet consisted of seventeen hundred vessels, which were to rendezvous at Boulogne. John also raised a large army of sixty thousand men and a considerable fleet, which latter he distributed at different points, and with which he hoped to prevent the landing of the French in England. The land force, which was encamped at Dover, might have proved invincible if it had been united by affection for the King and zeal for the country; but there were few in the army whom the King could trust. The people regarded him with horror as under anathema, the barons were disgusted by his tyranny, cruelty, and licentiousness, and the foul murder of young Arthur was not forgotten. John himself was an arrant coward; his superstitious fears had been aroused by the prophecy of one Peter, which had gained popular notoriety, that before Ascension day John would have ceased to be King. When, therefore, Pandolfo suddenly appeared at Dover desiring an interview, the panic-stricken wretch was prepared to give himself up to the persuasive words of the wily Italian, and made every concession that he demanded.

He agreed to submit entirely to the Pope's judgment, to acknowledge Langton as primate, to restore all the banished clergy to their estates, to make restitution of all goods and compensation for all damages, and to release every one who had been outlawed or imprisoned for adherence to the Pope. He would pay Peter's pence and an annual tribute of a thousand marks sterling.

The English barons were indignant. Most of them stood aloof from the King and refused to join him in his invasion of France. The bishops, and Langton among them, took sides with the barons against the papal legate. To Langton's honor, the churchman now gave way to the Englishman. A new legate, Nicholas of Tusculum, was sent to England, to whom John made formal submission at the high altar of St. Paul's, and formally resigned the kingdom of England and Ireland to the papal see. The legate was empowered to fill all vacant benefices; and he suspended many prelates and seized their property. The barons at last appealed to arms. John, in order to insure papal protection, took the cross. The barons armed and assembled at Northampton, and soon after obtained possession of London, and at Runnymede John signed the famous Magna Charta.

On the 24th of August, 1215, Innocent issued a bull declaring Magna Charta void because it infringed the rights of the King without the approval of the Pope as feudal lord. It is a notable point in history. The Pope of Rome formally declares the charter of English freedom invalid. The Hildebrandian idea squarely confronts the consciousness of independent nationality, brands it, and bids it down.

We return to the year 1212, which was marked by a unique development of the crusading spirit. In the village of Cloies, in France, there appeared in June of that year a shepherd boy named Stephen, endowed with a remarkable gift of speech, who announced that the Saviour had authorized him to preach the cross. He went through towns and cities singing, "Lord Jesus, help us again to the holy cross." His example stimulated other youthful preachers, who appeared with crosses, banners, and censers, and to whom children of both sexes joined themselves. They were freely entertained by the people, and when asked, "Whither are you going?" replied, "To God. Beyond the sea we are going to seek the holy cross." In spite of the remonstrances and restraints of parents, the children broke locks and scaled walls and joined the bands. The craze was especially violent in Burgundy and the adjoining German territory, and youths, maidens, old men, and many priests enlisted in their ranks. When Innocent heard of it he said, "These children put us to shame. While we sleep they bravely rally to win the Holy Land."

Several thousands of them marched to Marseilles, where they fell into the hands of two kidnappers, who offered to convey them over the sea. They embarked in seven large ships. Two of the vessels were wrecked on the island of San Pietro, not far from Sardinia, and all on board were lost, much more fortunate in this fate than their surviving companions, who were carried to Alexandria and sold as slaves. About twenty thousand assembled in Germany, and started to reach an Italian seaport. Clad in smocks, with staves and wallets, they crossed the Alps, with a lad for their leader barely ten years old, named Nicholas, the tool of a rascally father. Many were lost in the forests and wastes, and died of hunger and thirst, while others were robbed. Seven thousand reached Genoa, and passed on thence to seek another seaport, their numbers melting away as they advanced into Lower Italy. A small remnant reached Brindisi, where they were stopped by the bishop. Nicholas disappeared, and nothing more was heard of him. Their condition was pitiable. Some hired themselves as servants, others fell dead in the streets, and a few reached Rome. On the coast of San Pietro Pope Gregory IX. afterwards erected a church in memory of the first victims, called "the Church of the New Innocents," with a foundation for twelve clergy.

New causes for anxiety were continually emerging in the Latin empire in the East, and a new and urgent call to the rescue of the Holy Land again rang through the West from the apostolic throne. Nothing but the dream of a united Christendom with Rome at its head, of the Greek Church merged in the Roman, of the principalities of the East held as fiefs of the Roman Church, could have maintained Innocent's enthusiasm at so high a pitch, in the face of such formidable discouragements and such general apathy. Moreover, a crusade was a convenient expedient for diverting popular thought from dangerous channels, for placing at a safe distance a prince who threatened to be troublesome, and for furnishing the Pope with an army which, though enlisted for the holy war, might be serviceable for any other use to which he might have occasion to put it.

Accordingly, Innocent displayed all his former zeal and activity in promoting this latest enterprise. He even wrote to the Sultan of Damascus and Cairo, inviting him to give back the Holy City to the faithful, assuring him that the Lord was about to restore the heritage of Jesus Christ, and counselling him to avoid the effusion of blood and the desolation of his empire. He appealed by turns to the Patriarchs of Alexandria and Antioch, and to all the princes of Armenia and Syria. The bull of the crusade was sent into every province of Christendom; preachers were chosen to kindle popular interest, and promises of indulgence were freely dispensed.

The great council known as the Twelfth General Council assembled at the Lateran in November, 1215. In his call Innocent had announced that this assembly was to be according to the model of the ancient general councils, and not like the later councils, in which the East was not represented, and where a number of bishops merely assembled round the Pope to listen to his claims and to subscribe them. In this council the East was represented, though by Latin patriarchs., The western bishops appeared in great numbers. Deputies were present from the Kings of England, Germany, France, Aragon, and Hungary, and from Henry, the Latin Emperor of Constantinople, and the needs of the church and of particular countries were actually discussed.

The Pope opened the council with a sermon, in which he declared his readiness to apply in person to the princes for the relief of the Holy Land. Numerous decisions were reached; some on theological points, as the scholastic contest about the Trinity, others concerning the suppression of the Albigensian heresy, the stated observance of confession and the Eucharist, the prohibition of marriage within prescribed degrees. Jews and Saracens must wear different clothes from Christians; the crusade was to be diligently preached; crusaders who preferred it could go by sea from Sicily; Raymond of Toulouse was deprived of all his possessions, and was sentenced to pay an annual tribute of four hundred marks; and the whole territory captured by the crusaders in France was assigned to Simon de Montfort. Otto IV. ventured to send up his claim to the German crown, and was summarily disposed of. The English barons presented their complaints against John, but the ban over themselves was confirmed, and London was laid under interdict. The King of France was excommunicated. It is no wonder that when the results of this council, called two years in advance, were laid before the provincial synods, the disappointment was general. The decrees were, in fact, mostly repetitions of old canonical decisions, and the principal novelty was the Pope's introduction into a general council of dogmatic decisions on scholastic controversies.

Innocent III. died at Perugia, on the 16th of July, 1216, in the sixty-fifth year of his age, having been Pope for eighteen years and a half.

His administration surpassed those of all his predecessors. It carried Hildebrand's policy further than Hildebrand himself was able to carry it, and it did not terminate in the disaster which overwhelmed the close of Hildebrand's career. He was not as great a man as Hildebrand. He could never have originated Hildebrand's scheme, though he could and did carry it out with a vigor equal to that of Hildebrand himself. He was no less resolute, energetic, and uncompromising, and more flexible and versatile. He added nothing to the great outlines of Hildebrand's policy, and he used only the instruments and methods which Hildebrand and his successors had created. His moral life was untainted with the gross vices so common among the clergy, but he was as cruel as Hildebrand, and more treacherous. Rome never canonized him. She recognized in him "a king rather than a priest, a Pope rather than a saint." He was the enemy of evil rather than the fosterer of good. The Albigensian crusade is a deep and indelible stain upon his character, not only because of the horrible atrocities which his mandate and influence set in motion and perpetuated, but also because of his deliberate cruelty, treachery, and falsehood towards Raymond of Toulouse.

By training he was both a jurist and a theologian, and was not without classical culture. He was fond of preaching, and was much given to expounding Scripture in that allegorical style which marked the fathers of the second and third centuries. He was preëminently a man of affairs, and had immense power of sustained effort, and a singular facility in despatching business.

Through him the papal power may be said to have effectually impressed its theory of sacerdotal government upon Europe. If there was any period at which the Papacy could be said to rule the world it was during his pontificate; but that very fact makes the failure of the Hildebrandian theory the more conspicuous. Perhaps it does not imply exceptional obtuseness on Innocent's part that he did not detect the underlying tendencies of his own age. Perhaps no Pope could be expected to recognize these, or, if he did, to think for a moment that they carried any menace for the system which claimed for itself divine origin and sanction. Sunk in the dream of a universal papal empire, Innocent's eyes were closed to the dawn which was beginning to redden the sky, and its fresher breath did not penetrate his sealed windows. The Hildebrandian popes and their counsellors, possessed with the idea of secular sovereignty, and concentrating their attention upon secular agencies, had never accustomed themselves to mark the deeper, slower working of spiritual and intellectual forces.

Their kingdom, unlike the kingdom of heaven, which they fancied that they represented, came only with observation.

The middle age was well advanced, but, as Sabatier remarks, "he treated it as if it were only fifteen years old." Significant hints came to him from which he might have learned much. Ban and interdict were often impotent. The obedience of crusaders and princes to the mandates of the Pope was by no means absolute; he was often forced to disavow the proceedings of his legates, and men like Stephen Langton were his enemies. His crusade against heresy in southern France resulted in frightful bloodshed without killing the revolt against ecclesiastical authority. England, Venice, and Lombardy were too strong for him. Magna Charta was something which he could not annul by a decree. Beneath the Pope's feet the ground was being silently honeycombed, and the imposing fabric, planned by Hildebrand and built up by nineteen successive popes during nearly a century and a half, was in danger from its own height. The monstrous assumptions and unscrupulous methods of the Papacy had been slowly preparing a protest which was sure to make itself heard ere long; and the victorious uprising of the Lombard communities, the Constitutions of Clarendon, the Magna Charta, and the republican movement in Rome itself, revealed the existence and energy of an independent national consciousness which boded no good to the Roman hierarchy.

CHAPTER XXXIV.

THE POPES AND FREDERICK II.—THE PASTOUREAUX AND FLAGELLANTS—THE MENDICANT ORDERS.

HE efforts of Innocent's successors for nearly a century resulted in no new or larger development of the hierarchical principle. They were spent in the attempt to maintain it at the level to which Innocent had brought it. The principal interest of the three following pontificates—those of Honorius III. (1216–27), Gregory IX. (1227–41), and Innocent IV. (1243–51)—lies in the papal contest with Frederick II., the development of the Mendicant orders, the growth and influence of the universities, and the Inquisition.

The English historian Matthew Paris speaks of Frederick as "the wonder of the world." Mr. Freeman remarks that "there probably never lived a human being endowed with greater natural gifts, or whose natural gifts were, according to the means afforded him by his age, more sedulously cultivated. Warrior, statesman, lawgiver, scholar, there was nothing in the compass of the political or intellectual world of his age which he failed to grasp."[1] By

---

[1] "The Emperor Frederick the Second," "Historical Essays," First Series.

birth he was half Norman and half German; by birthplace, Italian; by residence, Sicilian; by temperament and education, Italian rather than German. Sensual and luxurious, he was also vigorous and brave in war, and astute in politics. Professing strict orthodoxy in religion and enforcing it in his legislation, lifelong contact with the Saracen and natural affinities with Islamite art and science made him tolerant of Islamism. By nature a free-thinker, his reverence for Christian truth and life as exhibited in the Roman Church was not enhanced by the examples of contemporary prelates, nor by the cruel injustice which he experienced at the hands of the Vicegerent of Christ.

At his coronation Innocent had exacted from the romantic, enthusiastic, and inexperienced youth a crusading vow, which proved to be the bane of his life and the root of his misfortunes. Both the performance of the vow and a quarrel with the Papacy were easily evaded under the administration of the mild and easy Honorius III.; but his successor, Gregory IX., an octogenarian, but in full command of his faculties, stern, irascible, of indomitable will, and with the highest views of the papal prerogative, at once assumed towards the young Emperor the attitude of tutor and guardian, and undertook to break him into submission. At his command Frederick at once proceeded to fulfil his vow, and embarked, only to return after a few days on a plea of sickness. Excommunicated for his disobedience, a second attempt was visited with a second excommunication, and his success in rescuing, by a treaty, Jerusalem, Nazareth, and Bethlehem from infidel hands, was met with papal denunciations for perfidy and contumacy, and for the reconciling of Christ and Belial, by the papal interdict upon the Holy City, and by the efforts of the Pope to stir up war and insurrection in the kingdom of Sicily. Gregory, however, was unable to counteract the admiration and sympathy created in Europe by Frederick's success in Palestine, nor could the papal forces resist Frederick's determined onslaught which scattered them in confusion.

The Treaty of San Germano, in 1230, under which the ban was removed, was followed by nine years of peace between the Emperor and the Pope, but also by the revolt of Henry, Frederick's son and vicegerent in Germany, in conspiracy with the Lombard states, the complete subjugation of which made Frederick master of Italy and threatened to reduce the Pope to a vassal of the empire. Another excommunication followed, a papal treaty with Venice, Genoa, and the confederated cities of Lombardy, and a war of words, in which both Emperor and Pope exhausted the vocabulary of invective. The papal thunders, however, fell upon indifferent ears. The avarice and rapacity of the Roman see had alienated western Christendom from the court of St. Peter. The Pope's allegations against Frederick were questioned and denied. Even the feeble Henry III. of England was moved to mild remonstrance; the English clergy flatly refused the levy imposed for the expenses of the Pope's contest with Frederick; Germany was indignant, and met the papal appeal with recommendations of peace; and Louis of France refused his aid and rebuked Gregory with plain words.

The Mendicant friars, the most active and dangerous arm of the papal service, were promptly driven by Frederick from his kingdom, and the English, French, and German commissioners to a council at Rome were intercepted and imprisoned.

The contest was taken up by Innocent IV., who soon was compelled to flee to France, where he met with a cold reception and was refused permission to reside in Rheims. He succeeded, nevertheless, in convoking a council in Rheims in June, 1246, at which Frederick was anathematized and his subjects released from their allegiance. Then the drama of conspiracy, intrigue, and violence continued to unfold itself for four more weary years: hard measure to the meddlesome friars who were busy in stirring up rebellion among Frederick's subjects; summons to revolt by the Pope; conspiracy of Sicilian and Apulian barons, and prompt and cruel execution of the conspirators; fruitless attempts at negotiation; then an anti-imperialist league in Germany, and Henry Raspe of Thuringia elected through the mandate and the money of Innocent, and anointed at Hochem, and soon after defeated and dead. From this time the star of the Hohenstaufen seemed to wane. The turning-point was the capture of Parma by the papal forces, followed by the seizure of Frederick's son, the brave Enzio, by the Bolognese, and the attempt to poison the Emperor by his chancellor.

Frederick died in 1250, pursued after death by papal maledictions and slanders, which represented him as dying unreconciled to the church, and his son Manfred as having hastened his death by smothering him with a pillow. In his last will he directed that all her rights and honors should be restored to the church on condition of her restoration of all the rights and powers of the empire. The church refused to regard this concession as other than the stubborn act of a rebel.

The death of Frederick did not destroy the hostility between the Papacy and the empire. The hatred of the Papacy towards the house of Hohenstaufen was implacable, and was carried into effect at fearful cost to Italy. Frederick's son Manfred seized the crown of Sicily and Naples, notwithstanding the Pope's declaration that "that sacrilegious race" had forever forfeited the throne, and held it, to the exclusion of Conradin, the young son of Conrad IV. of Germany. The Pope kept offering the crown to one and another, and it was at last accepted by Charles of Anjou, a younger brother of Louis IX. of France, who was furnished with money by the Pope to enable him to take possession. He defeated Manfred and assumed the sovereignty. The French rule by its cruelty and outrage was a curse to the southern kingdom, and in 1268, Conradin, now sixteen years of age, with Frederick of Austria, crossed the Alps in order to recover his inheritance, and was joined by the Ghibelline party in Italy. He defeated Charles at Scurcola in 1268, but lost his victory through Charles's cunning, and he and Frederick both fell into the hands of the French and were publicly executed.

In Conradin's death the house of Hohenstaufen, unrivaled in splendor among the houses of Germany, expired at the hands of the Gregorian Papacy. Under it the internal decomposition of the empire had become complete. Indeed, the Holy Roman Empire really fell with the death of Frederick II., whom Dante calls "the last Emperor of the Romans."[1] He was "the last prince in whose style the imperial titles do not seem a mockery; he was the last under whose rule the three imperial kingdoms retained any practical connection with one another, and with the ancient capital of all."[2]

The pontificate of Alexander IV., the successor of Innocent, was marked by two singular outbreaks of popular fanaticism. The first was that of the Pastoureaux, or "shepherds," an insurrection against the nobles and churchmen, which originated among the very lowest orders of society. In 1251 appeared a mysterious preacher known as the "Hungarian." He was an old man who carried in his clenched hand a paper which he pretended he had received from the Virgin Mary as his commission. He spoke Latin, French, and German, and wandered from town to town, preaching against the rich who suffered the Holy Land to remain in the hands of the infidels, and summoning the poor and the humble to rescue the sacred places. Great applause followed his attacks on the clergy and the Mendicant orders, whom he denounced as given over to lusts of the flesh and as being vagrants and hypocrites.

The peasants left their employments and thronged to him, until the multitude amounted to a hundred thousand. The movement drew to itself all the disorderly elements of society, and the vagabonds in

---

[1] "Convito," iv., 3.   [2] Freeman.

The Flagellants.

many cases brought arms with them. At Orleans they broke into the houses of the clergy and burned their books. At Bourges the Hungarian was killed in a tumult, and the citizens cut down the crowd of wretches. Some of their emissaries went to England and excited an uprising among some peasants there. Their leaders acted the part of bishops, blessed the people, sprinkled holy water, and celebrated marriages. Their spoliations of the clergy won them favor with the people, and prelates of high standing declared that so great a danger had never threatened Christendom since Mahomet. Simon de Montfort dispersed them at Bordeaux, threw their leader into the Garonne, and hanged many of them, and the movement was thus finally suppressed.

About ten years later broke out the inexplicable craze of the Flagellants, who first appeared at Perugia. The population was suddenly seized with a fury of penitence, which possessed all ranks and ages, and both sexes. The whole of Upper Italy was soon filled with tens of thousands of penitents, who walked in procession, stripped to the waist, praying God for mercy and scourging each other with leathern thongs until the blood marked their tracks. They marched through the cities by day and night in the sharpest cold of winter, preceded by priests with crosses and banners, to the churches, where they prostrated themselves before the altars. Thirty-three days, the number of the years of Christ's earthly life, was the usual period of the penance. Usurers and robbers restored their gains, and criminals confessed their transgressions. The movement spread throughout

Germany and Bohemia, but, like all similar ebullitions of ignorant fanaticism, soon ceased, and was even denounced as heresy.

But a far more serious and permanent development was that of the Mendicant orders. The monastic orders had long been an established feature of the Papacy and an important and powerful organ of its administration. They were diffused over Europe, and had amassed great wealth. They had rendered valuable services in rescuing extensive domains from desolation, in improving the art of agriculture, in preserving and reproducing the treasures of literature, and in furnishing shelter and medical aid to the unprotected and the sick. Their influence was felt in church councils; they had furnished more than one distinguished occupant of the papal chair, and their organization and discipline had contributed greatly to the efficiency of the hierarchical system. So greatly had the number of the religious orders increased during the last two centuries that the Fourth Lateran Council had prohibited any further multiplication. Any one desiring to adopt the monastic life must select one of the orders already established. Yet the very Pope who issued this decree himself sanctioned the creation of two new orders whose influence was destined to surpass that of all their predecessors.

By the end of the twelfth century it was apparent that the church could not maintain her grasp upon Christendom by force. It was equally apparent that her existing agencies could not or would not foster the spiritual life of the people. The profligacy and rapacity of the clergy repelled and disgusted them, and had not a little to do with driving them into those sects and heresies which the church in vain sought to repress. The monasteries, which, on their serene heights or in their lovely valleys, seemed to invite to praise and prayer and rapt meditation, were too often haunts of debauchery and rampant lust. Such charges as these cannot be laid to Protestant prejudice. The most plain-spoken and sickening exhibitions of these abominations proceed from churchmen. But granting all possible mitigations, allowing, as we may freely allow, that there was a better side to the monastic life, and that within those walls there were not a few whose piety was real and whose lives were pure, there was an evil in the monastic ideal itself.

For seclusion is not the true ideal of Christian life. Mere absence of temptation, if temptation can ever be absent, does not develop sanctity. The self-centred, isolated life of the recluse can never leaven society. Religion is made for contact, and attains its highest practical ends thereby. The crying needs of those wretched, trampled mediæval populations were not to be reached or relieved by the macerations or the ecstasies of the lonely devotee. If there is a danger in loving the world, there is also a danger in withdrawing from it. It is easier to retire into the wilderness than to mingle with and purify the common life of men. Piety spoils if it is shut up. The best way to increase it is to communicate it. The monk found that to immure himself in the monastery was not to escape temptation. The devil had a pass-key. [1]

---

[1] I know of no more powerful development of this truth than Georg Ebers's " Homo Sum."

There were men in that age who perceived and exposed the abuses of clerical life—men like Bernard and Gerhoch of Reichersperg and Peter Cantor; and Waldo's mission was an effort to evangelize the church itself. But there were also men who looked deeper and detected the radical error of the monastic ideal, and who had the courage to confront it with another and a more Christian ideal.

Some precursors of the great preaching orders appeared towards the end of the twelfth century, as Foulque de Neuilly, an obscure and imperfectly educated priest, to whom a preaching license was given by Innocent III., whom thousands flocked to hear, and who was especially successful in reclaiming dissolute women, for whom the convent of St. Antoine was founded at Paris. Durán de Huesca, the Catalan, was one of the leaders of the Waldensians in Aragon. With him originated the idea, afterwards developed by the Franciscans and Dominicans, of an order devoted to preaching and missionary work. His plan was submitted to Innocent III. and approved. It embraced strict chastity of life, absolute poverty, numerous fasts, prayer seven times daily, and a habit of white or gray with sandals. The learned were to devote themselves to preaching and reclaiming heretics. The care of the poor was to be the special duty of the order. This community, known as the "Pauperes Catholici," had established, by the year 1209, communities in Aragon, Narbonne, Béziers, Usez, Carcassonne, and Nismes. They disappeared in the Albigensian crusade, and were not heard of after 1212.

CHAPTER XXXV.

THE DOMINICANS AND FRANCISCANS.

HE Archbishop of Toulouse brought with him to the great Lateran council in 1215 a Spaniard named Domingo de Guzman, who desired permission to found a new order. He was a native of Calaruega, in Old Castile, and had been trained in the University of Palencia. He labored for a long time in Languedoc, where he showed that he could learn even from heretics, since he adopted a measure which they found very effective in disseminating their views—the foundation of institutions for the gratuitous education of young girls of gentle blood. The establishment of Prouille became a large and wealthy convent, which boasted of being the germ of the Dominican order.

Disappearing for eight years, he came into view again after the battle of Muret had destroyed the hopes of Raymond of Toulouse. In 1214 he was forty-four years of age, earnest, resolute, zealous, kindly, winning in manners, and given to the practice of severe austerities. In this year, Pierre Cella, a rich Toulousan, resolved to join him in his mission work, and gave a large house near Château Narbonnais, which for more than a hundred years remained the home of the Inquisition. A few gathered round him and lived as monks, devoting themselves to peaceful instruction. Foulques, the Bishop of Toulouse, as already noted, took Dominic with him to the Lateran council to obtain the Pope's permission to found a new order. Innocent hesitated, but the story runs that his doubts were removed by a dream, in which he saw the Lateran tottering to its fall, and a man whom he recognized as Dominic supporting it on his shoulders. He finally gave his consent on the condition that Dominic and his friends would adopt the rule of some established order, and Dominic selected that of St. Augustine.

The order was divided into provinces, with a provincial Prior over each and a general Master over all. Its members were trained to mix with the world, and were exercised in all the arts of persuasion. They were known as the Preaching Friars. The vow of poverty formed no part of the original foundation, and was not adopted until 1220, after the Franciscans had set the example. The chapter of 1228 prohibited the acquisition of lands or revenues. Innocent died before Dominic could reach Rome to receive the papal confirmation, but the sanction of the see was given by Honorius III. in 1216. Returning to Toulouse, Dominic immediately dispersed his followers on their mission of preaching in all parts of the world. He himself went to Rome, where he won many disciples. In Paris the order was granted the house of St. Jacques, and founded the famous convent of the Jacobins. In 1218 Dominic went to

Spain, and founded the first monastery of the order at Segovia and a second at Madrid. At Barcelona a respectable citizen devoted his house to the purpose.

He was now joined by his brother, and the two were summoned to Germany and went subsequently to Hungary, where the Patarines furnished a large field for their activity. Four years after the sixteen disciples parted at Toulouse, the order had sixty convents and was organized into eight provinces— Spain, Provence, France, England, Germany, Hungary, Lombardy, and Romagnuola. Dominic died in 1221, but the organization continued to grow, drawing into itself the best intellects of the age, and everywhere earning the respect and confidence of the people.

The founder of the Franciscan order was born at Assisi about 1182, and was the son of a rich merchant, Pietro Bernardone. He was baptized by the name of Giovanni, but his father chose to call him Francis. His youth was passed in dissipation, and he achieved distinction among his companions by his extravagances, though the influence of the Troubadours, whose productions appealed to courtesy and delicacy, kept him from coarseness and indecency. A violent illness in his twentieth year resulted in his conversion. He gave himself up to solitude and sympathetic ministration to the poor, and then went on a pilgrimage to Rome. On his return to Assisi he surrendered his patrimony, and devoted himself thenceforth to the work of preaching and ministering to the poor and sick, especially lepers. With his companions he retired to Portiuncula, in the vicinity of Assisi, where they constructed lodgings of boughs. When the community reached the number of twelve they went to Rome to obtain the Pope's approval of their organization. Innocent reserved his full approbation, but authorized them to continue their mission, and gave them his blessing, with a promise of full indorsement if they should prove successful. Portiuncula was formally ceded to them by the Benedictines, and there the first Franciscan convent was established.

Although they did not hesitate to receive alms on occasion, their rule was work and not beggary. After entering the order the brethren were to continue exercising their former callings or to learn one. For payment for their labors they were to accept only such food as was offered them, and if that was insufficient they might beg. A special feature of their organization was poverty. Readers will recall the praise of Francis which Dante, in the "Paradiso," puts into the mouth of Thomas Aquinas, a member of the rival order of Dominicans:

> "For he in youth his father's wrath incurred
> For certain Dame, to whom, as unto death,
> The gate of pleasure no one doth unlock;
> And was before his spiritual court
> *Et coram patre* unto her united;
> Then day by day more fervently he loved her.
> She, reft of her first husband, scorned, obscure,
> One thousand and one hundred years and more,
> Waited without a suitor till he came.
> . . . .
> But that too darkly I may not proceed,
> Francis and Poverty for these two lovers
> Take thou henceforward in my speech diffuse."[1]

[1] "Paradiso," xi., 58–75 (Longfellow's translation).

Institution of the Franciscan Order. 385

The number of his disciples constantly increased. They were recruited mostly from the young men of Assisi and its neighborhood, some of whom were nobles and some farmers. By 1216 the church had discerned in the new order a power which it was for its interest to utilize. Honorius III. offered it his protection, seeing in it an instrument for reviving the popular zeal for the crusades.

In 1219 Francis set out for the East to preach to the Mahometans. He was carried before the Sultan and was heard with the reverence which the Islamite pays to insanity. He passed through the Holy Land and the kingdom of Antioch, and then returned to Italy. Some of his order suffered torture and death at the hands of the Moors of Africa.

It will have been noticed that up to this time the order as such had received no formal papal recognition. It had been merely licensed as a preaching order, and its missions had been organized with the Pope's approval. Francis desired no more than this, but the papal court insisted upon precise and detailed regulations. Francis, after an interview with the Pope's legate, decided to go to Rome; and after conference there a bull was issued in 1220, constituting the Franciscans an order in the strictest sense, and thus inaugurating a new era in their relations with the church. The bull was the laying of the strong hand of the Papacy upon the Franciscans. From this time Francis resigned the mastership of the order. The final rule of 1223, in the attempt to assimilate the movement, transformed it from its original ideal. The association, which in the beginning was antimonastic, fell into the hands of the dogmatic and sacerdotal church, and was bent to its policy. Under the new rule the name of the order was the " Brothers and Sisters of Penitence."

The Mendicant orders were a startling innovation on the monastic theory. The essence of monasticism was selfish—the effort of the individual to secure his own salvation by repudiating all the duties and responsibilities of life. The spirit of the Mendicants was consuming zeal for the salvation of others. Into this movement large numbers of laymen were drawn by the institution of the " tertiary orders," through which laymen, without abandoning the world, were associated with the labors of the brethren. Upon a population generally ignorant, easily stirred to tempests of emotion, and groping blindly for something better than the church had given them, the influence of the Mendicants was profound. The Papacy recognized in them an agency far superior to any that had hitherto been known, for bringing its power to bear directly upon every corner of Christendom, for breaking down the independence of the local prelates, and for fighting the enemies of the secular hierarchy.

Privileges and exemptions were showered upon them, until they were rendered practically independent of the regular ecclesiastical organization. The rule that excommunication or anathema could be removed only by him who had pronounced it was altered in their favor. Bishops were required to give absolution to any Franciscan or Dominican who should apply for it, and Mendicant friars were authorized to absolve members of their own order from any censures inflicted on them. The members of the order were thus responsible only to their own superiors, and could undermine the power and influence of the local hierarchy and replace them with the absolute authority of Rome. By a series of bulls of Boniface VIII., in 1295, they were formally released from all episcopal jurisdiction, and the statutes of the orders were declared to be the only laws by which they were to be judged. Gregory IX., in 1241, granted them the privilege of living freely in the lands of excommunicates, and of receiving assistance and food from them. Therefore they could penetrate everywhere, and serve as secret emissaries in the interest of Rome.

Their efficiency was demonstrated in the long struggle with Frederick II. Frederick banished the Franciscans from Naples in 1229, as papal emissaries seeking to undermine the people's allegiance to the Emperor. When Gregory IX., in 1234, laid the Emperor under ban, he communicated the ban to the Franciscan friars for publication; and when Frederick was deposed by the Council of Lyons the Dominicans were employed to announce the sentence. Thus the Mendicants, originally a spiritual force in a movement against the corruption of the church and an evangelistic force in the interest of penitence and faith, were converted by the Roman see into an instrument of its own greed and secular tyranny. Gradually superseding the bishops in the publication or enforcement of papal mandates, they worked on the line of Hildebrand's purpose to weaken the episcopal power and to make everything centre in Rome. Commissions for the investigation or trial of abuses, formerly issued to bishops, were now issued to them, and the papal power was thus felt in every abbey and episcopal palace in Europe.

A fruitful cause of discord was their intrusion into the pulpit and the confessional. Preaching had been previously reserved for bishops, and had been much neglected, and lazy priests had ceased to concern themselves about the souls of their people. By Gregory IX., in 1227, the friars were empowered to preach, to hear confession, and to grant absolution. They gradually invaded every parish, to the immense disgust of the local priesthood and the serious diminution of their revenues. The matter was made worse by the fact that the people welcomed the ministrations of the intruders and preferred them to their own spiritual advisers. Their reputation for sanctity and the fervor of their preaching drew crowds to their ministrations. They were more skilful in the work of the confessional than the regular incumbents, and in the popular feeling superior virtue attached to their penances and absolutions.

Such intrusions naturally provoked antagonism between the regular clergy and the new orders, and matters came to an issue at Paris, which had welcomed Dominic's first missionaries, while the university had admitted Dominicans to its corps of teachers. Two of these refused to obey the order of the university authorities to suspend lectures on account of the murder of some students. The question was appealed to Rome, and the Mendicants were worsted. The university now represented the cause of the local clergy generally, and made an organized attempt to deprive the orders of the privileges which made them so dangerous. Innocent IV., who had issued briefs in their favor, now unexpectedly issued a bull forbidding them to receive in their churches on Sundays and feast-days the parishioners of others; to hear confession without the special license of the parish priests; to preach in their own churches before mass, and to preach in parish churches and when bishops preached or commissioned others to preach.

This was simply to annihilate both orders; but they were saved by the death of Innocent. His successor, Alexander IV., a warm friend of the Mendicants, at once revoked the bull, and decided the quarrel in favor of the Dominicans. The university was at last defeated and obliged to submit to the demands of the Mendicants, but their aggressions created a widely spread and determined hostility in all ranks of the clergy. Some fresh concessions by Martin V. roused the whole Gallican church, and Honorius IV. was finally won over, and was on the point of issuing a bull depriving the Mendicants of the right to preach and to hear confession, when his death interposed in their favor. The fight did not end until the sixteenth century, and then terminated in a compromise.

Both orders in course of time degenerated. Preaching for money early began among them. Their profession of poverty became a notorious farce, and their vow was evaded by vesting absolute ownership of all property in the Pope, and enjoying the returns, which was permitted by the rules. The property thus vested accumulated so that the two orders were the richest in Christendom. Their monasteries became palaces,

Bonaventura, in 1257, even while fighting for them against the University of Paris, lamented their avarice, idleness, excesses, and importunate beggary, their splendid palaces, and their greedy grasping after legacies and benefices. Their employment as political emissaries diverted them from their spiritual duties, attracted ambitious and scheming men into their ranks, and gave a secular character to their institutions; and the mutual hatred and jealousy of the two orders, and the unscrupulous means by which these were gratified, were a constant scandal and danger to the church.

CHAPTER XXXVI.

THE INQUISITION.

AN important part of the work of the Mendicant orders was the conversion and persecution of heretics. The Inquisition, as the most effective agent in this work, thus fell into their hands and was made their own. The foundation of this fearful institution is commonly ascribed to Dominic, but without sufficient reason, since the Inquisition, as a regularly constituted tribunal, had no existence until several years after his death. Neither can the Dominicans exclusively claim the questionable glory of organizing and perfecting the institution. They were convenient instruments whenever a crusade against heretics was set on foot, since their order was specially devoted to preaching and converting; and as converting gradually gave place to persecuting, they and the Franciscans were equally available and useful. Indeed, it would be difficult to fix a precise date at which the Inquisition may be said to have been formally founded.

The word itself gives a clue to its original character. It was a search, a scrutiny, an investigation. Heresy was not easy to discover. Many heretics were outwardly orthodox, and observed the forms and ceremonies of the church, and many of the local prelates were indifferent. Judicial torture was not employed in the earlier investigations of heresy. The "ordeal" was often applied—trial by handling hot iron, or floating or sinking in water, or swallowing a piece of consecrated bread; but this mode of trial fell into disrepute with the study of Roman law, and was peremptorily forbidden by Innocent III., and by the Lateran council in 1215. As the feudal system developed, the bishops acquired new powers in the administration of canon law, and the spiritual courts which were attached to every episcopate served as instruments for the investigation and suppression of heresy. The jurisdiction of these courts was strengthened by the study of Roman law after the middle of the twelfth century, and their principles and practice were greatly modified. The episcopal judge was commonly versed in both the civil and the canon law, and the ecclesiastical procedure was systematized in accordance with the rules of the civil process. Besides these courts there existed, theoretically, a system of general inquest for the detection of all offences, including heresy, founded upon the *missi dominici* of Charlemagne, who were itinerant officials commissioned to traverse the empire and inquire into all cases of disorder, crime, and injustice.

The church fell into the same system, which it carried out by means of the episcopal visitations. On the arrival of the bishop the whole body of the people of the parish was convoked, and seven men were appointed by him, who were sworn to reveal whatever they might know or hear of any offence which required investigation. These witnesses (*testes synodales*) became an established institution in the church, and furnished an organization well adapted for the discovery and investigation of heresy, though up to the time of the Albigensian crusade the ignorant and lazy prelates did not avail themselves of it, notwithstanding the exhortations of the Pope. A vigorous effort was made to utilize this organization in 1184, by Lucius III., who issued a decree requiring all archbishops and bishops to visit, at least once a year, every parish where there was suspicion of heresy, and to compel two or three good men to swear to reveal any reputed heretic or any one whose mode of life differed from that of the faithful in general. Those who were thus designated were to be summoned by the bishop, and if they failed to purge themselves were to be punished at his discretion. Obstinate heretics were to be handed over to the secular authorities.

This attempt failed. In 1209 the decree of Lucius was reënacted with the change that in every parish a priest should be added to the laymen who acted as local witnesses and inquisitors. This also was ineffectual. Two things contributed to the solution of the problem. One of these was the Mendicant orders. Special and permanent tribunals were required, which should be free from local jealousies or partialities, and the judges and examiners of which should be specially trained in the detection and conversion of heretics, and by their vows should be inaccessible to all allurements of wealth or pleasure. The second thing was the secular legislation against heresy in the edicts of Frederick II., from 1220 to 1239, which formed a complete and inexorable code of persecution founded upon the Lateran canons.

By these edicts, those who were suspected of heresy were required to purge themselves under penalty of deprivation of civil rights and of imperial ban. Heretics of all sects were outlawed. When condemned by the church, they were to be delivered to the secular power to be burned. If they should recant they were to be imprisoned for life. If they should relapse they were to be put to death, all their property was to be confiscated, and all their heirs were to be disinherited. The children to the second generation were to be ineligible to positions of emolument or dignity unless they should win favor by betraying their fathers or other heretics. Houses of heretics were to be destroyed and never rebuilt. All rulers and magistrates were to exterminate any persons whom the church should designate as heretics. When the papal Inquisition was commenced, Frederick, in 1232, placed the whole machinery of state at the command of the inquisitors, who were authorized to call upon any official to capture whomsoever they might designate as a heretic, and to hold him in prison until the church should condemn him, in which case he was to be put to death.

The coronation edict of 1220 was sent by Honorius to the University of Bologna, to be read and taught as a part of practical law; the most stringent enactments of this infernal legislation were incorporated into the civil code, and finally into the canon law itself. Coincidently with the Treaty of Paris in 1229, an ordinance was issued in the name of Louis IX., putting the royal officials at the service of the church for the suppression of heresy. Raymond of Toulouse, in 1234, was compelled to enact a statute which embodied all the principal points of Frederick's legislation, and decreed confiscation against every one who should fail, when called upon, to aid the church in the capture of heretics. In 1315 Louis le Hutin formally adopted Frederick's edicts, and made them valid throughout France. In Aragon, Don Jayme I., in 1226, issued an edict prohibiting all heretics from entering his dominions, and in 1234 instituted an episcopal inquisition, to be supported by the royal officials, in which for the first time appears a secular prohibition of the Bible in the vernacular. All persons possessing any books of the Old or New Testament in Romance are summoned to deliver them to their bishops within eight days, under penalty of fire.

As a papal organization, the Inquisition may be said to have taken shape in the commission issued by Gregory IX. in 1227, by which the prior of the Dominican house of Santa Maria Novella at Florence, with one of his brethren and a canon, was authorized to proceed judicially against the heretic Bishop Paternon and his followers, and to compel them to abjure, calling, if necessary, upon the clerics and laymen of the sees of Fiesole and Florence for aid. In 1235, when the project of an organized Inquisition throughout Europe was taking shape, Gregory appointed the Dominican provincial of Rome "Inquisitor" throughout his extensive province, which embraced both

Tuscany and Sicily. This district appears to have proved too large; and about 1240 we find the city of Florence under the charge of Frà Ruggieri Calcagni, who, in 1243, qualified as "Inquisitor of the Lord Pope in Tuscany."

The Inquisition was thus a development out of existing materials. Its permanent basis was the selection by the provincial bishop of certain men who exercised in their province the delegated authority of the Holy See, in searching out and examining heretics with a view to ascertain their guilt. The fixed organization was given by the bull of Innocent IV., issued on the 15th of May, 1252, a carefully considered and elaborate law which should establish the machinery for systematic persecution "as an integral part of the social edifice in every city and state." All rulers were to put heretics under ban in public assembly. Any one finding a heretic might seize him and take possession of his goods. Each chief magistrate, within three days after assuming office, must appoint, on the nomination of his bishop, two friars of each of the Mendicant orders, twelve good Catholics, with two notaries and two or more servitors, whose sole business should be to arrest heretics, seize their goods, and deliver them to the bishop or his vicars. Their wages and expenses were to be defrayed by the state; their evidence was receivable without oaths, and no testimony was good against the concurrent statement of any three of them.

They were to hold office for six months, and were entitled to one third of the proceeds of all fines and confiscations inflicted on heretics—a provision eminently adapted to stimulate their holy zeal and to repress any possible inclinations towards lenity. No statutes were to be passed interfering with their action; the ruler was bound, when required, to send his assessor and a knight to aid them, and every inhabitant, when called upon, must assist them under a heavy penalty for refusal. The state was bound to arrest all accused persons, to hold them in prison, to deliver them to the bishop or inquisitor under safe escort, and to execute within fifteen days all judgments pronounced against them. The ruler was, moreover, required to inflict torture on those who would not confess and betray all the heretics of their acquaintance. The proceeds of fines, commutations, and confiscations were to be divided into three parts; one going to the city, one to the assistants in the business, and the remainder to the bishops and inquisitors, to be expended in persecuting heresy!

This measure was to be inscribed on all local statute-books, together with all subsequent laws which the popes might issue, under penalty of excommunication of the officials and interdict upon the city. Rulers and their officials were to swear to its observance under penalty of loss of office, and any neglect in its enforcement was punishable as perjury, with perpetual infamy, a fine of two hundred marks, and suspicion of heresy, involving loss of office and disability for all official position in future. As an additional stimulant to diligence, every ruler, within ten days after assuming office, was required to appoint, on the nomination of the bishop or of the Mendicants, three good Catholics, who, under oath, were to investigate the acts of his predecessor and to prosecute him for any failure of obedience.

The right to abrogate any laws which might interfere with the Inquisition made it virtually supreme in all lands. Where such laws existed, the inquisitor was instructed to have them submitted to him, and if he found them objectionable, the authorities were obliged to repeal or modify them. Inquisitors were practically exempt from all supervision and responsibility. Even a papal legate was not to interfere with them or to investigate heresy within their inquisitorial districts. They were not liable to excommunication while in the discharge of their duties, nor could they be suspended by any delegate of the Holy See. In 1261 they were authorized to absolve each other from excommunication for any cause; which, as each inquisitor usually had an associate ready to perform this office for him, rendered them virtually invulnerable. They held themselves accountable to their superiors only for their acts as friars, and not as inquisitors; in the latter capacity they acknowledged responsibility to the Pope alone, and claimed that the power of removal could be exercised only in cases of inability to act through sickness, age, or ignorance. Their vicars and commissioners were entirely beyond any jurisdiction but their own.

My purpose is fulfilled in sketching the development of this institution. My plan does not include the history of its operations. Those who desire to study these have many sources of information at command, among which may be specially noticed the learned, elaborate, and deeply interesting " History of the Inquisition of the Middle Ages," by Henry C. Lea, a work composed from original sources, and to which I am principally indebted for the contents of this chapter.

Comment is needless. An ecclesiastical tribunal with all the resources of the civil power at its absolute command, subject only to the head of the church, who is thoroughly committed to its aims and methods, with the right to modify or abrogate civil enactments whenever they interfere with its operation, the evidence of its functionaries exempt from oath, entitled to a generous share of the profits of its confiscations, empowered to employ torture to extort confession or submission, with two vast organizations distributed in every part of Europe eager to carry out its behests to the letter, presents one of the most astounding and terrible phenomena in the history of either religion or secular legislation, from which one is prepared to expect the most colossal atrocities, and finds his expectation surpassed by the facts.

CHAPTER XXXVII.

THE UNIVERSITIES.

HE compactness and effectiveness of such an organization as the Inquisition, the ample response of the secular power to its demands, the terrible singleness of motive which animated it, the incorporation of its decrees into the civil and canon law, the perfection and simplicity of its machinery, and the wide range of its operation, are adapted to create discouraging impressions as to the degree of social development attained in the thirteenth century. It would seem at first sight as though the Hildebrandian idea had achieved a complete and decisive triumph; as though human life and human thought and the most precious individual and social interests were hopelessly at the mercy of hierarchical absolutism. Yet it is often under the most dreary tracts of history that we detect occasions for hope and promises of better things. The ice-floes are heaped in chaotic confusion and seemingly indissoluble rigidity, the frosty blue throws up its hard lines through the snows, the ice-needles glitter, yet the sun is telling; the icicles are beginning to drip, the ghastly heaps are changing their outline, and there is a cleft here and there through which one

catches a gleam of unfrozen water far down, and hears the sound of running streams.

Among the tokens of reviving life none were more significant or full of promise than the rising universities. The universities seconded the blow struck by the crusades at the feudal system, and were signs of the radical change in the constitution of western society. For, however historians may differ as to the indirect benefits reaped by Europe from the efforts of western Christendom to master the East, all are agreed as to the effect of the crusades in undermining the feudal system. Whereas Europe had been cut up into petty baronies, each with its own feudal lord, its own band of retainers, its own interests, and these interests endlessly conflicting with those of other baronies, the death of the barons in the crusading wars dissipated their estates and often extinguished their race, and the smaller fiefs were swallowed up in the larger. Political unity was thus promoted. The larger domains worked to counteract the spirit of anarchy. Many of the barons who did not die returned bankrupt in fortune, and their " poverty extorted from their pride those charters of freedom which unlocked the fetters of the slave, secured the farm of the peasant and the shop of the artificer, and gradually restored a substance and a soul to the most numerous and useful part of the community." [1]

The crusades, moreover, awakened a spirit of inquiry and a zeal for study which the universities both represented and promoted. The crusaders in the East came into contact with Saracen civilization,

[1] Gibbon.

which was superior to their own. They saw other lands, other races, other arts and sciences, the products of other industries. They discovered new opportunities for traffic, and the spirit of adventure and enterprise was stimulated. Their intellectual horizon was thus enlarged and their humanitarianism broadened. Greek books found their way from Constantinople. Greek culture, which had set its mark upon the empire of the Cæsars, had vanished from mediæval Europe: Greek philosophers and poets were cited only at second-hand, from Latin translations. Though portions of Aristotle had been known in Europe in the sixth century through Boethius, and later, in the eleventh and twelfth centuries, through Averrhoes and the translations of Spanish Christians and Jews, it was not until after the crusades, about 1270, that the western schoolmen possessed translations of all his writings, made either from Arabic versions from Spain or from Greek originals brought from Constantinople and other cities. Civilization owes a lasting debt to the Arabs for their preservation of Greek thought and its transmission to mediæval Europe.

Education had been confined almost entirely to the clergy. The cathedral schools, which attained their highest influence and reputation in the twelfth century, taught only what was necessary for the education of a priest or a monk. In the ninth century the course included grammar, logic, rhetoric, music, arithmetic, geometry, and astronomy; but all these were studied in their relations to theology. Music meant church chanting, and astronomy the method of calculating the date of Easter.

The era of the universities begins with the revival of the study of jurisprudence as derived from the laws of Justinian. About 1113 Irnerius opened a school of civil law at Bologna, and began to lecture on the Institutes and the Code of Justinian. His instructions were eagerly welcomed, since they met the need created by the rapid commercial and political development of the Lombard states. The new and more complex questions growing out of the freer life and larger intercourse of these communes demanded a larger range of legal knowledge than was required for the judgments of feudal barons and counts; and the rapid succession of municipal judges elected from the midst of the commonwealth required a fixed body of statutes and legal principles. The new spirit of the people refused to be satisfied with the mere dogmatic decisions of the individual judge. He must render a reason as well as a decision, and the reason must be something more than his individual opinion, and must be justified by precedent and formulated legislation.

Such a body of enactments and principles was at hand in the works of Justinian—the Code, the Pandects, and the Institutes. This prince had undertaken the stupendous task of arranging and digesting the Roman laws and legal opinions of ten centuries. In the first year of his reign his learned associates revised the ordinances since the time of Hadrian, as they were contained in the Gregorian, Hermogenian, and Theodosian codes, purging the errors and contradictions, retrenching the superfluities, and selecting the laws best adapted to the practice of the tribunals of his own age. The twelve books thus produced were known as the Code, and were confirmed by Justinian's signature, and transmitted to the magistrates of all the imperial provinces. These were followed by the Pandects, in fifty books, containing a digest of the principles of Roman jurisprudence; and these, again, by the Institutes, a condensation of the Code and Pandects, prepared as an elementary work for academical instruction and ordinary practice.

The law as thus codified by Justinian perhaps never became entirely unknown in the West;[1] but Justinian's "body" of law had become very scarce, so that, as we have already seen, Rome in the twelfth century had no copy of the Pandects in her libraries and was apparently ignorant of its existence. Justinian's Code had never been received in the Lombard states, a fact which makes the revival of the study in Lombardy the more significant.

The distinctly secular character of this study, as now revived at Bologna, naturally aroused the suspicion of the Papacy; but this was gradually allayed by the introduction of the study of the canon law also into the university curriculum, and by the great interest awakened in it. Down to the close of the thirteenth century Bologna was the principal school for the study of both civil and ecclesiastical law.

The University of Bologna, however, regarded as a single foundation, was not constituted until the close of the twelfth century. The more correct name

---

[1] Savigny's "Geschichte des Römischen Rechts im Mittelalter" (1831) endeavors to prove that the Roman law retained its vitality from the fifth to the thirteenth century.

previous to that time would have been "universities," since the term was originally applied to student-guilds. These arose out of the variety of nationalities represented among the students, and were formed for their protection in a foreign city. In 1158, by which time Lombardy was full of lawyers, Barbarossa granted to these guilds special immunities and privileges, among which was the permission for students to be tried in civil suits by their own judges. These privileges were gradually extended to all the other Italian universities, and, with the power of the organizations themselves and the fact that many of the students were men of mature age, enabled the students to extort many concessions from the citizens. In Bologna there were four of these "universities" or guilds, and as many or fewer, as the case might be, at Vercelli, Padua, and elsewhere. In the middle of the thirteenth century these confederations in each of the educational centres were blended, forming in each case the university.

The majority of the older Italian universities—Reggio, Modena, Vicenza, Padua, Vercelli—were, as has been said, outgrowths of the cathedral schools as well as departures from them under the impulse of new subjects of study and new methods of instruction. This was also true of the University of Paris, which became the model for those of central Europe and England. The universities, however, were not in antagonism to the Papacy, though occasional innovations might awaken the suspicion or call forth the censure of the popes. The Paris University was largely indebted to papal assistance for its survival, and came to be regarded as the great transalpine centre of orthodox theological teaching; and successive popes exerted themselves to cultivate friendly and confidential relations with it.

The interest awakened by the lectures of Irnerius was contagious, and rapidly spread from Italy over other parts of Europe. The jurisprudence of Justinian was expounded at Montpellier before the end of the twelfth century, and superseded the Theodosian code in the dominions of Toulouse; and Roman law according to Justinian became the rule of all tribunals in southern France.

Of the universities modelled after that of Paris, Oxford was the earliest, and the manner of its development was similar. The story which assigns its foundation to Alfred must be consigned to the region of myth. It probably grew out of the cloister schools of Osney and St. Frideswide, and entered upon a larger life when Vacarius, about 1140, under the protection of Theobald, the Archbishop of Canterbury, began to read lectures on civil law. Towards the close of the twelfth century, Giraldus Cambrensis describes Oxford as a place where the clergy in England chiefly flourish and excel in clerkly lore. By 1257 the deputies from Oxford to the King could speak of it as second only to Paris. The three earliest colleges were University (1249), Baliol (1263), and Merton (1264). The University of Cambridge arose somewhat later,[1] out of the schools of the church of St.

[1] A hot controversy broke out in the reign of Elizabeth as to the comparative antiquity of Oxford and Cambridge, the details of which are amusing. See Sharon Turner, "History of the Anglo-Saxons," vol. ii., bk. v., chap. vi.

Giles under the charge of the church canons, which were further developed in the new priory of Barnwell, to which they were removed in 1112. In 1224 the Franciscans established themselves in the town, and were followed some years later by the Dominicans. At the English universities, as at Paris, the Mendicants and other religious orders were admitted to degrees, a privilege not extended to them elsewhere until 1337. Their interest and influence in these institutions were proportionately great.

Not only in England, but everywhere, the study of the civil law was eagerly taken up by the clergy, and their influence contributed greatly to spread the knowledge of it over Europe. Their pride was stirred by the connection of the science with the name and empire of Rome. The diffusion of Roman law appeared to them to reflect lustre upon the great centre of their religion. But their interest was also of a much more practical character. Knowledge of the civil law was indispensable to them as holders of large properties, which were often endangered by the rapacity of barons and princes. As the knowledge of the age and the discipline of thought were mostly in their possession, the practice as well as the science of law fell largely into their hands. In like manner the clergy turned the universities to the interests of theology. The Mendicant friars obtained possession of some of the most important chairs in the chief universities of Europe, and gave a new impulse to all academical studies as well as to the study of theology. The orders which originally emerged as popular preachers and travelling evangelists aspired to become the leaders in scholastic theology. Of its five great leaders, Albertus Magnus and Thomas Aquinas were Dominicans, and Bonaventura, Duns Scotus, and William of Occam, Franciscans.

Besides the University of Paris, other universities arose in France at Montpellier, Toulouse, Orleans, Angers, Avignon, Cahors, Grenoble, and Perpignan. Paris was noted for theology, Orleans for jurisprudence, and Montpellier for medicine. The University of Toulouse was the first founded in any country by a papal charter, and arose out of the Albigensian persecution.

The feudal and the hierarchical order of the mediæval world were alike threatened by this new power. The very term " university " was a protest against feudalism, signifying as it did a community regarded in its collective aspect. The spirit and tendency of feudalism were separative, fostering a multitude of isolated and mutually hostile principalities, and emphasizing distinctions of birth, rank, property, or brute force. The universities, on the other hand, were not local but European. All Christendom was represented at Paris, Bologna, and Padua. The whole university world was bound together by a common language and a common interest in the same studies. The universities thus accomplished what both the church and the empire aimed at but failed to attain—the knitting of Christian nations into a vast community. Normans and Saxons mingled with Englishmen at Oxford, and read civil and canon law together, and the son of the noble was on the same footing with the Mendicant. The title to superiority was won by knowledge alone.

While the democratic union and interchange thus threatened feudalism, the intellectual movement menaced ecclesiasticism. Externally the universities were strictly ecclesiastical bodies. To mediæval thought education was represented by the clergy. We have noticed how largely even the study and practice of the civil law were absorbed by them. But within the universities a fermentation was going on which was already straining the old patristic and papal wineskins. Men were fast learning that there were other subjects of study than theology; other thinkers and writers than the church fathers; that there were other sides of truth than those exhibited by church dogma and exegesis, and other literature than the rubbish-heaps of Bede, Alcuin, and Walafrid Strabo. The Greek classics had begun to come in from the East, and Homer and Demosthenes were leading men into a new, fascinating, stimulating world of thought, and into the atmosphere of a fresh, vigorous, and unconstrained intellectual life. People were beginning to get hold of the fact that laymen could think as well as popes and bishops, and that the individual reason had its rights no less than the church.

The church was not blind to the danger. Her sense of it was behind the successful effort of the Mendicant orders to establish themselves in the universities. If she could not shut her eyes to the intellectual movement, she could at least try to turn it into her own channels and to her own purpose. Yet the ranks of the friars furnished the highest representative of the power of the movement in the person of Roger Bacon, whose life almost covers the thirteenth century. "From my youth up," he writes, "I have labored at the sciences and tongues. I have sought the friendship of all men among the Latins who had any reputation for knowledge. I have caused youths to be instructed in languages, geometry, arithmetic, the construction of tables and instruments, and many needful things besides."

The zeal and persistence with which Bacon devoted his life to the pursuit of science under enormous difficulties testify to the power of the new spirit which was stirring in his age. Without instruments or other means of experiment, without astronomical tables, which the poverty or the folly of those whom he employed prevented his constructing for himself, the works of Avicenna, Aristotle, Cicero, and other ancients out of his reach because of their immense cost, and some of them not to be had at any price, spending all his means in the attainment of wisdom, laboring in the face of the ignorant prejudice of the age against scientific studies, the "Opus Majus" saw the light at last, that work which comprised all the knowledge of his time on every branch of science which it possessed, "at once the Encyclopædia and the Novum Organum of the thirteenth century."

CHAPTER XXXVIII.

BONIFACE VIII.—COLLAPSE OF THE HILDEBRANDIAN PAPACY.

IN the space of the fifty-three years succeeding the death of Gregory IX., in 1241, the papal chair was occupied by fourteen popes, one of whom, Innocent IV., the immediate successor of Gregory, continued for thirteen years, and the rest for shorter periods, from seven years to a few months. We have already observed that the age of Hildebrand practically ends with Innocent III.; but before closing our task it will be interesting to note a few events in connection with the collapse of the Hildebrandian structure under Boniface VIII.

Benedetto Gaetani succeeded to the apostolic throne in January, 1295, on the abdication of the feeble Cœlestine V., with the title of Boniface VIII. He would seem to be an illustration of the old saying, "Whom the gods mean to destroy they first deprive of reason." The closing scene of the Hildebrandian Papacy is a succession of madman's freaks. Of a noble family, thoroughly versed in ecclesiastical jurisprudence, of commanding ability, with a large and varied experience acquired as a papal representative, and with a personal acquaintance with most of the monarchs of Europe, Boniface was crafty, rapacious, ambitious, with a conception of the papal prerogative as exaggerated as that of Hildebrand or of Innocent III., and a reckless arrogance in asserting it which surpassed even their insolent pretensions. Contemporary Christendom wrote him down in the words, "He came in like a fox, he ruled like a lion, he died like a dog."

In the magnitude of his papal conceit, in his rapacious greed for power, and in his blind and headstrong obstinacy, he preferred claims at which even the most daring of his predecessors would have hesitated, and thereby paved the way for his own ruin. With all his native ability and intimate acquaintance with the secular and ecclesiastical movements of his age, he seemed to be utterly blind to the intellectual and social forces which were gradually transforming European society. Among these were the growth of the royal power in France, the movement towards civil and religious freedom in England, the new intellectual energy and wider range of thought generated by the universities, and the growing power of the legal fraternity, who were fast trenching on the ground once occupied wholly by ecclesiastics, and were formidable at once by their learning and their *esprit de corps*.

The English common law was ranging itself alongside of the canon law; the clergy had been slowly pushed back from the civil administration; in France the lawyers had begun to get the upper hand in the parliaments, and as a class were the partisans of the royal as against the papal prerogative. They were now opposing to the hierarchy an erudition equal if not superior to their own, and confronting the canons of the church with civil canons of greater antiquity; and the clergy were beginning to abandon their secular immunities for the chartered liberties of the realm. These things Boniface either could not or would not see. He incurred the dangerous enmity of the great Franciscan order, not only by refusing to annul the provision of their charter which disqualified them from holding property, but also by seizing for his own use a large sum which they had deposited with bankers as the offered price of such abrogation. He thus alienated a society compactly united along its whole extent throughout Europe, with a great command over the popular mind and a close affiliation with the profoundest theology of the age.

Among the first incidents of his pontificate was his collision with the Colonnas, a powerful Ghibelline family of Rome, and represented by two cardinals in the conclave. The result was their overthrow and the destruction of their city, Palestrina; but their long-cherished and deadly vengeance never slumbered from that moment until it had accomplished the ruin of Boniface. In England and France the Pontiff had to deal with sovereigns of a very different type from John Lackland and Philip I. Edward I. of England was a politic and warlike king, brave, vigilant, and enterprising, a legislator who vigorously maintained the laws of his realm, and who has passed into history as the English Justinian. He was arbitrary, wilful, and imperious, able to keep a firm hand on his barons, an excellent organizer, tenacious of his rights, dogged, stubborn, and proud. Philip the Fair, like Edward, was a man of determined will and boundless ambition, wily, selfish, rapacious, remorseless, unscrupulous, and vindictive.

To these two Boniface threw down the gauntlet. He began by interfering in the war between them, which broke out about the time of his accession, declaring their alliances void, and imperiously enjoining a truce of a year. He then came to a clash with Edward on the taxation of the clergy, which Edward had carried to the extent of demanding a subsidy of half of their annual revenues. Philip also, probably emboldened by Edward's example, included the clergy in the common assessment. Boniface thereupon proceeded to an act which is phenomenal even in the voluminous history of human infatuation. He determined to sever the property of the church from all secular obligations, and to declare himself the one exclusive trustee of all property held throughout Christendom by the clergy, the monastic bodies, and even the universities; so that, without his consent, no grant or subsidy, aid or benevolence, could be raised on those properties by any sovereign in the world.

It may be easily conceived how such a claim was met by the kings of England and France. Edward's clergy proved refractory under his cruel assessment, and were outlawed in a body; while Philip struck the Papacy in a sensitive place by practically cutting off all French revenue to Rome. France was far too valuable an ally for Boniface to relinquish, and he adroitly explained his decree so as practically to annul it with reference to that kingdom. England had organized a powerful league against France. Neither party had paid the smallest attention to the truce commanded by the Pope, but both exhausted their resources in the strife; the limit of taxation had been reached in both countries, and both finally resorted to Boniface as mediator, and agreed to a treaty which practically recognized his authority. Scotland, too, sought his protection against Edward, and appealed to him as its liege lord and feudal proprietor. Edward, however, though ordered by Boniface to desist from the war with Scotland, took no notice of the command and accomplished the defeat of Wallace. The bull of Boniface addressed to Edward in 1299 affirmed that the kingdom of Scotland belonged in full right to the Roman Church and had never been a fief of England.

At this period occurred the famous Jubilee at Rome. Christendom was in a state of comparative peace. Palestine was irrecoverably lost, the holy places were once more in the hands of the infidels, and the West was now seized with a paroxysm of devotion to the shrines of Peter and Paul at Rome—a devotion not entirely disinterested, since it was stimulated by the hope of obtaining by pilgrimage to those shrines all the remissions and indulgences formerly granted to the crusaders. The Pope finally proclaimed from the pulpit of St. Peter's the desired privileges, and granted full absolution of all their sins to all Romans who, during the centenary year, should visit once a day, for thirty days, the churches of the apostles, and to all strangers who should do the same for fifteen days.

The roads from Germany, Britain, and Hungary were thronged with pilgrims. At times there were two hundred thousand strangers at Rome. To those who had made the long and weary journey to the East a pilgrimage to Rome seemed easy. The chronicler Ventura declares that the total number of pilgrims was not less than two millions. He describes the high price of lodgings, the scarcity of forage, and how men and women were trampled under the feet of the crowds. For the protection of pilgrims a barrier was erected along the middle of the bridge of St. Angelo, dividing those going towards St. Peter's and those returning. Dante, who was at this time about thirty-four years old, may have been one of the crowd. At any rate, he preserves a memorial of the occasion in the eighteenth "Inferno," where he uses the scene on the bridge to illustrate the two bands of sinners moving in opposite directions in the first circle of Malebolge. The Pope, Ventura continues, received from the pilgrims money past counting (*innumerabilem pecuniam*); for day and night two priests stood at the altar of St. Paul with rakes in their hands, raking in the treasure, all of which was at the absolute and irresponsible disposal of the Pope.

The Jubilee marked the zenith of the power and fame of Boniface. Everything seemed to favor the accomplishment of his vast schemes. Christendom had apparently submitted; the Colonnas were exiles. Sicily, it is true, was still in rebellion.

At this point we may briefly digress to sketch the course of events in Sicily after the death of Frederick II. After the death of Manfred, Frederick's son, Sicily passed, by the papal gift, into the hands of Charles of Anjou, the brother of Louis IX. of France; and the outrages of the French in the island ended in the Sicilian Vespers, in March, 1282, in which they were ruthlessly massacred. The kingdom was then offered by the Sicilians to Peter of Aragon, the husband of Manfred's daughter, and the dominion of Charles of Anjou was restricted to Naples. Through the long series of complications between the houses of Aragon and Anjou, in which the popes maintained the cause of the Angevines, the throne of Sicily finally devolved on Frederick, the younger son of Peter of Aragon. Boniface endeavored to accomplish Frederick's practical surrender of Sicily by arranging a marriage between him and Catherine Courtenay, the daughter of Philip, titular Latin Emperor of the East. By a confederation of the western powers, Frederick and Catherine were to be placed on the throne of Constantinople.

This bait, however, did not tempt Frederick. The Pope also concluded a treaty with Charles of Valois and James of Aragon, by which James abandoned the claim of Aragon to Sicily. Frederick refused to be bound by this treaty, and baffled all the attempts of the Pope, of whom James was only the half-hearted agent against his brother. Boniface finally summoned Charles of Valois to undertake the conquest, and was now, at the time of the Jubilee, hoping that his intervention would terminate the obstinate conflict with Sicily, and that Charles, by his marriage with the heiress of the Latin Emperor Baldwin, would restore the throne of Constantinople to the West and to the Roman see.

But Boniface was cordially hated. The Franciscans, as we have seen, were his enemies, and Charles of Valois proved a broken reed which pierced his hand. The Pope found in him a master instead of a vassal. Instead of driving Frederick from the throne of Sicily he concluded a peace with him, by which Frederick was to be left in undisturbed possession during his lifetime. He crushed the liberties of Florence and made the name of Boniface execrated throughout Italy. The Pope's interference in Scottish affairs was repudiated both by Edward and the English nation; and the quarrel with Philip, which had long been smouldering, now at last broke out into a furious flame. It has been truthfully said that this quarrel " is one of the great epochs of the papal history, the turning-point, after which, for a time at least, the Papacy sank into a swift and precipitate descent, and from which it never rose again to the same commanding height."

A bull concerning the dispute between France and England and the affairs of Gascony, and containing certain peremptory demands on Philip, was thrown by him into the fire, and Philip entered into alliance with the excommunicated Albert of Austria by a marriage contract between his sister Blanche and Albert's son Rodolph. Saisset, Boniface's legate to France, was seized and imprisoned on a charge of treason. Boniface issued a series of four bulls, the last of which practically contemplated a league of the entire French clergy against their King. Another, proclaimed early in the following year, rebuked Philip's oppression of his subjects, denied his right to the bestowment of benefices, and censured his presumption in subjecting ecclesiastics to civil jurisdiction. This document was publicly burned at Paris in the King's presence. All France espoused the cause of its sovereign. The States-General was summoned for the first time, and the chancellor, Peter Flotte, submitted several bulls issued by the Pope which withdrew the privileges conceded by him to the realm of France, summoned all the bishops and doctors of theology and law in France to Rome as his subjects and spiritual vassals, and asserted that the King held the realm of France, not of God, but of the Pope.

Each order of the States-General—the nobles, the clergy, and the commons—drew up its own address to the Pope. That of the nobles declared that they would never endure the Pope's claim of the temporal subjection of the King and the kingdom to Rome, nor his summons of the prelates of the realm to appear before him at Rome. The address of the clergy also protested, though in milder terms, against these claims as dangerous novelties. They had felt themselves embarrassed between their allegiance to the King and their allegiance to the Pope, and had asked permission to go to Rome to represent the whole case; but this had been peremptorily refused.

The Pope returned a wrathful answer to the address of the clergy, and rebuked them for their cowardice. About the same time a consistory was held at Rome, from which issued the famous bull defining the powers assumed by the Pope:[1] "There are two swords, the spiritual and the temporal; our Lord said

[1] The bull "Unam Sanctam," November 18, 1302.

not of these two swords, 'It is too much,' but, 'It is enough.' Both are in the power of the church: the one, the spiritual, is to be used *by* the church; the other, the material, *for* the church. . . . One sword must be under the other, the temporal under the spiritual. . . . We assert, define, and pronounce that it is necessary to salvation to believe that every human being is subject to the Pontiff of Rome." Finally the Pope's legate presented twelve articles to which the King's immediate assent was demanded, articles asserting the extreme papal claims and couched in insulting and menacing terms.

On the 12th of March, 1303, a parliament was convened at the Louvre, at which many of the French barons were present. William of Nogaret, an eminent professor of civil law, presented a catalogue of charges against Boniface, laying down the four following propositions: the Pope is not the true Pope; the Pope is a heretic; the Pope is a simoniac; the Pope is guilty of pride, iniquity, treachery, and rapacity. The document appealed to a general council, which Nogaret declared it to be the King's right and office to summon, and before which he professed his own readiness to substantiate the charges. To this bold proceeding—the arraignment of a Pope before a general council—the Pope replied with instructions to the Cardinal of St. Marcellinus to declare the King excommunicate; but the bearers of the letters were seized and imprisoned, and the legate was closely watched and allowed to receive no paper or visit without the King's knowledge. A second parliament was held at the Louvre, on the 13th of June, which declared that Christendom was in the utmost danger and misery through the rule of Boniface. Detailed charges of the most startling and repulsive character, some of them flagrantly false, were preferred against him, and the parliament gave its formal approval of the call of a general council for his arraignment.

Meanwhile the wrath and hatred of the Colonnas had never slumbered, and they had been patiently biding their time. Two of them had been openly received at the French court, and were in active co-operation with the lawyers; and it is not improbable that the charges against the Pope had emanated largely from them. Boniface retired to Anagni for the summer, and issued several bulls, among which was one depriving the French universities of the right to teach, or to grant any degree in theology or in canon or civil law. This privilege he declared to be derived entirely from the apostolic see, and to have been forfeited by their adhesion to the King. He then prepared to launch the sentence of excommunication. The document had been prepared and had received the papal seal; but Nogaret and Sciarra Colonna were in Italy, on the borders of Tuscany, not far from Rome, and had their secret emissaries in Anagni, and a band of lawless soldiers at their command.

On the 7th of September, Sciarra Colonna, with three hundred horsemen under the banner of France, swept through the streets of Anagni, with the cry, "Death to Pope Boniface!" They attacked the Pope's palace and set on fire a church by which it was protected. Boniface was seized, placed backwards upon a horse, and thus led through the town. His palace was plundered, and an enormous amount of treasure fell into the hands of Colonna's troops. Boniface was at last rescued by a company of horsemen from Rome, and was conveyed to the city, but only to be thrown into prison, and to die, baffled, broken-hearted, old, and execrated, on the 11th of October, 1303.

Dante, who had seen the liberties of Florence extinguished by Charles of Valois, and who had himself been driven into exile thereby, never loses an opportunity to lash Boniface VIII., though he distinguishes between the Pope and the man, and deprecates the outrage at Anagni upon the person of the Vicar of Christ. He has devised for him a unique and ingenious punishment in hell, where his legs appear protruding from a narrow stone well with an eternal flame playing along the soles of his feet. Every reader of the "Paradiso" will recall that tremendous passage where the whole heaven reddens with shame as St. Peter thunders his denunciation of Boniface:

> "Quegli ch' usurpa in terra il luogo mio,
> Il luogo mio, il luogo mio, che vaca
> Nella presenza del Figliuol di Dio,
> Fatto ha del cimiterio mio cloaca
> Del sangue e della puzza, onde 'l perverso,
> Che cadde di quassù, laggiù si placa.
> Di quel color, che, per lo Sole averso,
> Nube dipinge da sera e da mane,
> Vid' io allora tutto 'l ciel cosperso."[1]

---

[1] "He that usurps on earth my place, my place, my place, which is vacant in the sight of the Son of God, has made of my burying-place a sewer of blood and stench, whereby the Perverse One who fell from here above is appeased down there. With that color which by reason

Thus fell the Papacy of the middle ages. Thus the "stately palace-dome" decreed by Hildebrand collapsed and sank. Benedict XI., the immediate successor of Boniface, occupied the chair for only a few months, and was succeeded by Clement V. in 1305, who was committed to carry out the policy of France, and with that view fixed his seat at Avignon, where he and six succeeding popes resided for the sixty-eight years following. The papal court was the vassal of France. Its dissoluteness, luxury, pride, and rapacity were the talk of Europe, and its subservience to the political aims of the French crown alienated from it the sympathy of England and Germany. It is not strange that Roman Catholic historians should have given to this period the name of "the Babylonish captivity."

of the sun over against it paints a cloud at even or at morn, I beheld then the whole of heaven suffused."—*Paradiso*, xxvii., 22–30. See also " Inferno," xix., 13 ff.; xxvii., 70–85, 96–111; " Purgatorio," xx., 86 ff.; xxxii., 150; " Paradiso," xii., 90; xvii., 50.

CHAPTER XXXIX.

CONCLUSION.

E have been following the history of a theory, and the outcome of the history is a stupendous failure. Around the death-couch of Boniface VIII. the stately edifice of Hildebrand lies in ruins. For the larger part of the next century the Roman Church, its throne removed from its ancient seat of empire, plays the part of a vassal to the power against which it has so often thundered its interdicts.

We have seen that the idea of the Holy Roman Empire survived with more or less potency long after the reality had vanished; but the idea had taken on a new dress. There was still an empire; its centre was still at Rome; its spirit was the spirit of imperial absolutism; its aim was to grasp the world. But the Emperor wore the tiara instead of the crown; the state counsellors were cardinals; the prætors, archbishops; the lictors, monks. The Hildebrandian ideal was as truly that of universal dominion as was the ideal of the Antonines. The Pope was Pope not only of Rome, but of France, Spain, Hungary, Africa, Sardinia, and Cyprus.

The church-empire was essentially and intensely

secular, as much so as the empire of the Cæsars. It was religious chiefly as a means of secular acquisition. Religion was its second business, not its first. The orders of friars, with their extensive and often splendid establishments, were diffused over Europe, an army obedient to the call of the Pope. The Pope's legates penetrated into the cabinets of kings, and manipulated their civil policy. The Pope claimed the right to enthrone and dethrone kings, and emperors must kiss his feet and hold his stirrup. Armies of knights and infantry moved at his summons to subdue refractory provinces, and orders of priestly soldiers in mail marched at his bidding against the strongholds of the East. His treasury was plentifully supplied; revenue from the great kingdoms of the West and costly presents from Byzantine usurpers flowed into his coffers; knights and barons and petty princes held their possessions by his investiture, and swore fealty to him as their feudal lord. Feudalism was taken up into papal imperialism, and utilized for its aggrandizement.

The secret of the failure of Hildebrandianism lies in this claim to secular absolutism. This is the taproot in which all other causes of failure converge. As Müller well says: " With Gregory appear for the first time the terrible consequences of a development in which the church becomes a power of this world, which must maintain itself among other powers and subject them to herself in virtue of her divine calling, a task for which the instruments of the kingdoms of this world are indispensable, so long as the relation of the constant silent or open warfare between them subsists." The church was a " visible divinity," carrying the whole power and majesty of Christ. Its form and its essence were alike monarchical. As the church was universal, her rightful dominion was universal. The logic was simple: God is the rightful sovereign of the world; the church represents God; therefore the church is rightfully supreme over the world. The Pope is the divinely commissioned head of the church, therefore the Pope is above all earthly rulers: *Q. E. D.*

The conflict was between papal absolutism and imperial absolutism. The Papacy must be independent of the power of the state. The prohibition of lay investiture was designed to free the church from feudal alliance with the empire. The decree which abrogated the right of investiture by the temporal sovereign, which deposed and interdicted every bishop or abbot who received investiture from any layman, and imposed the same penalty on the Emperor or other secular ruler who should confer investiture with a bishopric, created a revolution in the whole feudal system throughout Europe in respect of the relation of the church to the state. It annulled the power of the sovereign over a large part of his subjects, and that the most influential part; it made all the great prelates and abbots, who were also secular princes, to a great degree independent of the crown, placed every benefice practically in the power of the Pope, and made him lord, temporal and spiritual, of half the world.

Hildebrand gives voice to this policy in one of his epistles:[1] "When God gave to Peter chiefly the

[1] Lib. iv., Ep. 2.

power of binding and loosing in heaven and in earth, he exempted no one and nothing from his power; he withdrew nothing from his power. For if one declares that he cannot be bound by the church, he denies that he can be absolved by its power; and whoever shamelessly denies this withdraws himself utterly from Christ. If the apostolic see is divinely endowed with the power to judge spiritual things, why not secular things?"

In the same line was Gregory's policy with regard to the bishops. He aimed especially to break the power of the metropolitans by assuming those privileges of nominating and consecrating bishops which had been vested in them by ancient ecclesiastical usage. He feared that the metropolitan office might acquire too much the character of a local Papacy. Cases which had been habitually referred to their decision he transferred to the jurisdiction of his legates. He sought in every way to bring the episcopate into complete dependence upon himself, and to make the relation of the bishops to the Pope that of a vassal to a suzerain.

The Hildebrandian policy failed after a fair trial for two centuries under conditions favorable to its success and under the leadership of men of genius and power. The edifice toppled by its own height, and fell, never to be rebuilt. The cause lay, not in external circumstances, but in the essential character of the theory itself. Such a theory could not finally succeed in the very nature of the case.

For, in the first place, the Hildebrandian idea of the church was essentially false. It was more nearly akin to the Old Testament theocracy than to the New Testament church. It was evolved by perversions of detached New Testament passages, such as "On this rock will I build my church"; "I will give thee the keys of the kingdom of heaven: whatsoever thou shalt bind or loose on earth shall be bound and loosed in heaven." From these was drawn the familiar dogma that Peter was the divinely appointed head of the church, and that the Roman Church as the church of Peter was absolutely supreme. Along with this went the assumption of Peter's episcopate of twenty-five years at Rome, which, to put the case in its mildest form, has a very doubtful historical basis. From such positions Innocent III. and Boniface VIII. drew the doctrines of the two swords and the two lights. The Old Testament was occasionally appealed to, to show, for instance, that priests were recognized in Scripture as gods. In the assertion of superiority to the secular power the Gregorian Papacy contravened the express declarations of the New Testament, which assign a distinct and legitimate sphere to the secular authority, affirming that there are things which belong to Cæsar no less than things which belong to God, and that the secular no less than the spiritual power is of divine ordination. These facts did not escape observation even in that age, and were more than once boldly thrown in the Pope's face.

The Hildebrandian theory was sustained by palpable forgeries. The right to hold landed property and to receive it by bequest, which was conferred by Constantine upon the church, was magnified into the claim that Constantine had granted to Pope Silvester

The Isidorian Decretals. 429

and his successors the free and perpetual sovereignty of Rome, Italy, and the provinces of the West. This preposterous claim, formulated about the middle of the eighth century, commanded the belief of Europe for seven centuries; and by this the Hildebrandian popes justified themselves for their unceremonious appropriation of any territory to which they might take a fancy.

With this forgery was associated another, equally impudent, the Isidorian Decretals. The old canon law was gradually modified and to some extent displaced by the new papal claims founded upon these fictions. The Decretals were intermingled with the canons and acquired equal authority with them, and their influence was diffused and strengthened by the great systematic collections of the canons and false Decretals made after the end of the ninth century. On these Gregory founded his theory of a papal theocracy, and the doctrine that all intercourse with the excommunicate was forbidden under penalty of excommunication. From this the deduction was easy that a prince banned by a Pope could no longer discharge his duties, and that his subjects, therefore, must be released from their allegiance. The right to dethrone princes was further deduced by Gregory from historical examples which were partly misunderstood and partly invented; such as the unhistoric deposition of the last Merovingian by Pope Zacharias, and the deposition of Valentinian and Honorius by Xystus III.

The advantage derived from the Isidorian Decretals was pressed and maintained in later pontificates by the formation of new collections of canons, incorporating later deliverances of popes and synods, such as the collections of Anselm of Lucca, Cardinal Deusdedit, and Gratian. The Gregorian system was, it is true, essentially contained in the Isidorians, but the later deliverances could be made more generally accessible by a condensed manual. Thus the theory of papal dominance was ever more firmly grounded and carried over to the succeeding generation by making the collections text-books in the canonical schools. The Papacy had a distinct advantage in that its law was written and formulated, while the national law was almost universally transmitted by word of mouth, and was therefore often loose and self-contradictory.

The Gregorian Papacy failed through its attempt to accomplish by force a class of results which can be reached only through the free, intelligent acquiescence of the individual will. It sought to do in the sphere of religion the selfsame thing which imperial Rome had done in the political sphere, and by the same means: to effect by external constraint what is feasible only through the power of unifying ideas and sentiments. A spiritual monarch sustained by physical force, holding his sovereignty by physical appliances and extending it by secular methods, is an essential contradiction and a palpable absurdity. The two conceptions are mutually repellent. In forsaking the spiritual power for the secular the church forfeited both. She perished by the sword because she took the sword; and in the prosecution of secular ends by secular means the ethical and spiritual factors of her life exhaled. Her policy encouraged the most dangerous passions of human nature. Pride, greed, falsehood, self-indulgence, were its legitimate outgrowths. Gregory did not perceive that the worldliness at which he struck with such vigor in his crusade against simony was being fostered by the principles of his own policy.

Nothing in the history of this age is more painful than the open defiance by the clergy of the Christian duty of veracity. A Pope is seen resorting to falsehood and treachery, as Innocent III. in his dealing with Raymond of Toulouse; or assuming the right to release subjects from their sworn allegiance to their sovereign, as Gregory VII. in the case of the subjects of Henry IV. The clergy, in the interest of the papal cause, encourage violations of the most sacred natural rights and duties. Mathilde's clerical partisans stimulate Conrad's rebellion against his father, and Pope Urban does not frown on an act which promises the alliance of Italy with the Papacy. Henry V. is absolved by Pope Paschal from his filial obligations and from the most solemn oaths to his father, and the rupture between father and son is blasphemously ascribed by the Pope to the inspiration of God. Paschal does not hesitate to break the formal treaty in which he has conceded to the German Emperor the right of investiture. Dean Milman has well remarked that "so completely was the churchman's interest to absorb all others, that crimes against nature not only were excused by the ordinary passions of men, but by those of the highest pretensions to Christian holiness. What Pope ever, if it promised advantage, refused the alliance of a rebellious son?"

The Hildebrandian Papacy was, in its conception, an unnatural institution. It was adapted to antagonize the social protections, obligations, checks, and balances which make society possible. An organization which claims divine sanction not only for its existence but for its supremacy over all secular institutions and authorities, a close corporation, choosing its own officers, denying the responsibility of its members to secular tribunals, wielding immense pecuniary power, and demanding from society a continuous revenue as its right, its property exempt from all interference of the civil power, clothed with authority to dissolve at will the obligations of child to parent and of subject to sovereign, empowered to control the choice of kings, to dethrone them on occasion, and to dictate their policy, with its agents in every court and an army of trained men separated from all natural and social ties at its beck—such an institution is a colossal monstrosity, a thing which no civilization can tolerate, and which carries in itself the seeds of its own destruction.

Such a theory, which was largely carried into effect, cannot be dismissed by saying that it is distinctively mediæval and concerns us only as an antiquarian curiosity. History is a unit, and the forces of one age are at work in every succeeding age. Humanity is one, and the phases of its development, whether in the patriarchal age, the first Christian century, the twelfth, or the eighteenth, are related to each other. That which commends itself to our attention in the history of this period is not the difference between Romanism and Protestantism. That difference is merged in the larger questions, what human nature will do under given circumstances, and how much strain it will bear; whether there is any power capable of controlling natural tendencies and directing them to beneficent ends, or whether history vindicates the principle of the French socialists, that man is a creature of circumstances, and that nature must be obeyed because she cannot be conquered.

As between Romanism and Protestantism, it is hardly safe for Protestantism to press the contrast. Protestantism has too much glass in its own house to be warranted in throwing stones at random. Not a few things popularly supposed to be peculiar to Romanism may be detected under other forms in Protestantism. The great fact is that the Romanist and the Protestant are alike human; the difference of environment is a subordinate fact. Archbishop Whately, over sixty years ago, with that hard, masculine common sense which distinguished him, went to the core of the matter in his essay on " The Errors of Romanism Traced to their Origin in Human Nature," and put the case in a sentence: " Whether a man be Papist or Protestant in name, let him chiefly beware of old Adam." History, even the history of the middle ages, proves that a man may be a Papist and at the same time a saint. History equally proves that a man may be a Protestant and exhibit the same lust for power, the same tyrannical instinct, the same persecuting spirit, the same disregard of veracity, the same indifference to fairness and justice, and the same bigoted adherence to traditional dogma which characterized certain of the Hildebrandian popes. The comparison of Hildebrand and Innocent III. with certain notable Protestant leaders is by no means out of place, and the resemblance is not wholly imaginary.

No doubt the system has something to do with shaping the man; but the fact remains that very few men, Papist or Protestant, are proof against the temptation to acquire power; and the temptation offered by ecclesiastical power is exceptionally strong. The respect and reverence which wait on the belief that a man is in confidential relations with heaven, that he holds the key to its rewards and punishments, and that he is empowered to declare its decrees, are things which appeal to susceptibilities very common in average human nature, and for which many a man is easily won to barter a large share of his manhood.

Human nature—yes. But how as to regenerate nature, Christianized nature, nature under a power which is supposed to offer resistance to temptation? Here emerges a question which a thoughtful man, even the most charitable, may find some difficulty in answering. It is this: In our estimate of a man's character and deeds, how much allowance is to be made for the age in which he lives, his social and religious environment, and the nature of his education? I speak not now of his theological beliefs, but of his ethics. A good deal of allowance is to be made, no doubt; only let us be careful not to commit ourselves to the conclusion that a man cannot rise above the level of his time. The average man does not as a rule, but we are not dealing now with average men. Leo IX., Hildebrand, Urban, Innocent III., Boniface VIII., were not average men.

Very much depends upon what standards of conduct are available for the men of any given period. No one would think of trying an Israelite, dancing round the golden calf, by the standard which he would apply to the Apostle John. No one would measure Seneca, Antoninus, or Epictetus by the moral and spiritual standard of the Apostle Paul. But here are exceptional men, ministers and leaders and teachers in the Christian church, with the Christian traditions and literature of twelve centuries behind them, which it is their special business to study; above all, with the New Testament in their hands, which in the matter of ethics is unmistakable, and in which a perfect ethical system is incarnated in the purest and noblest of mankind. They call themselves his ministers; they call him Lord; they give themselves out as his vicegerents; by their own voluntary profession they stand committed to his code of ethics, his spirit, his example. How much allowance is to be made for them, especially in the light of the fact that earlier and cruder ages than their own produced men, and many of them, who lived above the ethical level of their age and consistently followed the precept and example of him whose name they bore? Compare Hildebrand and John; Innocent and Paul; Boniface and Ignatius; Leo and Irenæus. Nay, the Hildebrandian period itself exhibits men of a higher moral type than these heads of the church—Bernard, Norbert, Anselm, and not a few others. What shall we say as to the amount of allowance due to the Hildebrandian popes? I shall not attempt to answer the question, but it is worth pondering. If it be asked whether the inconsistency is any less in the modern than in the mediæval church, it may be answered, Granting it is no less, so much the worse for the modern church.

Certain it is that with the sacred Scriptures in its hands, with the apostolic traditions behind it, with the New Testament code of ethics before its eyes, under the avowed commission of the Christ of love and peace and truth and purity, an opportunity was offered to the church of the Roman popes which, if it had been seized, might have changed the history of Europe. With the nations ready and waiting for some strong, moulding hand, and showing, by the readiness with which they responded to the appeal of every fanatical impulse, how easily they might have been led to respond to higher and purer appeals; with the church's magnificent organization spread over Europe; with a profound though superstitious reverence for the church already implanted in the popular mind and heart; with a dense ignorance which needed instruction; with rude manners and habits which pure Christianity could have refined, and gross vices which it could have rebuked and checked; with all the education and mental training of the age centred in the clergy—the church, by the very magnitude of her baleful achievement, showed what she might easily have done in the interest of truth and righteousness. As it was, " her lie, as all lies do, punished itself. The salt had lost its savor. The Teutonic intellect appealed from its old masters to God and to God's universe of facts, and emancipated itself once and for all. They who had been the light of Europe became its darkness; they who had been first became last, a warning to mankind to the end of time that on truth and virtue depends the only abiding strength."[1]

[1] Charles Kingsley, "The Roman and the Teuton."

INDEX.

Abélard, 162; career, 200 sq.; edition of works, 202 (footnote); philosophy and theology, 203 sq.; teachings condemned, 206; appears at Sens, 206; death, 206; influence, 206, 207.

Adalbert, Archbishop of Bremen, 58; conflict with Hildebrandians, 58; fall, 59; makes enemies of Saxons, 71.

Adelais. See Praxedis.

Adelheid of Vohburg, 223.

Adhemar, Bishop of Puy, 131.

Agnes, daughter of Duke of Tyrol, 295, 311.

Agnes, regency of, 39; jealousy of bishops, 56; enters Rome as penitent, 57; disregarded, 91; death, 99.

Alaric, 6.

Albert of Austria, 418.

Albert of Benevento, 285.

Albert of Sabina, 135.

Albertus Magnus, 185, 408.

Albigenses, 247, 303-305, 337 sq.

Alcantara, 162.

Alcuin, 196, 409.

Alessandria, 275.

Alexander, 11, 50; affronts Germans, 52; opposed by Lombards, 52; denounced by Benzo, 54; withdraws to Lucca, 55; acknowledged Pope at Augsburg, 57; proclaimed lawful Pope at Mantua, 59; at Rome, 59; relations to clerical marriage, 61; death, 63.

Alexander III., disciple of Abélard, 207; chosen Pope, 238; installed, 239; summoned by Barbarossa, 239; breach with Barbarossa, 240; excommunicates Barbarossa, 240; also Octavian, 240; opposed by Clugny, 241; refuses to attend Council of Pavia, 241; adverse decision, 241; excommunicated, 242; supported by English and French bishops, 242; by Council of Toulouse, 243; his victory a partial defeat, 243; recognizes Scotland's independence, 244; canonizes Edward the Confessor, 244; enters Rome, 244; flees, 244; in Paris, 246; annoys Barbarossa, 248; relations to Becket, 249 sq.; embarrassed by Becket, 251 sq.; urged to return to Rome, 252; relations to Henry II., 253 sq.; embarks for Rome, 254; names Becket as legate, 254; concessions, 255; driven from Rome, 260; further negotiations with Henry and Becket, 263; a "chameleon," 264; removes Becket's suspensions, 264; letters of suspension against Archbishop of York, etc., 266; demands of Henry renunciation of Clarendon articles, 267; recalls Becket, 267; an exile, 271; appealed to by Henry, 273; canonizes Bernard, 274; marriage of daughter of Henry, 275; terms with Barbarossa, 276 sq.; returns to Rome, 278, 279; fresh quarrels, 279;

Index.

submission of Calixtus, 280;
death and character, 280, 281.
Alexander IV., 376, 389.
Alexandria, apostolic patriarchate, 3.
Alexius Comnenus I., 109; leagues with Henry, 109, 111.
Alexius III., 311.
Alexius IV., 326.
Alfonso of Leon, 296.
Alice, Queen, 244.
Amadeus, 93.
Amalfi, 192.
Amauri, son of Montfort, 348.
Anacletus II., 174; attacks Innocent, 175; invites Lothair to Rome, 175; oppositions to, 175; banned by Synod of Liége, 175; in St. Peter's, 189; repulsed by Innocent and Lothair, 190; bribes Romans, 190; holds Lateran, 190; deposed by Council of Pisa, 191; abjured by Milanese, 191; titles Roger, 192; dies, 194.
Anagni, 276, 277.
Anastasius IV., 223.
Anathema, 74, 75.
Ancona, 275.
Angela of Foligni, 185.
Anselm, Bishop of Milan, 191.
Anselm, selected for Canterbury, 136; exiled, 136; quarrel with Henry I., 136, 137, 140; sent to Rome, 140; supports King, 143, 184, 198; a realist, 199, 200, 246.
Anselm of Badagio, 50; legate to Milan, 61. See Alexander II.
Anselm of Lucca, collections of, 430.
Antioch, apostolic patriarchate, 3.
Antonines, 4.
Apulia, Bishop of, 107.
Aquileia, Patriarch of, 104, 242, 284.
Aquinas, Thomas, 185, 384, 408.
Arabs, intellectual debt to, 402.

Aragon, homage to Innocent II., 176.
Arcadius, 4.
Arezzo, 146.
Arialdo, 50, 61.
Aristotle, 181, 196, 197, 402.
Arnaud of Citeaux, 318, 319, 339, 342.
Arnold of Brescia, 162, 214; expulsion, 215; released from ban, 215; the man of the hour, 215, 216, 224, 225; death, 227.
Arnoldists. See Arnold of Brescia.
Arnstadt, Assembly of, 353.
Augsburg, appointment of diet at, 92.
Ausch, Archbishop of, 318.
Autbert, 292.
Averrhoes, 402.
Avignon, 423.
"Babylonish captivity," 423.
Bacon, Roger, 409, 410.
Baldwin, 327, 329.
Baldwin II., King of Jerusalem, 333.
Bamberg, 192; Diet of, 270.
Ban, 74, 75.
Barbarossa, 221 sq.; relations to Papacy, 222; defiance, 223; march through Italy, 225; meets Pope, 225; reply to senate, 226; coronation, 227; attacked by Romans, 227; aims, 228; second marriage, 229; complaints of Pope, 230; vigorous proclamation against papal domination, 230, 231; subdues Milan, 233; Roncaglia, 233; "lord of the world," 233; affronted by Hadrian, 234; meeting of princes, 235, 236; rebukes Hadrian, 236, 237; breach with Alexander, 239, 240; excommunicated, 240; banned by Alexander, 242; fall of Milan, 245; annoyed by Alexander III., 248; supports Paschal III., 253; endorses Henry's defiance, 255;

Index. 441

expedition through Italy, 257; Monte Porzio, 258, 259; treaty with Rome, 261; withdraws from Rome, 261; revolt of Lombard cities, 262; attempts negotiations with Alexander, 270; with Louis, 270; again invades Italy, 275; defeat, 276; terms with Alexander, 276 sq.; relations to Lucius, 283; to Urban, 284; receives the cross, 289; peace with Clement, 289; opens crusade, 289; death and character, 289, 290; grants to student-guilds, 405.

Baronius, admits spuriousness of Isidorian decretals, 23; "Annales Ecclesiastici," referred to, 65 (footnote).

Basilica, Golden, 64.

Basilica of Constantine, 64.

Beatrix, daughter of Mathilde, marries Godfrey, 63; promises help to Hildebrand, 77.

Beatrix, daughter of Philip of Suabia, 350, 354, 357.

Beatrix, widow of Margrave Boniface, 37; seized by Henry, 38; released, 39; influenced by Hildebrand, 39; opposes Cadalous, 53.

Beatrix of Burgundy, 229; crowned, 260.

Bechelheim, 142.

Becket, 246 sq.; proposed canonization of Anselm, 247; quarrel with Henry, 248 sq.; relations to Constitutions of Clarendon, 249; appeal to Pope against council of realm, 251; visit to Pope, 251; resignation and reinstatement, 252; named legate, 254; anger at selection of legates, 263; suspensions removed, 264; appears at Montmirail, 264; bans Gilbert of London, 264; rebuked, 265; anger at proposed coronation of Prince Henry, 266; formal reconciliation with King, 266; letters of suspension against Archbishop of York, 266; recalled to England, 267; death and character, 268, 269.

Bede, 196, 409.

Beghards, 185.

Beguines, 185.

Bellarmine, admits spuriousness of Isidorian Decretals, 23.

Benedict IV., 12.

Benedict IX., 14; restored to throne, 15; sells Papacy to Gratian, 15; reappears, 20.

Benedict X., 43; flees, 45; captured and deposed, 45.

Benedict XI., 423.

Benedict of Nursia, monastic organization of, 7.

Benedictine reform, significance of, 161.

Benedictus Christianus, 169.

Benno, Archbishop, 144.

Benzo, Bishop of Albi, opposes Alexander II., 54; urges Honorius to hasten to Rome, 55.

Berengar, attacks Paschasius on the Eucharist, 31; burns his books, 46; final settlement, 100, 101.

Berengaria, 361.

Bernard of Clairvaux, contrasted with Hildebrand, 120, 162, 176; most important man of age, 177; sketch of life, 177 sq.; peculiar type, 180 sq.; contrasted with Hugo and Richard, 182; character, 185 sq.; letter to Emperor, 190; ambassador to Milan, 191; to Roger of Sicily, 194; opposes Abélard, 202, 205, 206; letter to Eugenius, 211; supports him, 211; attacks Arnold, 215; preaches second crusade, 217; its failure, 219; "De Consideratione," 219; death, 220; canonized, 274; describes state of religion in Toulouse, 300.

Bernard of Pisa. See Bernard of St. Anastasius.
Bernard of St. Anastasius, chosen Pope, 211; flees, 211; consecrated, 211; success, 212; two years' absence, 213; second crusade, 216; returns to Rome, 218; concession to senate, 218; leaves Rome, 220; relations with Barbarossa, 222; death, 223.
Bernardone, Pietro, 383.
Berthold of Carinthia, 92.
Berthold of Moravia, 289.
Besançon, Diet of, 230.
Béziers, Bishop of, 340.
Bible, prohibition of, 395.
Bishop of Rome. See Papacy.
Blanche, sister of Philip the Fair, 418.
Boethius, 196, 402.
Bohemond, 131.
Bologna, University of, 394, 404.
Bonaventura, 185, 390, 408.
Boniface, Margrave, 37.
Boniface III., 5.
Boniface VIII., 387, 411 sq.; quarrel with Philip, 418; "Unam Sanctam," 419, 420; charges against, 420; excommunicates Philip, 420; seizure and death, 421, 422, 428.
Bouvines, battle of, 346.
Bramante, 17 (footnote).
Brigitta of Sweden, 185.
Brixe, 106.
"Brothers and sisters of penitence," 386.
Bruno, Abbot of Clugny, 16.
Bruno, Bishop of Toul, nominated Pope, 21. See Leo IX.
Bryce, quoted in footnote, 10, 118.
"Bugari," 304.
"Bugres," 304.
"Bulgari," 304.
Cadalous, Bishop of Parma, 52. See Honorius II.
Calabria, Bishop of, 107.
Calatrava, 162.

Calcagni, Ruggieri, 396.
Calixtus II., 158; proposed agreement with Henry, 159; broken off, 160; excommunicates Henry, 160; approves Benedictine reform, 161; goes to Rome, 162; treaty with Henry, 163; reconciliation, 164; improvements in Lateran palace, 167; dies, 167.
Calixtus III., 262; acknowledged in Germany, 270, 277; deposed, 278; rebels, 279; submits, 280.
Cambrensis, Giraldus, 406.
Cambridge, University of, 406, 407.
Campiglia, Viscount of, 225.
Canosa, 93.
Cantor, Peter, 380.
Carcassonne, 341.
Cardinals, 46.
Carthusians support Alexander III., 241.
Cassiodorus, 196.
Castile, homage to Innocent II., 176.
Cathari, 162, 302 sq. See Albigenses.
Catherine of Siena, 185.
Celibacy, 25 sq., 60 sq.
Cella, Pierre, 381.
Cencius, family, 61, 76; plots, 84; seizes Hildebrand, 84, 157, 167, 168.
Charlemagne, 4; head of church, 6; ratifies "Donation of Pepin," 9; crowned, 10; disputes sovereignty of Rome, 10 sq.
Charles of Anjou, 375, 417.
Charles of Valois, 417, 418, 422.
Charles the Bald, 12.
"Charta Caritatis," 162.
Chasseneuil, 340.
Childeric III., 8.
Children's crusade, 364, 365.
Christian of Mainz, 252, 258, 262, 268, 275, 280, 282.
Christina Ebner, 185.

Cinthius, 62, 99.
Cistercians, 162, 178; support Alexander III., 241. See Bernard.
Cistercium, 161.
Citeaux, 161, 177 sq. See Bernard.
Civil law, 233, 400 sq.
Civitas Leonina, 44.
Clairvaux, 162, 178. See Bernard.
Clarendon, Constitutions of, 249, 272.
Clement II., 18, 20.
Clement III., 286 sq.; peace with Barbarossa, 289; death, 289.
Clement III., antipope. See Guibert of Ravenna.
Clement V., 423.
Clergy. See Papacy, Roman Church.
Clermont, Synod of, 131, 176.
Clugny, 16 sq., 161; against Alexander, 241.
Code. See Justinian, Theodosian, Gregorian, Hermogenian codes.
Cœlestine II., 170; disciple of Abélard, 207; repeal of French interdict, 210; death, 210; protects Arnold, 215.
Cœlestine III., 291 sq.; death, 299.
Cœlestine V., 411.
Cologne, Archbishop of, 163.
Cologne Diet, 137.
Colonna, Peter, 141.
Colonna, Sciarra, 421.
Colonna family, 413, 421.
Comba, E., "Waldo and the Waldensians," referred to, 301 (footnote).
Comnenus, Alexius. See Alexius.
Conceptualism, 203.
Concordat of Worms, 163 sq., 172.
Conrad, Archbishop of Mainz, 260.
Conrad, son of Henry IV., in Lombardy, 126; plots by Gregorians, 127; absolved from obligation to his father, 127; crowned King of Italy, 128; treaty with Urban, 130; death, 137.
Conrad III., 211, 212; rumored league with Constantinople, 218; appealed to by republicans, 219; death, 220.
Conrad of Hohenstaufen, 171; banned by Anacletus, 175; banned by Synod of Liége, 176; crowned, 191.
Conrad of Lützelhard, 279.
Conrad of Rabensburg, 323.
Conrad of Sabina, 223.
Conrad of Ürslingen, 294.
Conradin, son of Conrad IV., 375.
"Consolamentum," 303.
Constance, Treaty of, 235.
Constantia, French Queen, 240.
Constantia, wife of Henry VI., 283, 308, 313.
Constantine, 3; head of church, 6; "Donation of," 9, 10, 23, 48, 121, 428.
Constantine, Basilica of, 64.
Constantine, son of Michael, 109.
Constantinople, non-apostolic patriarchate, 4; imperial seat removed to, 5; Hildebrand's designs on, 79; taken by crusaders, 326, 351.
Constitutions of Clarendon, 249, 272.
Coronation edict, 394.
Corsi, 141.
Corso, Stephen, 141.
Council, Fourth Lateran, 26; Frankfort, 10; Twelfth General, 366, 367.
Courtenay, Catherine, 417.
Cremona, Council of, 244.
Crusades, first, 130 sq.; second, 216; third, 286 sq.; fourth, 310 sq., 323; fifth, 366; summoned by Hildebrand, 79; children's, 364, 365; in general, 401, 402.
"Cullagium," 25.

Cyprus, 296.
Damasus II., 20.
Damiani, Peter, author of "Gomorrhianus," 24, 28; cardinal, 42; "Epist. ad Card. Episcopos," referred to, 46 (footnote); opinion concerning German bishops, 50; opinion concerning Cadalous, 52, 53; representative of Hildebrandians at Augsburg, 57; legate to Milan, 61; dies, 63.
Dante, quoted, 4, 10; supposed reference to Mathilde, 154, 182; "celestial hierarchies," 185; portrait of Bernard, 186, 376, 384, 416, 422.
David of Augsburg, 185.
Decretals. See Pseudo-Isidorian Decretals.
Democrats. See Republicans.
Denys, St., 181.
Desiderius, abbot of Monte Cassino, 108, 111, 116; summoned to papal chair, 125; anathematizes Guibert, 125; dies, 126.
Deusdedit, Cardinal, collections of, 430.
Dieckhoff, "Die Waldenser im Mittelalter," referred to, 301 (footnote).
Dionysius, 181.
Döllinger, quoted, 10 (footnote).
Domingo de Guzman. See Dominic.
Dominic, 381 sq.; not founder of Inquisition, 391.
Dominicans, 381 sq.
"Donation of Constantine." See Constantine.
"Donation of Pepin." See Pepin.
Durán de Huesca, 380.
Durazzo, 109.
East and West, schism, 8.
Ebers, "Homo Sum," referred to, 379.
Ebner, Christina, 185.
Ebner, Margaret, 185.

Ebrard, 69.
Ecbert, 56.
Edessa, 217.
Edward I. of England, 413, 414.
Edward the Confessor, canonized, 244.
Eleanor, Queen of Henry II., 273, 293.
Election decree, 46 sq.
Elizabeth of Schönau, 185.
England, relations of Hildebrand to, 102; homage to Innocent, 176; relations to Alexander III., 246 sq.; war with France, 274; relations to Innocent III., 330, 359; to Boniface VIII., 414, 415. See William the Conqueror, Henry I., II., John, Alexander III., Innocent III., Paschal II.
Enzio, 374.
Erigena. See Scotus, John.
Erlembaldo, 50, 61, 76.
Eucharistic controversy, 30, 31, 100, 101.
Eudoxia, 65.
Eugenius III. See Bernard of St. Anastasius.
Excommunication, 74, 75.
Feudalism, 401, 408. See Papacy.
Flagellants, 377.
Flavians, 4.
Flotte, Peter, 419.
Flurchheim, battle of, 105.
Forchheim Diet, 96.
Foulque de Neuilly, 380.
Foulques, Archbishop of Toulouse, 345, 381, 382.
Fourth Lateran Council. See Council.
Francis, founder of Franciscans, 383 sq.
Francis of Assisi, 188.
France. See Louis VI., VII., VIII., IX., X., Philip I., II.
Franciscans, 382 sq., 413.
Frangipani family, 156, 167, 168, 210. See Cencius.

Frankfort, Council of, 10.
Frederick, son of Barbarossa, 289.
Frederick, son of Peter of Aragon, 417, 418.
Frederick I. See Barbarossa.
Frederick II., 297, 298; crowned at Palermo, 308, 353, 356, 357; crowned at Aachen, 358; character, 371, 372; relations to Gregory IX., 372; success in Palestine, 372, 373; quarrels with Papacy, 373, 374; death, 374; banishes Franciscans, 387; edicts of, 394.
Frederick of Austria, 375.
Frederick of Lorraine, 34; eludes Henry, 38; Abbot of Monte Cassino, 39; cardinal, 41; enthroned Pope, 42; death, 43.
Frederick of Rotenburg, 259.
Frederick of Suabia, 171; banned by Synod of Liége, 176; submits, 192.
Freeman, quoted, 268, 371, 376.
French church synod, 153.
Frêteval, 266.
Froude, "Life and Times of Thomas à Becket," referred to, 251 (footnote).
Fulda, Abbot of, 163.
Fulk of Neuilly, 323.
Gaetani, Benedetto, 411.
Gebhard, Bishop of Eichstadt, 37.
Gelasius II., 156; insulted, 157; flees, 157; consecrated, 158; excommunicates Gregory VIII. and banns Henry, 158; again attacked and flees, 158; death, 158.
Gensa of Hungary, 82.
Genseric, 6.
Geoffrey, Archdeacon of Norwich, 360.
Geoffrey, son of Henry II., 273.
Gerard, Archbishop of Florence, 44.
Gerard of Bologna. See Lucius II.

Germans. See Henry III., Henry IV., Alexander II., Leo IX., Damiani, Hildebrand, etc.
Geroch of Reichersperg, 240, 380.
Gertrude, 185.
Ghibelline, 357.
Giacomo della Porta, 17 (footnote).
Gibbon, quoted in footnote, 10, 401.
Giesebrecht, quoted, 88 (footnote).
Gieseler, "Ecclesiastical History," referred to in footnote, 23, 122.
Gilbert of London, 251, 264, 265.
Gildas, St., 202.
Giovanni, 383.
Giraldus Cambrensis, 406.
Gluber, Rudolph, 14 (footnote).
Godfrey of Lorraine, 34; marries Beatrix, widow of Margrave Boniface, 37; stirs up revolt against Henry, 38; increasing power, 39; seats Nicholas II., 44; mediates between Alexander and Honorius, 55; supports opposition to Adalbert, 59; death, 63.
Godfrey, son of above, marries Beatrix, 63; promises help to Hildebrand, 77; murdered, 91.
Godfrey of Vendôme, 128.
Golden Basilica, 64.
Gotelin, Count, 252.
Gratian, collections of, 430.
Gratian, deputy to Becket, 265.
Greeks defeat crusaders, 351.
Gregorian code, 403.
Gregorovius, quoted in footnote, 7, 8, 10, 18, 63, 117, 152, 208.
Gregory, Cardinal, 194.
Gregory II., 8.
Gregory VI., 15.
Gregory VII. See Hildebrand.
Gregory VIII., 285, 286.
Gregory VIII., antipope, 158; attacked by Calixtus, 162; brought to Rome, 162; death, 163.
Gregory IX., 348, 365, 372; rebellion against, 373; privileges

to Mendicants, 387, 388; Inquisition, 395.
Gregory of St. Angelo, 174. See Innocent II.
Gregory of Vercelli, 57, 69.
Gregory the Great, recognized head of Rome, 7; wealth, 8, 139.
Guelf, 357.
Guibert of Ravenna, 52, 55; displaced, 57; plots, 76 sq.; instigates Lombards, 90; excommunication renewed, 100; chosen Pope, 106; marches with Henry to Rome, 108; Lombards acknowledge him, 108; enthroned, 114; in Rome again, 116; anathematized by Desiderius, 125; expelled from Rome, 127; called back, 127; death, 134.
Guido, Archbishop of Milan, 61.
Guido, Cardinal, 217.
Guido di Castello. See Cœlestine II.
Guido of Cremera. See Paschal III.
Guido of Palestrina, 321, 322.
Guido of Valate, 50; resignation, 83.
Guido of Vienna, 153, 158. See Calixtus II.
Guiscard, Robert, 34, 47; condemned by Nicholas, 48; receives fiefs of Holy See, 48; sustains election of Alexander II., 51; fealty to Hildebrand, 70; anathematized, 74; overtures by Hildebrand, 90; leagues with Hildebrand, 106; doubleness, 108; attacks Durazzo, 109; returns, 110, 111; aids Hildebrand, 112; forces entrance into Rome, 114.
Guzman, Domingo de. See Dominic.
Hadrian I., claims allegiance, 9; letter to Charlemagne, 9.
Hadrian II., married, 26.

Hadrian IV., 223, 224; agrees to crown Barbarossa, 225; expedition against William of Sicily, 228, 229; alliance with William of Sicily, 229; negotiations with Barbarossa, 230, 231; concessions, 232; affronts Barbarossa, 234; summons Milan to revolt, 235; meeting of princes, 235, 236; rebuked by Barbarossa, 236, 237; dies, 237; gives Ireland to Henry II., 271.
Hagenau, 289.
Hallam, "View of State of Europe in Middle Ages," referred to, 335 (footnote).
Hanno, Archbishop of Cologne, 56; convenes council, 57; supplanted by Adalbert, 58; heads opposition to Adalbert, 59; summons council at Mantua, 59.
Harnack, "Dogmengeschichte," quoted, 182 (footnote); on Abélard, 207.
Hartzburg, 72.
Héloïse, 201.
Henry, Archbishop of Rheims, 270, 271.
Henry, Bishop of Augsburg, 56.
Henry, brother of Baldwin, 330.
Henry, son of Frederick II., 373.
Henry, son of Henry II., crowned, 266; recrowned, 272; rebellion, 274.
Henry, son-in-law to Lothair, 192.
Henry I. of England, 26, 140, 143; meets Innocent II., 176.
Henry II. of England, relations to Alexander III., 242, 243, 246; quarrel with Becket, 248 sq.; agrees to acknowledge Paschal III., 253; asks pardon of Alexander, 253; defiance of Pope, 254; threatened by Pope, 265; formal reconciliation with Becket, 266; renunciation of Clarendon articles demanded, 267; recalls Becket, 267; rela-

tions to Ireland, 271; murder of Becket, 271; penance, 272; appeals to Pope to compel obedience of children, 273; rebellion, 274; reconciliation with France, 288; third crusade, 288.

Henry III. of England, 373.

Henry III., Emperor of Germany, 14; enters Rome, 16; relation to Clugny, 17; right of nominating Pope, 18, 19; coronation, 18; gives lands to Normans, 34; seizes Beatrix and Mathilde, 38; death, 39.

Henry IV., Emperor of Germany, receives absolution from Hildebrand, 1; asked to nominate Pope, 49; abducted by Hanno, 56; apprised of Hildebrand's election, 66; defied by Hildebrand, 69, 70; penitential letter to Hildebrand, 71; treaty with Saxons, 72; diet of princes, 72; deputation to Rome, 72; conspires with Milan, 76, 77; defeats Saxons, 82; master of Germany, 82; breaks with Gregory, 83 sq.; summoned to Rome, 83; ordered to call council, 85; at Worms, 86; seeks confederates in Italy, 86; commands Hildebrand to renounce pontificate, 87; anathematized, 88; new Synod at Worms summoned, 91; treats with Diet of Tribur, 92; promises obedience to Pope, 92; crosses Mount Cenis, 93; suppliant at Canosa, 94; terms of submission, 95; demand for abdication, 96; asks to be crowned King of Italy, 96; evades Hildebrand's requisition to appear at Forchheim, 96; returns to Germany, 97; confiscates domains of Welf, 97; proposed conference with Rudolph, 98; battle of Melrichstadt, 100; goes to Würzburg, 104; defeated at Flurchheim, 105; again deposed, 105; pays homage to Guibert, 106; invasion of Saxony, 107; ban renewed, 107; march to Rome, 107; receives crown of Italy, 108; attacks Mathilde's garrisons, 108; leagues with Alexis, 109; again besieges Rome, 109; division of his army, 110; enters city, 111; appeals against Hildebrand, 111; synod to decide claims, 112; nobles bribed to desert him, 113; declares Hildebrand deposed, 113; crowned and receives patriciate, 114; threatens to destroy Mathilde, 126; siege of Mantua, 127; deserted by Conrad, 128; defection of Italian cities, 128; effect of charges of Praxedis, 130; four years' peace, 137; excommunication renewed by Paschal, 138; deserted by son Henry, 142; imprisoned by Henry, 142; resigns, 142; death, 143.

Henry V. of Germany, 137; deserts his father, 142; alliance with Paschal, 142; imprisons his father, 142; King, 143; bethrothal to Matilda, 145; sets out for Rome, 145; allegiance of Mathilde, 145; concessions of Paschal, 147; enters Rome, 149; German bishops refuse terms, 150; riot, 150; gallantry in Rome, 151; takes Pope prisoner, 151; royal investiture, 151, 152; coronation ceremonies, 152; declared excommunicated, 153; celebrates father's obsequies, 155; marriage with Matilda, 155; desertions, 155; goes to Rome, 155; failure there, 156; attacks Gelasius, 157; banned by Gelasius, 158; agreement with Calixtus, 159; broken off, 160; excommunicated, 160; treaty with Calixtus, 163, 164; reconciliation, 164; dies, 171.

Henry VI. of Germany, 270; marriage, 283, 284; coronation at St. Peter's, 291; relations to Sicily and Papacy, 292; imprisons Richard I., 293; master of Italy, 294; crusade, 296; ambition, 296; death, 298.

Henry of Lausanne, 300.

Henry of Lower Lorraine, 349.

Henry of Rheims, 274.

Henry of Saxony, 227.

Henry of Thuringia, 374.

Henry the Lion, 227.

Henry the Proud, 192, 357 (footnote).

Heresies, 299 sq., 391 sq.

Hermann, Count of Luxembourg, chosen King of Germany, 109; dies, 126.

Hermogenian code, 403.

Herzog, " Die Romanischen Waldenser," referred to, 301 (footnote).

Hildebrand, absolves Henry, 1; his ideal the imperial ideal, 3; monk of Clugny, 17; chaplain to Gregory VI., 19; life sketched, 19 sq.; views on relation of empire to Papacy, 21; accompanies Bruno to Rome, 21; superior, monastery of St. Paul, 28; chief man in Rome, 35; heads deputation to Henry, 36; ambassador to Agnes, 43; enlists Gregory against Benedict X., 44; treaty with Normans, 45; policy with Normans, 47; assembles cardinals to elect Anselm of Badagio, 50; chancellor, 53; denounced by Benzo, 54; triumph over Germans, 59, 60; hailed Pope, 65; nature of election, 66; policy, 67 sq.; claims on Spain, 68; defiance against Henry, 69, 70; inaugurated, 70; relations to Guiscard, 70; to Michael, 70; to Landolfo, 70; to Richard of Capua, 70; commands Henry to submit Saxon revolt to papal legates, 71; refuses to help Henry against Saxons, 73; blows at simony, 73 sq.; summons against Saracens, 73; first great reform synod, 74; opposition, 75 sq.; threatens France, 78, 79; letter to Henry concerning Constantinople, 79; letters to Denmark, 79, 80; lay investiture, 80, 81; imprisoned by Cencius, 84; escape, 85; condemned at Worms, 86; proclaimed usurper, 87; anathematizes Henry, 88; laid under ban by Lombards, 90; summons Germany to choose new King, 91; disregards oath to Empress, 91; sets out for Augsburg, 93; takes refuge in Canosa, 93; refuses to release Henry from ban, 94; terms of submission, 95; refuses crown of Italy to Henry, 96; overreaches himself, 96; requires Henry's attendance at Forchheim, 96; attitude towards Rudolph, 98 sq.; relation to Berengar, 100, 101; relations to England, 102, 103; to Rudolph, 104; again deposes Henry, 105; his decree, 105; authority renounced at Mainz, 106; leagues with Guiscard, 106; aids Michael, 107; agitation at Henry's approach, 108; encyclical, 110; escapes to St. Angelo, 111; general excommunication, 112; people revolt, 113; declared deposed, 113; freed by Guiscard, 115; goes to Salerno, 115; last encyclical, 116; suggests successor, 116; death and burial, 117; character and policy reviewed, 118 sq., 427 sq.; quoted, 426, 427.

Hildegard of Bingen, 185.
Hohenstaufen, 4, 171; fall of, 375, 376.
Holy Roman Empire, 4; Dante's political ideal, 4; a fiction, 4, 275, 376, 424.
Honorius, Emperor, 4, 6, 429.
Honorius II., 170; trouble with Monte Cassino, 172; quarrel with Roger of Sicily, 173; Neapolitan monarchy, 173, 174; dies, 174.
Honorius II., antipope, 52; chancellor, 53; enters the Leonina, 55; withdraws to Parma, 55; at St. Angelo, 58; deserts St. Angelo, 59.
Honorius III., 347, 371, 372, 382, 385.
Honorius IV., 389.
Horace, quoted, 208.
Hubald of Ostia, 282.
Hubert, papal legate to England, 103.
Hubert of Canterbury, 296, 310, 330.
Hugo, Abbot of Clugny, 17, 95.
Hugo, Cardinal, 275.
Hugo Candidus, 65, 86, 106.
Hugo of Lyons, 116, 143.
Hugo of St. Victor, 182, 188.
Hugolino of the Holy Cross, 350.
Humbert of Crivellis, 283.
"Hungarian," the, 376, 377.
Hyacinth, Cardinal, 291.
Ingeborg, 295, 311.
Ingelheim, 142.
Innocent I., 6.
Innocent II., 174; escapes from Anacletus, 175; deserted by Frangipani, 175; escapes to France, 175; reversal in favor of, 176; meets Henry of England and Lothair, 176; pronounced Pope by Synod of Liége, 176; homage at Synod of Rheims, 176; privilege to Cistercians, 189; charter to Clairvaux, 189; meets Lothair, 189; enters Rome, 189; gives possessions of Mathilde in fief to Lothair, 190; leaves Rome, 190; at Melfi, 192; quarrel over Monte Cassino, 192; bigotry, 195; beaten by Roger, 195; treaty with Roger, 195; lack of candor, 195; Tivolese yield, 209; revolution, 209; secular power lost, 209; dies, 209.
Innocent III., 2, 306 sq.; relations to empire, 308; reforms, 308, 309; bans, 309; crusade, 310; absolutism, 312; Philip of Suabia and Otto IV., 313 sq.; attacks heresy, 318, 319; favors Otto, 319 sq.; defied by German bishops, 322; fourth crusade, 323 sq.; Constantinople, 326 sq.; absence from Rome, 329; relations to England, 330 sq.; novel mandate, 332; rebukes Templars, 336; Albigenses, 337 sq.; breaks with Otto, 350; negotiations with Philip, 350; excommunicates Otto, 355; enlists Philip II. against Otto, 356; suppor's Frederick II., 357; excommunicates John, 360 sq.; deposes John, 362; Magna Charta, 364; Twelfth General Council, 367; death and character, 368–370; Dominicans, 382; Franciscans, 384; forbids "ordeal," 392, 428.
Innocent III., antipope, 280.
Innocent IV., 374, 389; inquisition, 396.
Inquisition, 391 sq.
"Insabbatati," 301.
Interdict, 75.
Investiture. See Lay Investiture.
Ireland, 271.
Irene, wife of Philip of Suabia, 325.
Irnerius, 403.
"Iron age," 12.

450 Index.

Isaac, Emperor of Constantinople, 325, 326.
Isidore, Bishop of Seville, 22.
Isidorian Decretals. See Pseudo-Isidorian Decretals.
Isidorus Mercator, 22.
Jacobi, quoted, 101 (footnote).
Jacquot, F., "Défense des Templiers," quoted, 336.
James of Aragon, 417.
Jayme I., 395.
Jerome, on celibacy, 26.
Jerusalem, non-apostolic patriarchate, 4; conquered by crusaders, 133, 134; capture of, by Saladin, 285.
Jews under Roman empire, 168.
Joannicius, 351.
John, Abbot of Struma, 262.
John, King of England, 314, 319, 331, 359; excommunicated, 360; outrages, 361; defiance, 361; deposition, 362; cowardice, 363; submission, 363; Magna Charta, 364.
John XII., deposed, 12.
John XIX., 14.
John de Gray, 330, 331.
John Mincius, 43.
John of Gaeta. See Gelasius II.
John of Porto, 88.
John of Sabina, 15.
John of St. Paul, 299.
John Scotus. See Scotus, John.
Jordan of Capua, 110, 111.
Jordanes, brother of Anacletus II., 210.
Jubilee at Rome, 415.
Julius of Palestrina, 252.
Justinian, closes Athenian schools, 196; code of, 403, 404, 406; Institutes of, 403, 404; Pandects of, 233, 403, 404.
Kamba, 171.
Kingsley, Charles, quoted, 436, 437.
La Ferté, 162.
Lambert of Ostia. See Honorius II.
Lando of Sezza, 280.

Landolfo, 50, 61, 70.
Landulph V., 47.
Lanfranc, on Eucharist, 31, 102, 135.
Langen, "Geschichte der Römischen," etc., referred to in footnote, 66, 67, 88, 101, 241.
Langensalza, battle of, 82.
Langton, Stephen, 331, 359, 360, 361, 363.
Lascaris, Theodore, 351.
Lateran church, 64.
Lateran Council. See Council.
Lateran Synod, 167. See Roman Synods.
Lateranus, Plautius, 64.
Lay investiture, 80, 81, 134, 136, 144, 163 sq., 234, 426.
Lea, Henry C., "A History of the Inquisition," referred to, 399 (footnote).
Legates, 122.
Legnano, 275.
Leo, son of Benedictus Christianus, 169.
Leo III. crowns Charlemagne, 10.
Leo VIII. established by Otto, 12.
Leo IX., 2; enthroned, 22; use of Isidorian Decretals, 23; a reformer, 24, 28 sq.; great religious visitation, 29; attacks Normans in Italy, 34; captivity and death, 35.
Leo of the Holy Cross, 350.
Leo the Great, 5, 7.
Leo the Isaurian, 8.
Leopold of Austria, 289, 293.
Lewis of Thuringia, 155.
"Li Poure de Lyod," 301.
Liégers, reply to Paschal, 139.
Lightfoot, J. B., quoted, 5 (footnote).
Lillebonne, Synod of, 25.
Lingard, quoted, 102 (footnote).
Lisieux, Bishop of, 247.
Loiseleur, "La Doctrine Secrète des Templiers," referred to, 336 (footnote).

Lombard, Peter, 207.
Lombards, invasion, 7; defeat, 9, 276, 279. See Hildebrand, Guibert, etc.
Lombards, sect. See Arnold of Brescia.
London, Synod of, 253.
Lothair, Cardinal. See Innocent III.
Lothair, son of Trasimund. See Innocent III.
Lothair III., 171; concessions to Pope, 172; invited to Rome, 175; meets Innocent II., 176; assists him, 189; crowned, 189; receives possessions of Mathilde in fief, 190; compelled to leave Rome, 190; acknowledged by Milanese, 191; asked to free Sicily of Roger, 192; march through Italy, 192; quarrel with Pope, 192; dies, 194.
Lothair of Bonn, 292.
Louis VI., 176.
Louis VII., 216; relations to Alexander III., 242, 243, 246, 270; conspires with Prince Henry, 273, 274; death, 280.
Louis VIII., 345, 347, 348.
Louis IX., 373; ordinance of, 395.
Louis X. See Louis le Hutin.
Louis le Hutin, 395.
Louvre, parliament at, 420.
Lucca, Bishop of, 176.
Lucca, treaty with Henry V., 145.
Lucius II., negotiates with Roger, 210; trouble with Roman Commune, 211; appeals to Conrad, 211; death, 211.
Lucius III., 282, 283; anathematizes Waldenses, 302; inquisition, 393.
Madgeburg Centuriators, 23.
Maginolf, 141, 152.
Magna Charta, 364.
Magnus, Albertus, 185, 408.
Magyars, invasion of, 12.

Mainz, Archbishop of. See Christian, Conrad.
Mainz, assembly of bishops, 106; Diet, 137.
Manes, 302.
Manfred, Bishop, 214.
Manfred, son of Frederick II., 374, 375.
Manichæism, 302, 303.
Mantua, 127; Council of, 59.
Manuel of Constantinople, 248, 257.
Margaret, wife of Prince Henry, 272.
Margaret Ebner, 185.
Maria, daughter of Philip of Suabia, 349.
Markwald, 294, 307, 313.
Marozia, 14.
Martène, Ed., quoted, 7 (footnote).
Martens, quoted, 88 (footnote).
Martin V., 389.
Mathilde, daughter of Margrave Boniface, 37; seized by Henry, 38; released, 39; influenced by Hildebrand, 39; her castles, 93; interview with Henry, 94; entreats for him, 95; faithful to Hildebrand, 110; in peril, 116; marries Welf, 127; fanaticism, 127; twenty years' treaty with Italian cities, 128; separates from Welf, 132; swears allegiance to Henry V., 145; death, 154; character, 154.
Matilda, 145.
Maurice Burdinus. See Gregory VIII.
Maurice of Braga. See Gregory VIII.
Maurillac, 346.
Mazzolinus, 208.
Mechthild of Hackeborn, 185.
Melrichstadt, battle of, 100.
Mendicant orders, 374, 376, 378 sq., 386.
Metz, Bishop of, 92.

Michael, Emperor, 70, 107.
Milan, 49, 50; attitude towards Rome, 60; subdued, 233; fall of, 245.
Military orders, 162.
Milman, quoted, 7 (footnote), 47 (footnote), 81, 82 (footnote), 431, 432.
Milo, legate to Raymond VI., 339.
Mincius, John, 43.
Mirbt, Carl, "Die Wahl Gregors VII.," referred to in footnote, 66, 67, 87; "Die Absetzung Heinrichs IV.," etc., referred to in footnote, 88.
"Missi dominici," 392.
Moisson, 159.
Monasticism, 379, 386.
Monastier, "Histoire de l'Église Vaudoise," 301 (footnote).
Monte Cassino, monastery of, 7; consecration of new basilica, 63, 172, 192.
Monte Mario, 55.
Monte Porzio, battle of, 258.
Montesa, 162.
Montfort. See Simon de Montfort.
Montmartre, 265.
Montmirail, 264.
Montpellier, University of, 408.
Moray, Bishop of, 243.
Morimond, 162.
Morosini, Thomas, 328.
Mount St. Geneviève, 202.
Mourzoufle, 326.
Müller, "Kirchengeschichte," quoted, 16 (footnote), 425.
Muston, Alexander, "L'Israel des Alpes," quoted, 301 (footnote).
Mysticism, 181 sq. See Bernard.
Narbonne, 302, 346.
Neapolitan monarchy, 173, 174.
Neoplatonism, 183.
Neulodi, 244.
Newman, Cardinal, quoted, 196.
Nicholas, Abbot, 172.
Nicholas, the boy leader, 365.

Nicholas I., 27.
Nicholas II., 44; convokes council at Rome, 46; league with Normans, 48; death, 49.
Nicholas of Albano. See Hadrian IV.
Nicholas of Tusculum, 363.
Nominalists, 198, 199.
Norbert of Xanthen, 187, 188; opposes Abélard, 202.
Nordhausen, 350.
Normans, influence of, 32 sq.; treaty with Hildebrand, 45; increasing power, 47; alliance with Rome, 48.
Northmen, invasion of, 12.
Novara, 145.
Octavian, Cardinal, 227; chosen Pope, 238; enthroned, 239; begs help of Barbarossa, 239; excommunicated by Alexander III., 240; supported by Clugny, 241; acknowledged by Council of Pavia, 241; opposed by Council of Toulouse, 243; recognition reaffirmed by Council of Cremona, 244; banned at Tours, 247; death, 250.
Octavian of Ostia, 292.
Oddo, Cardinal, 225.
Oderisius, Abbot, 172.
Odillo, Abbot of Clugny, 16, 20.
Offa, King, 102.
"Opus Majus," 410.
"Ordeal," 392.
Orleans, University of, 408.
Othbert, 143.
Otho, Cardinal, 263.
Otho of Bavaria, 56.
Otto, Palgrave, 232.
Otto III., 12.
Otto IV., 313, 314; supported by Innocent, 319 sq.; takes oath to Innocent, 321; proclaimed King, 321; weakness, 332, 349; resists overtures of legates, 350; recognition and pledges, 353; betrothal, 353; coronation, 354;

imperial rights in Italy, 354; quarrel with Pope, 355; excommunicated, 355; waning cause, 356; marriage, 357; death, 358.
Otto of Bavaria, 230.
Otto of Nordheim, 71.
Otto of Ostia, 116; named for Pope, 126; submission of Sancho, etc., 127; shrewd policy, 127; quits Rome, 127; returns, 128; holds Synod of Piacenza, 129; treats with Conrad, 130; preaches crusade, 131; triumph and death, 133; character, 133.
Otto of Wittelsbach, 352.
Otto the Great, 4, 12.
Oxford, University of, 406.
Pallium, 136.
Pandects, 233, 403, 404.
Pandolfo, papal legate, 361, 363.
Papacy, subject to empire, 6; secular character, 6; first temporal sovereign, 7; forces in establishment of supremacy, 7, 8; supreme arbiter, 8; under Charlemagne, 11; effect of feudal system on, 11; in tenth century, 12; administration of Leo IX., 22, 29 sq.; Council of Rome concerning election, 46, 47; secular power lost, 209; fall of mediæval, 423. See Papal Absolutism.
Papal absolutism, 1 sq., 67, 68, 88, 89, 123, 312, 425, 426; reasons for failure, 430. See Papacy, Roman Church.
" Paraclete," 202.
Paris, University of, 388, 389, 405.
Parma, capture of, 374.
Paschal II., monk of Clugny, 17, 134; theory of crusade, 135; renews excommunication of Henry, 138; quarrel with Henry I. of England, 140, 141; quarrels with Colonnas and Corsi, 141; abandons Rome, 142; alliance with Henry V., 142; concessions to Henry I., 143; receives commissioners from Henry V., 144; prohibits lay investiture, 145; agrees to surrender temporalities, 147; failure of German bishops to agree, 149; riot, 150; seized by Henry, 151; yields right of royal investiture, 151, 152; denounced, 152; hides, 152; breaks treaty, 153; confirms decrees of French synod, 154; also of Vienna synod, 155; flees, 155; returns, 156; dies, 156; relation to Citeaux, 161.
Paschal III., 251, 252; installed, 260; dies, 262.
Paschasius, views on Eucharist, 30.
Pastoureaux, 376.
" Patarenes," 35, 304, 383.
Pataria, 50, 76, 165.
Paternon, Bishop, 395.
" Patrician," 9.
Paul of Palestrina. See Clement III.
Paul of Samosata, 303.
Paulicianism, 303.
" Pauperes Catholici," 380.
Pavia, Council of, 239, 241.
Pedro of Aragon, 319, 341, 344 sq.
Pepin, coronation of, 8; "Donation of," 9.
Peter, Cardinal, son of Peter Leonis, 169, 170, 174. See Anacletus II.
Peter, St., in Rome, 428.
Peter Cantor, 380.
Peter Leonis, 169.
Peter Lombard, 207.
Peter of Albano, 104.
Peter of Amiens, 130.
Peter of Aragon, 417.
Peter of Pisa, 194.
Peter the Hermit, 130.
Peter Waldo, 301.
Peter's pence, 102.

Philip, Archbishop of Cologne, 270.
Philip I. of France, 74.
Philip II. of France, 280, 288, 292, 293, 295, 310, 311, 315, 319, 338, 356, 362.
Philip of Suabia, son of Barbarossa, 297, 308, 313 sq., 321, 326; offers to Innocent, 331; recrowned, 332; overpowers Cologne, 333; success, 349, 350; absolved, 350; death, 352.
Philip the Fair, 413, 414, 418 sq.; excommunicated, 420.
Phocas, 5.
Piacenza Synod, 86, 90, 129.
Pierleone, 169.
Pierleoni family, 168.
Pierre Cella, 381.
Pierre de Castelnau, 319, 338, 339.
Pierre de Bruys, of Embrun, 300.
Pierre de Palais. See Abélard.
Pietism, 181 sq. See Bernard.
Pietro Bernardone, 383.
Pisa, Council of, 191.
Pisa, treaty with Henry V., 145.
Plautius Lateranus, 64.
Pontigny, 162.
Pontremoli, 145.
"Poor of Lyons," 301.
Pope. See Papacy, Papal Absolutism.
Poppo of Brixen, 20.
Portiuncula, 384.
Præmonstrants, 188.
Praxedis, 129, 133.
Preaching Friars, 382.
Preger, art. "Theologie, mystische," referred to, 181 (footnote).
Protestantism contrasted with Romanism, 433, 434.
Prouille, 381.
Prutz, Hans, "Geheimlehre und Geheimstatuten des Tempelordens," referred to, 336 (footnote).

Pseudo-Isidorian Decretals, 22, 23, 121, 429.
Ptolemæus, 156.
Quedlinburg, 350.
Rainald, Chancellor, 232.
Rainald of Cologne, 256 sq.
Rainald of Dassel, 253, 255.
Rainer, Cardinal, 309.
Rainer. See Paschal II.
Ranke, quoted, 102 (footnote).
Ratisbon, Diet of, 145.
Ravenna, Archbishop of, 175.
Raymond VI., 317, 319, 338, 339, 342 sq.; death, 348; condemned at Twelfth General Council, 367; forced to adopt edicts of Frederick II., 395.
Raymond VII., 347, 348.
Raymond of Béziers, 340, 341.
Raymond of Daventry, 302.
Raymond of Toulouse, 131.
Raynal, Abbot of Monte Cassino, 193.
"Real Presence," 30, 31, 100, 101.
Realists, 198, 199.
Reform Synod. See Hildebrand.
"Regale," 166.
Reginald of Canterbury, 330, 331.
Republicans, 209 sq., 218, 222, 226.
Rhadagaisus, 6.
Rheims, Synod of, 176; Council of, 374.
Richard I. of England, 273, 292, 293, 296, 310, 314.
Richard of Aquitaine, 275.
Richard of Aversa, 47, 48.
Richard of Capua, fealty to Hildebrand, 70.
Richard of St. Victor, 182.
Robert, Abbot of Mclesme, 161.
Robert, King of France, 17.
Robert Guiscard. See Guiscard, Robert.
Robert of Capua, 173, 190, 192.
Robert of Flanders, 139.
Roboald of Milan, 191.

Index. 455

Rodolph of Austria, 418.
Roger of Sicily, 130, 173, 190; anathematized, 191; titled by Anacletus, 192; sues for peace, 192; escapes, 192; hears embassy, 194; excommunicated, 195; conquers Innocent and receives Sicily as fief, 195; negotiates with Lucius, 210; wiliness, 218; rumored league with France, 218; marriage of daughter, 284.
Roger of York, 248, 249, 251, 266, 267.
Roland of Parma, 87.
Rolf, 32.
Roman law, 400 sq.
Roman Church, early dominance, 5; threefold ground of primacy, 5; subordinate to empire, 5; opposing the state, 8; clergy refuse vassalage, 11. See Papacy, Papal Absolutism, Celibacy.
Roman synods, 80, 87, 99, 100, 105, 153, 154, 194, 280.
Rome, apostolic patriarchate, 3; world's metropolis, 4; condition in eleventh century, 15; again metropolitan city, 60; sacked by Guiscard, 115; delivered from papal dominion, 209; under interdict, 224; independent, 286, 287.
Roncaglia, 233.
Roscelin, 199, 200.
Rudolph of Suabia, 82, 92; elected King, 97; annointed, 97; opposition to, 97; proposed conference with Henry, 98; acknowledged, 105; death, 107. See Henry IV.
Ruggieri, Calcagni, 396.
Rusticus, 113.
Rutherius, 27.
Sabina, 228.
Saisset, 418.
Saladin, 285.
San Germano, 373.

Sancho I. of Portugal, 296.
Sancho of Aragon, 127.
Sancho the Great, 17.
Santa Maria, monastery of, 19.
Saracens, invasion of, 12, 33; advance of, 73.
Savigny, "Geschichte des Römischen Rechts," etc., referred to, 404 (footnote).
Saxo of Anagni, 170.
Saxons, revolt of, 71, 72. See Henry IV., Henry V., Rudolph, etc.
Scartazzini, quoted, 154 (footnote).
Schaff, Philip, quoted in footnote, 5, 121.
Schism between East and West, 8.
Scholasticism, 181, 195 sq.
Scotland appeals to Boniface, 415. See Alexander III.
Scotus, John, attacks Paschasius on Eucharist, 30; translates Dionysius, 180; scholasticism, 181, 182, 197, 408.
"Semper Augustus," 4.
Senate, Roman, 213, 226.
Sens, Synod of, 206.
"Shepherds," 376.
Sicilian Vespers, 417.
Sicily, 416, 417. See Henry VI., Frederick II., Roger of Sicily, William of Sicily, etc.
Siegfried, Archbishop of Metz, 56.
Silvester III., 15.
Silvester IV., 141.
Simon de Montfort, 341, 342, 346, 347, 367, 377.
Simony, 24, 25, 28.
Siricius, Pope, on celibacy, 26.
Soissons, Assembly of, 362; Council of, 202.
Solomon of Hungary, 82.
St. Gildas, 202.
St. Jacques, Paris, 382.
St. Marcellinus, Cardinal of, 420.
St. Peter ad Vincula, 65.
St. Victor, school of, 182, 187.

Stanley, Dean, "Life and Letters," referred to, 93 (footnote).
States-General, 419.
"States of the Church," 9.
Stephen, Abbot of Citeaux, 161, 162.
Stephen, Cardinal, 50.
Stephen, Sir James, quoted, 120.
Stephen II., 8.
Stephen IX. See Frederick of Lorraine.
Stephen the Norman, 157, 168.
Stephen the shepherd boy, 364.
Stieler, Paulus, and Caden, "Italy from the Alps to Etna," referred to, 93 (footnote).
Storrs, R. S., "Bernard of Clairvaux," referred to, 187 (footnote).
Strabo, Walafrid, 409.
Suidger. See Clement II.
Susa, Marchioness of, 93.
Sutri, Bishop of, 109.
Swen of Denmark, 79.
Silvester, Pope, 428.
Synod, French church, 153.
Synod, Lateran, 167. See Roman Synods.
Synods, Roman. See Roman Synods.
Tancred, 131.
Tancred, brother of Constantia, 292, 295.
Tedaldo, nominated Archbishop of Milan, 83, 100, 110.
Templars, 162, 333 sq.
Tertiary orders, 386.
"Testes synodales," 393.
"Texerants," 304.
"Textores," 304.
Theobald, 170.
Theobald of Canterbury, 406.
Theodore Lascaris, 351.
Theodoric of St. Rufina, 135.
Theodosia, 14.
Theodosian code, 403, 406.
Theodosius, legate to Raymond VI., 342, 344, 345.

Therese, Princess, 297.
Thomas à Becket. See Becket.
Thomas Aquinas, 185, 384, 408.
Thomas Morosini, 328.
Thomson, Richard, "Historical Essay on the Magna Charta," referred to, 331 (footnote).
Thuringia, 71.
Tivoli, 208, 209, 213, 228, 287.
Toulouse, 243, 343 sq.
Toulouse, University of, 408.
Tours, Council of, 246.
Transubstantiation, 30, 31, 100, 101.
Tribur, Diet of, 92.
Trollope, F. E., translation of "Italy from the Alps to Etna," 93.
Troyes, Council of, recognizes Templars, 333; Synod, 144.
Turner, Sharon, "History of the Anglo-Saxons," referred to, 406 (footnote).
Tusculum, 287, 291.
Tusculum, Counts of, 14.
Twelfth General Council. See Council.
Ulrich of Padua, 104.
"Unam Sanctam," 419.
"Universal Bishop," 5.
"Universals," 198, 199.
Universities, 400 sq.
Urban II., monk of Clugny, 17. See Otto of Ostia.
Urban III., 283 sq.
Vacarius, 406.
Val Louise, 300.
Valentinian III., 5, 429.
Vandals, 6.
Vaudois, 301.
Vaughan, Robert A., "Hours with the Mystics," referred to, 181 (footnote).
Venice, in Fourth Crusade, 324 sq.; peace of, 277, 278, 280.
Ventura, describes jubilee, 416.
Verona, Council of, 302.
Vèzelai, 217.
Victor, St., school of, 182, 187.

Index. 457

Victor II., 37, 39; death, 40.
Victor III. See Desiderius.
Victor IV., 194. See Octavian, Cardinal.
Villemain, "Histoiré de Grégoire VII.," referred to, 21 (footnote).
Vivian, deputy to Becket, 265.
Von Hammer, "Mines de l'Orient," referred to, 336 (footnote).
Waiblingen, 357.
Walafrid Strabo, 409.
Waldenses, 301, 302, 346.
Waldo, Peter, 301.
Wallace of Scotland, 415.
Welf, 357.
Welf, the younger, 127; separates from Mathilde, 132.
Welf of Bavaria, 92; domains confiscated, 97.
Werner of Ancona, 141.
Westcott, B. F., "Religious Thought in the West," referred to, 181 (footnote).
Whately, quoted, 433.
Wibald, 219.
Wichmann, Bishop of Zeitz, 222, 223.
Wigbert, 110.
William, Archbishop of Tyre, 287, 288.
William, Duke of Aquitaine, 16.
William II. of Sicily, 255, 284.
William of Apulia, 173.
William of Burgundy, 73.
William of Champeaux, 201; modification of views, 204.
William of Dijon, 17.
William of Nogaret, 420.
William of Occam, 408.
William of Pavia, 263.
William of Scotland, 274.
William of Sicily, 224; subjection, 229; answer to papal legates, 232; conspiracy, 238 sq.; summoned to answer for conspiracy, 242, 254; death, 255.
William of Thierry, 205.
William of Utrecht, 86, 91; sudden death, 91.
William Rufus, 136.
William the Conqueror, 25, 102, 103.
Worms, Synod of, 86; Concordat, 163 sq., 172.
Würzburg, Assembly acknowledges Innocent, 176; Diet, 253, 297.
Würzburg, Bishop of, 92.
Xystus III., 429.
Zacharias, Pope, 8, 429.
"Zaptati," 301.
Zara, 324, 325.

THE ANTE-NICENE CHRISTIAN LIBRARY.

JUST PUBLISHED, in 4to (540 pp.), price 12s. 6d. *net*,

AN ADDITIONAL VOLUME

CONTAINING

RECENTLY DISCOVERED MSS.

AND

ORIGEN'S COMMENTARIES ON MATTHEW AND JOHN.

EDITED BY

PROFESSOR ALLAN MENZIES, D.D.,
ST. ANDREWS UNIVERSITY.

THE GOSPEL OF PETER (By Professor ARMITAGE ROBINSON)—THE DIATESSARON OF TATIAN—THE APOCALYPSE OF PETER—THE VISIO PAULI—THE APOCALYPSES OF THE VIRGIN AND SEDRACH—THE TESTAMENT OF ABRAHAM—THE ACTS OF XANTHIPPE AND POLYXENA—THE NARRATIVE OF ZOSIMUS—THE APOLOGY OF ARISTIDES—THE EPISTLES OF CLEMENT (complete Text)—ORIGEN'S COMMENTARIES ON MATTHEW AND JOHN, etc.

EDINBURGH: T. & T. CLARK, 38 GEORGE STREET.

T. and T. Clark's Publications.

In Twenty-four handsome 8vo Volumes, Subscription price £6, 6s.,

ANTE-NICENE CHRISTIAN LIBRARY.

A COLLECTION OF ALL THE WORKS OF THE FATHERS OF THE CHRISTIAN CHURCH PRIOR TO THE COUNCIL OF NICÆA.

EDITED BY PROFESSOR ALEXANDER ROBERTS, D.D., AND PROFESSOR J. DONALDSON, LL.D.

CONTENTS:—Apostolic Fathers, one vol.; Justin Martyr, Athenagoras, one vol.; Tatian, Theophilus, The Clementine Recognitions, one vol.; Clement of Alexandria, two vols.; Irenæus and Hippolytus, three vols.; Tertullian against Marcion; Cyprian, two vols.; Origen, two vols.; Tertullian, three vols.; Methodius, etc., one vol.; Apocryphal Gospels, Acts, and Revelations, one vol.; Clementine Homilies, Apostolical Constitutions, one vol.; Arnobius, one vol.; Dionysius, Gregory, Thaumaturgus, Syrian Fragments, one vol.; Lactantius, two vols.; Early Liturgies and Remaining Fragments, one vol.

Any Volume may be had separately, price 10s. 6d.

In Fifteen Volumes, demy 8vo, Subscription price £3, 19s.,

THE WORKS OF ST. AUGUSTINE.

EDITED BY MARCUS DODS, D.D.

CONTENTS:—The 'City of God,' two vols.; Writings in connection with the Donatist Controversy, one vol.; The Anti-Pelagian Writings, three vols.; 'Letters,' two vols.; Treatises against Faustus the Manichæan, one vol.; The Harmony of the Evangelists, and the Sermon on the Mount, one vol.; On the Trinity, one vol.; Commentary on John, two vols.; On Christian Doctrine, Enchiridion, On Catechising, and On Faith and the Creed, one vol.; 'Confessions,' with Copious Notes by Rev. J. G. PILKINGTON.

Any Work may be had separately, price 10s. 6d. per Volume.

SELECTION FROM
ANTE-NICENE LIBRARY AND ST. AUGUSTINE'S WORKS.

MESSRS. CLARK now offer a Selection of Twelve Volumes from either or both of those Series at the Subscription Price of THREE GUINEAS *net* (or a larger number at the same proportion).

T. and T. Clark's Publications.

HISTORY OF THE CHRISTIAN CHURCH.
By PHILIP SCHAFF, D.D., LL.D.

1. **APOSTOLIC CHRISTIANITY, A.D. 1–100.** Two Vols. Ex. demy 8vo, price 21s.
2. **ANTE-NICENE CHRISTIANITY, A.D. 100–325.** Two Vols. Ex. demy 8vo, price 21s.
3. **NICENE AND POST-NICENE CHRISTIANITY, A.D. 325–600.** Two Vols. Ex. demy 8vo, price 21s.
4. **MEDIÆVAL CHRISTIANITY, A.D. 590–1073.** Two Vols. Ex. demy 8vo, price 21s.
5. **THE GERMAN REFORMATION.** Two Vols. Ex. demy 8vo, price 21s.
6. **THE SWISS REFORMATION.** Two Vols. Ex. demy 8vo, price 21s.

'Dr. Schaff's "History of the Christian Church" is the most valuable contribution to Ecclesiastical History that has ever been published in this country. When completed it will have no rival in point of comprehensiveness, and in presenting the results of the most advanced scholarship and the latest discoveries. Each division covers a separate and distinct epoch, and is complete in itself.'

Now complete, in Five Volumes 8vo, price 10s. 6d. each,
INDEX Volume (100 pp. 8vo), price 2s. 6d. *net*,

HISTORY OF THE JEWISH PEOPLE IN THE TIME OF OUR LORD.
By Dr. EMIL SCHÜRER,
PROFESSOR OF THEOLOGY IN THE UNIVERSITY OF KIEL.

FIRST DIVISION, in Two Vols., **POLITICAL HISTORY OF PALESTINE from B.C. 175 to A.D. 135.**

SECOND DIVISION, in Three Vols., **INTERNAL CONDITION OF PALESTINE IN THE TIME OF CHRIST.**

'Under Professor Schürer's guidance we are enabled to a large extent to construct a social and political framework for the Gospel History, and to set it in such a light as to see new evidences of the truthfulness of that history and of its contemporaneousness. ... The length of our notice shows our estimate of the value of his work.'—*English Churchman.*

'Messrs. Clark have afresh earned the thanks of all students of the New Testament in England, by undertaking to present Schürer's masterly work in a form easily accessible to the English reader. ... In every case the amount of research displayed is very great, truly German in its proportions, while the style of Professor Schürer is by no means cumbrous, after the manner of some of his countrymen. We have inadequately described a most valuable work, but we hope we have said enough to induce our readers who do not know this book to seek it out forthwith.'—*Methodist Recorder.*

N.B.—This work is issued in THE FOREIGN THEOLOGICAL LIBRARY, from which selections of Eight Volumes may be had for Two Guineas.

T. and T. Clark's Publications.

'*The most important contribution yet made to biblical theology.*'—EXPOSITOR.

In Two Volumes 8vo, 21s.,

THE TEACHING OF JESUS.

By HANS HINRICH WENDT, D.D.,
ORD. PROFESSOR OF THEOLOGY, HEIDELBERG.

TRANSLATED BY REV. JOHN WILSON, M.A., MONTREUX.

Copyright by arrangement with the Author.

'Our advice is to all students and clergy to buy this book. Treat it as a spiritual unfolding of our Lord's teaching, trusting it as far as it goes, and thanking God for so bright a ray of spiritual sunshine out of what has so often been a murky cloud.'—*Church Bells.*

'Every section opens out for us fresh views of the great and wondrous depths of the teaching of Jesus, and gives us the persuasion that there is in that teaching fresh worlds yet to be discovered. We are grateful to Dr. Wendt for the great work he has done.'—*The Thinker.*

'Dr. Wendt's work is of the utmost importance for the study of the Gospels, both with regard to the origin of them and to their doctrinal contents. It is a work of distinguished learning, of great originality, and of profound thought. The second part (now translated into English), which sets forth the contents of the doctrine of Jesus, is the most important contribution yet made to biblical theology, and the method and results of Dr. Wendt deserve the closest attention. . . . No greater contribution to the study of biblical theology has been made in our time. A brilliant and satisfactory exposition of the teaching of Christ.'—Prof. J. IVERACH, D.D., in *The Expositor.*

'Dr. Wendt has produced a remarkably fresh and suggestive work, deserving to be ranked among the most important contributions to biblical theology. . . . There is hardly a page which is not suggestive; and, apart from the general value of its conclusions, there are numerous specimens of ingenious exegesis thrown out with more or less confidence as to particular passages.'—Prof. W. P. DICKSON, D.D., in *The Critical Review.*

'In introducing Professor Wendt's work to English readers, the publishers have done a service to theology in this country second only, if indeed second, to that rendered by the issue of Professor Driver's famous " Introduction."'—*Literary World.*

www.ingramcontent.com/pod-product-compliance
Lightning Source LLC
Chambersburg PA
CBHW051847300426
44117CB00006B/292